DONNA KOOLER'S

encyclopedia *of* crochet

A LEISURE ARTS PUBLICATION

DONNA KOOLER'S

encyclopedia
of
crochet

A LEISURE ARTS PUBLICATION

10 9 8 7 6 5 4

Library of Congress Cataloging-in-Publication Data
Kooler, Donna
Donna Kooler's Encyclopedia of Crochet
"A Leisure Arts Publication"

I S B N :   1 - 5 7 4 8 6 - 2 8 2 - 0

4

contributors

produced by

published by

LEISURE ARTS

If you have questions or comments
please contact:

LEISURE ARTS CUSTOMER SERVICE
P.O. BOX 55595
LITTLE ROCK, AR 72215-9633
www.leisurearts.com

KOOLER DESIGN STUDIO, INC.
399 TAYLOR BLVD. SUITE 104
PLEASANT HILL, CA 94523
kds@koolerdesign.com

PRINTED IN THE U.S.A. BY
R.R. DONNELLEY & SONS, CO.
WILLARD, OHIO

stitchers
EDWARD BARRALL (THE KNITTING ROOM),
MARIANNA FORRESTAL, ROSITA HERRICK,
JO ANN MOSS, KATHERINE MANCINHO,
NANCY NEHRING, SHARON RYMAN,
KATHLEEN STUART, SCOTT WINEGARDEN

models
CAREN ANDREWS, MALIKA ANDREWS,
RUTH ATKINSON, JENNIFER FOYE,
MADELINE ROSE FOYE,
THEA DORA JO HANNER, MISSY MITCHELL

creative director
DONNA KOOLER

editor in chief
JUDY SWAGER

encyclopedia editor
JO LYNN TAYLOR

text editor
SHELLEY CARDA

pattern editor
NANCY NEHRING

book design & production
NANCY WONG SPINDLER

project manager
PRISCILLA TIMM

writers
TEXT: SHELLEY CARDA
COLOR: LINDA GILLUM
PATTERN GALLERY: NANCY NEHRING

editors
PROJECTS: SHELLEY CARDA, JOAN CRAVENS,
NANCY NEHRING, ANN E. SMITH
TEXT: KIT SCHLICH, JOAN CRAVENS
INDEX: JOAN CRAVENS

illustrations
DIAGRAMS: JO LYNN TAYLOR
CHARTS: DONNA YUEN
COLOR WHEELS: JESSICA MAIN

project designers
RUTH ATKINSON, SHELLEY CARDA,
ARLINE FISCH, MARSHA HINKSON,
KATHLEEN POWER JOHNSON,
GWEN BLAKLEY KINSLER, MELISSA LEAPMAN,
NANCY NEHRING, ANN E. SMITH, JACQUELINE YOUNG

photography/color separator
DIANNE WOODS, BERKELEY, CA

photo stylists
BASHA HANNER
SUSAN WEINSTEIN

foreword

If I could choose only one book to take to a desert island, *Donna Kooler's Encyclopedia of Crochet* would be the one! I've been crocheting both for pleasure and professionally for many years, and how I wish I had had this elegant book when I began. Here at last is the definitive history of crochet, with wonderful photos and facts solving the mystery of the origins of this beautiful craft. Each step and technique is clarified with diagrams so clear that you will feel you have an expert teacher sitting beside you. Whatever you might want to know about crochet, you will find it in this comprehensive book! Those who love symbol crochet, or have wanted to learn this innovative method of pattern writing, will be delighted with the presentation of the symbol language and symbol charts as well as words accompany nearly every project. The book is a feast for the eyes, with gorgeous photos tempting you to try project after project. A complete glossary of crochet stitches guides you to the mastery of stitches from the basic to the unusual. This book will definitely go to the desert island with me; and I might even take along a crochet hook or two and a bale of yarn!

Jean Leinhauser, President
American School of Needlework

acknowledgements

Without the knowledge, creativity and love of crochet by so many, this book could not have been written. I wish to thank the following individuals for their contributions: Shelley Carda for her authenticated research into the history of crochet and Nancy Nehring for her wonderful pattern gallery. Donna Yuen for her amazing charts and Jo Lynn Taylor for the hundreds of diagrams she so painstakingly created. Thanks to all the designers for their creative designs, and the stitchers who reproduced them so accurately Nancy Wong Spindler for her beautiful book design and Dianne Woods for the glorious photos. Kit Schlich, Judy Swager, and Joan Cravens for editing material written by so many and allowing us to speak with one voice. To Marsha Hinkson and everyone who had a part in creating the Encyclopedia of Crochet, *my heartfelt thanks for a job well done.*

And last but not least, thank you to Linda Gillum and Priscilla Timm for twenty-five years of personal and professional support, and friendship.

Donna Kooler

contents

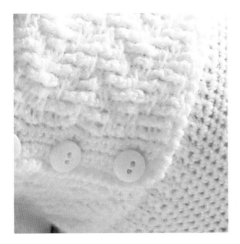

beginnings

crochet basics

projects

beyond the basics

projects

pattern gallery

for your information

CROCHET is the art of using a hook to make loops into a shape. The soothing rhythm of the activity makes it an ideal accompaniment to daydreaming and may well explain how crochet readily adapts itself to an amazing variety of uses. This versatile and deceptively simple technique has produced an entire clan of offspring, from supremely decorative to steadfastly functional.

Done with fine thread, crochet imitated, and then supplanted, the finest European needle laces. Done with warm wool, crochet provided both a creative outlet and warm, sturdy clothing. Crochet fed the starving at the same time it celebrated women's acquisition of leisure, wealth, and education. Crochet embodies the philosophy of "do it yourself," but it also accompanied the birth of the Industrial Revolution, mass production, and the consumer society. Yet crochet has never been mechanized; it is still always done by hand.

The boundaries of crochet are elusive. For just about every thread or cord created, there has been an equal and enthusiastic response with the crochet hook. Anything flexible enough to be hooked is fair game for the inventive crocheter. Leather lacing becomes shoes and sandals, wire becomes jewelry, and synthetic fibers become hats, bags, or anything else you can dream up. The secret lies in the ability of crochet to be a descriptive line for drawing or a three-dimensional object, either firm or flexible. If you can figure out a way to shape it, you can make it with crochet.

Naturally, so agreeable and versatile a craft has a host of fans, male and female, young and old, traditional or *avant garde.* You can immerse yourself in the most historical of forms, copy patterns from the past, and create innumerable lovely variations. You also can cut loose with a hook and a concept and end up doing something completely different. Yet it will still be crochet: easily understood, endlessly adaptable. In the end, and again at the beginning, it comes down to the simplicity of a hook and a strand.

Crochet sampler book (c. 1900) stores small samples of crocheted lace patterns for later reference. From the collection of Gwen Blakley-Kinsler. Photograph by Joe Coca.

A RECENT "OLD" TECHNIQUE

Handiwork is a comfortable way of turning our modern hands to the work of our ancestors. After all, anything done by hand is as old as time itself, isn't it? Especially something as fundamental as crochet… hooking a thread through a loop. Alas, in this imperfect world progress is not always a logical flow from simple to complex. Odd as it may seem, crochet is the gift not of antiquity, but of the Industrial Revolution.

Crochet seems to have sprung, fully formed like Aphrodite, from ladies' magazines in the 19th century. The earliest known printed crochet patterns are from 1824, from the Dutch magazine *Pénelopé*, published from 1821–1833.[1]

THREADS OF HISTORY

An enormous amount of physical evidence about early textiles still exists, including textiles themselves. Even in the Stone Age, weaving and other textile techniques were complex and sophisticated. But there is no early physical evidence of crochet implements or fabrics. It is important to realize that not all hooks are crochet hooks, and the existence of a hook does not establish the existence of crochet. The prime example of this is the drop spindle with a hooked top.

Spinning, the oldest fiber craft, is known as early as 20,000 B.C.[2] Drop spindles with hooked tops, to hold fibers during the spinning process, are seen in the Neolithic period (7000–2000 B.C.).[3] Though evidence of fabric is abundant, there is no evidence of crocheted fabric in this period.

Imprints of fiber structures in pottery have been cited as proof of the early existence of crochet among the Pima Indians.

But the imprints are merely a misinterpretation of both textile construction and pottery-making techniques, and do not indicate the existence of crochet at an early date.[4]

The earliest known written reference to crochet using wool dates from 1812. Elizabeth Grant's *The Memoirs of a Highland Lady* mentions "shepherd's knitting" as a method of making warm hats, waistcoats, and drawers from homespun wool, using a hook made from an old comb.[5] This could have been an established old craft in cold climates, but there is no artifact or writing to indicate its existence prior to the 19th century.

A WINTER GIFT

In an early book of needlework patterns, *A Winter Gift for Ladies, Being Instructions in Knitting, Netting, and Crotchet* [sic] *Work, containing the newest and most fashionable patterns from the latest London edition. Revised and edited by an American Lady,* printed in 1847 by G. B. Zieber and Company of Philadelphia, we find some clues to the novelty of crochet. First, the spelling is wobbly. This indicates that the activity of crocheting was not old enough to have a fixed name in English.[6] That means it was rather new in 1847.

The next interesting fact is that *A Winter Gift* gives knitting and netting patterns without any instruction as to how knitting and netting are performed. They are assumed to be part of a lady's needlework skills, so only the patterns are given. But very careful instructions are given on the precise method of doing crochet. Only three stitches are given: single crochet and double stitch (the British terms for what we refer to now as slip stitch and single crochet), and the muffatee stitch. The muffatee stitch is worked like a slip stitch, but through the front loop only. It also lists items for which the muffatee stitch is used: mittens, baby shoes, gaiters, and gloves.

There are only three patterns for crocheted items: two purses to be worked in silk and a gentleman's cap in several colors of Berlin wool. In the instructions for a long purse, the lady is instructed to turn her crocheting at the end of a row, so we learn that crochet was done back and forth, as well as in rounds.[7] The gentleman's cap calls for a coarse ivory crochet hook; the openwork purse calls for a steel one, so there was already some choice of hook sizes.

Godey's Lady's Book also used the term "crotchet" before 1848, from its first introduction of the craft in July–December 1846, volume 33, until January–June 1848, volume 36. From 1848 on, the word "crochet" seems to be standard.

NUN'S LACE

Even in recorded history, written references to crochet-like techniques are not dependable. Language is imprecise when a non-craftsman tries to describe fabric structure. There are mentions of "cheyne lace" (and other assorted spellings) in 17th- and 18th-century inventories and descriptions. This is sometimes taken as evidence of the existence of crocheted thread lace, no doubt because a chain of loops is fundamental to crochet. But the "chain" part of the name merely indicates a chain stitch done on a fabric base,[8] first as needle embroidery and later as tambour work, a form of embroidery done with a hook in the 18th century. Chain embroidery seems to have originated in the East, being referred to as Turkish, Persian, and even Chinese.

It is unlikely that early lace called "nun's work" or "nun's lace" was crochet because there simply is no extant crocheted lace prior to the second half of the 19th century. Supposing that "nun's lace" would most likely be found in Catholic altar-linen archives, Danish scholar Lis Paludan investigated the altar cloths and vestments at St. Peter's Basilica in Rome. The earliest example of crocheted lace there dates to about 1900. In the altar linen and vestment collections of other historical Roman Catholic churches throughout Italy, she found not a single piece of crocheted lace dating earlier than the second half of the 19th century. There were numerous examples of needle and bobbin laces, many dating from the 16th century, but nothing crocheted was found that could be dated earlier than the latter half of the 19th century.[9] It is reasonable to conclude that "nun's lace" was simply the generic description of any lace produced by nuns and that before the mid-1800s none of it was crocheted.

WHAT TOOK SO LONG?

Prehistoric fiber artists produced complex weaving and basketry while apparently overlooking something as simple as crochet. Even given the possibility that only a human from the period of written history could have invented crochet, knitting appears about four centuries earlier than crochet,[10] though the two are very similar. Why did crochet not show up until the 19th century, just before machines turned crafts into hobbies?

The reason may be that people preferred more economical fabric-creating techniques.

Crochet uses an enormous amount of thread to produce fabric structures which can be much more economically produced by the ancient techniques of *netting, sprang,* single-needle looping techniques such as *nalbinding,* or even *knitting.* All these techniques produce stretchy, flexible fabrics which have a more even and consistent thickness than crocheted fabric. The twisting and layering of thread required to produce crochet consumes far more thread than the same area of knitted, netted, or looped cloth.

In pre-industrial society, making fabric to meet only the most basic of human needs was "the most time-consuming single industry."[11] Time expended to make fabrics beautiful was not considered wasteful, since all fabric making techniques consumed time. Time was not yet money; it simply *was.* Artisans made beauty an integral part of a product because making something beautiful was pleasing.[12] Redundant and unnecessary use of materials, on the other hand, was simply wasteful. This may explain why crochet appears quite late as a fiber technique.

The almost simultaneous invention of machine-made thread and crochet are reasonable when you consider that only when thread is inexpensive can there be widespread popularity of a craft which uses thread lavishly. When crochet did finally appear, unrestrained by thrift, it had multiple personalities because it is wonderfully adaptable and can be used in a number of creative ways. When the cost of materials was not a limiting factor, crochet blossomed into an entire family tree, almost overnight.

A WEALTH OF THREAD

In 1770, James Hargreaves's patent for the spinning jenny stood the textile world on its head. This device could spin 16 threads at once, unlike the modest output of a single spinner at a single wheel.

The next technological leap forward was the invention in 1793 of the saw cotton gin by Eli Whitney. The saw gin was specifically designed to process medium- and short-staple (1 inch) cotton fibers being grown in abundance in the southern United States. There already was mechanical processing of the long-staple cottons (what we today call Egyptian or Pima cotton), but the processing was very slow, able to clean only two bales of cotton a day. This made the long-staple cotton as much a luxury fiber as silk, and it was used for much the same purposes—brightly colored embroidery thread and fabrics—because cotton takes dyes much more readily than linen does.

Flax was the fiber commonly used for non-woolen clothes. Flax grows in many climates, but the processing of flax for linen production is lengthy, requiring rotting (also known as *retting*) of the stem, removing all the stem particles, and breaking the fibrous remains into long strands. With the saw gin, cotton bolls could be quickly and efficiently stripped of their seeds and then as quickly spun by the spinning jenny. This put vast quantities of inexpensive, sturdy cotton thread into the marketplace. A wealth of thread meant that cloth manufactur-

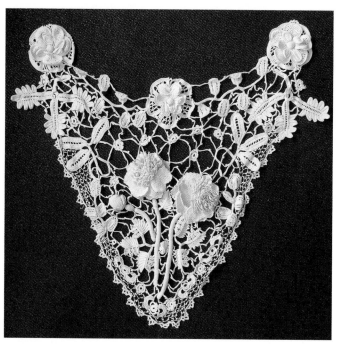

Modesty piece for open neckline; Irish crochet, cotton, c. 1910. From the collection of Lacis.

ers could make cloth less expensively. And with the money saved on fabric, women could do something frivolous with thread. Now a thread-hungry craft like crochet was not limited by the cost of materials; it could take its place in a world craving novelty and ornamentation of dress.

WEARING WEALTH

True to human nature, one of the most significant uses of technology is for fashion. Fashionable clothing is a distinguishing trait of wealth and power, and it is very agreeable to be rich and powerful, or at least to look rich and powerful. An example of the impact of technology on wealth is seen in the history of lace, which figures largely in the history of crochet.

The lavish use of lace from the Elizabethan period (1558–1603) is well documented in writing and in portraiture. The cost of materials combined with the cost of labor made lace prohibitively expensive, affordable only to the nobility. But after the invention of the spinning wheel in the late 15th century, the spread of spinning technology dropped the cost of thread. With more efficient thread production the cost of lace dropped to a level the prosperous merchant class could afford; they bought lace and wore it, just like the nobles. Sometimes lace was made of silver and gold,[13] to be exclusive, but this did not stop the merchants for long. They always ended up wearing lace too, even gold and silver.

Sumptuary laws prohibiting the commoners' wearing of upper class finery were passed early and repeatedly in many countries,[14] specifically to keep commoners unfashionable. Such laws were withdrawn when it became obvious that they were being ignored.

So the gentry resorted to making a fashion of phenomenally complex laces which took years to create and cost a king's ransom. It worked, for a while. The exquisite laces of the 17th and 18th centuries are legendary. The art of smuggling fine laces also kept pace and is a fascinating study in human nature.[15] But the Industrial Revolution completely changed fiber technology, fashion, wealth, and power. Not only were spinning machines invented, lace-making machines were invented. Now beautiful lace could be had quickly and inexpensively. It was not handmade, but it was lace, and everyone could afford it.

WHERE DID HOOKS COME FROM?

The specific parent of modern thread crochet is generally believed to have been tambour work, a form of embroidery that uses a hooked needle to pull fine thread up through fabric held tightly in a hoop, or tambour (drum).[16] It was known in Turkey, Persia, and India, (and China, if we may believe advertising from 1764, promoting "the new Chinese needlework").[17] Tambour work produced a simple, flowing chain stitch, which was very popular throughout the 18th century. There are numerous examples of delicate tambour hooks, called *crochet* ("little hook") in France, from as early as 1700.[18] These hooks were really hooked needles which were clamped into beautifully made handles of such materials as ivory, bone, silver, tortoise shell, mother-of-pearl, and agate. Ladies looked graceful and attractive while they were using them, which was essential to a leisure activity.[19]

When the supporting fabric was removed, hooking a chain stitch "in the air" produced the foundation chain needed for all subsequent crochet stitches.[20] Cotton thread could stand up to the tug of a hook pulling it through the loops of each stitch, unlike the brittle, scarcely-spun linen lace thread.[21]

According to Paludan,[22] crochet hooks, unlike tambour hooks, do not have sharp points to pierce fabric. There were both crochet hooks and tambour hooks stored inside a number of the early 19th-century tambour hook handles, secured interchangeably by means of a wing nut, indicating that both tambour work and crochet were being done. It seems that the technology of genteel needle arts provided the inspiration for all that crochet would become.

But the wisdom of hands surpasses the speculation of scholars. American designer and author Nancy Nehring has a collection of antique tambour and crochet hooks with which she has experimented extensively, with surprising results. The above-mentioned sets of crochet and tambour hooks really contain only tambour hooks: pointed hooks for woven fabric and blunt hooks for tambour work on tulle. As Nehring points out,[23] the wing nut used to attach hook to handle makes it impossible to use the hook as anything other than a tambour hook. Crochet cannot be done without the wing nut interfering, but the wing nut is essential to tambour work. So the development of crochet from tambour embroidery is not a reasonable theory. Furthermore, Nehring has experimented with early Scottish hooks specifically made for crochet. The stitches possible with the early crochet hooks are limited to the shorter stitches (chain, slip stitch, single crochet)[24] used in early patterns for purses, caps, and utilitarian articles.

Despite the use of silk in the early patterns, tools and stitches used in the earliest crochet seem to come from shepherd's knitting. Flat shepherd's hooks produce just the stitches used before the advent of crocheted lace.[25]

How did rural Scotland meet with the parlors of Europe, or vice versa? At the beginning of the 19th century, soldiers and sailors from all over the British Isles made their way through Europe to fight Napoleon Bonaparte's empire building. Shepherd's knitting would have been very useful in wartime, since common soldiers of the past had to supply many of their own necessities and all of their own comforts. A useful technique such as shepherd's knitting would not have gone unnoticed, either by soldiers marching across Europe or by the rural folk where armies encamped. We may never know if crochet went to Europe or came from it, but by 1824 there was enough interest to put a pattern for a crocheted silk purse into a very fashionable European ladies' magazine.

A SAMPLING OF HOOKS OLD AND NEW, FROM TOP TO BOTTOM: (1) Handy Hook, marbleized plastic, US design patent 256629 (1980), 1999; (2) hook fashioned from rib bone, probably seal or walrus, Eskimo, 1900–1950; (3) steel hook with silver and gold metalwork handle, type associated with Victorian necessities, 1880–1900; (4) breaching whale, carved whale bone (not baleen), by Kate Lebherz-Gelinas, 2001; (5) William Ross hook, steel needles set in pot metal (pewter) handle, US Patent 215979, 1879; (6) apple twig hook, by Pam Moller, 1999; (7) African porcupine quill set in silver, steel needle, 1860–1890; (8) Queen Victoria golden jubilee commemorative hook, handle stamped with significant dates in her life: born 1819, crowned 1838, married 1840, jubilee 1887, steel needle set in brass, British patent Rd. No. 67730, 1887; (9) 3 needles swing on hinged handle, sheath with transfer lithography (paint on metal); to use a needle, sheath is removed, one of three different needles is rotated down and the sheath replaced, 1870–1935; (10) celluloid hook in imitation tortoise shell, 1900–1935; (11) steel hook with mother-of-pearl handle, type found in Victorian necessities, 1880–1900; (12) steel needle mounted in handle of black paint on iron, brass ball and chatelaine ring on end, 1860–1880; (13) carved bone with large flat grip, Eskimo, 1900–1950; (14) carved bone with clenched fist and hammer; painted design includes red fingernail polish, 1860–1880; (15) double-ended steel needle mounted in painted iron handle, British registration mark, 21 Nov 1868; (16) interchangeable screw-in needle in gold plated handle, multiple needles in various sizes provided with handle, 1860–1870; (17) interchangeable needle in agate handle, split brass collar with screw-on cap to hold needle, multiple steel needles in various sizes provided with handle, 1860–1880; (18) scrimshaw fish, fossilized mammoth ivory, Eskimo, Queen Charlotte Islands, 1900–1950; (19) steel hook in sterling silver handle, type found in Victorian necessities, 1900–1915; (20) early crochet needle in tambour hook style, removable steel needle, brass mount with screw-on cap, carved bone handle with hollow end and screw-on cap to hold additional needles, 1850–1870; (21) carved ivory shepherd's knitting hook, silver plate is a 1" gauge, 1840–1880; (22) steel needle with steel wound wire handle, 1870–1890; (23) carved bone sewing souvenir; this one is from Montmartre, France, although the same souvenir was available at many different tourist attractions; it combines crochet hook, needle case (inside hollow umbrella), and Stanhope (microscopic photographs mounted on end of a magnifying glass rod) held in fist, 1870–1890; (24) bone Tunisian hook, 1860–1900. From the private collection of Nancy Nehring.

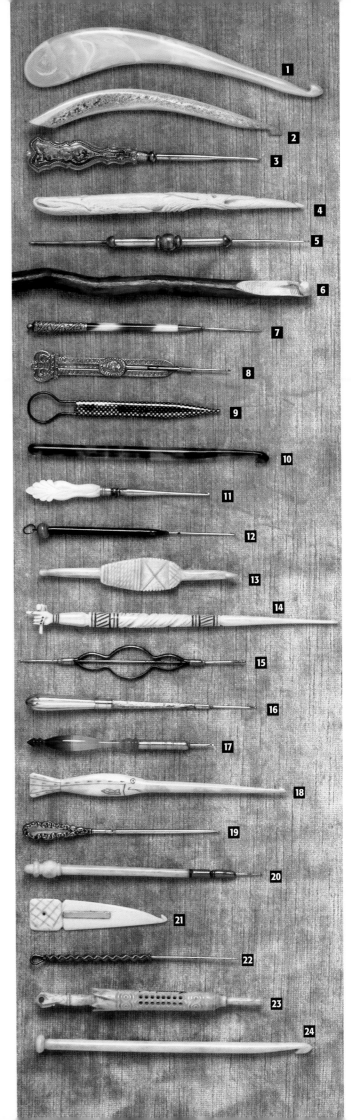

Bullion-stitch cap; cotton with silk bows. American (Southern), second half of 19th century. Private collection.

A PATTERN FOR SUCCESS

While France was busy getting rid of an emperor and the rest of Europe was recovering from him, America was busy becoming wealthy. The newly settled land hadn't lost much during the American Revolution or The War of 1812 because there wasn't much to lose. But Americans were intent on making up for lost time by taking full advantage of agriculture and industry, and on all fronts there was prosperity.

One of the first uses of the new wealth was education, and male and female children alike were sent to school. No longer was literacy the education for males and needlework the education for females; even girls could learn to read. Because of this, the printing trade grew vigorously, and printing presses poured out materials promoting virtue and industry.

Much of the industry promoted was needlework. A bare minimum of clothing was no longer the rule of thumb, because there was wealth and even a little spare time, since factories (European and American) were producing yarn, thread and cloth. The ladies knew how to knit and sew, but surely they needed fresh inspiration and ideas! Printers rushed to fill the void with periodicals such as *Godey's Lady's Book* and *Peterson's Magazine*, along with innumerable books and guides with homemaking and child-rearing advice, medical information, recipes, and, of course, needlework patterns. Fashions began to change at breakneck speed, virtually every year. The changes were carefully documented in fashion journals and magazines so that ladies would know just how unfashionable they had become. Of course, instructions and patterns for making one fashionable again were provided in the same publications, often continued in subsequent issues.

MAKING THE PURSE-STRINGS

The ladies of America began to crochet the reins of consumer power. Purses for the lady of the house were among the first articles made with the new, extravagant craft of crochet. Abundance was celebrated by instructions for purses made of silk floss and gold thread.[26] Ladies needed elegant bags to display the wealth that was shifting into their delicate hands.

Children's books with lessons in manners and morality were published, and knitting and crochet patterns were included in the books for little girls. They learned to clothe their future families by clothing their dolls. Tiny mittens, hats, stockings, and underwear all were produced from patterns in books for little girls. They established at an early age the habit of looking to publications for new styles and instructions.

Books promoting healthy lifestyles warned against the dangers of keeping infants too warm. Lacy, crocheted cotton hats allowed fresh air to circulate and cooled little heads, preventing dangerously fevered brains, dropsy, and hair loss.[27] (See the photo, left.) Garments and shoes were still crocheted of wool, of course.

Health-promoting hair pomades of macassar oil and bone marrow became very popular. This led to the development of defensive doilies and absorbent antimacassars to protect upholstered furniture from greasy stains.

CONSPICUOUS LEISURE

Essential to the health of a household was the presence of beauty. Once the necessities were provided, beauty could be produced in abundance. Books reminded readers of the dangers of idleness, and decorative needlework was indicative of a civilized and moral culture.[28] So spare time was enthusiastically turned to the service of wholesome, soothing beauty. The Protestant ethic met the Industrial Revolution. Bright crocheted pillows, bolsters, candlestick covers, linen hampers, pen-wipers, pincushions, lamp mats, lampshades, piano shawls, table covers, and abundantly tasseled everything added to the atmosphere of unrelenting industry in service of beauty. Conspicuous leisure became an acceptable alternative to idleness.[29]

Perpetual productivity required immense creativity on the part of designers, who were kept busy inventing new necessities and "elegancies" that could keep needlewomen (and girls) from even a moment of unproductive time. Such was the demand for novelties that the same patterns often were published more than once. For example, a mat of three-dimensional, multi-colored pansies was published once in 1875, twice in 1876, and frequently thereafter. It still crops up today in pattern collections. Patterns for striped bolsters and pillows known as *brioche* were everywhere. Lace designs were stolen verbatim, frequently and shamelessly, copyrights notwithstanding. Sometimes the pirates waited as much as half a year before publishing the patterns, but often they published within weeks, sometimes even before the lawful licensee had time to do so.[30]

THE PRICE OF PROGRESS

Inexpensive and trouble-free materials were no cause for rejoicing to those whose livelihood came from linen. At the same time that ginning and spinning technologies made fine thread easily affordable, they also helped to wipe out the highly developed linen industry. The ability to make 16 threads instead of one made skilled linen spinners obsolete. They were replaced by the spinning jenny.

The spinning jenny produced a tough, tightly spun thread, but the spinning jenny was completely unsuited to brittle linen fibers. Within a generation the skills for producing linen fibers 1/150 of a millimeter thick were lost, and with them the lace threads spun of only seven of these fibers. The very loosely twisted lace threads for the fine, soft laces of the 17th and 18th centuries could no longer be made, even if the market for them existed.[31]

Lacemakers no longer had to work in dank, dark cellars to produce fine, white lace. In fact, many of them no longer had work at all; the French Revolution had eliminated vast numbers of lacemakers, along with much of the demand for fine laces.

When the Emperor Napoleon reintroduced the fashion for handmade lace at court, it was countered by the invention of lacemaking looms, so everyone could afford lace again. The few independent lacemakers left were organized into companies, and by the 1830s the lace manufacturers of Belgium and France had switched to cotton thread.[32]

With the advent of undemanding cotton threads, lacemaking could also be pursued as a leisure activity rather than as a profession. American ladies were encouraged to take up the art of lacemaking themselves, so that they could produce their own frills and ruffles in their spare time. Coupled with the desire to create beauty was the intent to liberate lacemakers from the abuses of the handmade lace industry. The treatment that lace makers endured from their employers was so abominable that decency demanded the rejection of foreign lace and the production of lace at home on the basis of simple morality. A book from 1844, *The Lace Runners,* quotes a lace manufacturer, asked why he paid his workers wages they could not live on. He stated plainly that he expected the women to supplement their incomes by prostitution.[33]

So patterns from Europe and cotton thread helped housewives crochet beautiful laces during leisure moments to add the touch of virtuous perfection to their wardrobes. Not only did crochet wear like iron, it could be thoroughly cleaned.[34] Detachable collars and cuffs, an important part of the middle class housewife's wardrobe, afforded a sturdy luxury. Beauty had to be practical.

IRISH CROCHET

The wealth and leisure created by the Industrial Revolution were offset by the abject poverty of people whose labor had been made obsolete. Economic hardships brought about by war and efficiency underscored the disaster of the Irish Potato Famine and the lace which rose from it like a guardian angel.

In 1845, Ursuline nuns at the Presentation Convent in Blackrock, County Cork, taught new techniques of thread cro-

Irish lace collar, last quarter 19th century. Courtesy of Carole's Cache, Arlington, VA. Photograph by Dee Dun.

chet to the local women and children.[35] When the Irish potato crop failed in 1846 and again in 1847, and people were starving, Susannah Meredith established the Adelaide Industrial School in Cork to teach the art of making crocheted lace and alleviate the economic distress of Ireland. Other Irish and English ladies established crochet schools and convents in the north and south taught crochet techniques to anyone who wanted to learn. The organizations or their founders also arranged the sales of finished pieces and the distribution of the proceeds.[36]

When Queen Victoria accepted a gift of the laces and wore them, Irish crochet was instantly fashionable. Ladies who had no objection to being both fashionable and charitable outfitted themselves in Irish crochet from head to toe. The affordability of the cotton laces, in addition to their sturdiness, also made them very popular with the rising middle class. Practically everyone could afford this handmade lace, if only a collar or cuffs. For once, buying lace was virtuous and actually earned the lacemakers enough to live on. Some earned enough money to survive the Great Famine; some, enough to emigrate.

Despite the popularity of wearing Irish crochet, making Irish crochet was not widespread in 19th-century America. A few immigrant lacemakers worked on commission and a few taught the techniques.[37] It may be that most never again wanted to make laces associated with horrible memories of destitution and starvation, or perhaps they didn't want to take the bread out of the mouths of those they left behind.

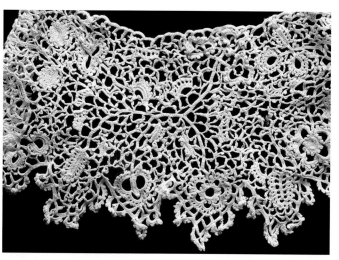

Crochet mimicking early 17th-century Italian needle lace, c. 1850. From the collection of Lacis.

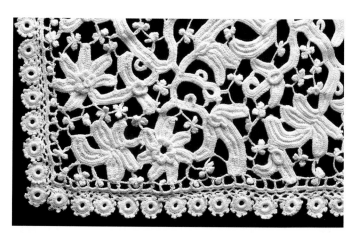

Venetian rose point lace, mid-17th century. From the collection of Lacis.

HOW IT GREW

There were several stages to the development of Irish lace. Initially the pieces were like the popular patterns published in ladies' magazines: "edgings and small articles worked in one piece."[38] Crochet artists then began to imitate the expensive needle laces of Europe. They made discrete, delicate motifs, that were joined with the bars or twisted threads of needle lace.[39] The imitation of needle laces by means of thread and a tiny hook quickly gained fame as Irish crochet.

The next stage was lace formed of motifs with high relief produced by crochet over a padding of heavier threads. These motifs were connected by needle-lace stitches, and finally, by crochet chains.[40] Irish crochet became a rich, dense lace instead of the delicate lace it had originally imitated. Because rich and dense were the Victorian aesthetic, Irish crochet became still more fashionable.

Designs originally adapted from popular Venetian *gros point* or rose point laces changed as local artists began to make their own designs. With such designs as the shamrock and the layered rose, a distinctive, regional lace emerged. Regional

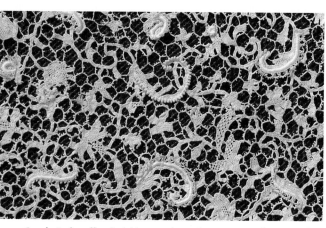

TOP: Crocheted cuff mimicking early 17th-century Italian Coraline needle lace, c. 1850. BOTTOM: Venetian rose point lace, mid-17th century. Both from the collection of Lacis.

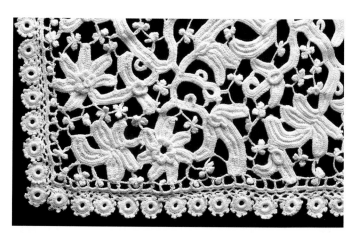

TOP: Irish crochet cuff mimicking 17th-century Venetian lace; c. 1840. BOTTOM: Gross point lace; appliquéd dimensional Irish crochet, late 19th century. Both from the collection of Lacis.

Irish crochet mimicking dimensional 17th-century Venetian lace, c. 1840. From the collection of Lacis.

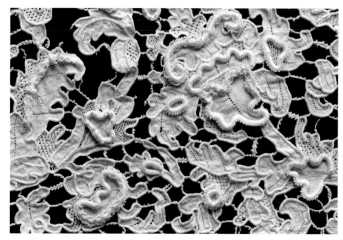

Spanish gross point lace, mid-17th century. From the collection of Lacis.

characteristics continue to this day, as in the Clones knot from the town of Clones in the northern County Monaghan.[41]

Credit for the invention of the Irish lace crochet techniques has been claimed by and for several gifted needlewomen and designers, among them the enormously talented Mlle. Eleanore Riego de la Branchardière. This prolific lace artist published books of thread crochet techniques and lace designs from 1846 until 1887.[42]

Mlle. Riego, as she was known, was instrumental in popularizing Irish crochet in England. She was gifted in design and in translating designs into instructions for reproducible results—something very rare in the early years of needlework publication.[43] While most of the needlework books gave directions which might or might not end up like the illustrations, Mlle. Riego's instructions were methodical and precise and allowed the art of crocheted lace to be disseminated to all who could afford the book. This, along with her taste and her knowledge of needle-lace motifs, enabled her to design consistently beautiful but novel laces.

The freedom of the Irish lace workers to develop their own motifs and designs was one reason that they quickly developed a recognizable and highly individual lace.[44] This was also its weak point. When famine was at the door, workers maintained a desperately high level of design and workmanship. Once the international taste for Irish crochet had been established, workmanship and originality fell off in the struggle to meet an overwhelming demand. When the famine was over, charitable organizations gradually disbanded and were replaced by an influx of distributors who were there for their own profit. This hastened the decline in workmanship.

Some workers chose to work only easy pieces, since they could be finished with less effort and in less time.[45] Poorly paid designers turned their talents elsewhere, and later designs were not as beautiful as the early ones based on the best European laces. By 1855 the popularity of Irish crochet had fallen off, but it was revived in the 1870s with new designs, high standards of production,[46] and the availability of cotton after the American Civil War.

Revived in the 1880s by an infusion of talented designers into schools with high technical standards, Irish crochet was again the rage from 1890–1910.[47] Featured by such famous dress designers as Paquin, the demand for Irish crochet was so great that skilled Irish lace workers were brought to France, Germany, and Austria to teach the techniques and establish more manufactories to meet the demand.[48] But fashion is fickle, and the wild success of the ballet *Scheherazade* in 1910, with Diaghilev's exotic Ballet Russe, turned the eyes of fashion to the Orient. Then Europe was brought to a shuddering halt by the devastation of World War I, which stilled (temporarily) the demand for fashion of any kind.

CROCHET IN AMERICA

While Ireland revolutionized the world of lace, America took crochet to heart and heartland. As America was becoming a nation, crochet was becoming a pastime; everywhere that America went, crochet went, too. Home decoration was full of needlework, and crochet hinted at luxury. The adaptability and versatility of crochet led to all sorts of variations. Filet crochet worked from a grid pattern was a natural offshoot of Berlin wool work. It was used for wall decorations of wholesome sentiment such as the Lord's Prayer or Home Sweet Home.

American crochet became a beloved needle art that accompanied the pioneers. There were few pleasures or diversions for those who left civilization and faced the wilds of the Western Reserve, the prairies, and the Great Plains. Functional sewing was a constant, but crochet was entertainment. A little thread or yarn produced beauty in a harsh land where women were considered a civilizing influence.

There were fluffy wool garments with fanciful names such as nubias and fascinators (scarves and mufflers), pelerines (shoulder capes), shawls, and numerous fleecy fashion accessories. Women also crocheted underwear, petticoats, and anything else to keep out the brutal cold. The Great Plains added a dimension to winter that no one really wanted to experience. Insulating twists and layers of crochet were a defense against winds that swept down from the arctic.

Crocheters also produced yards of lace to trim undergarments (eight feet was an average petticoat circumference) and bed and table linens. Hand-sewn muslin sheets and pillowcases were edged with crocheted lace representing untold hours of labor. True to its sturdy nature, much crocheted pioneer lace has survived to this day.

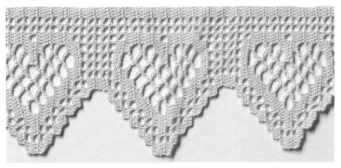

Filet and lacet crochet edging for a pillowcase, designed by Nancy Nehring (see page 211 for the pattern).

IN THE OLD WORLD

Other countries had long traditions of beauty from which to draw. This was as true of the folk arts as it was of the *salons* of the upper classes. But the versatility of crochet, which made it so popular in America, also was appreciated elsewhere. This contributed once again to the annoyance of the gentry. The innovative beauty of Irish lace had been no threat because the peasants were making something pretty for the wealthy. How could that be a threat? Things had always worked that way. The fact that wearing crochet at all started out as charity could only make crochet less of a threat.

It was no threat until peasants began to abandon activities marking them as peasants and took up the activities enjoyed as conspicuous leisure by the wealthy. Once again we find the old "rabble in lace" issue, and rather than settle it, the Industrial Revolution made it worse. Suddenly machine-made goods were standard fare, available to all.

This upstart side of crochet was demonstrated in 19th-century Denmark. Crochet let the peasants on the farm dress like aristocrats. This was a matter of some distress to ladies used to peasants looking like peasants. In 1873 the wife of a wealthy Danish landowner kicked open a hornets' nest when she published a letter in the local paper which criticized rural women for daring to prefer crochet over more appropriate and traditional peasant activities of spinning, weaving, knitting, darning, linen sewing, and patching. But she gave away her real objection by complaining, "…when Madam embroiders or crochets, her maid thinks that she too has the right to do the same."[49]

Crochet had conquered the hands of peasants and gentlewomen alike. This is the mark of an art which knows no bounds. Its decorative and functional qualities were quickly adapted to urban fashion as well as folk costume. Apron lace, lace caps, purses, ornament for jackets, skirts, warm underwear such as petticoats, and vests all were made from the ever-obliging crochet.

IN THE HINTERLANDS

In some places crochet was so popular that it made the area famous. *Crochet de Bosnie,*[50] or Bosnian crochet, is simply rows of slip stitch with a foreign name (remember the muffatee stitch?). It may have arrived in Bosnia by way of the Crimean War (1853–56) and stayed on, making itself indispensable.

Tunisian crochet (also known as the Afghan stitch) is a hybrid of crochet and the long, hooked knitting needles of Turkey and Greece. It has characteristics of both knitted and woven fabric, allowing rich patterning and sturdiness to be combined with ease of construction and portability. It is worked back and forth on one hook, with the stitches picked up on the hook in the first row, and dropped off as they are worked in the second row. Whether this was developed long ago from knitting by nomadic Berbers or was a local adaptation of French colonial crochet remains to be discovered, but it has identified North Africa as a land of crochet. Wherever it started, as part of the international crochet vocabulary it has been reinterpreted. It is now generally identified with bright, luxurious throws under which we snuggle, far from the Sahara.

MODERN TIMES

In 1918 hostilities of World War I ended and the diligent knitting of wartime ceased. Needlework of leisure began to peep from laps and handbags once again, and crochet resumed its place as the functional diversion. The lace industries of Europe were decimated, but women began to replace the devastation of war with things of beauty.

The women who had worked while men were in the trenches, or who had worked alongside the trenches themselves, did not suddenly become sedentary. They took part in tennis, golf, swimming, and stayed in the workforce, too. Clothing for women became more business-like, but trim exteriors did not mean that women abandoned lace entirely. Instead, the lace went out of sight, onto underwear.

The war that leveled so much also leveled the world of needlework. Irish crochet, which women once had allowed other women to make for them, became something they now made for themselves. Books were published with patterns familiar from earlier times, with techniques revived and revised into a hobby.

The Roaring Twenties enticed young women to turn their hands to making scandalous scanties. Crochet designers published books of trims and insets for underwear and boudoir apparel, since most ladies' undergarments were still made at home. The laces of the period are just as feminine as the needle laces of earlier times, but sleek and modern and used with

Crocheted cotton brassiere, American, 1920. Private collection.

restraint. Instead of yards of lace for a petticoat, a few inches at the neck of a chemise or a dainty touch on a pair of step-ins was just enough.

The pink crocheted brassiere (above), worked and worn by a daring American bride in 1920, is so utterly modern that it might be a design in a current summer fashion magazine. It tells the story of crochet perfectly: crochet is always on the forefront, both of fashion and technology.

Accessories of the '20s were well served by crochet, too. The tiny cloche hat could be endlessly adapted and improved upon by crochet. Little brims, intriguing textures, and flower adornments could all be produced at whim by a hook. Lace gloves were whipped up with traditional Irish roses or Art Deco details. The delight of crochet was that it could be old-fashioned and *avant garde* equally well.

The Depression made small things luxuries once again. Thread companies published and republished patterns for lace edgings, tablecloths, and bedspreads. Trim, unfussy collar and cuff patterns made a new fashion statement out of an old dress. Young ladies who had not learned to crochet took up the skill and made it sleek and part of the times. Instead of working an Irish crochet edging in size 100 thread, they dispensed with the individual motifs, used size 30 thread, and made the beautiful grounds the focal point of the lace. We are still enchanted with this "bare bones" lace.

After December 7, 1941, and America's entry into World War II, there wasn't much time for innovation in fashion, except to make it short and sweet. The less material used on non-essentials, the better, so crochet was saved for special things: a touch of lace, a luxurious scarf, a cheerful hat. After the war, home and hearth had first claim on crochet. Tablecloths and edgings for pillowcases, handkerchiefs, and towels were again luxuries that women allowed themselves.

Once yarn was liberated from the confines of olive drab socks it became the stuff of highly innovative crochet designers. For those too industrious to have bowls of wax fruit on the dining room table, a bowl of *crocheted* fruit was a monument to careful shaping, shading, and persistence. Novelties in yarn were a post-war tribute to the joys of domesticity, and young wives of the '50s created baby layettes, loopy slipper and mitten creatures, and enough afghans to blanket the Himalayas.

Crochet remained domesticated until the 1960s. Then rebellious children, who had grown up seeing their mothers and grannies crochet everything establishment, picked up hook and yarn, rope, or anything else they could get their hands on. They went out on tangents that no one had even dreamed existed. They began crocheting baskets, turning granny squares into octagons, and making clothing which had no patterns and used most of the rainbow. Men again took up the hook and began to crochet cowboy hats, briefcases, and Grecian urns.

What is 21st century crochet like? If you haven't picked up a hook for a while, let me warn you: crochet doesn't stop at treble anymore. It doesn't stop at anything. Hook met wire, and thread mesh became the stuff of King Midas' dreams. The hook has conquered the dazzling world of metal. Where can it go from here?

High fashion has been keeping an eye on the crafty hook, and carefree, post-'60s crochet is becoming *haute couture*. New York fashion designers realize that un-mechanized crochet is perfect for people who again want exclusive, handmade goods.

Everything we thought we could do with crochet isn't nearly creative enough. Crochet can do more… we just haven't thought of it yet. 🌀

Crocheted cotton gloves, French, early 20th century. Private collection.

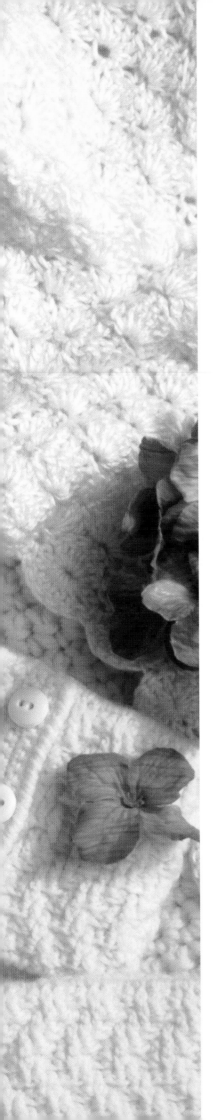

crochet basics

 If you have never crocheted before, welcome to Crochet Basics. This is where you will develop the skills to turn a strand of fiber into anything you like. The first steps are small, easily understood, and easily mastered. If you like to celebrate new skills with projects, turn to the back of this section each time you have learned a new stitch. We have projects which take the simplest of skills and make them simply beautiful, simply fun, or simply too tempting to pass up. If you don't need a hot pad, there is a budding chef somewhere who dreams of it.

Basics alone let you make things to grace you from head to toe. Choose from socks that will skip from season to season, a lacy shell for a special evening, or a tam textured with traditional cables.

Draw loop through luxurious loop to make a wrap so rich with color and glittering tassels that it could warm an arctic night. Or take the granny square of afghan fame, and turn it into a child's delight, updated with a handsome edging. Simple things remind us that accomplishment starts and finishes with the soothing satisfaction of creativity.

If you can't wait to put hand to hook, don't wait! Learn the stitches now, as you think about the project you will choose first. Read about tools and materials when you need to select yarn, and work a gauge swatch for your first project. Turn to the finishing techniques and touches that will mark your achievements. We'll be waiting for you.

FREQUENTLY USED ABBREVIATIONS

beg	beginning
CC	contrast color
ch(s)	chain(s)
ch sp	chain space
cl(s)	cluster(s)
cont	continue
dc	double crochet
dec(ing)	decrease(ing)
ea	each
est	established
hdc	half double crochet
hk	hook
in(s)	inch(es)
inc(ing)	increase(ing)
MC	main color
pat st	pattern stitch
prev	previous
rem(ing)	remain(ing)
rep(s)	repeat(s)
rnd	round
RS	right side
sc	single crochet
sk	skip
sl	slip
sl st	slip stitch
sp(s)	space(s)
st(s)	stitch(es)
tog	together
tr	treble crochet
WS	wrong side
YO	yarn over

ABBREVIATIONS USED IN THIS BOOK

B	bobble
bb-dc	back bead double crochet
bb-sc	back bead single crochet
bb-sl st	back bead slip stitch
bb-tr	back bead treble crochet
b-ch	bead chain
beg	beginning
BL	back loop
BP	back post
BPdc	back post double crochet
BPdc	back post double crochet
BPhdc	back post half double crochet
BPsc	back post single crochet
BPtr	back post treble crochet
BPtrtr	back post treble treble crochet
C	crossed stitch
CC	contrast color
ch(s)	chain(s)
ch-	chain or space already made
ch sp	chain space
cl(s)	cluster(s)
cm	centimeters
cont	continue
dc	double crochet
dc-picot	double crochet picot
dec(ing)	decrease (ing)
dsc	double single crochet
dtr	double treble crochet
E	extended
ea	each
EOR	every other row
est	established
F	Forward row
fb-sc	front bead single crochet
fb-sl st	front bead slip stitch
FL	front loop
FLO	front loop only
FP	front post
FPdc	front post double crochet
FPdtr	front post double treble crochet
FPhdc	front post half double crochet
FPsc	front post single crochet
FPtr	front post treble crochet

FPtrtr	front post treble treble crochet
hdc	half double crochet
hk	hook
in	inch(es)
inc(ing)	increase(ing)
L	linked stitch
lp(s)	loop(s)
MC	main color
pat st	pattern stitch
prev	previous
R	Return
rem	remain(ing)
rep(s)	repeat(s)
rnd	round
RS	right side
Rev sc	reverse single crochet
S	spike
sc	single crochet
sc-picot	single crochet picot
Sdc	spike double crochet
sk	skip
sl	slip
sl st	slip stitch
sp(s)	space(s)
Ssc	spike single crochet
st(s)	stitch(es)
Str	spike treble crochet
tch	turning chain for height
Tdc	Tunisian double crochet
Thdc	Tunisian half double crochet
Tks	Tunisian knit stitch
tog	together
Tps	Tunisian purl stitch
tr	treble crochet
trtr	treble treble
Tsl st	Tunisian slip stitch
Tss	Tunisian simple stitch (afghan stitch)
Ttr	Tunisian treble crochet
TwTss	Twisted Tunisian simple stitch
WS	wrong side
YB	yarn back
YF	yarn forward
YO	yarn over

READING SYMBOLS

Each symbol represents a single, specific stitch. Groups of stitches on a chart show the actual structure of a crochet design. Stitches worked together have linked symbols to show that they are joined.

Patterns are charted row by row and read as if from the front of the fabric, bottom to top. Follow the numbered rows alternately from the right or left as you turn the work. In this book, alternate rows and rounds are shown in different colors to better indicate in which row a stitch is worked. Repeats are shown with a bracket below the section of the chart which can be repeated as needed for width. For more about reading symbols, see next page.

CHART SYMBOLS FOR CROCHET PATTERNS

Instructional

- Start
- direction of next row
- end/ bind off

Basic Stitches

- slip stitch (sl st)
- chain (ch)
- single crochet (sc)
- half double crochet (hdc)
- double crochet (dc)
- treble crochet (tr)
- double treble* (dtr)
- treble treble* (trtr)

Front Loop Stitches (FL)

- slip stitch in front loop (FLsl st)
- single crochet in front loop (FLsc)
- half double crochet in front loop (FLhdc)
- double crochet in front loop (FLdc)
- treble crochet in front loop (FLtr)
- double treble crochet in front loop* (FLdtr)

Back Loop Stitches (BL)

- slip stitch in back loop (BLsl st)
- single crochet in back loop (BLsc)
- half double crochet in back loop (BLhdc)
- double crochet in back loop (BLdc)
- treble crochet in back loop (BLtr)
- double treble crochet in back loop* (BLdtr)

Extended Stitches

- double single crochet (dsc)
- extended half double crochet (Ehdc)
- extended double crochet (Edc)
- extended treble crochet (Etr)

Locked Crossed Stitches

- locked crossed half double crochet
- locked crossed double crochet
- locked crossed treble crochet*

Spike Stitches

- spike slip stitch (Ssl st)
- spike single crochet (Ssc)
- spike half double crochet (Shdc)
- spike double crochet (Sdc)

Post Stitches

- front post slip stitch (FPsl st)
- back post slip stitch (BPsl st)
- front post single crochet (FPsc)
- back post single crochet (BPsc)
- front post double crochet (FPdc)
- back post double crochet (BPdc)
- front post treble crochet (FPtr)
- back post treble crochet (BPtr)
- front post double treble crochet (FPdtr)
- back post double treble crochet (BPdtr)

Fans and Shells: Increases (inc)

- increase one single crochet
- increase two single crochets
- increase one double crochet
- increase two double crochets (three double crochet shell)
- five double crochet shell
- increase two front post double crochet
- increase two back post double crochet

Clusters: Decreases (dec)

- decrease one single crochet (sc2tog)
- decrease two single crochets (sc3tog)
- decrease one double crochet (dc2tog)
- decrease two double crochets (dc3tog) (three treble crochet cluster)
- decrease one treble crochet (tr2tog)
- decrease two treble crochets (tr3tog) (three treble crochet cluster)
- three strand puff
- four strand puff
- five strand puff
- centered puff
- centered cluster

Bobbles, Popcorns and Puffs

- three strand puff
- four strand puff
- five strand puff
- puff in back loop
- puff in front loop
- three half double crochet (hdc3tog)
- three double crochet (dc3tog)
- three treble crochet (tr3tog)
- five treble crochet (tr5tog)
- three double crochet popcorn
- three treble crochet popcorn
- five treble crochet popcorn

Other Stitches

- corded reverse single crochet
- corded reverse single crochet in front loop
- winding stitch
- picot
- single crochet picot

Tunisian Stitches

- simple or Afghan stitch (Tss)
- knit stitch (Tks)
- purl stitch (Tps)
- return stitch (R)
- top loops
- top front loop
- top back loop
- incomplete double crochet
- incomplete treble crochet

Crochet Through Multiple Layers

- slip (sl)
- single (s)
- half double (hd)
- double (d)

Note: Symbols used in charts may be distorted to improve readability. Refer to written instructions for clarification.

* Double treble and taller stitches are indicated by one line in the center of the symbol for each yarn-over.

AMERICAN AND BRITISH STITCH NAMES

There are two systems for naming crochet stitches: American and British. This book uses American. The American system names a stitch on how many times you yarn over and draw through 2 loops. The British system names stitches on the basis of how many total times you yarn over and draw through, including the loop drawn up after inserting the hook. So identical British stitches sound one step longer than American stitches. If your pattern doesn't provide a key, check for the slip stitch. The British system has no stitch by this name.

AMERICAN	BRITISH
Slip stitch	Single crochet
Single crochet	Double crochet
Half double	Half treble
Double	Treble
Treble	Double treble
Double treble	Treble treble

READING INSTRUCTIONS AND SYMBOLS

Many instructions provide both written and symbol versions, and they are both useful, even if you prefer one to the other. If you come to a confusing part in your preferred version, look at the other for clarification. Both kinds of instructions assume you are right-handed.

WRITTEN INSTRUCTIONS may look like obscure code when you read them for the first time. They are actually a shorthand to indicate stitches or actions. Written instructions use abbreviations and punctuation symbols to define logical groups, either repeated operations or small groups of stitches that make up a distinct pattern. They use as little writing as possible to save space and to keep instructions clear and methodical. The abbreviations are defined at the beginning of each pattern or each book of patterns. Any special techniques also will be explained there.

Repeated groups of instructions are given working names used throughout the instructions, for example, "Leaf Cluster," or "Buttonhole." These also may be explained the first time they appear in the text and then referred to by working names thereafter.

BRACKETS AND PARENTHESES group related information, indicating alternate measurements or stitches to substitute according to the size garment you are working. For example:

"Sizes S (M, L, XL); 10 (15, 20, 25) sts; 2 (4, 6, 8) inches"

They group a series of instructions which are to be repeated as a whole: *(sk 4 ch, 5 dc in next ch) across the row* means that you will leave 4 chains unworked; in the 5th chain you will work 5 double crochets. Repeat the entire process, skipping 4 chains and then working 5 double crochets in the next stitch, as many times as indicated (in this case, as many times as fit in the row).

Brackets and parentheses can be used separately, to indicate grouped steps, or they can be nested within each other to separate subsets of instructions, where each group is being repeated within the context of a whole piece. Several examples:

[(A series of buttonholes) worked while you are also shaping the center front] of the left side of a cardigan.

[(The picot) at the tip of a petal] repeated 6 times around a ring for a flower.

Brackets and parentheses can also contain explanations needed at that point.

Stars, asterisks, daggers [★, *, †] (or any other symbol) serve the same basic function as brackets and parentheses: to set apart a group of stitches or actions that will be repeated as a whole. Generally these symbols define repeats for the row, rather than the whole piece.

STITCH PATTERNS make an overall patterned fabric. To make swatches and original designs from stitch patterns, calculate the starting number of chains (sometimes called Base Chains) using whole repeats of the pattern stitch plus extra stitches for the edges, written as "Multiple of x stitches + y." If you wish to make a swatch that repeats the pattern four times across the width of the fabric, multiply the number of repeats you want by the first number in the formula. Then add the second number (the + y part), to keep the pattern repeats lined up vertically.

For example, if a pattern is a "Multiple of 8 stitches + 2," to repeat the pattern 4 times, (4 repeats x 8 stitches = 32 stitches) + 2 more stitches. 32 + 2 = 34 total stitches: so chain 34 to begin.

Sometimes there is a third number in the formula (e.g., Multiple of 8 + 2 + 1). The third number (+ 1) provides the height needed for the first row. This number may be omitted from the formula and found instead as a turning chain in the instructions for the first row.

FOUNDATION ROWS are the rows which "set the stage" between the base chain and the actual pattern rows. Usually they are simply a few rows of plain crochet into which clusters or long stitches are worked. Sometimes they are called foundation rows and row by row instructions are given. In this case the instructions will tell you to repeat only the rows of pattern stitch, for example, "Repeat rows 3–12 for the desired length." At other times you are just told to make a chain and work back across it, and then the numbered pattern rows begin.

SYMBOLS show the actual structure of a crochet design. Each symbol represents a single, specific stitch. Groups of stitches are arranged on a chart to show their relationships to each other. A stitch is placed over the stitch or chain in which it is worked. Increases are shown with the correct number of stitches placed over one stitch. Stitches worked together have linked symbols to show that they are joined.

A medallion chart shows the center ring with successive rounds arranged from the center outward. A lengthwise pattern is charted row by row and read as if from the front of the fabric, bottom to top. Read rows alternately from the right end or the left end of the chart as you turn the work. Row numbers appear on the left or right side of the chart, indicating the first stitch of the row. Foundation rows may or may not be labeled on a chart, but if they are, the chart will show where the pattern rows begin.

In this book, base chain rows are shown in black. Alternate

rows and rounds are shown in different colors to better indicate in which row a stitch is worked. This is especially helpful in complex lace patterns and medallions. Repeats are shown with a bracket below the section of the chart which can be repeated as needed for width.

CHARTS AND WRITTEN INSTRUCTIONS clarify each other. If written directions don't adequately explain a point, look at the chart and vice versa. Some things are almost impossible to chart, such as cylinders, and some things are much easier when read from a chart, such as lace. Both symbols and written instructions have their advantages; used together they can answer virtually any question you may have about a stitch or pattern.

GAUGE

Correct gauge is the difference between a treasured heirloom and a yard sale bargain. The correct size of your finished project depends on gauge. Gauge depends on the size of the hook, the size of the yarn, and how tense you are on any given day. Make a decent-sized gauge swatch; 20 rows x 20 stitches is reasonable. The number of stitches for a swatch may be recommended in the instructions, on the yarn label, or may be determined by the pattern repeat number (see previous page).

The hook size suggested for a pattern is just a place to start. You may work more tightly or loosely than the person who wrote the pattern. You need to work at *exactly* the gauge the pattern requires in order to reproduce it accurately.

Gauge is composed of two parts: stitch gauge and row gauge. Stitch gauge is the number of stitches in a given length of a row, for instance 4 stitches/inch. Row gauge is the height of a number of rows, for instance 3 rows/inch.

Resist the temptation to take it easy and skip the gauge swatch. Work whatever pattern stitches are called for by the pattern, then block and measure them precisely. Partial stitches matter: a half-stitch per inch is the difference between a sock for you and one for your baby.

Make swatches until your stitch gauge is correct. Change hooks until you find one that allows you to make the gauge. If you can't make the gauge with your usual brand of hook, try another brand. Tiny things like a hook's shape and finish make a difference.

When working at the correct gauge you should be able to insert the hook in a stitch comfortably. If you can't, try a different hook.

The row gauge is important, but if you repeatedly obtain the stitch gauge and never quite get the row gauge, you can usually adjust lengths as you work.

Be sure to pull out enough yarn at the beginning of a row to complete the row so you don't have to constantly tug a length of yarn from the ball during a row. Tension on the working yarn will stretch it, making the gauge incorrect.

STRESS SHOWS UP IN YOUR WORK. After a difficult day check the gauge as you crochet to make sure you aren't working more tightly than usual. Check the gauge frequently on a long or complicated project, and change hooks when your gauge is off.

Swatches used to test gauge make great hot pads. Tests made with synthetic yarns should not be used for hot pads since they might melt.

BUY AN EXTRA BALL OF YARN TO WORK SWATCHES. Don't pull out your test swatch and use the yarn in your project from misguided motives of thrift. Your swatch is a test run. Use it to check your gauge, but don't stop there. Work a couple of swatches to learn any new pattern stitches in your project. Throw a test swatch in the washer if you expect to wash the finished project. You will never regret taking the time to learn about the yarn you think you want. How long will you mourn the cashmere sweater that used to fit you and now fits a doll? Use old swatches as hot pad or afghan squares. Partial balls of yarn are great for small projects, donations to charitable programs, or cat toys.

PLAN AHEAD!

Before you begin a new row, unwind enough yarn to complete the new row, or next cluster if you are working motifs. Make this a habit to keep your tension constant. The tug of short yarn will change your tension and make the crochet uneven.

The second reason is that you will find out *before* you run out of yarn that you don't have enough to finish the row. It is false economy to use half a row of yarn and to have an unnecessary join in the middle of a row, and you will have two ends to hide in the middle of the row. Make the join at the end of the preceding row. Cut the extra yarn off and use it for seams, markers, surface embroidery, or stash it away for granny squares.

CROCHET TOOLS

HOOKS

Hooks—especially antique hooks—can be made of just about anything: bone, ivory, horn, silver, brass, pewter, wood, mother of pearl, and tortoise shell. You name it, you can find it. Modern hooks are metal, plastic, or wood.

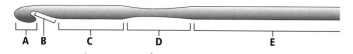

A = tip
B = throat
C = shaft The diameter of "C" is the measure of the hook.
D = grip
E = handle

ANATOMY OF THE HOOK

HOOK SIZES The diameter of the *shaft* of a crochet hook determines the size of the stitch since the loop is formed around the shaft.

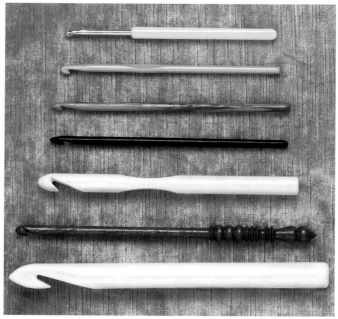

Assorted crochet hooks: metal, wood, and plastic.

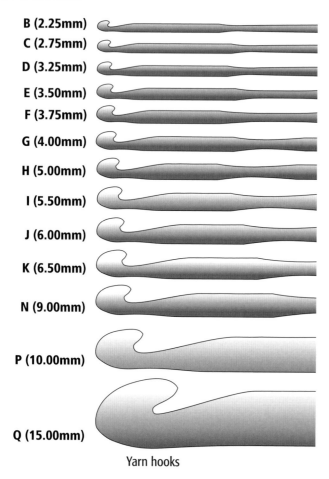

Yarn hooks
B (2.25mm)
C (2.75mm)
D (3.25mm)
E (3.50mm)
F (3.75mm)
G (4.00mm)
H (5.00mm)
I (5.50mm)
J (6.00mm)
K (6.50mm)
N (9.00mm)
P (10.00mm)
Q (15.00mm)

The size of the *hook* determines the size of yarn you can use. Hooks are divided into two basic groups: yarn hooks and steel (thread) hooks. Yarn hooks are made of aluminum, plastic, or wood. They generally are used for larger diameter yarn. They are also used for wire. Steel (thread) hooks as the name implies are made of steel and are used for thread.

Yarn hook sizes are written in metric sizes (2.25–15.00mm); letters (B–Q, Q being the largest); and

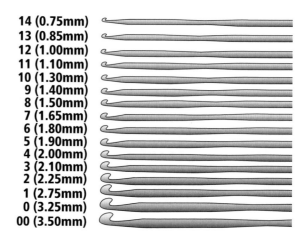

Steel (thread) hooks
14 (0.75mm)
13 (0.85mm)
12 (1.00mm)
11 (1.10mm)
10 (1.30mm)
9 (1.40mm)
8 (1.50mm)
7 (1.65mm)
6 (1.80mm)
5 (1.90mm)
4 (2.00mm)
3 (2.10mm)
2 (2.25mm)
1 (2.75mm)
0 (3.25mm)
00 (3.50mm)

sometimes by number (B = 1 or 2, and so forth). You may find any of these markings stamped on the hooks.

Steel hooks range from size 14 (= .75 mm) to size 00 (= 3.5 mm). Steel hook sizes overlap in the 2.25–3.50 mm range with yarn hooks. You may find either or both markings on the grip. A good hook gauge will have all these markings to help you "translate" the sizes of your hooks.

BRITISH VS. U.S. VS. CONTINENTAL HOOKS

Until very recently, there has been no attempt to standardize hook sizes from one country to another. Older British and American hooks went by their own sizing, depending on the manufacturer. Now there is an attempt to make hooks conform to common metric sizes. If you are using an older hook, don't depend on the size stamped on the grip. To save a lot of potential frustration, test the hook in a metal hook gauge. This is a good idea even with new hooks.

It may be that your grandmother's hook does not match any modern size, but that is not all bad. There are advantages and disadvantages to standardized sizes. If you are having

26

trouble matching your gauge to the required gauge of a pattern, one of these old hooks may be just what you need. Treasure your old hooks, even if they never help you make gauge; muffler sizes are not critical, and you can use a historic hook just for the pure pleasure of carrying on a tradition.

OTHER TOOLS

A METAL HOOK GAUGE is the only tool that can tell you what size your hook is. You can stretch out a paper or plastic gauge, but a metal gauge won't lie. Don't just go by the size stamped on the hook; always check the size of your hook with a metal gauge.

MARKERS remind you where you made changes, increases, decreases, or anything else you want to find easily. They can be safety pins (without coils), paper clips, split rings, scrap yarn or thread, or sleek plastic arrows made for the purpose. It is nice to have an assortment for different jobs. Make them a habit so you don't have to count through a row to find out if you forgot a decrease.

BOBBINS hold small quantities of yarn. They are essential for multi-colored work, when small lengths of five different colors can, while you are not looking, become one big knot.

ROW COUNTERS keep count of rows mechanically. Some people love them, others never use them.

CLOCKWISE FROM UPPER LEFT: Line magnifier, Susan Bates Knit Check, wool needles, darning set, darning needles, tape measure, row counter, bobbins, scissors, thread cutter.

NOTE PAD AND PENCIL are handy whether you use a mechanical row counter or not. Besides making a note of where you stopped, you will sometimes want to change a pattern to suit yourself. Make a habit of immediately writing down a change you made during the course of a row. Otherwise you may not remember that you modified one sleeve until *after* you have assembled the garment.

THE YARN LABEL

The manufacturer's label is one of your most important tools. It's the only place you can find everything you need to know about the product. Every piece of information is designed to help you choose the yarn or thread that will give you a perfect finished product. Before you fall in love with a yarn, read the label. Look for the following:

FIBER CONTENT is basic, but it is amazing how many people choose yarn without ever looking at what it is made from. If you want to make felted slippers, avoid resin-coated, no-shrink wool, even if it is in the wool section.

INTERNATIONAL YARN LABEL SYMBOLS

 4x4"
10x10cm

30M or S
40 R

The manufacturer's suggested gauge/tension with the suggested needle size. This block of knitting stitches can be translated to read: In stockinette stitch, 30 stitches (S) [in French—Mailles (M)] and 40 rows (R) will equal 4" x 4" (10 x 10 cm).

 F/4mm

Manufacturer's suggested crochet hook size in metric and/or US sizes.

 3½-4mm

(5-6)

Manufacturer's suggested knitting needle size in metric and/or US sizes.

 Hand wash in lukewarm water only

 Hand wash in warm water at stated temperature

 DO NOT wash by hand or machine

 Machine wash in warm water at stated temperature, cool rinse and short spin; more delicate handling

 Machine wash in warm water at stated temperature, short spin

 40°C

Machine wash in warm water at stated temperature

 Bleaching permitted (with chlorine)

NO Bleach

or

DO NOT dry clean

May be dry cleaned with flourocarbon or petroleum based solvents only

May be dry cleaned with perchlorethylene or flourocarbon or petroleum based solvents

May be dry cleaned with all solutions

 Press with cool iron   Press with warm iron

 Press with hot iron    DO NOT press

WEIGHT AND YARDAGE are not the same thing. If you are planning to substitute one brand for another, you need to be sure that one 50 gram ball has 100 meters, just like the other brand; a substitute with 75m/50gms will give you an unpleasant surprise, even in a muffler.

Different dyes weigh more than others; if you don't check the yardage you could run short, even if you bought the right total weight. If the ball is labeled only with the weight, get a spare or two. Better yet, buy yarn that tells you the yardage.

CLEANING, BLEACHING, DRYING, AND IRONING TEMPERATURES are shown in internationally recognized symbols (see chart at left). Don't take chances; even yarns with guarantees require proper handling.

PLY AND TWIST actually make a difference in your choice or yarn. (See the following Yarns, Threads and Fibers section for explanations of these terms). If you choose a 4-ply *woolen* spun (which does not mean wool fiber) instead of a 4-ply *worsted* spun, your yarn will pill and wear badly. If worsted is what you need, make sure worsted is what you buy; you would do better buying a 1-ply worsted, even if the ply number is different, than buying a woolen-type.

YARN CLASS (SIZE) has replaced the confusing and esoteric ply and twist classification system. Yarn is now categorized by the working diameter of yarn, which is the way most people look for yarn. (See the following page for explanations.)

GAUGE AND HOOK SIZES are now appearing on most labels. If the gauge and hook size recommended for the yarn surprise you, rethink your choice of yarn. A thin-looking yarn may take a 6mm hook because of the fuzzy fiber.

THE PRODUCT NUMBER AND DYE LOT are stamped somewhere on the label. Whatever you end up buying, purchase it all from the same dye lot. Minute color differences not apparent under store light will be blatant in natural light. Even whites do not always match. Different products, even from the same manufacturer, come in different shades of white. If you are matching a fabric, take it with you and match it under natural light.

Some synthetic yarns have no dye lot because consistency in manufacture makes it possible to keep the colors true from batch to batch. But it is still a good idea to purchase all the yarn for a project at one time because stores run out and companies discontinue colors and products.

KEEP THE LABELS! If you love the yarn, keep a label so that you can reorder. If you crochet a project as a gift, send a label—and some extra yarn for mending—along with the gift. The recipient will need to know how to launder it.

YARNS, THREADS, AND FIBERS
SPIN, PLY, AND SIZE

Yarn and thread are made up of strands that have been twisted together to form a larger diameter. The different ways fibers are spun, the number of strands, and the specific qualities that come from these differences determine what you can do successfully with a particular product.

SPIN tells you the arrangement of the fibers while they were being spun and also tells you something about the tightness of the twist of each strand.

IN WORSTED YARNS, fibers are parallel to each other and to the length of each strand (ply). Few fiber ends will be exposed to the surface of the yarn, which means it will be smooth and will not pill or fuzz easily. The threads are smooth and tightly twisted, forming a very sturdy yarn. Worsted yarn is good for garments that take a lot of abrasion, such as mittens and socks.

IN WOOLEN-SPUN STRANDS, fibers are spun crosswise to the length of the thread, so that the fibers form a vortex around a core of air. This gives the yarn good insulating properties. The strands are loosely packed and softly spun, so that the air-catching spaces are not squeezed shut. These warm yarns are good for garments that do not get a lot of abrasion, such as vests, baby garments, hats, and afghans. "Germantown" refers to a soft, woolen-spun yarn, 3- or 4-ply.

SPECIALTY YARNS have other qualities that define the yarn, such as bouclé, eyelash, slub, chenille, and so forth, and are chosen for appearance.

PLY refers to the number of spun strands twisted together to make up a yarn, usually two, three, or four. The number of plies does not tell you the diameter of the yarn because a ply can be large or small. Ply does not indicate either the type or size of yarn. (See the sizes below right.)

Ply has a great deal to do with how yarns wear, and what their shapes are. Yarn is not just "plain round."

To see the differences, take a piece of rope, fold it in half, and twist it; that is 2-ply. It is not very round, and each ply has a lot of surface exposed, which means that each ply gets a lot of wear. Fold the rope in quarters and twist it; that is 4-ply. The plies fit together, and each ply has most of its surface hidden. Folded into eighths, the rope is now as tightly packed as industrial cables.

YARN SIZES are a potential source of confusion, so several systems based on the diameter of yarn have been devised. One classifies yarns into five categories by the approximate diameter of the yarn:

A = fingering or fine-weight yarns, good for thin socks and light baby clothes

B = sport or medium-weight yarns, good for indoor sweaters, baby things, dresses, and suits

C = worsted-weight or knitting yarns, good for outdoor sweaters, hats, mittens, afghans, and slippers

D = bulky-weight yarns, used for rugs, heavy jackets, and crafts

E = extra-bulky-weight yarns, used mostly for rugs

(1) Caron, Cuddle Soft, 3-Ply Yarn; (2) Red Heart, TLC 3-Ply Yarn; (3) Red Heart, 4-Ply Yarn; (4) Lion Brand &Yarn, Wool-Ease Thick & Quick, 2-Ply Yarn

Sport-weight yarn is a diameter of yarn, and it is frequently two-ply. It could have eight ply and still be a sport-weight yarn if the diameter were the same. It is smaller than so-called knitting worsted and larger than fingering or sock yarn.

Knitting worsted is frequently 4-ply, but there is single-ply knitting worsted with the same diameter as the 4-ply. And there are 4-ply silk yarns which are nowhere near the diameter of knitting worsted but which have the same tough qualities.

Some manufacturers also have a DK, or Double Knitting size, which falls between sport yarn and worsted weight.

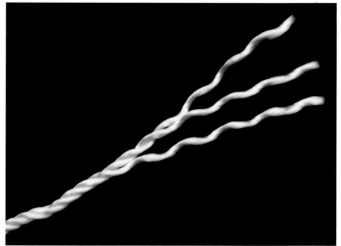

Sample of a 3-ply cotton thread.

The other system categorizes yarns into six classes, determined by the number of stitches per 4-inch swatch of knitted stockinette stitch. The smaller the number, the smaller the yarn:

1 = fine = 29–32 sts
2 = light = 25–28 sts
3 = medium = 21–24 sts
4 = medium-heavy = 17–20 sts
5 = bulky = 13–16 sts
6 = extra-bulky =9–12 sts.

Lace-weight yarns are ultra-fine, generally knit up at 40 stitches to 4 inches or more, and fall outside of both systems.

When in doubt, look on the label to see what stitch gauge and hook size is recommended. If it varies widely from what your project requires, buy one ball and make a test swatch.

SUBSTITUTIONS must be made with care. Knowing the class of yarn is not enough. Substitutions are risky and require that you take into account the length per ball as well as the diameter of the yarn.

Substituting one diameter of yarn for another is generally not a good idea. Making the gauge work is difficult, and calculating how much yarn you need is even harder.

When substituting one brand of yarn for another, be careful to check the yardage. For example, 50 grams of yarn, 100 meters long will not give you the same amount of yarn as 50 grams, 80 meters long.

When substituting a different fiber of the same diameter, consider carefully whether the two fibers will act the same. Cotton, linen, and ramie (see page 33) are not stretchy and will not act the same in a sweater ribbing as wool or acrylic. Mohair will not show off your stitches the way a reeled silk yarn will.

(1) Mimosa Cashmere, Cashmere & Nylon Blend; (2) Trendsetter Yarns, Dali, Cashmere; (3) Belangor, French Angora Rabbit Hair; (4) Karabella Yarns, Lace Mohair; (5) Moco Yarns, Musk Ox Qiviut; (6) Moco Yarns, Musk Ox Qiviut, Australian Merino, and Silk; (7) Himalaya Yarn Co., Tibet Recycled Silk; (8) Judi & Co., Hand-Dyed Rayon Raffia; (9) Hemp

When uncertain, buy one ball of yarn and work several test swatches to see if what you want the yarn to do is, in fact, what the yarn does. Check for stitch definition, shrinkage, abrasion (pilling), or any other quality important in the finished product.

WEIGHT AND MEASURE EQUIVALENTS

These are the approximate equivalents of measurements commonly found on yarns and threads:

1 cm = 0.4 in.
10 cm = 4 in.
1 m = 1.1 yds.
100 m = 109 yds.
1 kg = 2.2 lbs.
1 g = 0.04 oz.
25 g = 0.9 oz.
50 g = 1.75 oz.
100 g = 3.5 oz.

FIBERS

There are common properties in various groups of fibers, and these will help you understand some of the variables in yarns and threads. Your choice of fibers will help to determine the character of your finished project. The more you know, the fewer surprises you will have.

PROTEIN FIBERS

Protein fibers come from animal hair and insect cocoons and have common properties. They are absorbent, weaker when wet, and tolerate acidic conditions, so they are best washed with mild detergents. They take dyes well and can be dyed brilliant colors. Protein fibers tolerate mild alkali conditions, including ammonia, so they can also be washed with soap, borax, and ammonia solutions. They are poor conductors of electricity and build up static charges in dry climates. The fibers are elastic but damaged by stretching. Protein fibers resist creasing.

WOOL is the most widely known animal fiber, usually shorn from the sheep; a few breeds shed their coats and are plucked. There are hundreds of breeds of sheep, each with a distinctive wool character. Merino and Rambouillet are known for fine, soft fleeces. Other types are Mountain and Hill breeds, Longwool and Lustre breeds, and Shortwool and Down Sheep. There are also regional breeds, such as Shetland sheep, descended from ancient Northern breeds, whose fine wool is renowned for the beautiful laces made from it.

MOHAIR comes from the Angora (Ankara) goat, which is shorn twice a year. Kid mohair, from goats up to 18 months old, is a fine, lustrous, and affordable luxury fiber. Adult mohair can be as fine as cashmere or quite hairy, depending upon the individual goat. It is very durable.

(1) Klaus Koch Kollection, Clip, Wool; (2) Eisaku Noro, Wool; (3) Karabella Yarns, Merino Irrestringibile, Wool; (4) Eisaku Noro, Wool; (5) Rowan, Wool Cotton; (6) Rowan, Biggy Print, Wool; (7) Anny Blatt, Wool & Kid Mohair Blend; (8) Mountain Colors Hand-Painted Yarns, Mohair, Wool & Nylon Blend

CASHMERE comes from Kashmir goats, whose downy winter undercoat is plucked in the spring. A number of other "down" goats have plucked undercoats. They used to be found primarily in Central Asia, but other countries are beginning to breed these goats.

ANGORA rabbits produce fibers for angora yarn. The fur is either plucked or shorn. It is frequently spun with a strand of silk or wool for a yarn which sheds less, is less costly, but which has the same silky texture of the soft fur. Angora felts easily.

THE LLAMA FAMILY is distantly related to the camel. There are two domesticated members of the group, the llama and the alpaca. The llama's rather coarse coat is used for utilitarian items rather than clothing. The alpaca is bred for its fine, silky fleece, which is used for clothing.

VICUÑA AND GUANACO come from undomesticated and protected members of the llama family. Their furs are extremely rare and costly.

CAMEL HAIR is the winter undercoat collected from the Bactrian (two-humped) camel of the Gobi desert. It is very fine, soft, and lusterless. Occasionally it is available in knitting yarns.

QIVIUT is the shed winter coat of the musk ox, which produces only about six pounds per year. Finer than vicuña and extremely rare, this luxury fiber is collected in the wild and is good for light but extremely warm garments. It is increasingly available from Eskimo cooperatives and specialty yarn sources.

SILK, extruded by the silk worm for its cocoon, is unwound in a single strand. It comes principally from cocoons of *Bombyx mori* moths.

There are several other species of moths whose cocoons are used for wild silk, called Tussah. After the moth has emerged from the cocoon, the short fibers (which cannot be reeled) are spun into yarns. The waste silk from the combing process, called noil, is sometimes combined with wool, cashmere, or other fibers for textured yarns.

Wool and angora's elasticity contributes to felting and shrinking, which can be either desirable or disastrous depending on the result desired. Other hair fibers felt and shrink to a greater or lesser degree, depending on the animal.

Both animal fibers and silk produce warm fabrics, but wool actually gives off heat when wet. Silk does not, and its lightness and absorbency make it comfortable in hot weather. Hair fibers are susceptible to insect damage and are also damaged by prolonged exposure to sunlight; silk is not. Because of their shared properties, all protein fibers combine well in yarns.

(1) Rowan Denim, Cotton; (2) Berrroco, Glace, Rayon Viscose; (3) Noro, Ganpi Abaka Tape, Ganpi Abaka, Rayon & Nylon Blend; (4) Trendsetter Yarns, Sunshine, Viscose Rayon & Polyamide Nylon Blend; (5) Muench Yarns, Cleo, Viscose & Metal Blend; (6) Muench, Touch Me, Viscose & Wool Blend; (7) GGH, Esprit, Polyamide Nylon; (8) Trendsetter Yarns, Shadow, Polyester; (9) Trendsetter Yarns, Charm, Polyester; (10) Anny Blatt, Victoria, Polyamide Nylon; (11) Gedifra, Mambo, Acrylic & Nylon Blend; (12) Anny Blatt, Ketmie, Polyamide

NATURAL CELLULOSE FIBERS

Cellulose fibers can be either natural or synthetic. The natural sources are from plant leaves, long stem (bast) fibers, and seed fibers. The most common natural cellulose fibers are cotton, flax (linen), hemp, and ramie. The fibers are hollow and absorb water readily, which makes them cool to the touch and pleasant to wear in hot climates. The spun fibers lie in one direction, giving cellulose threads a luster.

Cellulose fibers are stronger when wet than dry, and can take high temperatures, scrubbing, and abrasion. They also tolerate alkali conditions well, but are susceptible to acids, particularly hot acids. Bleach with chlorine (sodium hypochlorite), or by simmering in a soap solution (not detergent). Yarns combining both protein and cellulose fibers are difficult to maintain; the method used to clean one fiber harms the other.

LINEN is produced from flax, which was first cultivated by the ancient Egyptians. Flax is a tall grass whose stem is broken, rotted, and beaten away to release the long fibers. The longest of these are combed and made into line flax, while the shorter waste fibers are called tow. Both can be made into smooth yarns which become shinier and softer the more they are worn. If you have a yarn with stiff, crunchy linen fibers, try wetting it thoroughly, freezing it, and then ironing it while it is still frozen. This will soften it by driving steam into the core of the fiber. The process also works for linen garments.

COTTON was originally cultivated in India, spread to China, and has been adopted by every warm climate. Egypt is famous for its long-staple cottons. Less than 2" long, the soft fibers must be very tightly spun to hold together but produce fine threads with a bright luster, ideal for lace and other work to showcase the detail of individual stitches. The luster and vivid jewel tones possible with dyes make cotton threads popular for clothing and accessories.

RAMIE is the stem fiber of a nettle called China grass, which has been cultivated in Asia for millennia. The fibers are beaten and scraped from the bark, dried, and degummed by boiling in alkaline solution. The lustrous, bleached fibers dry very quickly and are resistant to mildew. Somewhat stiff, the fibers are often found mixed with linen or cotton in yarns.

REGENERATED CELLULOSE FIBERS

All man-made fibers are, strictly speaking, synthetic. But fibers made from regenerated natural fibers are no longer classed as synthetics; they are now called natural fibers. These fibers fall into two categories: regenerated cellulose and cellulose acetate. Cellulose, frequently in the form of wood chips, is broken down and regenerated to produce viscose rayon, referred to as viscose or as rayon.

RAYON has properties similar to those of cotton and blends well with other cellulose fibers, but it is weaker when wet and abrades more easily. Rayon combined with wool tends to felt or mat together when machine washed and dried.

LYOCELL (TENCEL®), a new regenerated cellulose fiber, is similar to rayon and has a light, silky texture. In hand-knitting yarns, it is found primarily in blends.

CELLULOSE ACETATE, commonly known as acetate, was developed after World War II. Its qualities are quite different from rayon and natural cellulose fibers and more like those of synthetic fibers. It melts at 446 °F, is not absorbent (so it will drip dry), and resists creasing.

SYNTHETIC FIBERS

Synthetic fibers are made from substances that are not fibers, but that are made into fibers by chemical means. Long-chain polymer molecules of coal and oil by-products are combined into continuous molecules. These long strands are synthetic fibers, extruded much the same way silk fibers are. Synthetics have the shared properties of great strength and elasticity. They are light, do not absorb moisture (which makes them difficult to dye, but they drip dry), and resist abrasion. Because they hold static charges, they soil more easily than natural fibers and are harder to clean.

NYLON (a polyamide), the first and most famous synthetic fiber, is followed closely by polyamids, a subgroup of polyamides with less-rigid properties.

POLYESTER, which comes in a number of varieties under a number of names such as Dacron, is a very fine fiber often used in commercially woven fabrics and high denier knits. In hand-knitting yarns these fibers are found in metallic and textural blends.

ACRYLIC fibers are a form of vinyl and come under various trade names, such as Orlon. Knitting yarns with acrylic fibers have the hand properties of wool yarn. Acrylic is more flammable than nylon and polyester, though there are some types with good flame resistance. Acrylic is less elastic than nylon and polyester, so garments may distort if not cared for properly.

POLYPROPYLENE draws moisture away from the skin, doesn't develop static easily, and is a good insulator. It is spun into soft yarns and blends.

Threads are covered in detail in the Thread Crochet chapter (page 76). 🕸

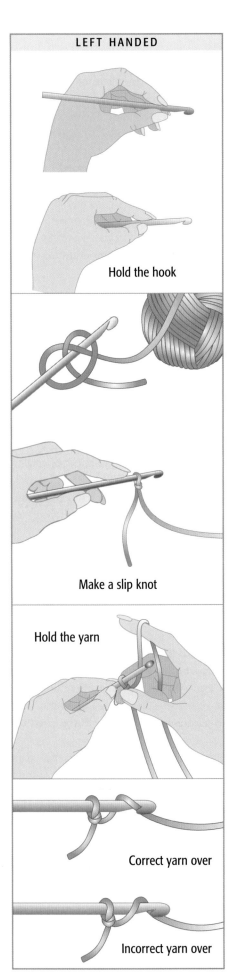

Hold the hook

Make a slip knot

Hold the yarn

Correct yarn over

Incorrect yarn over

GETTING STARTED
HOLDING THE HOOK AND YARN

HOLD THE HOOK like a pencil or under the palm of the hand, like a knife, whichever position is more comfortable. Practice both grips, and change if your hand gets tired.

MAKE A SLIP KNOT to start the chain. Leaving a 4-inch tail of yarn, make a circle of yarn with the working yarn (from the skein) under the circle. Insert the hook under the working yarn. Pull the working end of the yarn to tighten the loop until it fits the hook, but slides easily on the shaft.

HOLD THE YARN in the hand not holding the hook. Let the yarn run loosely under the palm and over your index finger. Use your thumb and second finger to hold the tail of yarn on the hook.

It is important that the yarn slide smoothly from your hand to the hook without being stretched or taut and that your hand is relaxed.

YARN OVER (yo) occurs at least once in every stitch. Bring up the working yarn behind the back of the hook, and lay it back to front across the shaft, just above the hook. DO NOT wrap the yarn from front to back. Stitches depend upon a correct yarn over.

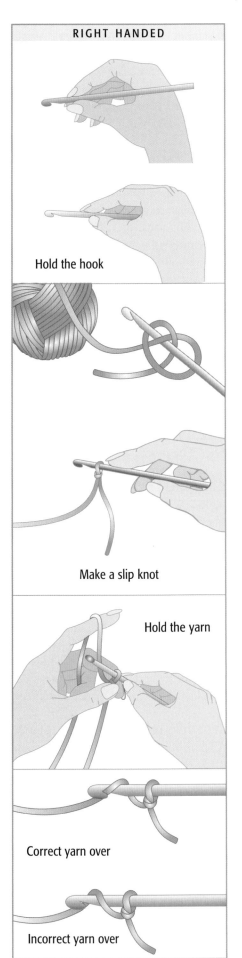

Hold the hook

Make a slip knot

Hold the yarn

Correct yarn over

Incorrect yarn over

34

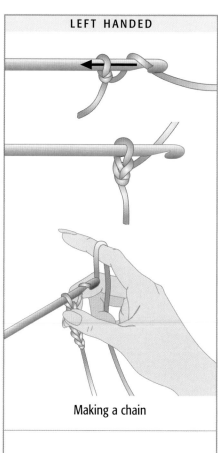

Making a chain

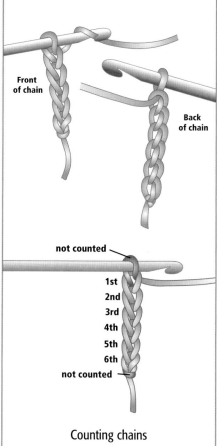

Front of chain

Back of chain

not counted

1st
2nd
3rd
4th
5th
6th

not counted

Counting chains

MAKING A CHAIN

MAKING A CHAIN (**ch**) starts with a yarn over. Catch the yarn in the hook and pull it through the loop on the hook. Each time you do this you make one chain. You may need to turn the hook a bit to pull the yarn over through easily. Keep the chains loose enough to insert the hook for other stitches. The shaft of the hook should slide comfortably in the chain.

Make chains until the stitches are even. To control the tension of the stitches, each time you make a stitch reposition your thumb and middle finger to hold the chain closest to the hook.

COUNTING CHAINS starts at the first chain after the hook. The front of the chain looks like a line of Vs. The back of the chain has a ridge running down its length. You can feel as well as see the difference between the front and back of a chain. Run your thumb down the spine (back loop) and count the bumps, or count the Vs on the front. The slip knot is never counted as a chain, nor is the loop still on the hook.

An easy way to keep track of how many chains you have made is to insert a marker into every 10th chain. If a project starts with a long chain, chain a few extra in case you miscount. It is easier to pick out the extra chains than to re-do the entire length.

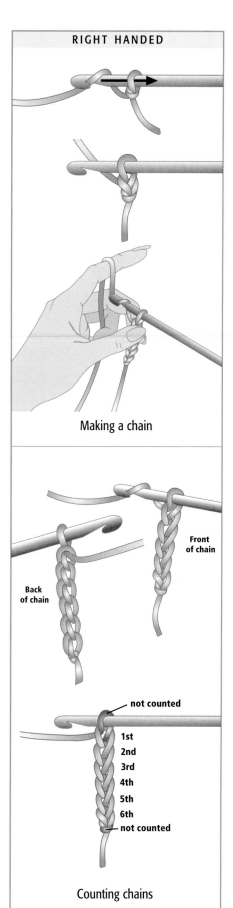

Making a chain

Front of chain

Back of chain

not counted

1st
2nd
3rd
4th
5th
6th

not counted

Counting chains

35

36

LEFT HANDED

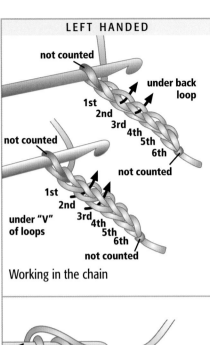

Working in the chain

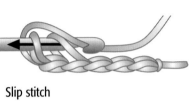

Slip stitch

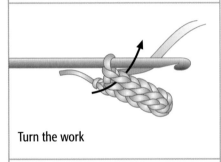

Turn the work

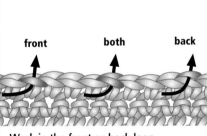

Work in the front or back loop

WORKING IN THE CHAIN begins by turning a chain over and inserting the hook, front to back, under the back loop of the second chain from the hook, or under either one or both loops of the V.

SLIP STITCH

SLIP STITCH (**sl st**) by first inserting the hook in the second chain then yarning over and drawing a loop through that chain and the chain on the hook. There will be one loop left on the hook when you have completed one stitch. This is true of all crochet stitches, unless the directions specifically tell you otherwise. Continue to slip stitch in each chain.

When looking at a slip stitch you see both the front and back loops. The stitch is in the form of a sideways V (or >). The top of the stitch is the back loop and the bottom of the stitch is the front loop.

Project for slip stitch: Decorative Hot Pad; see page 53 for instructions.

TURN THE WORK at the end of a row. Insert the hook under the V of the second slip stitch. Yarn over, and draw one loop through both the slip stitch and the stitch on the hook.

WORK IN THE FRONT OR BACK LOOP means working in the front or back strand of a stitch, instead of working in both. Insert the hook under the back or front bar of a stitch, yarn over, and draw through. Work a few rows of each to see the differences. Working in the front and back of stitches is used throughout crochet to produce interesting patterns.

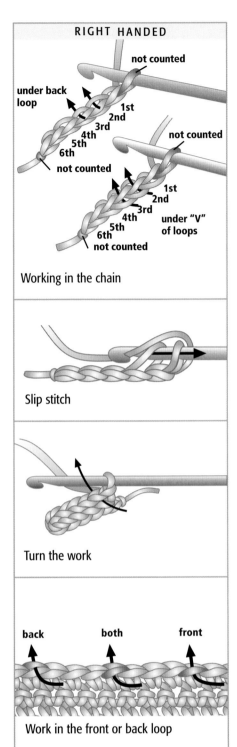

RIGHT HANDED

Working in the chain

Slip stitch

Turn the work

Work in the front or back loop

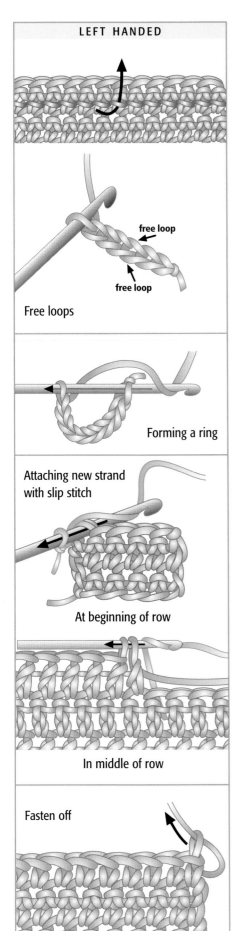

Free loops

Forming a ring

Attaching new strand
with slip stitch

At beginning of row

In middle of row

Fasten off

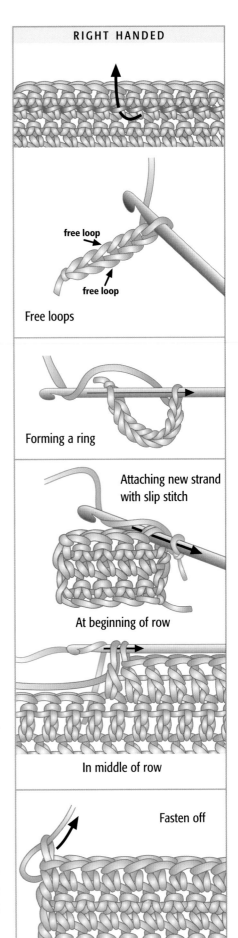

Free loops

Forming a ring

Attaching new strand
with slip stitch

At beginning of row

In middle of row

Fasten off

FREE LOOPS occur when you work in the back or front loop of a stitch: the unused loop is called a free loop. Any unworked stitch has two free loops. Free loops of lower rows can be crocheted into for patterns and color work.

FORMING A RING is needed for motifs and round projects. To make a basic ring, chain 8, insert the hook in the first chain, yarn over, and slip stitch through the first chain and the chain on the hook.

ATTACH A NEW STRAND OF YARN WITH SLIP STITCH at the beginning of a row, make a slip knot in the new yarn and place the loop on the hook. Insert the hook through the last stitch made, yarn over, and slip stitch through the stitch.

Attach a new strand of yarn in the middle of the row with a slip stitch or begin in the last loops of the preceding stitch. Work the stitch up to the last yarn over. (The last yarn over in a stitch may be the only yarn over, such as in the slip stitch.) Hold the new yarn behind the crochet and work the last yarn over with the new yarn. This completes the stitch with the new strand. If the new strand of yarn is a different color, the next stitch will be the new color. Work in the loose ends when you have finished the piece. You can also crochet a few stitches with the new strand and a loose end.

FASTEN OFF after completing the last stitch. Cut the yarn and pull it through the last loop on the hook. Work the tail into the seam or the edge. ❀

37

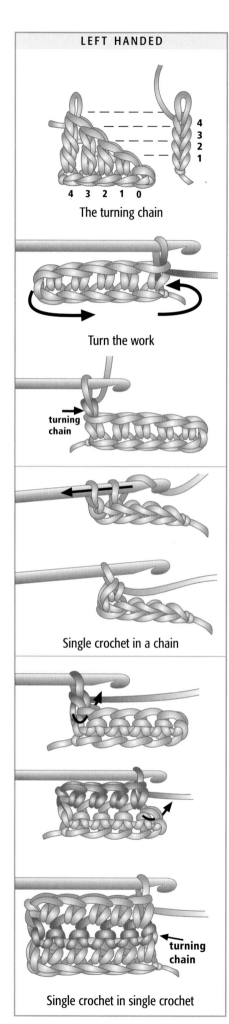

LEFT HANDED

The turning chain

Turn the work

turning chain

Single crochet in a chain

Single crochet in single crochet

BASIC STITCHES

Basic stitches differ in height, and the height is established at the beginning of a row.

THE TURNING CHAIN (tch) creates the height of a new row. Even work in the round requires chains for height even though the work is not turned. Don't confuse the last loop of a row with a turning chain. The turning chain is the first stitch of a new row.

TURN THE WORK first so that your hook is again at the beginning of the row and you will not confuse the two, though some instructions write the turning chain at the end of a row.

A single crochet is one stitch high, so there will be one turning chain. A half double crochet is 2 stitches high, a double crochet 2 or 3 stitches high, and so forth. Work chains as required.

You may require fewer or more turning chains than recommended to accommodate the height of a row. Work the number of chains you need, no matter what the instructions say.

SINGLE CROCHET

SINGLE CROCHET (sc) IN A CHAIN Insert the hook into the back loop of the second chain from the hook (skipping the first chain = 1 turning chain for height). Yarn over and draw up a loop (two loops on the hook). Yarn over again and draw it through two loops, leaving one loop on the hook. This forms a single crochet. Work across the chain. Turn.

SINGLE CROCHET IN SINGLE CROCHET Chain 1 for height. Insert the hook under both bars of the first stitch. Yarn over and draw up a loop. Yarn over again and draw it through two loops. One loop remains on the hook.

Work a single crochet in each stitch of the row, ending with one single crochet in the last stitch of the row. There should be exactly as many stitches in this row as in the row below; don't work in the turning chain. Count to be sure, and make this a habit as you work.

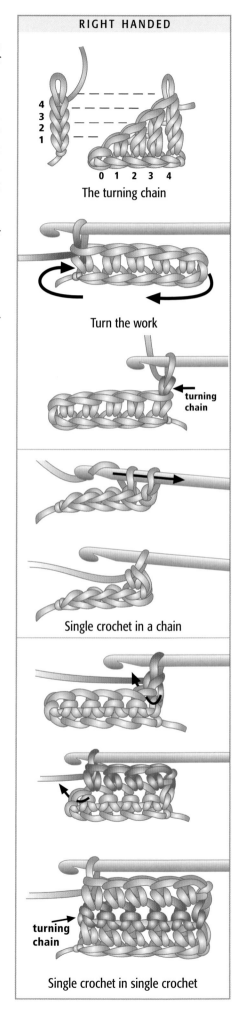

RIGHT HANDED

The turning chain

Turn the work

turning chain

Single crochet in a chain

turning chain

Single crochet in single crochet

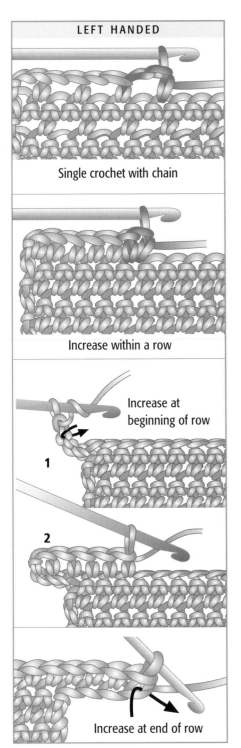

Single crochet with chain

Increase within a row

Increase at beginning of row

1

2

Increase at end of row

SINGLE CROCHET WITH CHAINS

A single chain stitch surrounded by chain stitches produces a hole. A row of alternating chains and single crochets makes an eyelet path to hold a ribbon or a drawstring. Alternating chains and single crochet in rows makes an all-over pattern called seed stitch.

INCREASES AND DECREASES add or subtract stitches and are used to shape garments and create decorative patterns. When used to shape a garment, the change will be placed exactly where it is needed: for example, to create a flare at the hipline. There are different methods of working an increase and decrease, depending on whether it is in the middle or at the end of a row.

INCREASE (**inc**) WITHIN A ROW: work two (or more) stitches into one stitch. The illustration shows an increase worked in single crochet, but the method can be used with any stitch.

INCREASE AT THE BEGINNING OF A ROW: start at the end of the preceding row. Chain the desired number of increased stitches plus the turning chains for height. Turn and work into the chain as you would a starting chain. Complete the row as usual.

The chain increase is useful for adding several stitches at once. Pair it with the *increase at the end of a row* for matched increases.

INCREASE AT THE END OF A ROW: yarn over as needed for the height of stitch you are using. Insert the hook into the base of the last stitch made and draw up a loop. Work the stitch as usual. The illustration shows this used with a single crochet, but it can be worked in any stitch.

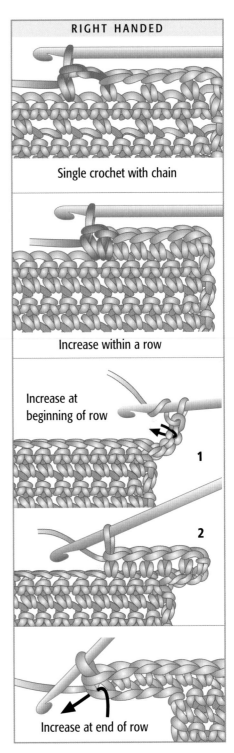

Single crochet with chain

Increase within a row

Increase at beginning of row

1

2

Increase at end of row

39

WHAT TO DO AT THE END OF A ROW

Work edge stitches (turning chains) in one of two ways depending on the application you plan to use. Using the Open Stitch Family as an example (Fig. 1), the chart shows the turning chain worked outside of the main body of stitches. For garments, work the turning chains outside the main body of the stitch so that the pattern repeats continuously across seam lines. Fig. 2 shows the turning chain worked within the main body of stitches. When you want even sides on a rectangular piece such as in a blanket, work the turning chain within the main body of stitches. You can convert the patterns in the gallery from one type of turning chain to the other depending on your application.

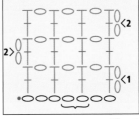

Fig. 1

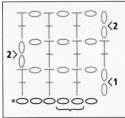

Fig. 2

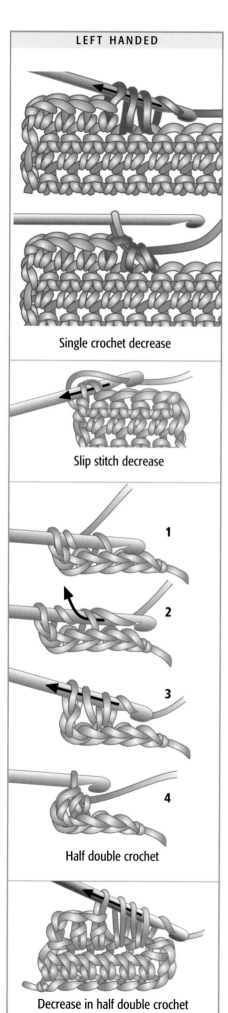

LEFT HANDED

Single crochet decrease

Slip stitch decrease

1

2

3

4

Half double crochet

Decrease in half double crochet

TO DECREASE (**dec**), work two or more stitches together. Start the decrease one stitch before the decrease occurs. Work the stitch up to the last yarn over, leaving two loops on the hook. Begin the next stitch and work as usual up to the last yarn over. Yarn over and draw through *all* the loops on the hook. This completes both stitches with a smooth and inconspicuous decrease.

A SHORT ROW will decrease stitches at the end of a row. Just skip the stitches you want to decrease, turn, chain for height, and start the new row.

USE A SLIP STITCH DECREASE to decrease stitches at the beginning of a row. Work slip stitches (which are virtually invisible) into the stitches to be decreased. Then chain for height, and work across the row.

Projects for Single Crochet: Mufflers; see page 57 for instructions.

HALF DOUBLE CROCHET

HALF DOUBLE CROCHET (**hdc**) is a half-step taller than single crochet. It is often used for garments because it drapes beautifully and is warm and cozy.

Chain 2 for turning chain. Yarn over once *before* inserting the hook. Insert the hook and draw up one loop (three loops on hook). Yarn over and draw the yarn through all three loops.

DECREASE WORKED IN HALF DOUBLE CROCHET (**hdc dec**) is worked over two stitches, just as the single crochet decrease. Yarn over, insert the hook in the stitch and draw up one loop (three loops on hook). Without completing the first stitch, yarn over, insert the hook into the next stitch, and draw up a loop (five loops on hook). Yarn over and draw the yarn through all five loops on the hook. This completes two half double crochets and one decrease.

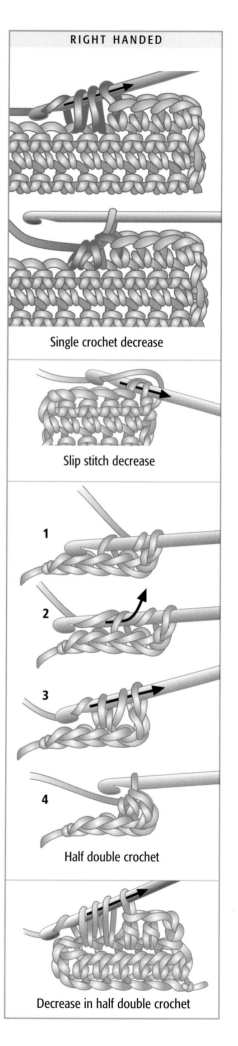

RIGHT HANDED

Single crochet decrease

Slip stitch decrease

1

2

3

4

Half double crochet

Decrease in half double crochet

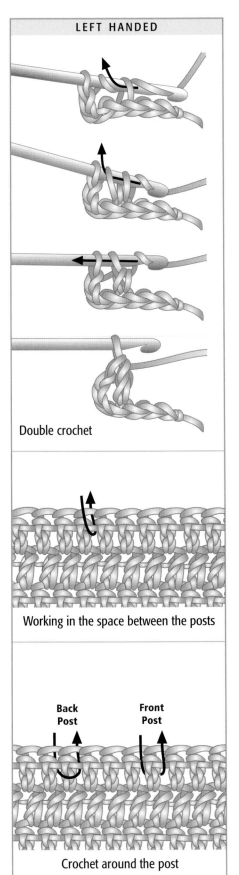

Double crochet

Working in the space between the posts

Back Post **Front Post**

Crochet around the post

DOUBLE CROCHET

The turning chain for double crochet (dc) is 2 or 3. As in the half double crochet, yarn over once before you insert the hook into a stitch. Draw up one loop (three loops on the hook). Yarn over, draw through two loops (two loops remaining). Yarn over again and draw through the remaining two loops to complete the stitch.

WORKING IN THE SPACES BETWEEN THE POSTS (the columnar part of the stitch) is an alternative to working in the horizontal bars of the stitches. Working in the space offsets the stitches, so that there is a brickwork effect instead of perfect vertical lines of stitches. This is shown in symbol charts by offsetting the stitch symbols, so that they appear in the spaces between the stitch symbols of the preceding row. (See the Shallow Stitch, page 135, for an example.)

When working in the spaces, the stitch gauge is wider and requires a looser foundation chain, so work it with a larger hook. The row gauge is shorter because the hook is inserted lower in the preceding row; you may need to adjust the turning chain height.

CROCHET AROUND THE POST adds textural interest. To work around a post, insert the hook on one side of the post and bring it out on the other side, then draw up yarn around the post. Using front post stitches and regular stitches will create a raised surface on the front of a fabric. Back post stitches recede when seen from the front. Using both back and front post stitches will make raised stitches on both sides of the fabric for highly textured patterns, and is very effective with long stitches and with crossing stitches.

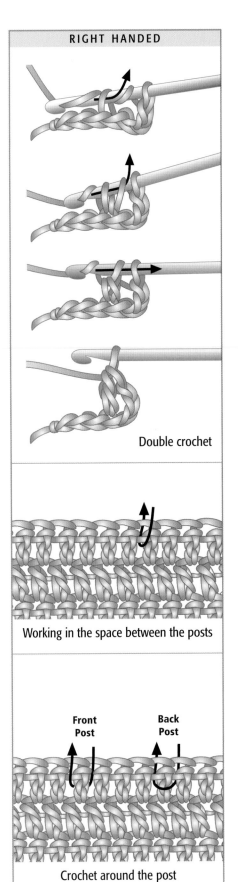

Double crochet

Working in the space between the posts

Front Post **Back Post**

Crochet around the post

41

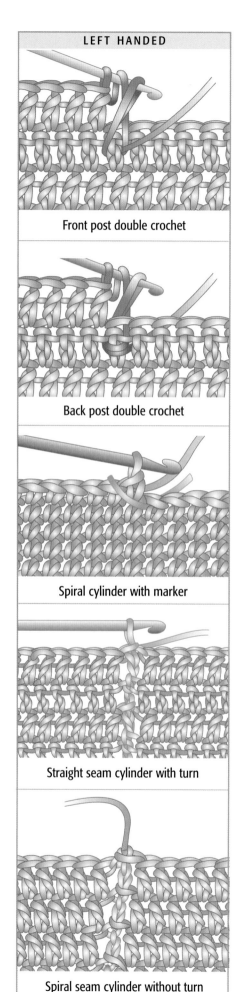

Front post double crochet

Back post double crochet

Spiral cylinder with marker

Straight seam cylinder with turn

Spiral seam cylinder without turn

FRONT POST DOUBLE CRO-CHET (FPdc): Yarn over once. Insert the hook from the front, around the post, coming out again at the front. Yarn over and draw up one loop. Complete the double crochet as usual. This will create a raised stitch on the front of the fabric.

BACK POST DOUBLE CRO-CHET (BPdc): Yarn over once. Insert the hook from the back, around the post, coming out again at the back. Yarn over and draw up a loop in the back of the piece, and complete the stitch as usual. This will create a raised stitch on the back of the fabric.

MAKING SHAPES

Now that you know how to do increases and decreases your work can become round, or square, or any other shape you want to make it. Cylinders are easy, and pancakes are not much harder.

SPIRAL CYLINDER is worked in single crochet. Chain 20, then work back across the row in single crochet. Join the two ends by working a single crochet in the first single crochet. Continue in a spiral, working a single crochet in each single crochet. At the beginning/end of the round, put in a marker to help count the rounds. Each time you come to the marker, work the stitch and replace the marker in the new row.

STRAIGHT SEAM CYLINDER, shown here in double crochet, can be worked in any stitch. Chain 20, slip stitch into first chain to join. Chain 3 for height. Work one double crochet in each chain, until you come to the end of the round. Slip stitch the last double crochet to the first double crochet to join.

Round 1: Chain three for height. Turn to reverse direction. Slip stitch to join. Repeat Round 1 for the desired height.

Working the cylinder with turns at the end of each round will give you a straight seam and even rounds, in case you want to make stripes. If you do not reverse direction every round, your rounds will be even, but the seam will spiral around the cylinder as you work.

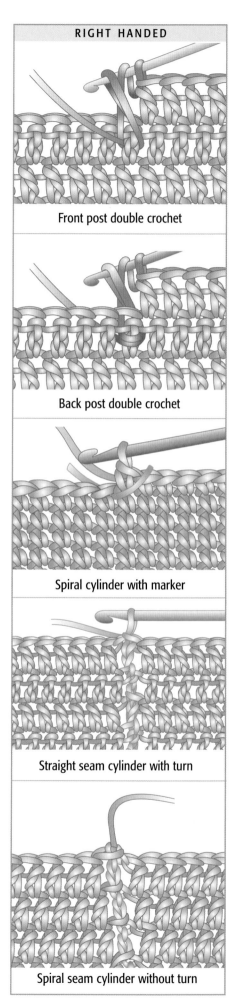

Front post double crochet

Back post double crochet

Spiral cylinder with marker

Straight seam cylinder with turn

Spiral seam cylinder without turn

Making a round

MAKING CORNERS

Sometimes you need a corner—in a ripple pattern or an afghan square, for example. Regularly spaced increases or decreases let you do this. An increase repeated in the same place in each row will make a corner as you progress. So will a decrease worked at the same place in each row, but the corner will turn in the other direction. Mark the center stitches of your bends, and repeat the same group of increases or decreases at the marked stitches, every row. Alternating increases and decreases creates decorative ripple patterns.

To make a circle into a square, four equally spaced chains or increases become corners. Working increases into these corners allows you to both increase the size of your square and retain the corners. This is the basis for the classic granny square. If you want something more than a square, put in 6 or 8 corners. The technique is the same: mark the center of the increase and repeat the increase each row.

ROUND AND FLAT

Sometimes crochet is an art, but making things round and flat strays into geometry. This formula works with single, double, and treble crochet.

Make a ring: Make a chain, ideally larger than three chains for ease of working, but if three is what you need, use three. Slip stitch in first chain to join.

Round 1: Chain for height. Count that as the first stitch. Work two stitches in every chain of the foundation chain. Slip stitch to join. Or, work the stitches over the ring, and catch in the tail of yarn as you are doing it.

Round 2: Chain for height, count it as a stitch, and again work two stitches in every stitch in the round. Slip stitch to join.

Round 3: Chain for height, count it as the first stitch, *work two stitches in the first stitch, one in the second stitch* and repeat this alternation around. Slip stitch to join.

Round 4: Chain for height and count it as the first stitch. *Work two stitches in one stitch, then work one stitch in each of the next two stitches*. Repeat from * to * around the ring. Slip stitch to join.

Round 5: Chain for height, count as

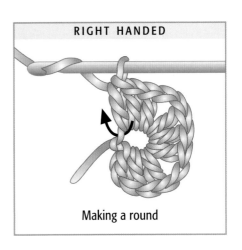

Making a round

the first stitch. *Work two stitches in one stitch, and then work one stitch in each of the next 3 stitches*. Repeat from * to * around. Slip stitch to join.

Round 6: Chain for height, count as the first stitch. *Work two stitches in one stitch, then work one stitch in each of the next 4 stitches*. Repeat from * to * around. Slip stitch to join.

Continue in this fashion, increasing the number of single stitches worked in between the "two in one stitch" stitches. Eventually you will need more "two in one" stitches, at which point you put in "two in one" stitches as required to keep your circle flat. This is where the geometry shifts to art. Keep laying the circle down to make sure it is flat. If you find you need a stitch more or a stitch less per round, do what you need to do.

Projects for Double Crochet: Button Top Socks and Granny Square Poncho; see pages 54 and 58 for instructions.

turning chain →

Treble crochet

TREBLE CROCHET AND LONGER

TREBLE CROCHET (**tr**) The turning chain is 4. Yarn over twice before inserting the hook. Draw up a loop (four loops on hook). Yarn over and draw through two loops, three times.

DOUBLE TREBLE (**dtr**) This is the longest stitch of the standard crochet vocabulary. It is called a double treble because it uses the same number of yarn overs as a double crochet (1) plus a treble crochet (2) or 3 yarn overs.

Turning chain of 5. Wrap the yarn around the hook three times before inserting it into a stitch. Then yarn over and work off two loops, four times.

LEARNING THE TERMINOLOGY

Do you recognize a pattern? Stitches are named by the number of times you yarn over and draw through two loops. You do it once for a single crochet, twice for a double, and three times for a treble. The pattern of *yarn over—draw through two loops, repeat until all the loops are gone*—is the norm.

Stitches which do not follow this pattern have different names, so that you can tell they are not standard. For example, look at the half double crochet: yarn over and draw through three loops, once.

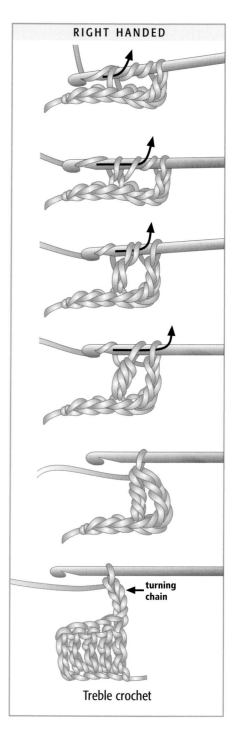

← turning chain

Treble crochet

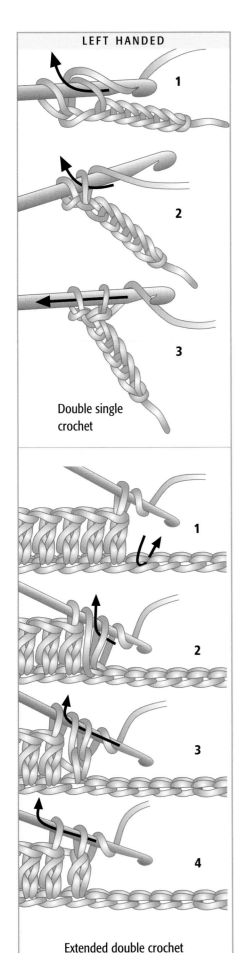

Double single crochet

Extended double crochet

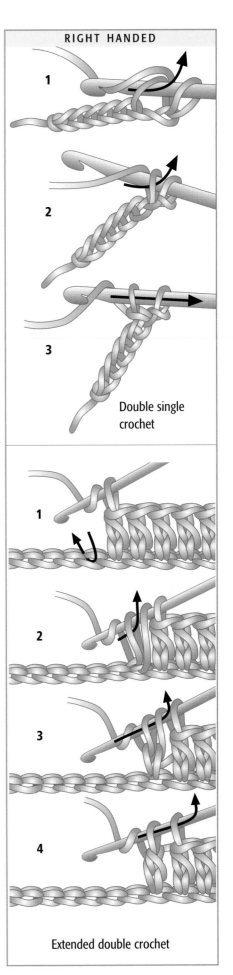

Double single crochet

Extended double crochet

EXTENDED STITCHES

EXTENDED STITCHES (**Edc, Etr, etc.**) occur when you draw a yarn over through only one loop. Extended stitches, also known as half-step stitches or Elmore stitches, are used when the normal stitch falls short or long. Once you have learned the method, invent and adapt as needed for making a stitch exactly the right length. Adjust the turning chain as needed, either by working it loosely or by making an additional chain.

DOUBLE SINGLE CROCHET (**dsc**) is a traditional extended stitch, with no E attached to the name. Insert hook and draw up a loop (two loops on hook). Yarn over, draw through *one* loop (two loops on hook). Yarn over and draw through the last two loops on hook.

EXTENDED DOUBLE CRO-CHET (**Edc**) starts out like a regular double crochet. Yarn over once and insert the hook. Draw up a loop (three loops on hook), yarn over and draw through *one* loop (three loops on hook). Yarn over, draw through two loops, twice. If you have done this in a row of regular double crochet, you will see that the extended stitch is a half step longer than the others.

No doubt this will give you ideas. If you need to connect something just a bit out of reach in a lace join or an afghan row, an extended stitch may bridge the gap.

PERFECT CURVES are easy with extended stitches (for example: sc, hdc, dc, Edc, tr, Etr, tr, Edc, dc, hdc, sc). Use them in color patterns for the perfect wave. Use them in fitting garments for a smooth curve at the armhole or the neckline. Just remember that the extended stitch technique will extend whatever stitch you choose.

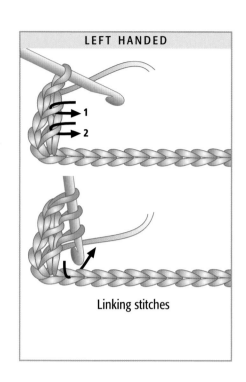

Linking stitches

ADDITIONAL TECHNIQUES

LINKING STITCHES are useful to connect the sides of long stitches. You can do this with anything except single crochet. It is shown here in treble crochet.

Insert the hook into the horizontal loops of the preceding stitch, drawing up a loop at each horizontal bar in turn, in place of yarn overs. In a treble crochet, draw up two loops this way before you insert the hook into the stitch below (three loops on hook). Draw up the loop from the stitch below (four loops on hook). Then work as usual: yarn over and work off two loops, three times. The stitch will be connected to the side of the preceding stitch.

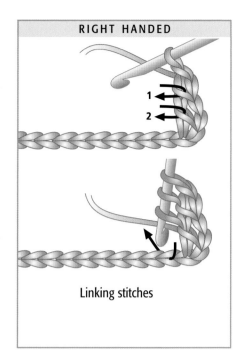

Linking stitches

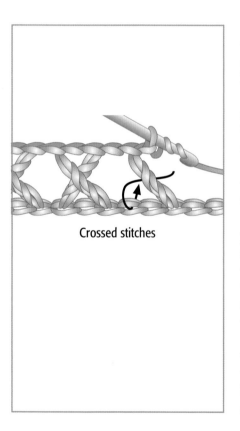

Crossed stitches

CROSSED STITCHES allow you to skip over stitches and rows to create dazzling diagonals. They work best with long stitches, so try them with trebles.

1st leg: Yarn over twice, skip a stitch, and insert your hook in the second stitch beyond where you would normally insert it.

Yarn over and work off two loops, three times. The treble stitch is at a tilt. Chain one stitch between the legs.

2nd leg: Yarn over twice. Work with your hook behind the first leg of the stitch. This time insert your hook *back* two stitches, directly below the origin of the first leg. Yarn over and complete the stitch as usual, chain 1. The next stitch is the first leg of another X.

Work crossed stitches across intervening rows of stitches for color or textural interest. Extended stitches give a bit more length to cross several rows of crochet.

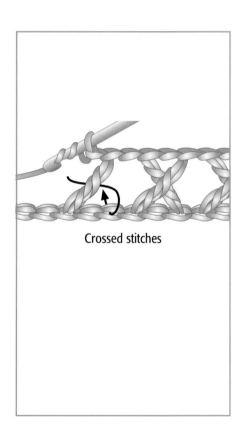

Crossed stitches

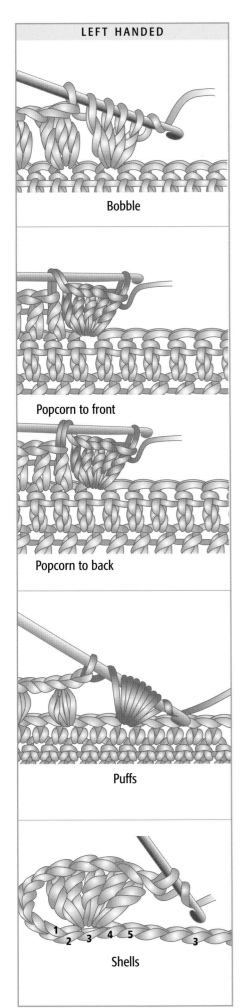

Bobble

Popcorn to front

Popcorn to back

Puffs

Shells

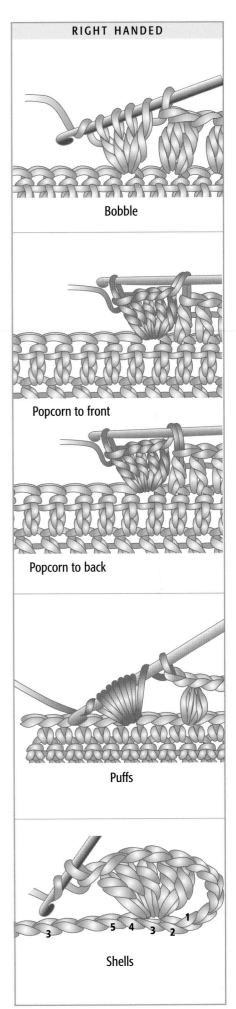

Bobble

Popcorn to front

Popcorn to back

Puffs

Shells

CLUSTER STITCHES are groups of stitches in one stitch or space, gathered at the top or the bottom, or sometimes both. They are really just glorified increases and decreases that do not change the stitch count of the row. Clustered stitches are crochet classics because they are easy to make and beautiful. Group them with other stitches for an endless variety of patterns, both lacy and solid.

BOBBLES, POPCORNS, AND PUFFS are all counted as one stitch because they begin and end in the space of one stitch, but bulge out in the middle.

BOBBLES are similar to popcorns, but drawn together at the top through all the loops. Work each stitch to the last loop, but *leave the last loop on the hook* while you are working the rest of the stitches in the bobble. Then, yarn over and draw a loop through all the loops on the hook to complete the stitch.

POPCORNS are worked like increases: each individual stitch is completed. Remove the hook from loop of the last stitch of the popcorn, reinsert it from the top of the first stitch into the loop. Then gather the stitches by drawing the loop through the tops of the first stitch. Popcorns can be made to pop out of either side of the work, depending on the side of the work you reinsert the hook into to gather the stitches.

PUFFS are similar to bobbles, but fluffier. Instead of working five entire stitches at the bottom, you draw up a loop and yarn over five times through the base stitch, and keep all the loops on the hook. Complete by making a yarn over and drawing it through all the loops on the hook. Puffs are loopier than bobbles and popcorns, and look more like clouds than raspberries.

SHELLS (also called *fans*) are groups of stitches worked into the same base stitch. Each stitch in a shell is counted as if it stood alone. Compensate for width by skipping stitches on either side of the center. Five double crochet in a shell are counted as five stitches: two on either side, and one in the middle stitch (or space) where all the stitches are worked. Two unworked stitches fall on either side of the stitch containing the shell.

47

GRACEFUL ENDINGS

Weaving in a lot of ends can seem tedious. Whenever possible, avoid weaving in the middle of a piece by attaching new strands at the beginnings of rows. Leave a long tail to sew seams, or work over the tails with a decorative border.

But sometimes it's inevitable: you have to work in an end. Use either a crochet hook or a large tapestry needle. Thread the yarn in the tapestry needle and use the needle to follow the curves of edge strands for a few inches. Fasten the tail around a strand in the center of a stitch. Make sure the edge stretches before cutting off the excess.

Or, insert a crochet hook under one strand of an edge. Catch the tail and wrap it around the strand to blend it in. Repeat the process in each edge loop until you have worked in 3 inches of yarn or more. Then insert the hook into the center of a stitch to catch the yarn around an interior strand. Stretch the edge and clip the excess yarn.

BLOCKING YOUR WORK

Blocking prepares garment pieces for assembly or tidies a garment after it has been laundered. If you want a garment that fits, check your stitch gauge frequently. If a garment doesn't fit before you block it, don't expect miracles from blocking.

Before you do anything, read the label on the yarn you used and do exactly what it says. The laundering instructions below are no substitute for the manufacturer's instructions.

EASY-CARE YARNS that can be dried in a dryer don't need to be blocked. Wash the pieces and dry them flat, or smooth them lightly with an iron following the instructions on the yarn

label. If you decide to iron, use a damp press cloth over the crocheted pieces to keep from damaging the yarn. Then join the pieces neatly. When you wash the item later, turn it inside out (to decrease visible pilling), and dry it in the dryer with minimal drying time and heat.

PROTEIN FIBER YARNS (wool, silk, etc.) should be laundered with mild detergent and tepid water.

CELLULOSE FIBERS (cotton, linen, ramie) clean best with soap and hot water.

COLORFAST means the dye will not run or bleed. If you are not sure if your fiber is colorfast, wash a test swatch in a bowl. If the dye is not colorfast and you have a multicolor garment, lay the pieces on an old towel. Using an iron and a press cloth, lightly smooth the pieces before assembling, and then dry-clean forever after. If the garment is one color, you can launder it carefully by itself, but be prepared for fading.

DRY THE PIECE(S) FLAT so the yarns don't stretch. Follow this same process for an unfinished or finished garment: First, squeeze out excess water by rolling the garment in a bath towel and walking on it. Then arrange it flat on a drying rack. Use a mesh drying rack or a dry towel on a counter. Shape to the finished measurements written in the instructions or to the drawn outline of the finished garment.

When almost dry, cover the piece with a light press cloth (to protect the fibers) and hold a steam iron or steam wand over the pieces to fluff the yarn and remove any curl at the edges. When the pieces are thoroughly dry, join them using your favorite method.

PROTEIN-FIBER LACE items generally need to be stretched to reveal the open spaces. Stretch the piece to the finished measurements (or to the point you want, if you make up your own pattern). Steam-fluff while still damp, before joining.

CELLULOSE-THREAD LACES can be starched during the final rinse or spray-starched when ironed. Three-dimensional laces, such as Irish lace roses, should be dried upside down in a thick towel to preserve the shapes; press the flat parts, if you like. Flat laces may be pinned out and allowed to dry or

ironed while damp. Lace edgings should be spray-starched and pressed when you press the garment. They don't need to be pinned out if you stretch them as you iron them.

A WORD OF CAUTION

Blocking is no remedy for a badly fitting garment. Changes made by blocking last only until the next laundering, if that long. Most blocking (especially to make things seem smaller) is quickly undone by body heat and normal humidity.

JOINS AND SEAMS

The ideal seam is invisible and flat, with no internal bulk. You can use different kinds of seams in the same garment as needed. On side seams you generally work from the hem or cuff to the armhole. When working a shoulder seam, work from the neck out (if there is a jog you can cover it with the sleeve).

WEAVING SEAMS FROM THE RIGHT SIDE allows you to see the seam as you make it. This is especially helpful when you have stripes or pattern stitches to match.

Thread a tapestry needle with 18–24 inches of yarn. Abut the two edges and pin them every 4 inches or so with coil-less safety pins. Work on a flat surface. Bring the needle up through the bottom chain on one side and insert it down in the equal and opposite stitch of the opposite piece. Bring up the needle in the next convenient stitch on the same piece. On the other side in the equal and opposite stitch, insert the needle down, and bring it up in the next convenient

---

LEFT HANDED

Woven seam

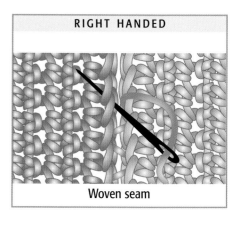

RIGHT HANDED

Woven seam

stitch a few threads on. The stitch length between where you insert the needle and bring it up on each side should be in proportion to the gauge of the work. You don't want gaps, but you don't want puckers, either. Draw the yarn only tight enough to keep the edges together, not tight enough to distort the crochet stitches. The stitches will be virtually invisible and the horizontals should match. Hide the tails on the wrong-side edges. On stepped edges ignore the steps and work in a straight line, turning the corners inside. Steam them flat later.

SLIP STITCHES join pieces neatly and easily, but each stitch must be loose enough to allow the seam to stretch. They are useful on internal stepped edges, because you can work in a straight line.

Pin the pieces together using large T-pins which won't get lost in the yarn. Draw up the slip stitch one stitch in from the edge, to keep the seam from being bulky. Insert the hook into the next stitch, and draw up a double loop (yarn and the yarn tail) through the first slip stitch. Depending on the thickness of the yarn, continue drawing up double loops until the tail is used up, then work with the single strand. If the double strand is too bulky, leave the yarn tail on one side, and draw up single loops for the seam, then work in the tail with a tapestry needle. If you run out of yarn before finishing the seam, cut a 24-inch strand and start again where you left off.

SINGLE CROCHET joins are good for decorative external seams but make bulky internal seams. It does not work well on stepped edges. On row ends the seam should be only as deep as the turning chain or first stitch post.

Pin the pieces, wrong sides together. Draw up a slip loop at the beginning of the seam on the front of the work. Yarn over and draw through a loop at the edge of the pieces. Insert the hook in the next opening along the edge, draw up a loop at the edge, yarn over, and continue making single crochet down the seam. Work the tail along with the yarn strand, thread it through the edge loops, or hide it inside the seam with a tapestry needle.

WHIPSTITCH works well for sewing straight-edged seams together. With the right sides together, insert the needle through the abutting loops of the edge stitches of the two pieces. At either end of the seam, secure the yarn and thread the tails into the stitches. ❧

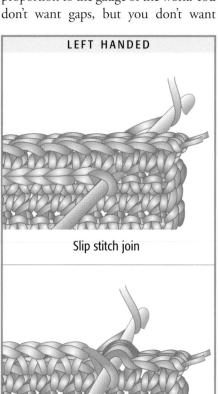

Slip stitch join

Single crochet join

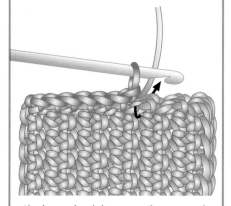

Single crochet join across the row ends

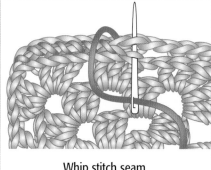

Whip stitch seam

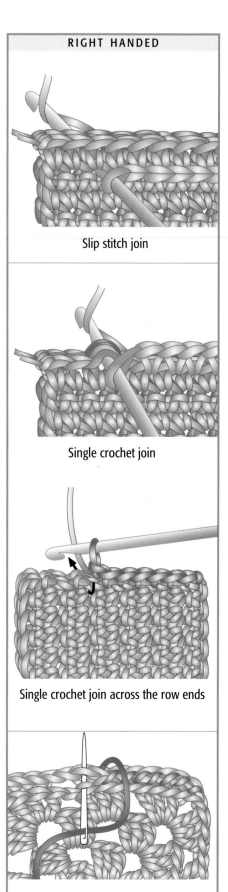

Slip stitch join

Single crochet join

Single crochet join across the row ends

Whip stitch seam

49

wrapped in love

Crochet takes a tasseled, high-fashion turn in a stole of luxurious mohair-blend yarn with added metallic sparkle. Any novice can master the half-double crochet that makes up the body of this inviting, snuggly wrap.

DESIGN BY MELISSA LEAPMAN
Skill level: Beginner
Finished project size: 30" x 70"

MATERIALS

Westminster Fibers/Jaeger, Odessa, 65% mohair/31% acrylic/4% polyester metal (50 grams/207 yards per ball): 15 balls of Cherise (168)

Size F/5 (4.00mm) aluminum crochet hook or size needed to obtain gauge

Size E/4 (3.50mm) aluminum crochet hook

60 small glass beads

Large-eyed sewing needle

GAUGE

In **Body Pattern** with larger hook, 22 sts and 12 rows = 4" (10.2cm)

Take time to check your gauge.

STITCH PATTERN

This simple wrap is made using only half double crochet stitches. A subtle vertical rib is created in this piece by "stacking" front and back loop stitches. The terms *front loop* and *back loop* are relative to the side facing you. Whichever side of your work faces you, the loop closer to you is the front loop and the loop farther away is the back loop. When you turn your work over, what was the front loop becomes the back loop, and vice versa.

⬭	chain (ch)
T	half double crochet (hdc)
↧	half double crochet in the front loop (hdc in front lp)
⊥	half double crochet in the back loop (hdc in back lp)

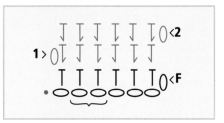

LEFT HANDED

hdc in front lp
hdc in back lp

Row 1: half double crochet alternating in front and back loops

INSTRUCTIONS

Multiple of 2 stitches +1.

Beginning at the lower edge using larger hook, ch 386.

Foundation Row (RS): Hdc in 2nd ch from hook and in each ch across — 385 sts; turn.

Row 1: Ch 1, hdc in front lp of first hdc; * hdc in back lp of next hdc, hdc in front lp of next hdc; rep from * across; turn.

Rep Row 1 until piece measures approximately 30" from beg. Fasten off.

FINISHING

EDGING: With the RS facing and smaller hook, join yarn with sl st in first hdc at right edge. Ch 1, 3 sc in same sc as join for corner, sc in each hdc across and work 3 hdc in next corner. Sc evenly along 3 rem sides, working 3 sc in each corner. At end; join with sl st in first sc.

Rnd 2: Ch 1, sc in same sc as joining, 3 sc in next sc. Sc in each sc around working 3 sc in each corner. At end, join and fasten off.

TASSEL CAPS (make 4): With smaller hook, ch 3. Work 9 hdc into third ch from hook — 10 sts. Do not join. Working in continuous rnds, hdc in each hdc around for 6 more rnds. Leaving a 16" tail, fasten off.

TASSEL

TASSEL STRANDS: Wrap yarn 35 times around a 6" piece of cardboard. Cut strands at one end, and tie them together in the center, leaving an 8" tail. Cut yarn ends and trim evenly.

BEADS: Thread one bead onto the 16" tail left from the Tassel Cap. Whipstitch it through both loops of one hdc on last rnd of cap. Repeat from * around pulling tightly after applying each bead. Fasten off.

TASSEL ASSEMBLY: Draw the 8" tail saved from securing the tassel strands through the center of cap. Thread 5 beads onto the tail. With the tail, join to corner of stole.

Rep this method for making and joining the remaining 3 tassels. ✺

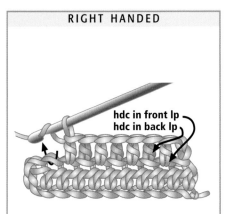

RIGHT HANDED

hdc in front lp
hdc in back lp

Row 1: half double crochet alternating in front and back loops

Tassle detail

Melissa Leapman has worked as a freelance designer with many leading ready-to-wear manufacturers and design houses in New York City. She takes commissions for contemporary designs from yarn companies such as Reynolds, Plymouth, and Brown Sheep. See her other designs on pages 58, 61, and 98.

MATERIALS

Lion Brand Kitchen Cotton, Article #760, worsted weight cotton yarn (5 ounces/236 yards per ball): one ball Maize (186)

Size C/2 (2.75mm) aluminum crochet hook or size needed to obtain gauge

GAUGE

20 sts and 21 rows = 3" (7.6cm)

Take time to check your gauge.

STITCH PATTERN

Working in solid slip stitch makes a very dense fabric. which is why this hot pad is ultra-thick. The project is worked in a continuous spiral around the base chain. The pattern stripe, created by working slip stitches in 10 front loops, then in 10 back loops, is a multiple of 20. The stripes become diagonal because the pattern is worked on a chain which is a multiple of 10 stitches + 1. If the chain were a multiple of exactly 10, the stripes would be straight up and down.

NOTES

Read about slip stitches on page 36. This project is worked in rounds. **Do not chain-1 or join rounds.**

INSTRUCTIONS

Multiple of 20 stitches + 9.

Ch 50.

Foundation: Sl st in 2nd ch from hook and in each ch across — 49 sts. Working along opposite edge of Foundation, sl st in each ch across — 49 sts or 98 total sts.

Rnds 1–55: * Sl st in front lp of 10 sts, sl st in back lp of 10 sts; rep from * around and around.

FINISHING

Holding WSs together, fold hot pad in half. Sl st through back lps across the top and through both layers to close opening. Hanging Loop: Ch 15; join with sl st in 15th ch from hook. Fasten off and conceal ends. 🌼

Nancy Nehring is a nationally recognized author, teacher, and designer. See her other designs on pages 100 and 105.

decorative hot pad

This elementary crochet lesson yields a project that's a cut above other beginners' hot pads. Bold diagonal stripes add surface interest to this easy-to-make example of Bosnian crochet. Try one in a color that strikes your fancy.

DESIGN BY NANCY NEHRING

Skill level: Beginner

Finished project size: 7" x 8"

⬭ chain (ch)

⬬ slip stitch (sl st)

⌣ slip stitch in the front loop (sl st in front lp)

⌢ slip stitch in the back loop (sl st in back lp)

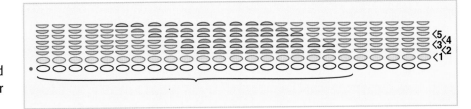

button top socks

A pair of jaunty socks offers the intermediate crocheter a lesson in shaping a garment with increases and decreases. Decoratively zigzagged, buttoned cuffs feature simple buttonholes and plenty of eye appeal.

DESIGN BY JACQUELINE YOUNG
Skill level: Intermediate
Finished project size: Women's medium (shoe size 6–8) or large (shoe size 8–10)

MATERIALS
Stahlwolle, Socka, 75% wool/25% polyamid yarn (50 gr/225 yards per ball): 3 balls of Natural (8013)
Crochet hook size B/1 (2.25mm) for medium; size C/2 (2.75mm) for large
2 split ring markers
Six ⅜"-diameter buttons
Tapestry needle

GAUGE
30 sc with B hook = 4" (10.2cm) worked in rnds for medium size.
28 sc with C hook = 4" (10.2 cm) worked in rnds for large size.
Take time to check gauge.

TO WORK GAUGE SWATCH: With appropriate hook for desired size, ch 30 with B/1 hook for medium (28 with C/2 hook for large), join with sl st in beg ch, sc in each ch around. Work in rnds on these 30(28) sc sts until piece measures 2" from beg. Piece should measure 2" across.

STITCH PATTERN
Charting the construction of a cylinder, especially shaped as elegantly as these socks, is a practical impossibility. These socks offer you a survey of shaping techniques: The inner cuff is a rectangle, seamed at the back of the leg. The foot features an opening for the heel, which you work in rounds after the rest of the foot is complete. The toe decreases in a spiral into smooth, perfect toes. Last comes the outer cuff, which forms a rectangle starting from the top edge of the inner cuff. Alternating front and back post stitches creates the decorative zigzag pattern.

INSTRUCTIONS
INNER CUFF (worked vertically):
Row 1: Using appropriate hook, ch 25. Sc in 2nd ch from hook and each remaining ch across — 24 sc; turn.

Rows 2-64: Ch 1, sc in first sc, sc in back loop only of next 22 sc, sc in last sc, turn. On last row do not fasten off, fold cuff in half with RS tog, working with a loose tension, sl st Row 1 and Row 64 tog. Turn cuff RS out. (Sl st seam is center back of cuff and beg of rnds.)

UPPER FOOT
Rnd 1: Sc in each row around, do not join — 64 sts. Place marker on first st to indicate beginning of rnds. Move marker up for each new rnd.

Rnds 2–9: Sc in each sc around.

Rnd 10 (preparation for heel): Sc in 48 sts, ch 32 loosely (this makes 16 sts on each side of center back), sk next 32 sts, sc in next sc (this is the 17th st past the marker) — heel opening made.

Rnd 11: Sc in each sc around and sc in each ch around — 64 sts.

Continue working in rounds until foot measures 4" (5") from heel opening or 4" less than desired length of foot.

TOE SHAPING

Continue to mark first stitch of each rnd.

Rnd 1: (Sc in 6 sc, sc2tog) 8 times — 56 sts.

Rnds 2–3: Sc in each sc around.

Rnd 4: (Sc in 5 sc, sc2tog) 8 times — 48 sts.

Rnds 5–6: Sc in each sc around.

Rnd 7: (Sc in 4 sc, sc2tog) 8 times — 40 sts.

Rnds 8–9: Sc in each sc around.

Rnd 10: (Sc in 3 sc, sc2tog) 8 times — 32 sts.

Rnds 11, 13, 15: Sc in each sc around.

Rnd 12: (Sc in 2 sc, sc2tog) 8 times — 24 sts.

Rnd 14: (Sc in 1 sc, sc2tog) 8 times — 16 sts.

Rnd 16: Sc2tog 8 times — 8 sts.

Rnd 17: Sc in each sc around. Leaving an 8" tail, fasten off. Close toe by weaving tail through rem sts, pull up to gather and fasten off.

HEEL

With RS facing, beg at center back, work 1 sc in each ch and sc around heel opening, making 1 sc in each corner — 66 sts. Mark corners sts with split ring markers.

Rnds 1–14: (Sc in each sc to 1 st before marked st, remove marker, sc3tog, replace marker in st just worked) 2 times, sc in each rem sc to end of rnd. At end of Rnd 14, fasten off, leaving a length of yarn to close heel. Invisibly sew heel seam.

STITCH PATTERN FOR CUFFS

Cuffs are joined to the top edge of the inner cuff facing on the sock using a foundation row of double crochet stitches. The ribbed pattern is then formed using pairs of alternating front and back post double crochet stitches.

OUTER RIGHT CUFF

With RS of inner cuff facing, join yarn with sl st on outer top edge of cuff. Ch 3 (counts as dc); work 61 dc along on upper edge of inner cuff — 62 sts; turn.

Row 1: Ch 2 (counts as dc); * 1 FPdc in each of next 2 dc, 1 BPdc in each of next 2 dc; rep from * ending dc in tch. Turn.

Row 2: Ch 2 (counts as dc); 1 BPdc in next st, * 1 FPdc in next 2 sts **, 1 BPdc in next 2 sts; rep from * ending last rep at **, 1 BPdc in next st, dc in tch; turn.

Row 3: Ch 2 (counts as dc); * 1 BPdc in next 2 sts, 1 FPdc in next 2 sts; rep from * ending dc in tch; turn.

Row 4: Ch 2 (counts as dc); 1 FPdc in next st, * 1 BPdc in next 2 sts **, 1 FPdc in next 2 sts; rep from * ending last rep at **, 1 FPdc in next st, dc in tch; turn.

Row 5: Rep Row 3.
Row 6: Rep Row 2.
Row 7: Rep Row 1.
Row 8: Rep Row 4.
Repeat rows 1–8 for pattern.
Work 16 rows in pattern, fasten off.

OUTER LEFT CUFF

Reversing side, work as a mirror image of Outer Right Cuff.

OUTER CUFF BUTTON BANDS

Row 1: With RS facing, attach yarn at side edge of outer cuff, ch 1, work 24 sc evenly spaced on side edge of cuff; turn.

Rows 2–5: Ch 1, sc in each sc across; turn. At the end of Row 5, fasten off.

To work band with buttonholes repeat rows 1–5, working 3 buttonholes spaced evenly on 3rd row as follows: Ch 1, sc in next 3 sts. * Ch 2, sk next 2 sts, sc in next 7 sts; rep from * 2 times more, ending last rep with sc in last 3 sts, fasten off.

FINISHING

Work 1 row of reverse sc (see page 73) around outer cuff edge. Sew buttons opposite buttonholes. 🕸

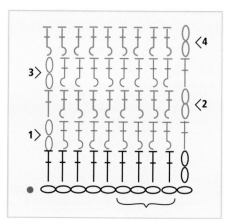

⬭	chain (ch)
⬯	slip stitch (sl st)
+	single crochet
⊤	double crochet (dc)
⌇	front post double crochet (FPdc)
⌇	back post double crochet (BPdc)

Jacqueline Young learned to crochet from her paternal grandmother and by her teens was creating her own original crocheted garments, preferring to develop her own patterns. See her other designs on pages 108 and 114.

RED MUFFLER

MATERIALS

Bernat, Chenille, 100% acrylic yarn (40 grams/85 yards per ball): 3 balls of Scarlet (17044)

Size I/9 (5.50mm) aluminum crochet hook or size needed to obtain gauge

GAUGE

In **Seed Stitch**, 26 sts and 21 rows = 6" (15.2cm)

Take time to check your gauge.

BLUE MUFFLER

MATERIALS

Mondial, Ciniglia Filo di Scozia, 100% cotton yarn (50 grams/100 meters per ball): 2 balls of Blue (526)

Size H/8 (5.00mm) aluminum crochet hook or size needed to obtain gauge

GAUGE

In **Seed Stitch**, 22 sts and 21 rows = 5" (12.7cm)

Take time to check your gauge.

STITCH PATTERN

This simple pattern stitch alternates a chain with a single crochet, then reverses it each row so that the single crochet is always worked into the chain space. This produces diagonal openwork stripes throughout the piece. Both mufflers are worked identically. The only differences are the yarn and number of chains used to start.

Because of the thickness of the chenille yarns, the usual chain-1 turning chain for single crochet has been increased to chain-2.

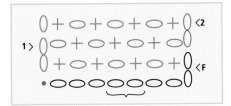

⬯	chain (ch)
+	single crochet (sc)

INSTRUCTIONS

Multiple of 2 stitches + 1.

Each turning ch-3, sk, and sc counts as one stitch.

Foundation: Ch 27 for red muffler or 23 for blue muffler. Sc in 3rd ch from

mufflers

An open seed-stitch pattern adds interesting texture to these almost-twin mufflers—warm, winter fashion statements for adults or children. Wonderfully soft to the touch and easy to crochet, either variation will help you develop consistency in your work.

DESIGN BY SHELLEY CARDA
Skill level: Beginner
Finished project sizes: 50" x 6" (red); 44" x 5" (blue)

hook; * ch 1, sk 1 ch, sc in next ch *; rep from * across; turn. 13sc/26 total sts for red muffler or 11sc/22 total sts for blue.

Row 1: Ch 3 (counts as tch), sk 1sc; * sc in next ch-1 sp, ch 1. * Repeat from * to * across.

Rep Row 1 to desired length (red model is 50"; blue model is 44"). Fasten off and conceal ends. ✡

Shelley Carda holds an M.A. from Indiana University in Early Christian and Byzantine Art. After a decade as a Middle Eastern archaeologist, she began to seriously pursue her interest in fiber arts. In addition to crocheting and knitting, she designs liturgical vestments and lectures in history. See her other design on page 102.

granny square poncho

Multiple granny squares recall a traditional afghan pattern, here transformed into a child's multicolored poncho. First combine the double-crochet squares, then learn to shape the neckline and finish the lower edge. Be sure to work it in your little girl's favorite color scheme.

DESIGN BY MELISSA LEAPMAN

Skill level: Beginner (granny squares); intermediate (neck border and hem edge)
Finished project size: Child's 4–8 (10–14).
Instructions are for smaller size, with changes for larger in parentheses.

MATERIALS

Plymouth's Encore, worsted weight yarn, (200-yd./100gm. ball): 1 (2) ball(s) of Yellow (215) for color A; 1 ball of Light Mauve (2340) for color B; 1 ball of Mauve (958) for color C; 3 (4) balls of Khaki (2282) for color D
Size H/8 (5.00mm) aluminum crochet hook or size needed to obtain gauge
Yarn needle

GAUGE

Each square measures 3¼" across.
Take time to check gauge.

STITCH PATTERN

The basic granny square begins with a ring that becomes square when you add chain increases at the corners in the first round. Shells of 3 double crochets increase by 1 along each edge in each round. Join the squares into 3-dimensional garments or traditional afghans by sewing or crochet. There are hundreds of variations of the basic square, and almost as many ways to arrange them.

⬯ chain (ch)

⬭ slip stitch (sl st)

┬ double crochet (dc)

aran isles muffler & tam

Named for the beautiful style of knitting from Ireland's Aran Isles, this tam and muffler set teaches the intermediate crocheter how to add puff-stitch embellishment to these durable winter essentials.

DESIGN BY ANN E. SMITH
Skill level: Intermediate
Finished project sizes: Muffler—50" x 8" excluding fringe; Tam—20" circumference

MATERIALS

Lion Brand Wool-Ease Sportweight, Article 660, 80% acrylic/20%wool yarn (435 yards per ball): 2 balls of Fisherman (099). (Two balls will make both tam and muffler.)
Size H/8 (5.00mm) aluminum crochet hook or size needed to obtain gauge
For Tam only:
Size G/6 (4.50mm) aluminum crochet hook

○   chain (ch)

+   single crochet (sc)

┬   double crochet (dc)

┬   front post double crochet

⬭   six-strand puff stitch

GAUGE

In Muffler Body Pattern, 15 sts and 18 rows = 4".
For Tam, with larger hook,15 sts and 17 rnds = 4".
Take time to check your gauge.

STITCH PATTERNS

Single crochet forms the basic fabric of the muffler and tam, while front post double crochet stitches rise above the surface. The post stitches are worked around each other, creating continuous cables which form diamonds and frame puff stitches.

To become familiar with the patterns and techniques, use the chart to make the muffler first. The tam, worked in a spiral from the top down, uses these same stitches to form both decorative patterns and ribbing.

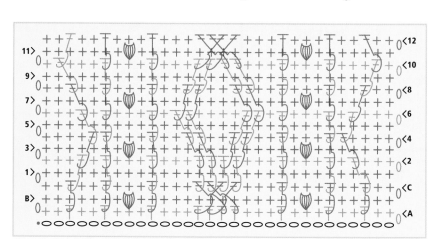

Fringed muffler

MUFFLER INSTRUCTIONS
Beginning at the lower edge, ch 31.

FOUNDATION
Row A (RS): Sc in 2nd ch from hook and in next ch; dc in next ch, sc in next 2 ch, (dc in next ch, sc in next 3 ch) twice. Dc in next 4 ch, (sc in next 3 ch, dc in next ch) twice, sc in next 2 ch, dc in next ch, sc in last 2 ch — 30 sts; turn.

Row B: Ch 1, sc in first 7 sts, puff st in next st, sc in next 14 sts, puff st in next st, sc in last 7 sts; turn.

Row C: Ch 1, sc in first 2 sc, FPdc over dc in row A, sk sc behind FPdc, sc in next 2 sc, FPdc over dc, sk sc behind FPdc, sc in sc, sc in puff st, sc in sc, FPdc over dc, sk sc behind FPdc; sc in next 3 sc, sk next 2 dc, FPdc over next 2 dc, FPdc over first and then over second skipped dc, sk 4 sc behind 4 FPdc, sc in next 3 sc. FPdc over dc, sk sc behind FPdc, sc in sc, sc in puff st, sc in sc, FPdc over dc, sk sc behind FPdc, sc in 2 sc, FPdc over dc, sk sc behind FPdc, sc in last 2 sc; turn.

BODY PATTERN
Work FPdcs around FPdcs two rows below. Throughout pattern, sk the sc behind the FPdc.

Row 1 (WS): Ch 1, sc in each st across; turn.

Row 2: Ch 1, sc in 3 sc, FPdc over FPdc, sc in next sc, FPdc over FPdc, sc in next 3 sc, FPdc over FPdc, sc in next 3 sc, (FPdc over FPdc) 4 times, sc in next 3 sc; FPdc over FPdc, sc in next 3 sc, FPdc over FPdc, sc in next sc, FPdc over FPdc, sc in last 3 sc; turn.

Row 3: Ch 1, sc in first 7 sts, puff st in next st, sc in next 14 sts, puff st in next st, sc in last 7 sts; turn.

Row 4: Ch 1, sc in first 4 sc, (FPdc over FPdc) twice, sc in next sc, sc in puff st, sc in next sc, FPdc over FPdc; sc in next 2 sc, (FPdc over FPdc) twice, skipping 2 sc behind 2 FPdc, sc in each of next 2 sts, (FPdc over FPdc) twice, skipping 2 sc behind 2 FPdc, sc in next 2 sts; FPdc over FPdc, sc in sc, sc in puff st, sc in sc, (FPdc over FPdc) twice, sc in last 4 sc; turn.

Row 5: Rep Row 1.

Row 6: Ch 1, sc in 3 sc, FPdc over FPdc, sc in next sc, FPdc over FPdc, sc in next 3 sc, FPdc over FPdc; sc in next sc, (FPdc over FPdc) twice, skipping 2 sc behind the 2 FPdc, sc in next 4 sts, (FPdc over FPdc) twice, skipping 2 sc behind the 2 FPdc, sc in next sc; FPdc over FPdc, sc in 3 sc, FPdc over FPdc, sc in sc, FPdc over FPdc, sc in last 3 sc; turn.

Row 7: Rep Row 3.

Row 8: Ch 1, sc in 2 sc, FPdc over FPdc, sc in 2 sc, FPdc over FPdc, sc in sc, sc in puff st, sc in sc, FPdc over FPdc; sc in next 2 sc, (FPdc over FPdc) twice, skipping 2 sc behind 2 FPdc, sc in next 2 sc, (FPdc over FPdc) twice, skipping 2 sc behind 2 FPdc, sc in next 2 sc. FPdc over FPdc, sc in sc, sc in puff st, sc in sc, FPdc over FPdc, sc in 2 sc, FPdc over FPdc, sc in last 2 sc; turn.

Row 9: Rep Row 1.

Row 10: Ch 1, sc in sc, FPdc over FPdc, sc in 3 sc, FPdc over FPdc, sc in next 3 sc, FPdc over FPdc; sc in next 3 sc, (FPdc over FPdc) 4 times, skipping 4 sc behind 4 FPdc, sc in next 3 sc; FPdc over FPdc, sc in 3 sc, FPdc over FPdc, sc in 3 sc, FPdc over FPdc, sc in last sc; turn.

Row 11: Rep Row 3.

Row 12: Ch 1, sc in 2 sc, FPdc over FPdc, sc in 2 sc, FPdc over FPdc, sc in sc, sc in puff st, sc in sc, FPdc over FPdc; sc in next 3 sc, sk 2 FPdc, FPdc over next 2 FPdc, FPdc over first and then over second skipped FPdc, sk 4 sc behind 4 FPdc, sc in next 3 sc; FPdc over FPdc, sc in sc, sc in puff st, sc in sc, FPdc over FPdc, sc in 2 sc, FPdc over FPdc, sc in 2 sc; turn.

Rep Rows 1–12 for Body Pattern to approx. 50" from beg. Rep Rows 1–2. With WS facing work fringe as follows: Sl st in first st, ch 24; (sl st in next st, ch 24) across ending sl st in last st. Fasten off.

LOWER FRINGE
With the WS facing, join yarn with a sl st in first Foundation ch, ch 1. Sc in same ch as joining and in each ch across; turn. Sl st in first sc, ch 24; (sl st in next sc, ch 24) across ending sl st in last sc and fasten off.

TAM INSTRUCTIONS
Do not join rnds.
Beginning at the top of the crown with larger hook, ch 2.

Rnd 1: 7 sc in 2nd ch from hook.

Rnd 2: 2 sc in each sc around — 14 sts.

Rnd 3: Rep Rnd 2 — 28 sts.

Rnd 4: (Sc in next sc, dc in next sc) around.

Rnd 5: * 2 sc in sc, FPdc over dc, (2 rows below and remember to sk st behind the FPdc), sc in next sc, FPdc over dc; rep from * around — 35 sts.

Rnd 6: * Sc in each of next 2 sc, sc in top of FPdc, FPdc over 2nd FPdc, FPdc over first FPdc; rep from * around for 7 times.

Rnd 7: * Sc in sc, in front lp of next sc [sl st, ch 5, sl st in 5th ch from hook — bobble made (B)], sc in next sc, FPdc over FPdc, in next FPdc (sc in top of FPdc, FPdc over FPdc); rep from * around for 7 times — 42 sts.

Rnd 8: *2 sc in 2nd sc before B, sc in rem back lp behind B, 2 sc in next sc, ch 1, sk FPdc, sc in sc, ch 1, sk FPdc; rep from * 7 times – 56 sts.

Rnd 9: (Sc in 5 sc, FPdc over FPdc, sc in sc, FPdc over FPdc) 7 times.

Rnd 10: * Sc in 2 sc, B in next sc, sc in 2 sc, ch 1, sk FPdc, sc in sc, ch 1, sk FPdc; rep from * around 7 times.

Rnd 11: * 2 sc in 2nd sc before B, sc in next sc, sc in rem back lp behind B, sc in next sc, 2 sc in next sc, sc in ch-1 sp, sk FPdc, FPdc over next FPdc, FPdc over skipped FPdc; rep from * 7 times — 70 sts.

Rnd 12: (Sc in 7 sc, sk 1 sc, FPdc over FPdc, sc in top of next FPdc, FPdc over same FPdc) 7 times.

Rnd 13: * 2 sc in sc, sc in next 2 sc, B in next sc, sc in 2 sc, 2 sc in next sc, ch 1, sk FPdc, sc in sc, ch 1, sk FPdc; rep from * 7 times — 84 sts.

Rnd 14: (Sc in 4 sc before B, sc in rem back lp of B, sc in 4 sc, sc in ch-1 sp, FPdc over 2nd FPdc, FPdc over first FPdc) 7 times.

Rnd 15: (Sc in 9 sc, sk 1 sc, FPdc over FPdc, sc in top of next FPdc, FPdc over same FPdc) 7 times.

Rnd 16: * 2 sc in sc, sc in next 3 sc, B in next sc, sc in 3 sc, 2 sc in next sc, ch 1, sk FPdc, sc in sc, ch 1, sk FPdc; rep from * 7 times — 98 sts.

Rnd 17: (Sc in 5 sc before B, sc in rem back lp of B, sc in 5 sc, sc in ch-1 sp, FPdc over 2nd FPdc, FPdc over first FPdc) 7 times.

Rnd 18: (Sc in 11 sc, sk 1 sc, FPdc over FPdc, sc in sc in top of next FPdc, FPdc over same FPdc) 7 times.

Rnd 19: * 2 sc in sc, sc in next 4 sc, B in next sc, sc in 4 sc, 2 sc in next sc, ch 1, sk FPdc, sc in sc, ch 1, sk FPdc; rep from * 7 times ——112 sts.

Rnd 20: (Sc in 6 sc before B, sc in rem back lp of B, sc in 6 sc, sc in ch-1 sp, FPdc over 2nd FPdc, FPdc over first FPdc) 7 times.

Rnd 21: (Sc in 13 sc, sk 1 sc, FPdc over FPdc, sc in top of FPdc, FPdc over

Tam rim

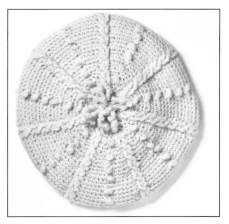

Tam crown

same FPdc) 7 times.

Rnd 22: * 2 sc in sc, sc in next 5 sc, B in next sc, sc in 5 sc, 2 sc in next sc, ch 1, sk FPdc, sc in sc, ch 1, sk FPdc; rep from * 7 times — 126 sts.

Rnd 23: (Sc in 7 sc before B, sc in rem back lp of B, sc in 7 sc, sc in ch-1 sp, FPdc over 2nd FPdc, FPdc over first FPdc) 7 times.

Rnd 24: (Sc in 15 sc, sk 1 sc, FPdc over FPdc, sc in top of next FPdc, FPdc over same FPdc) 7 times.

Rnd 25: * 2 sc in sc, sc in next 6 sc, B in next sc, sc in 6 sc, 2 sc in next sc, ch 1, sk FPdc, sc in sc, ch 1, sk FPdc; rep from * 7 times — 140 sts.

Rnd 26: (Sc in 8 sc before B, sc in rem back lp of B, sc in 8 sc, sc in ch-1 sp, FPdc over 2nd FPdc, FPdc over first FPdc) 7 times.

Rnd 27: (Sc in 17 sc, sk 1 sc, FPdc over FPdc, sc in top of FPdc, FPdc over same FPdc) 7 times.

Rnd 28: * sc2tog, sc in next 6 sc, B in next sc, sc in 6 sc, sc2tog, sc in next (FPdc, sc, and FPdc); rep from * 7 times — 126 sts.

Rnd 29: *Sc in 7 sc before B, sc in rem back lp of B, sc in next 10 sc; rep from * 7 times – 126 sts.

Rnd 30: (sc2tog, sc in each of next 11 sc, sc2tog, sc in each of next 3 sc) 7 times — 112 sts.

Rnd 31: (Sc in next 6 sc, B in next sc, sc in 9 sc) 7 times.

Rnd 32: (Sc2tog, sc in next 4 sc, sc in rem back lp of B, sc in next 4 sc, sc2tog, sc in next 3 sc) 7 times - 98 sts.

Rnd 33: (sc2tog, sc in next 7 sc, sc2tog, sc in next 3 sc) 7 times — 84 sts.

Rnd 34: (sc2tog, sc in next 2 sc, B in next sc, sc in next 2 sc, sc2tog, sc in next

3 sc) 7 times — 70 sts.

Rnd 35: (Sc in next 2 sc, sc2tog, sc in rem back lp of B, sc in next 6 sc) 7 times.

Rnd 36: Change to smaller hook. In next sc, sl st and ch 3; dc in each sc around; join with a sl st in 3rd ch of beg ch-3.

Rnd 37: Ch 3; * BPdc over next dc, FPdc over next dc; rep from * around ending with BPdc over last dc; join with a sl st in 3rd ch of beg ch-3.

Rnd 38: Ch 3; * BPdc over BPdc, FPdc over FPdc; rep from * around ending with BPdc over last BPdc; join.

Rnds 39–40: Rep Rnd 38.

Rnd 41: Ch 5, sl st in 5th ch from hook for B; * sc in top of next post st, in next st (sl st, ch 5, sl st in 5th ch from hook for B); rep from * around ending with sc in last st. Join and fasten off.

TOP

With the RS facing, join yarn with a sl st in sp between 2 sc from Row 1. Ch 1, sc in same sp and in next 5 sps. Sl st in first sc; * (ch 5, sl st in 3rd ch from hook) 5 times, ch 2, sl st in same sc **, sl st in next sc; rep from * around ending last rep at **. Leaving a long tail, fasten off. Wrap tail several times around all loops, close to the tam. Secure in place. 🏵

Ann E. Smith has been involved in textiles for over 17 years, including working as a crochet pattern editor for publications, yarn companies and individual designers. She wrote the popular column "The Professional Touch" for *McCall's Crochet* magazine.

beyond the basics

 We are sure that long before you finished your first muffler you realized the worlds of possibility crochet offers. If you already have several more projects in mind, Beyond the Basics is just what you need to help you realize your dreams.

Crochet with multiple colors has been a tradition since the beginnings of crochet. You can try your hand at an opulent afghan positively stuffed with color, since the technique of hiding other colors within each stitch allows you to switch colors easily, then hide them again whenever you wish.

If you just can't wait to blend color and texture, mingle stripes and bobbles in a baby wrap so delightful that you might want to make another one for yourself.

Enter the glittery realms of jewelry, accessories, and whatever strikes your fancy. Bejewel a pair of hearts or make a bride's bag as dazzling as a happy smile. Create an amulet necklace to tote tiny trinkets. Or, go to great lengths creating beautiful chains from a spectrum of wires.

Follow the winding thread to a treasury of lace techniques that put the secrets of heirloom lace in your own hands, from exquisite pillowcase lengths to a rose medallion for your dressing table or an Irish-crochet rose for your buttonhole.

Let us lead you to still more fascinating foreign crochet techniques with a Tunisian crochet pillow embroidered in the colors of a Tunisian garden and a Tunisian-stitch vest for a child.

Top off your collection with a multicolored coat. Far from being the end of your travels, it marks the beginning of your adventures in the world of creative crochet. *Bon voyage!*

Choose a project, then choose the colors. Color delights the eye and speaks to the heart. But how do you decide among all the wonderful color selections? You might look outdoors to the colors of nature in all the seasons. You will find everything from earth tones to flamingo pink and brilliant turquoise. Butterflies, rocks, trees, and flowers can inspire you. Let nature guide you; then, use the information below to help you express yourself.

THE COLOR WHEEL

Use the color wheel as a starting point for creating your own color combinations. Primary colors are red, blue, and yellow. Halfway between the primary colors are the secondary colors: orange, green, and violet. All the colors between the primary and secondary colors are intermediate colors.

COLOR TERMS

PURE COLOR is undiluted, intense, and brilliant. The use of pure color creates excitement and energy.

Pure color

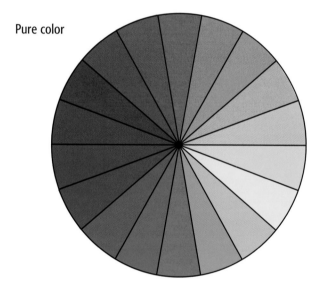

TINT is pure color with white added. Pastels are tints. A tinted color conveys a feeling of softness and delicacy.

Tint

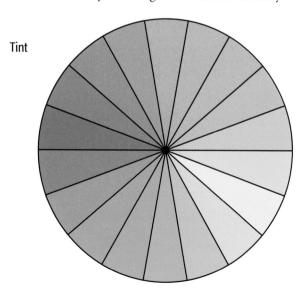

SHADE is pure color with black added. Shades have depth and richness. They include the warm hues of autumn and the deep blue tones of night.

Shade

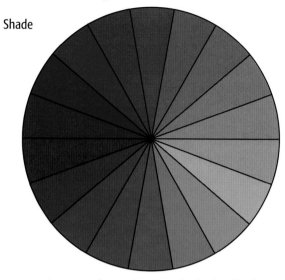

TONE is pure color, a tint, or a shade that has been grayed. Tones are subdued, subtle colors. Tones enhance the colors around them.

Tone

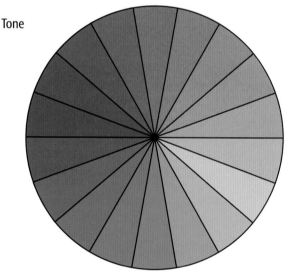

INTENSITY refers to the degree to which a pure color has been tinted, shaded, or toned.

High intensity   Low intensity

VALUE of a color refers to its darkness or lightness. The contrast between the values of colors can be very strong, such as black to white, or very subtle, such as yellow to white.

Value

Contrast

COLOR SCHEMES

Colors can be combined in endless ways. Certain types of combinations will always produce pleasing results. Deciding on a color scheme depends on your project. Home décor items usually are based on the colors in the home. Wearing apparel often is based on the color preferences of who will be wearing it. Choose colors you love and have fun finding new ways of combining them with other colors.

Decide what mood or feeling you want to convey. Warm colors such as red, orange, and yellow suggest heat. They can be fun and exciting to work with. Cool colors convey a wintry mood, relaxing and subtle. Choose the type of color that will enhance the feeling you want: pure color, tints, shades or tones. Allow one type to dominate. The next consideration is value. How dark and light the colors are in each project affects the feeling of the piece. Strong contrasts in value are dramatic. Low contrasts in value are calming.

The following color schemes will help you explore ways to combine your favorite colors. In all the color schemes below, the colors can range from bright and pure to grayed and subtle. The values can also range from very strong to very soft.

MONOCHROMATIC schemes use colors from the same "family." Choose one color from the color wheel and use different values, tints, tones, and shades to create a color scheme. Monochromatic color schemes are cohesive and sophisticated.

In these two examples, the pure colors green and red (center squares) darken when shaded (at left) and lighten when tinted (at right).

COMPLEMENTARY colors are opposite each other on the color wheel. Allow one of the colors to dominate. For example, if red is the dominant color, use a touch of green to complement it.

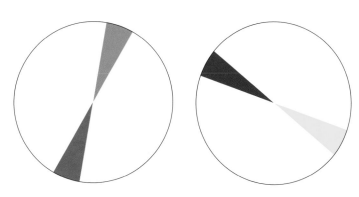

Complementary colors

ANALOGOUS colors are next to each other on the color wheel. Choose three to seven colors that are side by side. Include tints, tones or shades with intense colors for a dynamic color scheme. Vary the values of the colors you have selected to add interest to your color scheme.

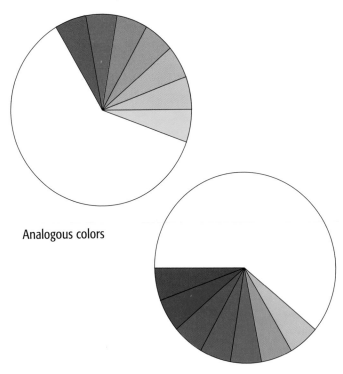

Analogous colors

SPLIT-COMPLEMENTARY color schemes use an analogous combination of colors with an added twist: a complementary color. The color of your complement will be opposite the mid-color of your analogous color group. If the analogous color scheme is made up of red, red orange and orange, the compliment would be blue-green. Split-complimentary color schemes are among the most beautiful.

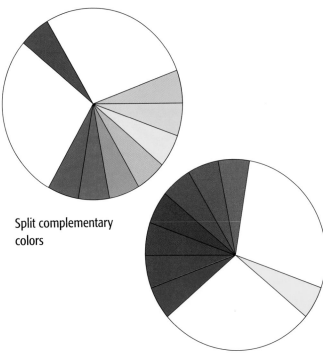

Split complementary colors

71

CROCHETING WITH COLOR

Choosing a project and a color scheme is fun, but it is even more enjoyable translating color to yarn. Holding the yarn in your hand and combining type and texture is a joy. From rich and chunky to soft and silky, the texture of your yarn will also affect color. The way light reflects from the fibers will change the perception of color. Base your final selections on what stirs your heart, because working with the yarns and colors you love is sure to produce a successful design and project.

TWO COLORS IN A ROW are twice as much fun as one. Attach a second color the same way you attach a new thread. Work up to the last two loops of the preceding stitch or row. Draw up the new color and complete the stitch. The next stitch will be the new color.

GAUGE is as important in color work as it is everywhere else. When you are starting a new project, work your test swatches exactly as you will work the project. If you are using two colors and cutting the thread at the end of each row, work the test swatch that way. If you will be using hidden color, reverse single crochet, or any of the other techniques explained below, be sure that you do it in the swatch. Your gauge will change with each technique or added strand of yarn. Avoid disappointment later by making a good test swatch at the beginning.

Following a charted or graphed design creates pictures with squares of color or space (see Filet Crochet, page 78). Each square of the graph is defined as a certain number of stitches to be worked in the color indicated. As you crochet, "carry" the other thread until you need it, then pick it up when the design calls for that color. The chart defines whether odd-numbered rows are the right or wrong side.

Worked in single crochet, hidden strand color produces thick, sturdy pieces because every stitch is worked around another strand of yarn. It can be adapted to any number of uses. You can carry more than one color this way, but each strand will pad your stitches, and more than two colors can become unwieldy.

Diagonal pull occurs with all crochet worked in one direction. In a circular piece it won't be as noticeable as in a flat piece. Flat pieces can be blocked back to a rectangle after laundering, or you can simply ignore the problem—a slanting afghan is no less cozy.

To eliminate diagonal pull, use the Reverse Single Crochet techniques described in the Tapestry Crochet section (opposite).

TECHNIQUES FOR WORKING IN COLORS

HIDDEN-STRAND METHOD In this traditional way of carrying two colors throughout a row, the strand not in use is hidden inside a single crochet. Carry the hidden strand from the beginning of the row. As with any color work, the technique is most successful when yarns are of equal thickness.

SWITCHING STRAND METHOD Pick up the hidden color as you would a new strand of yarn. One stitch before you want the new color to appear, drop the old color to the inside, along the top of the preceding row. Pick up the new color from the back as a yarn over, and draw it through the last two loops of the stitch. The next stitch will be the new color. This allows you to alternate two colors with no loose ends or strands in the middle of a row.

If you want both colors in the next row, work the turning chain in the color of the first stitch and work the first single crochet around the hidden color. If skipping a row or two, run the unused color along the edge. Carry it by wrapping it around the turning chain of each row. If not using the color for several rows, cut it and reattach it.

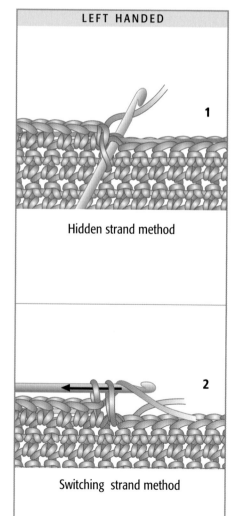

LEFT HANDED

1

Hidden strand method

2

Switching strand method

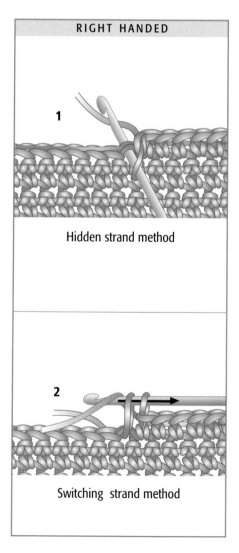

RIGHT HANDED

1

Hidden strand method

2

Switching strand method

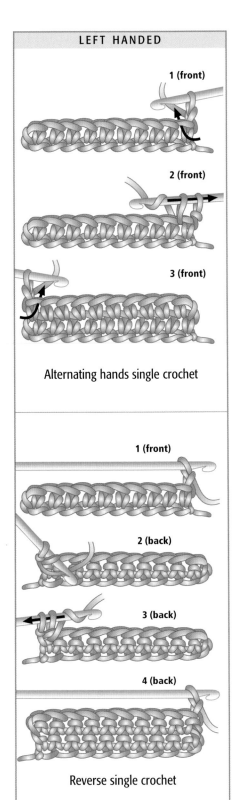

1 (front)

2 (front)

3 (front)

Alternating hands single crochet

1 (front)

2 (back)

3 (back)

4 (back)

Reverse single crochet

TAPESTRY METHOD

Tapestry crochet is a specialized form of the hidden-strand technique. It is worked in one direction or with directional stitches for very precise designs, such as bird or animal motifs. Tapestry crochet makes precise images because all the bumps are on the back of the fabric. The front side of the work is smoother, which gives this kind of work a right side and a wrong side (see the Lap of Luxury project on page 96).

ROUND WORK, flat or cylindrical, worked in a continuous round can be made following a charted pattern.

SINGLE-DIRECTION stitching can be used for flat pieces. Instead of turning the work, simply cut the yarns at the end of every row. Go back to the beginning of the row, and start again from the same end. Do this every row. For a built-in fringe leave a 6"–8" tail of yarn at each end of the row.

ALTERNATING HANDS SINGLE CROCHET allows you to work back and forth across a row without turning the piece. Work from left to right one row, and from right to left the next row.

Before you dismiss the idea, think of not having to turn that king-sized afghan after each row. You will also be able to work longer before tiring because both hands share the work.

REVERSE SINGLE CROCHET (**Rev sc**) allows you to work backwards across a row. This will eliminate bias pull and still give you the clarity of the tapestry crochet technique

Work from the back if you prefer to always work in one direction. Alternating a row of regular single crochet with a row worked from the back will give the fabric a smooth right side necessary for tapestry crochet. On alternate rows simply modify the way you insert the hook for single crochet.

Carrying the yarn in *front* of the work, insert the hook from the back of the stitch and draw up the first loop to the back. Yarn over and finish the stitch as usual. At the end of the row, turn the work. Work the next row of single crochet in the usual way.

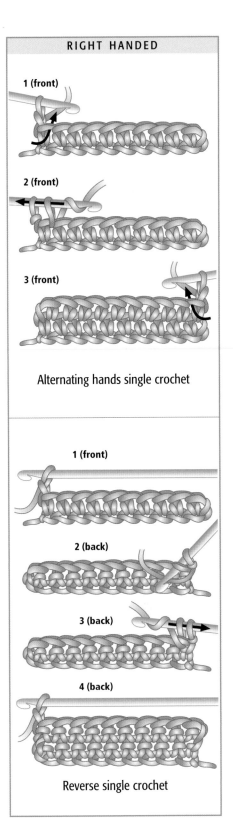

1 (front)

2 (front)

3 (front)

Alternating hands single crochet

1 (front)

2 (back)

3 (back)

4 (back)

Reverse single crochet

73

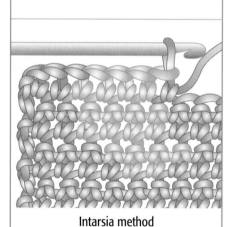

Stranding method

Intarsia method

STRANDING METHOD

Stranding carries yarn behind the piece, picking up for a stitch of that color. A "float" of yarn lies loosely along the back of the work.

In order to keep the floats from being too snag-able, every few stitches catch up a float inside a new stitch. This is rather like hidden-strand color, but the float is only contained within one stitch, rather than all of the stitches. The color will show on the front only when used to crochet a stitch.

Carrying the float at the front of the work introduces it as a design element. In this case, the securing stitches will form a design across the floats, producing a brocade effect.

INTARSIA METHOD

Intarsia is an Italian word meaning *inlay*. Use this technique to make a color motif in one specific area. Attach a bobbin or short strand of the new color where the motif begins. Use it for the motif stitches in each row. The background color floats behind the motif. The bobbin hangs behind the piece when the motif is not being worked.

If using several strands, keeping the colors closely wound on bobbins keeps the yarns from tangling when not in use. Catch up loose ends as you work other stitches, or thread them in when you finish the work.

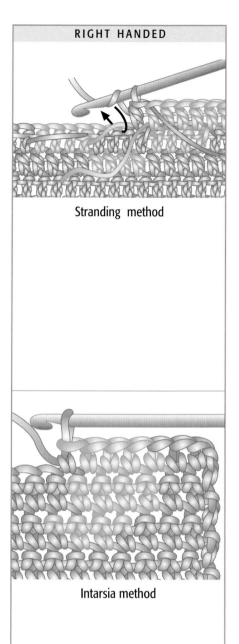

Stranding method

Intarsia method

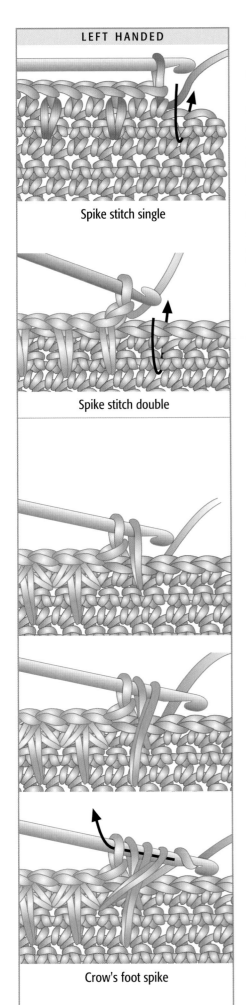

Spike stitch single

Spike stitch double

Crow's foot spike

SPIKE STITCH METHOD

SPIKE STITCHES, also called dropped stitches, (for example, Ssc = spike single crochet, Sdc = spike double crochet, etc.) also called dropped stitches, are an excellent way of making a vertical or angled dash of color or texture from one row to a lower row. While a color change is not essential, it is enormously gratifying to see a dash of color appear in rows already completed. Worked singly or in clusters, spikes should be worked loosely, so they don't draw up the rows they cross.

You cannot begin spike stitches in the first row. So begin by crocheting two rows of single crochet. Change color, chain for height, and work two single crochets as usual. On the third single crochet, insert the hook into the space of the single crochet two rows below, yarn over, and draw up the new color to the level of the new row, making sure the yarn is not too tight across the lower rows. Yarn over and work the rest of the single crochet as usual. Continue the pattern of *2 sc, one Ssc* across the row.

For a touch of color that is not a stripe, use a slip stitch instead of the single crochet, and spike the color unobtrusively.

CROW'S FOOT SPIKE: You can work the spikes diagonally across rows and in clusters. A cluster of spikes to successive stitches in different rows gives a crow's foot effect.

Projects for color work: Lap of Luxury, Baby Bobbles, and Philosopher's Coat; see pages 96, 98, and 124 for instructions. 🌐

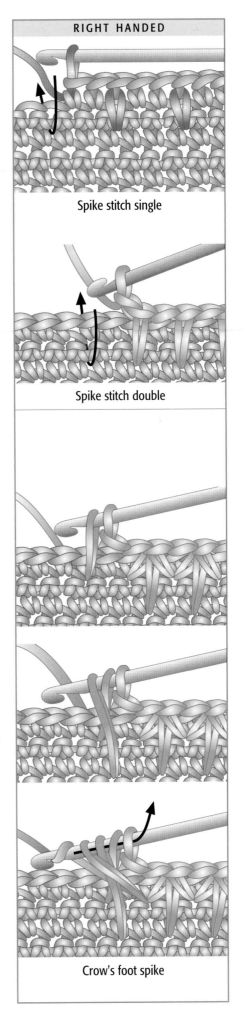

Spike stitch single

Spike stitch double

Crow's foot spike

75

THREAD CROCHET

The smoothness of thread is well coupled with crochet, whose intricate twists can be seen and appreciated when worked in thread. From evening bags crocheted with shining silk to kitchen rugs crocheted with cotton warp, there is more to thread crochet than lace. But lace comes to mind first.

Lace uses the double trebles you thought you would never need, fans straight stitches into shells, and catches them with chains. Filet crochet can make scrolls out of squares and pictures that are half air.

Though the stitches will be familiar, crochet with thread requires tighter tension. Looping the thread around your index finger an extra time should be enough, but you can also loop the thread around your little finger for greater control.

Symbol diagrams allow you to see the structure of lace in complete detail. Most lace patterns, especially in foreign publications, are printed only in symbol diagrams. If you can read symbols, the world's finest designs are at your fingertips.

MATERIALS

There is a wealth of thread to choose from, but there are only a few different types of threads. As you become familiar with thread crochet you may wish to experiment with different types, or you may find the thread you love and never change.

SAMPLE GAUGES FOR CLASSIC THREADS

6-ply Crochet Cotton	U.S. Hook Size	Size of Swatch
No. 5	7	3" x 3" = 33 dc x 15 rows
No. 10	8	3" x 3" = 36 dc x 16 rows
No. 20	9	3" x 3" = 40 dc x 16 rows
No. 30	10	3" x 3" = 45 dc x 18 rows
No. 40	11	3" x 3" = 47 dc x 19 rows

THREAD SIZE

Cotton and linen threads do not have the peculiarities of worsted and woolen spin. But there are some things to consider if hours of work are to produce the heirloom of your dreams.

SIZE (diameter) is the basic measure of a thread. It makes the difference between a doily for your dresser or your patio.

Thread sizes range from 100 (finest) up to 16, 12, 10, 8, 5, and 3. After that they become yarns and have such vague names as "kitchen cotton," "rug yarn," and trade names for specific products such as "Sugar 'N Cream." Linen threads come in the same sizes, written with the ply after the size, such as 10/2. Try different threads when you test new patterns, so

(1) DMC, Cebelia #30; (2) DMC, Cordonnet Special #10; (3) DMC, Cordonnet Special #20; (4) DMC, Cebelia #20; (5) DMC, Special dentelles #80; (6) DMC, Cordonnet Special #40; (7) DMC, Cebelia #10; (8) DMC, Cordonnet Special, Ecru #100; (9) Flora Cotton #10; (10) Manuela, Cotton #20; (11) Handy Hands, Cordonnet #50; (12) Flora Cotton #20; (13) Lacis, Silk Lace Thread; (14) Kantklosgaren, Egyptisch Katoen cotton; (15) J & P Coats, Knit Cro-Sheen #10; (16) Miami Baumwolle Cotton

that you know their properties. Your book of lace swatches and notes can be an heirloom (see the example at right).

OTHER PROPERTIES OF THREAD

Thread is not simply big or small. Just as in yarn, there are other considerations in addition to size.

PLY is the number of separately twisted strands in a single thread; it is not a unit of size (see photo, page 30). Ply affects the roundness of thread, its tensile strength, the way it wears, and how it catches the light.

There are crochet threads from 2-ply (pearl cotton) to 8-ply (Fil d'Ecosse). Classic crochet cotton is 6-ply, tightly twisted,

Crochet sampler book from the collection of Gwen Blakley Kinsler.

HOOK SIZES FOR SELECTED COTTON THREADS		
	HOOK SIZE	
	Intl.	U. S.
COTTON THREAD		
(Three-cord, four-cord, six-cord or uncorded: 20grams/¾ oz. per ball.)		
No. 3	1.75	4
No. 5	1.50	8
No 10	1.50	8
No. 15	1.25	10
No. 20	1.25	10
No. 30	1.25	10
No. 40	1.00	12
No. 50	1.00	12
No. 60	0.85 or 0.75	13 or 14
No. 70	0.75	14
No. 80	0.75	14
No. 100	0.60	16
SPECIALTY YARNS (50 grams/1¾ oz. per ball)		
Fil d'Ecosse (8-ply or 6-ply special twist)		
No. 5	1.50	8
Pearl Cotton (2-ply long staple cotton, loosely twisted)		
No. 5	1.90	5
No. 8	1.50	8
Knitting Cotton (6-ply long staple cotton with a high sheen)		
No. 4	2.00	4
Soft Knitting Twist (5-ply long staple cotton, matte finish, loosely twisted)		
No. 4	2.25	2
No. 6	2.00	4

and hard wearing, but 3-ply bedspread cotton also is commonly used.

STAPLE means the length of a fiber, but since long fibers are also thinner, it indirectly refers to fineness. Cotton fibers are roughly categorized as long (1⅜") or short (1") staple. Because of their length and tensile strength, long-staple threads (such as Egyptian and Pima) can be more finely and softly spun than short-staple cottons.

TWIST refers to how tightly twirled the fibers are. It affects the hardness and flexibility of threads and their soft or crisp characteristics. Tightly twisted threads are crisp and hold the fibers tightly, preventing fraying from clouding the luster and clarity of the thread.

Seemingly identical threads may actually be quite different from one another. For example, DMC Cebélia is softly twisted and drapes beautifully; it would be a good choice for a comfortable lace collar. On the other hand, DMC Cordonnet Spécial is firmly twisted, and would produce a crisp lace for an edging.

MERCERIZED COTTON has been boiled in sodium hydroxide (lye), which shrinks, de-fuzzes, and increases luster of the thread. Most threads are mercerized; look for it on the label. Non-mercerized cotton will shrink, fuzz, and not behave the way you are used to cotton behaving.

STRAIGHT LACES

Straight laces are worked in rows, rather than in rounds. They can be used both as trim and pictures. In some laces the length of the foundation chain is the length of the finished piece, and these are often worked directly on the edges of handkerchiefs and linens. This is the natural home of the shell stitch, which can scallop an edge like nothing else.

Some designs use the foundation chain as the width; pattern repeats make the piece longer rather than wider. This lets you choose the length as you work.

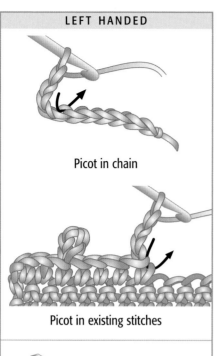

Picot in chain

Picot in existing stitches

Forming the mesh

Forming the block

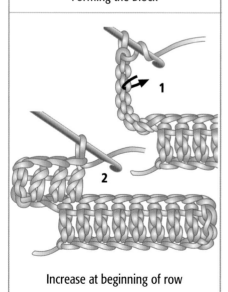

Increase at beginning of row

PICOTS

Picots are used extensively in crocheted lace, and there are a lot of variations. The two basic types are picots made as you work a chain and picots worked into existing stitches.

PICOTS IN CHAINS are simply a thread cul-de-sac. As you work the chain, loop back 3 or 4 chains (depending on what looks nice) and connect with a slip stitch.

PICOTS IN EXISTING STITCHES are worked from a base of a single crochet or other stitch. When you complete the base stitch, chain 3 or 4, slip stitch back into the base stitch, and continue the row.

FILET CROCHET

Filet crochet is a graphed (charted) design worked in "solid and space." Once you understand how to form the mesh, filet crochet can depict anything that can be graphed with black and white squares, which explains its diversity and popularity. Decreases and increases at the beginnings and ends of rows allow you to shape the edges.

FORMING THE MESH is a square grid of double crochets and chain stitches.

FORMING THE BLOCK The first stitch and last stitch of each square define the space; the middle two stitches color it in with double crochet to make the block, or it can be left blank with chains. Gauge is measured in meshes per inch.

The turning chain, 3 chains high, is always counted as a design stitch. When you work the turning chain, if the first square of the row is an open square, the turning chain will be 5 chains: 3 chains = the first double crochet, and 2 chains = the following two blank spaces.

INCREASES AT THE BEGINNING OF ROW work additional chains to increase: 3 for each mesh base +3 for height. After that, work from the chart.

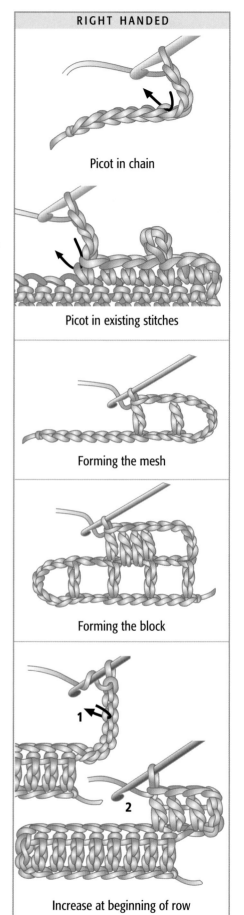

Picot in chain

Picot in existing stitches

Forming the mesh

Forming the block

Increase at beginning of row

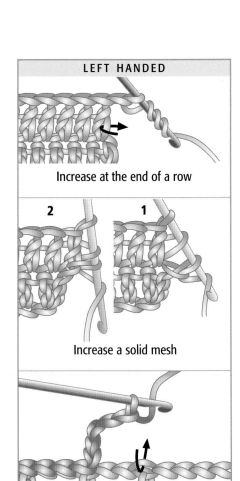

Increase at the end of a row

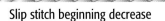

Increase a solid mesh

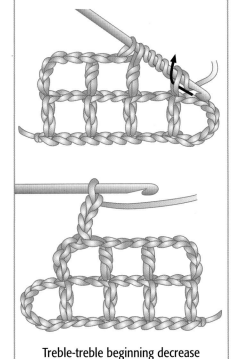

Slip stitch beginning decrease

Treble-treble beginning decrease

INCREASE AT THE END OF A ROW, work increases into the base of the previous stitch. For an open mesh, * chain 2, yarn over 3 times and work a double treble (see page 44) in the base of the preceding mesh * Repeat from * to * once for each mesh increased.

INCREASE A SOLID MESH, * work an extended double crochet into the base of the preceding stitch * three times.

DECREASES

A SLIP STITCH BEGINNING DECREASE can be worked with the invisible slip stitch. Instead of making a turning chain, slip stitch across to where you wish to work the first mesh of the row. Begin the mesh with a 3-chain out of the last slip stitch. Work the next two stitches according to the chart.

A TREBLE-TREBLE BEGINNING DECREASE is very useful for working one open mesh, especially if you are working with ultra-fine thread. Though it is worked on the end of the preceding row, it is still a beginning decrease.

This may be the only time you need to work a treble treble. It is worth knowing. It works just like a regular treble, just a bit longer. Yarn over 4 times and work off the loops two by two. This will happen six times, which equals six chains. After turning the work, work a treble treble, one mesh to the left in the row below. (For left-handed workers, one mesh to the right.)

At the end of working the treble treble you will end up back where you began. You are positioned to work the chain 3 to begin the next row. Continue according to the chart.

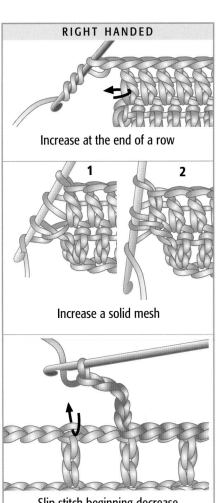

Increase at the end of a row

Increase a solid mesh

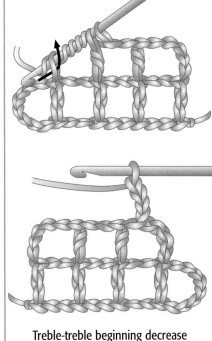

Slip stitch beginning decrease

Treble-treble beginning decrease

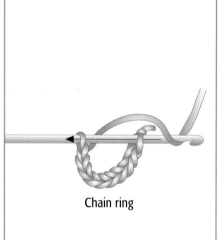

Solid mesh decrease

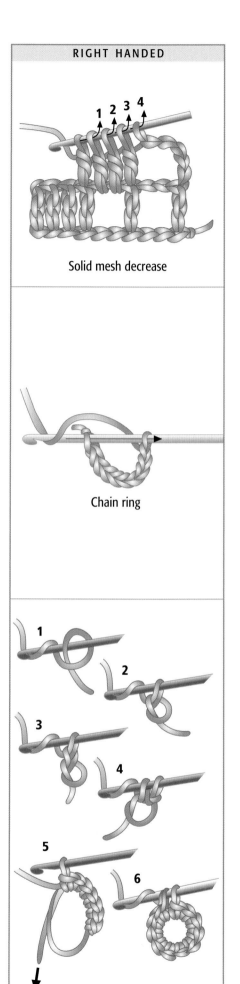

Solid mesh decrease

END OF ROW DECREASES

SOLID MESH DECREASE uses the familiar decrease on four stitches at once. Simply work each of the last 4 double crochets until two loops each remain on the hook. Then yarn over and work off two loops at a time, ending up centered over the double crochet where you began. Turn and make 3 chains to begin the new row.

Project for Edging: Delicate Filet Edging; see page 100 for instructions.

ROUND MOTIFS AND DOILIES

MOTIFS (medallions) are worked in the round, though they may be squares or octagons. They are joined to each other at the end of the project, when a second pattern may be used at the corners.

DOILIES are also worked in the round. Other design elements, worked separately, may be joined into the main piece as it expands.

FORMING A RING

THE CHAIN RING is made by working a chain and joining it into a circle with a slip stitch. Then work into it or around it, catching up the tail as you go. If you are working into individual stitches, this is the ring you must use.

THE ADJUSTABLE RING is especially useful if you need a very small ring. It allows you to work the stitches in a larger diameter ring, and then pull the tail of thread to decrease the diameter.

Start as if you are making a slip knot. Instead of drawing a loop through the center and pulling it tight; just leave the thread circle as it is and draw up a chain for height to begin the first round. It does not matter that the thread circle is much bigger than you want the ring to be—pulling on the tail of thread will tighten the circle when you have made enough covering stitches. Insert the hook back into the thread circle, yarn over, draw up a loop, and work a single crochet around the thread. Continue working single crochet around the thread circle and tail of thread. Pull the tail to draw the loop tight and slip stitch to join.

Chain ring

Chain ring

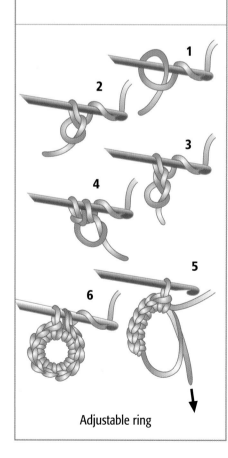

Adjustable ring

Adjustable ring

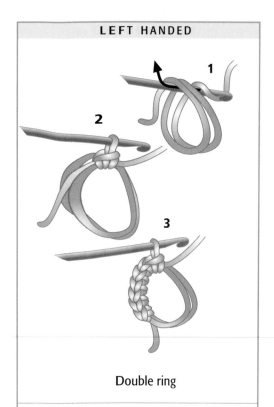

Double ring

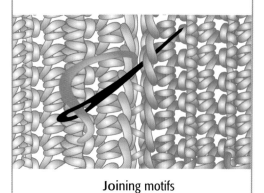

Joining motifs

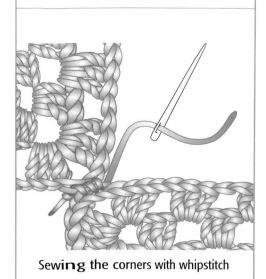

Sewing the corners with whipstitch

A DOUBLE RING is simply a thicker center ring. Start with a thread circle, wrapping the thread around twice. Draw up the first loop, chain for height, and proceed with single crochets over the ring.

JOINING MOTIFS

Joins for straight seams are covered in "Joins and Seams" (see page 48), but joining motifs is almost an art form. Feel free to improvise artistically.

SEWING THE CORNERS is the simplest way to join motifs. Lay the motifs out on a table, with all the right sides up. Check this twice to avoid unpleasant surprises. Work from the right side of the motifs, so that you will know if your stitches are invisible.

Thread a tapestry needle with the same thread you used for the motif. Knot the thread and draw the needle through a convenient corner stitch of the first motif to hide the knot. Take the second motif and insert the needle *from the right side,* coming out the back. Take the third motif and insert the needle *from the right side,* coming out the back. Repeat this on all the motifs, always making the stitch from the right side. Make the last stitch in the first motif. Make a discrete knot, then bury the needle in another convenient cluster stitch and cut the thread.

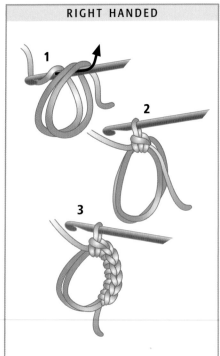

Double ring

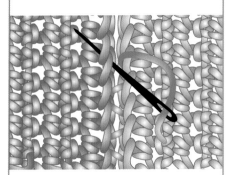

Joining motifs

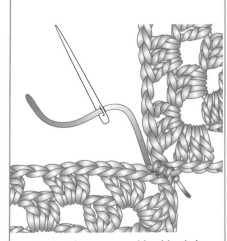

Sewing the corners with whipstitch

lap of luxury

A rich tapestry of navy, wine and teal adds drama to a thick and cuddly afghan. Easy enough for a beginner, it offers a lesson on how to crochet using multiple colors.

DESIGN BY MARSHA HINKSON
Skill level: Beginner
Finished project size: 40" x 58" excluding fringe

MATERIALS

Lion Brand Wool-Ease Thick & Quick, Article #640, 80% acrylic/20% wool yarn (6 ounces/108 yards per ball): 7 balls of Navy (110) for MC; 5 balls each of Claret (143) for color A and Pine (182) for color B

Size N/15 (9.00mm) aluminum crochet hook or size needed to obtain gauge

GAUGE

In Tapestry Crochet, 9 sts and 8 rows = 4" (10.2cm).
Take time to check your gauge.

NOTES

Work the afghan with each row as a right side row. Do not turn at the end of rows.

When working over the unused strand, carry it loosely along top of previous row.

The afghan will stretch along the bias when worked in all RS rows; follow instructions for blocking (see Finishing, below).

STITCH PATTERN

This afghan hides the unused strand of color inside the other single crochet stitches in the row, making color changes quick and neat. The only yarn ends are at the ends of each row, and become fringe. To review the hidden color and tapestry crochet techniques, turn to pages 72 and 73.

INSTRUCTIONS

Foundation: Leaving a 10" tail at beginning, with MC, ch 91. Sc in 2nd ch from hook and in each ch across — 90 sts. Leaving a 10" tail, fasten off. **Do not turn.**

Row 1 (RS): Leaving a 10" tail of MC and A, with the RS facing, join MC with sl st in first sc at right edge, ch 1. Working over color A strand, with MC, sc in same sc as joining and in each of next 9 sc, changing to color A. * With A, sc in next 10 sc and work over the MC strand; with MC, sc in next 10 sc and work over the color A strand. Rep from * across; at end, leaving a 10" strand of each color, fasten off.

Rows 2–10: Rep Row 1.

Row 11 (RS): Leaving a 10" tail of B and MC, with RS facing, join B with sl st in first sc at right edge, ch 1. Working over color MC strand, with B, sc in same sc as joining and in each of next 9 sc, changing to MC. * With MC, sc in next 10 sc and work over the color B strand; with color B, sc in next 10 sc and work over the MC strand. Rep from * across; at end, leaving a 10" strand of each color, fasten off.

Rows 12–20: Rep Row 11.

Row 21: Leaving a 10" tail of A and MC, with the RS facing, join A with sl st in first sc at right edge, ch 1. Working over MC strand, with A, sc in same sc as joining and in each of next 9 sc, changing to MC. * With MC, sc in next 10 sc and work over the color A strand; with A, sc in next 10 sc and work over the MC strand. Rep from * across; at end, leaving a 10" strand of each color, fasten off.

Rows 22–30: Rep Row 21.
Rows 31–40: Rep Rows 1–10.
Rows 41–50: Rep Rows 11–20.
Rows 51–60: Rep Rows 1–10.
Rows 61–70: Rep Rows 11–20.
Rows 71–80: Rep Rows 1–10.
Rows 81–90: Rep Rows 21–30.
Rows 91–100: Rep Rows 11–20.
Rows 101–110: Rep Rows 1–10.

FINISHING

JOINING: With the RS facing, join MC with sl st in first sc at right edge of Row 110. Ch 1, sc in same sc as joining and in each sc across. Fasten off.

BLOCKING: Place afghan onto a flat, padded surface, pinning to measurements. Cover with damp towels and leave until dry.

FRINGE: Beginning at corner, take 2 tails through st, leaving a small lp; take tails through the lp and pull up to form a knot. Rep for each set of 2 tails across each end. ✿

Marsha Hinkson has been a member of the Kooler Design Studio for the past eleven years as an expert on counted-thread work and embroidery. Her needlework interests and talents include designing easy-to-crochet afghans.

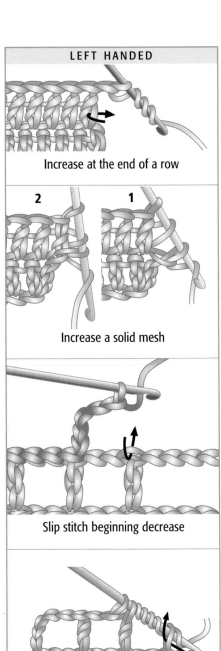

Increase at the end of a row

2 1

Increase a solid mesh

Slip stitch beginning decrease

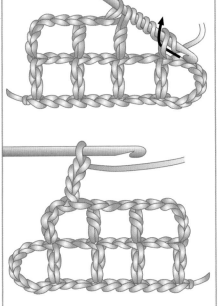

Treble-treble beginning decrease

INCREASE AT THE END OF A ROW, work increases into the base of the previous stitch. For an open mesh, * chain 2, yarn over 3 times and work a double treble (see page 44) in the base of the preceding mesh * Repeat from * to * once for each mesh increased.

INCREASE A SOLID MESH, * work an extended double crochet into the base of the preceding stitch * three times.

DECREASES

A SLIP STITCH BEGINNING DECREASE can be worked with the invisible slip stitch. Instead of making a turning chain, slip stitch across to where you wish to work the first mesh of the row. Begin the mesh with a 3-chain out of the last slip stitch. Work the next two stitches according to the chart.

A TREBLE-TREBLE BEGIN-NING DECREASE is very useful for working one open mesh, especially if you are working with ultra-fine thread. Though it is worked on the end of the preceding row, it is still a beginning decrease.

This may be the only time you need to work a treble treble. It is worth knowing. It works just like a regular treble, just a bit longer. Yarn over 4 times and work off the loops two by two. This will happen six times, which equals six chains. After turning the work, work a treble treble, one mesh to the left in the row below. (For left-handed workers, one mesh to the right.)

At the end of working the treble treble you will end up back where you began. You are positioned to work the chain 3 to begin the next row. Continue according to the chart.

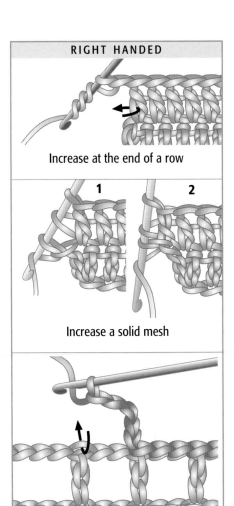

Increase at the end of a row

1 2

Increase a solid mesh

Slip stitch beginning decrease

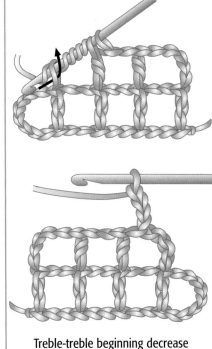

Treble-treble beginning decrease

79

LEFT HANDED

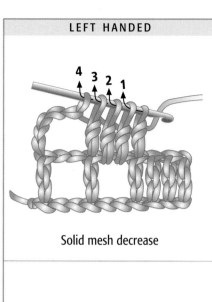

Solid mesh decrease

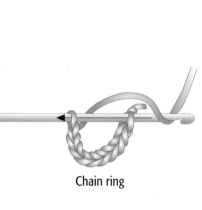

Chain ring

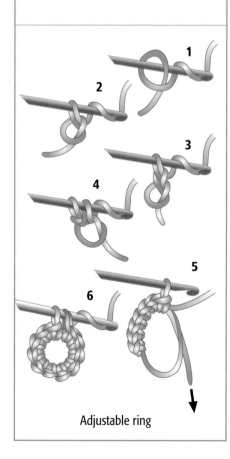

Adjustable ring

END OF ROW DECREASES

SOLID MESH DECREASE uses the familiar decrease on four stitches at once. Simply work each of the last 4 double crochets until two loops each remain on the hook. Then yarn over and work off two loops at a time, ending up centered over the double crochet where you began. Turn and make 3 chains to begin the new row.

Project for Edging: Delicate Filet Edging; see page 100 for instructions.

ROUND MOTIFS AND DOILIES

MOTIFS (medallions) are worked in the round, though they may be squares or octagons. They are joined to each other at the end of the project, when a second pattern may be used at the corners.

DOILIES are also worked in the round. Other design elements, worked separately, may be joined into the main piece as it expands.

FORMING A RING

THE CHAIN RING is made by working a chain and joining it into a circle with a slip stitch. Then work into it or around it, catching up the tail as you go. If you are working into individual stitches, this is the ring you must use.

THE ADJUSTABLE RING is especially useful if you need a very small ring. It allows you to work the stitches in a larger diameter ring, and then pull the tail of thread to decrease the diameter.

Start as if you are making a slip knot. Instead of drawing a loop through the center and pulling it tight; just leave the thread circle as it is and draw up a chain for height to begin the first round. It does not matter that the thread circle is much bigger than you want the ring to be—pulling on the tail of thread will tighten the circle when you have made enough covering stitches. Insert the hook back into the thread circle, yarn over, draw up a loop, and work a single crochet around the thread. Continue working single crochet around the thread circle and tail of thread. Pull the tail to draw the loop tight and slip stitch to join.

RIGHT HANDED

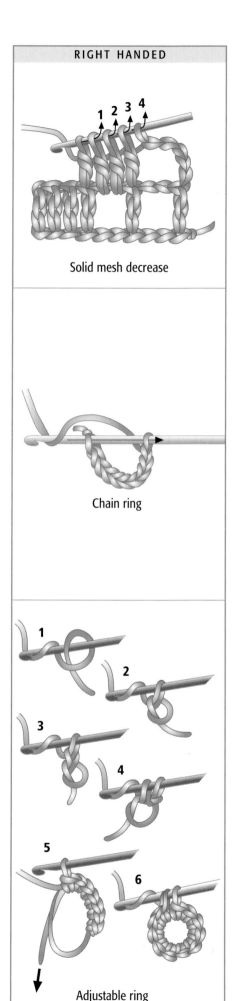

Solid mesh decrease

Chain ring

Adjustable ring

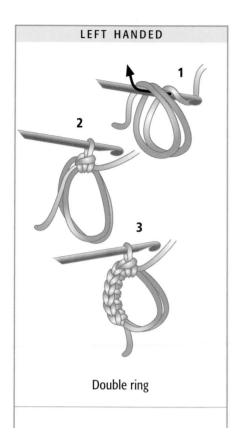

1

2

3

Double ring

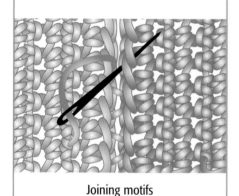

Joining motifs

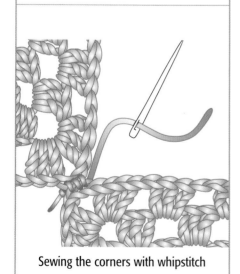

Sewing the corners with whipstitch

A DOUBLE RING is simply a thicker center ring. Start with a thread circle, wrapping the thread around twice. Draw up the first loop, chain for height, and proceed with single crochets over the ring.

JOINING MOTIFS

Joins for straight seams are covered in "Joins and Seams" (see page 48), but joining motifs is almost an art form. Feel free to improvise artistically.

SEWING THE CORNERS is the simplest way to join motifs. Lay the motifs out on a table, with all the right sides up. Check this twice to avoid unpleasant surprises. Work from the right side of the motifs, so that you will know if your stitches are invisible.

Thread a tapestry needle with the same thread you used for the motif. Knot the thread and draw the needle through a convenient corner stitch of the first motif to hide the knot. Take the second motif and insert the needle *from the right side,* coming out the back. Take the third motif and insert the needle *from the right side,* coming out the back. Repeat this on all the motifs, always making the stitch from the right side. Make the last stitch in the first motif. Make a discrete knot, then bury the needle in another convenient cluster stitch and cut the thread.

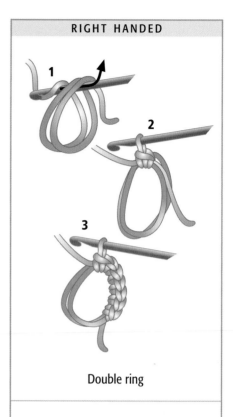

1

2

3

Double ring

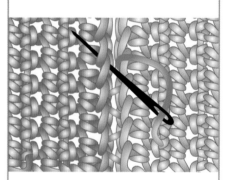

Joining motifs

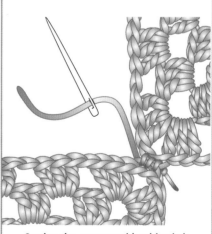

Sewing the corners with whipstitch

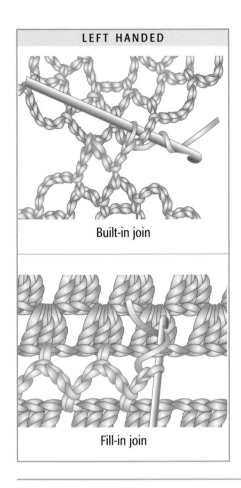

LEFT HANDED

Built-in join

Fill-in join

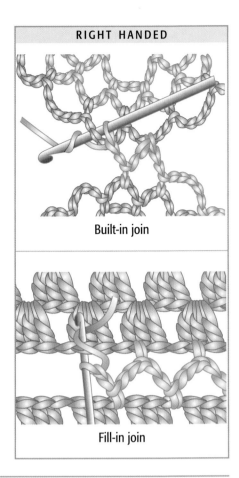

RIGHT HANDED

Built-in join

Fill-in join

THE BUILT-IN JOIN is designed into some motifs, so that the last round of one motif joins two motifs. This eliminates the entire sewing process. Clever designers know that crocheting is much more fun than hiding knots.

THE FILL-IN JOIN can be invented to fill in spaces between motifs. Round motifs on square grids and octagonal motifs have large corner spaces. These can be filled with chain flowers, worked from a central ring.

Fake it. If you like a motif without a built-in join, consider devising your own. Picots or edges can be caught together with clusters worked from a central stem chain. (Remember that after you finish the cluster you will need to get back to the stem.)

Project for motifs: Virginia Roses; see page 102 for instructions.

IRISH CROCHET

Irish crochet was invented to reproduce European needle laces comparatively quickly and inexpensively. True Irish crochet is far too complex a discipline to be covered in one chapter, or even in one book. The lace is characterized by densely worked, individual floral motifs, joined by delicate chain-stitch grounds.

Most modern Irish crochet is only an allusion to the original art. But certain motifs and techniques are recognized everywhere as being of Irish origin. Learning them allows us to carry on the thread of this distinctive, traditional art with familiar stitches. Motifs become even more striking by being heavily padded at the centers or edges. The simple technique can be used in any motif to create the play of light and shadow. Remember that highly textured and three-dimensional patterns are not suitable for tablecloths.

FLOWER AND LEAF MOTIFS
(CORDED & UNCORDED)

There are hundreds of flower and leaf motifs, and we have included some in the Pattern Gallery (see page 196 for a

good example). The classic Irish rose motif is included in a project (see page 105). None of the motifs is padded, but you may pad the leaves if you wish.

Use several strands of crochet thread for padding. Working single crochet around another thread should be familiar from the tapestry crochet color technique (see page 73).

GROUND PATTERNS/EDGING/INSERTION

Delicate chain trellises with picots like swelling buds hold botanical motifs together. But the lovely traditional grounds are often used alone as edgings and inserts now. We have included examples of both in the Pattern Gallery (see pages 187 and 188).

JOINING MOTIFS

Most traditional ways of joining motifs have fallen into disuse:

Motifs were placed on muslin, face down, and regular grounds were crocheted across the entire expanse of fabric, catching in the motifs.

Motifs were placed face up on muslin, and grounds were chained randomly from motif to motif to catch in the edges.

Modern ways of joining motifs set them in a simple mesh, with a few picots to soften the straight lines of the chains. This can be worked in a length, with the motifs joined on one side to make an edging. Or, enlarge motifs into mesh squares or medallions, which creates a much more regular fabric for tablecloths and bedspreads.

Project for Irish crochet: Irish Roses; see page 105 for instructions.

specialty crochet

Detail of Wedding Keepsake beaded bag; project instructions on page 108.

BEAD CROCHET

Bead crochet is all the fun of crochet combined with glimmer, glitter, and glitz. Dress up your favorite stitches, lace or otherwise, with anything from glass to metal. Use beads to add a monogram or subtle pattern, or scatter a few crystals like stars. The stitches are the same basic crochet stitches you already know. If a technique seems confusing, try it without the beads for a few rounds or rows until you understand the stitch structure.

BEADS

Beads come packaged in grams, kilograms, or strung in hanks. Experiment with different sizes and types before you buy hanks of something unfamiliar. Start your adventures in bead crochet with relatively large beads: a size 6 or 8.

ROCAILLE BEADS (SEED BEADS) are commonly used in beaded crochet, since they fit nicely between segments of crochet stitches. They come in sizes 1° (large) to 15° (tiny). Sizes are also sometimes written 1/0 or 15/0.

TRUE CUTS rocailles with one cut surface come in sizes 8°, 11°, 13°, and 15°. ("Charlottes" are specifically size 13° true-cuts). Two- and three-cuts have (respectively) two and three cut surfaces, and come in sizes 9°, 10°, 11°, and 12°. The facets add extra sparkle to your work, and the beads come in hundreds of colors.

WHITE HEARTS are rocailles with a white hole, which brightens the vivid colors even more.

DELICAS OR MIYUKI DELICAS are a specific Japanese variety of rocailles, made at the Miyuki plant. These elegant beads are laser-cut cylinders with thin walls and large holes, and are the most expensive beads made. They come in small (11°) and large (8°) sizes, and are sold only by the gram.

UNICAS are a less expensive and less precise imitation of Delicas and come only in size 14°.

CZECH ROCAILLES come from a bead-making tradi-tion that originated in the Middle Ages, and are known for their clarity, colors, and shape. They have small holes and thick walls. They come in over 2000 colors, and are sold in hanks or by weight.

BUGLE BEADS (long tube beads) are not commonly used in crochet, except perhaps in fringes, because the shape of the bead does not lend itself to crochet stitches. Use two seed beads for the effect of a bugle bead.

MATERIALS AND TOOLS

THREADS Choose a smooth, firmly-twisted thread for your crochet work. Cotton threads in sizes 30, 20, 10 or pearl size 8 work well. Silk buttonhole twist wears very well and comes in colors to complement the rainbow of bead hues. Beads sliding along thread will fray it, and a hard twist will fuzz less.

HOOKS should coordinate with the thread, as in regular crochet. If you are working a pavé ("paved") piece, with a bead on every row, remember that the hook will also need to fit between the closely packed beads. For a guideline, a size 6 or 7 steel hook works well with 8° beads and size 10 thread.

BEADING NEEDLES are longer and thinner than sewing needles. You can choose from fixed-eye needles, or flex-ible-eye needles. The flexible-eye needles stretch out for easier threading, and then collapse to squeeze through the beads. This is convenient, but the eyes break after repeated uses. Fixed eyes are longer and thinner than those in sewing needles, but are easily threaded using a needle threader.

FLOSS (Nymo) for threading beads onto the crochet thread can be found in the bead section of your store.

NEEDLE-NOSED PLIERS are useful for breaking off beads that are threaded out of order. It is easier to sacrifice a bead than to restring 100, especially when doing multi-color work. When you break off beads, be sure to wear eye protec-tion. Or you can cut the thread, slip off the bead, and reattach the thread.

THREADING THE BEADS

KNOTLESS THREADING Use a beading needle with a long eye and beading floss (a needle threader is handy). Cut a foot of floss and thread both ends into the eye to make a loop. Insert the end of your crochet thread into the floss loop, and bend the cut end down. Pick a few beads up on the needle and gently slide them down the floss and onto the crochet thread. If you come to a bead with too small a hole to slide onto the crochet thread, slip the thread out of the loop and remove the bead.

TIE THE FLOSS TO THE THREAD if the crochet thread slips from the loop a lot. If you come to a bead with too small a hole to slide onto the crochet thread, cut the floss and remove the bead.

A SHOELACE END may sometimes be necessary when the beads just won't fit over the doubled crochet thread. Use "super glue" (cyanoacrylate) or nail polish to stiffen the end of the thread, shoelace style, for a self-needle.

THREADING ORDER in multi-color work is in reverse order: the first bead on is the last bead used. If you are working from a chart, threading order is determined by the direction in which you read the rows.

ALTERNATE ROW BEADING: the beads will always be counted from the same edge in the pattern graph.

IN THE ROUND: the beads will always be counted in the same direction in the pattern graph.

EVERY ROW: Count the beads from the left in one row and from the right in the next row, depending upon whether you are working on the right or wrong side of the fabric.

MISTAKES HAPPEN in counting, and you may miss a bead or two. Crochet to a point close to the mistake, where you can conveniently cut the thread, then restring a few beads, insert the missing one, and reattach the thread. Or you can sew on a bead later, though the bead will not be flush with the others. If you are doing pavé work, this will be very noticeable.

If you have too many beads, break them off carefully with the pliers, and wipe up the glass dust with a damp cloth.

AVOID FRAYED THREAD when threading hundreds of beads. Thread and work about a hundred beads at a time. Break the thread at the end of a row to thread the next batch of beads. Be sure to mark on the graph or pattern where you have stopped. While working, push the beads back so you have just enough thread to crochet. There is no point in pushing beads back six feet if you only need six inches. Keep the beads you need handy on your index finger, and slide them into place as required.

BEAD CROCHET BASICS

Beads are no fun unless they end up where you want them. A bead naturally slides to the back of a stitch: in tall stitches you can even choose which segment of the stitch will hold the bead.

You can also place beads on the front. Mixing and matching front and back techniques allows you to put a bead on either side, so that you can work beads every row.

To insure precise bead placement, the yarn over must be correct. Just hooking the thread from the front may cause a misplaced bead. Hold the bead in place with your thumbnail if it shifts around while you are working a stitch. Draw the loops up tightly; keep yarn overs short to prevent a bead from shifting.

Making a bead sampler is a good way to try all the different beading techniques and stitches and is well worth the time and effort before you start an actual project. Keep row ends tidy with a beadless selvage stitch.

BEAD CHAIN (b-ch): Start with one chain and use one bead for each subsequent chain. Slide the bead up to the hook, yarn over, and draw the loop through.

BEADS ON THE BACK: The techniques explained on the following page allow beads to fall to the back of the stitch (work). Work beads on the wrong side rows to place beads exactly where you need them on the front side.

LEFT HANDED

Knotless threading

Front of chain

Back of chain

Bead chain

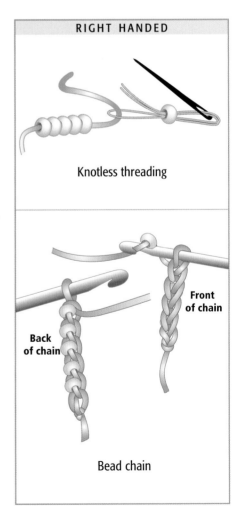

RIGHT HANDED

Knotless threading

Back of chain

Front of chain

Bead chain

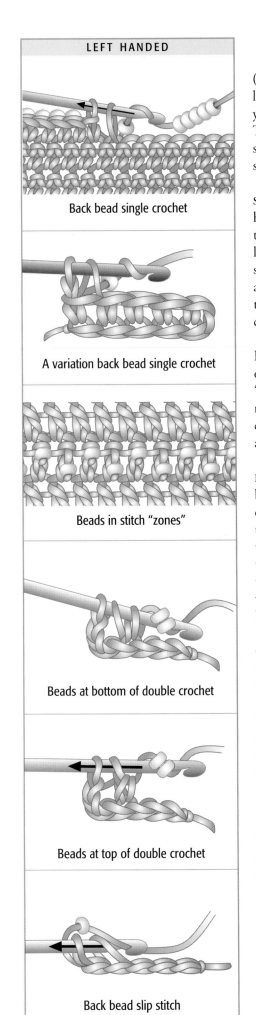

Back bead single crochet

A variation back bead single crochet

Beads in stitch "zones"

Beads at bottom of double crochet

Beads at top of double crochet

Back bead slip stitch

BACK BEAD SINGLE CROCHET (bb-sc): Insert the hook and draw up a loop; slide the bead up against the hook; yarn over and draw through both loops. The bead will be in place on the other side of the fabric when you finish the stitch.

A VARIATION BACK BEAD SINGLE CROCHET is to insert the hook, push the bead against the hook, then yarn over, and draw through both loops. This slants the bead in the opposite direction from the first method. For a herringbone pattern, alternate rows of this variation with rows of bead single crochet.

BEADS IN STITCH "ZONES": Placing beads between any two yarn overs in a stitch anchors them in that "zone" on the back of a stitch. By alternating upper and lower zone beads you can place beads in a zigzag pattern across a single row.

BEADS AT BOTTOM OF DOUBLE CROCHET: To put two seed beads on the bottom half of a double crochet, yarn over, insert the hook, draw up a loop. Slide the beads tight against the hook, yarn over and draw through two loops: two beads will be in place in the bottom zone. (At this point you can work the stitch as a double or a half double crochet.)

BEADS AT TOP OF DOUBLE CROCHET: To put two (more) beads at the top of a double crochet, slide two beads up against the hook, yarn over and draw through the last two loops; these beads will be in the top zone of the double crochet. This works in treble and taller stitches as well. It does not work on the front of a stitch.

BACK BEAD SLIP STITCH (bb-sl st) produces a very densely packed beading. Insert the hook, push a bead up against it, yarn over and draw through both loops. Worked inside out in a small spiral, this stitch will make a beaded cord: Chain 5. In the first chain, insert the hook from the inside out (the thread will be in the center of the ring throughout). Push a bead against the hook, yarn over, and draw through both loops. Repeat around in a spiral for the desired length.

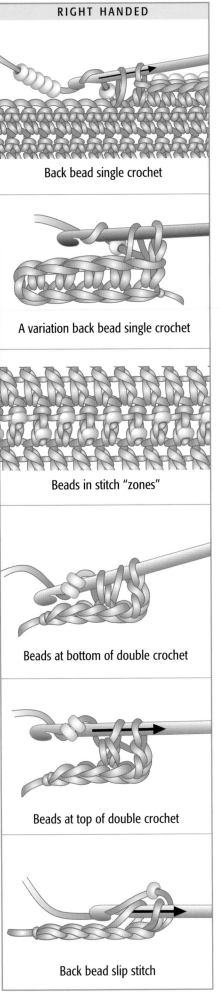

Back bead single crochet

A variation back bead single crochet

Beads in stitch "zones"

Beads at bottom of double crochet

Beads at top of double crochet

Back bead slip stitch

85

LEFT HANDED

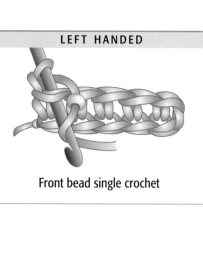

Front bead single crochet

Front bead double crochet

Front bead slip stitch

BEADS ON THE FRONT stitches will put beads on the work facing you, though not in stitches taller than double crochet. The direction of twist in crochet stitches limits the placement of front beads to the base of the stitch. To keep a bead on the front, the thread with the bead needs to be in place before you begin the process of yarn over and work off, whatever stitch you are working.

FRONT BEAD SINGLE CROCHET (**fb-sc**): To work a single crochet with a bead facing you, slide a bead into place against the hook. Insert the hook from the back to the front, working in the space or through the stitch. Draw up a loop, yarn over, and draw through 2 loops.

FRONT BEAD DOUBLE CROCHET (**fb-dc**): Slide the bead against the hook, then yarn over. Insert the hook, draw up a loop, and slide the bead over the hook to the front of the yarn over (the front of the stitch). Yarn over and draw through two loops, twice. This stitch also can be worked as a front bead half double crochet.

FRONT BEAD SLIP STITCH (**fb-sl st**): produces very densely packed beading. Insert the hook from back to front (wrong side to right side), push a bead up against the hook, yarn over, and draw through both loops.

PAVÉ ROWS: alternate rows of back and front bead single crochet with a bead in every stitch.

Projects for bead crochet; Wedding Keepsake and Beaded Heart Pins; see pages 108 and 112 for instructions.

RIGHT HANDED

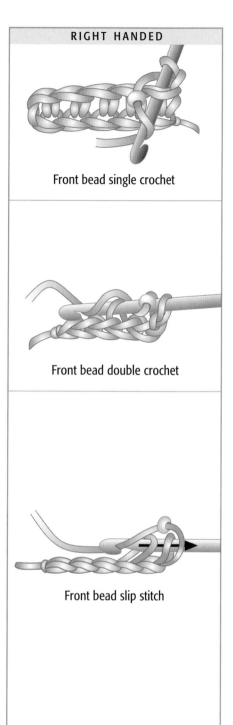

Front bead single crochet

Front bead double crochet

Front bead slip stitch

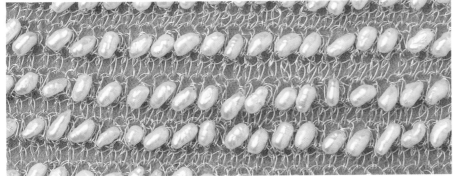

Detail of sterling silver wire crochet and freshwater pearls. From the collection of Nancy Nehring.

WIRE CROCHET

Crochet with wire is crochet with light. Wire catches the light in its coils and tosses it back at us. Here tradition yields to innovation, and rules are bent. The stitches are familiar, but light years away from layettes and warm mittens.

Unforgiving wire requires our closest attention, but tiny kinks and twists reward our imperfections with plays of light and shadow. Instead of longing for perfect curves, appreciate the calligraphic quality of a line in space, full of character and personality.

MATERIALS

Resist the temptation to use the smallest crochet hook you can find. A nice aluminum size G or H will do very well, even if you are using fine wire. The idea is to show off the structure of the stitch, not keep out the wind. Dedicate a hook to wire, since working with wire will scar it. You will also need wire cutters and needle-nosed pliers.

When choosing wire, bend a few different gauges (diameters) of wire to see how flexible they are: the higher the gauge number, the thinner the wire. A gauge of 22 is too thick. Start with 30-gauge soft brass wire. Copper will work, but soft brass is more flexible.

TECHNIQUES

Wire makes the rules. Wire doesn't wrap around your hand, it has its own tension, and you do what wire allows… or else you outsmart it.

If you pull wire off the spool the way you do thread, it will kink like a corkscrew. Instead, work with the wire in front of you and pull the wire perpendicular to the spool so that it isn't pre-kinked. If you are using a coil of wire and don't want it to go *sproing!* immediately, wrap a twist tie around it and release a few coils as you need.

Try out wire crochet with a sampler of stitches to see what works and what doesn't. Form stitches in different ways to see what effects you can create. Deliberately work some stitches to be as open as possible, and then see how tightly you can work the same stitch. Tension takes on a whole new meaning when it is built into the materials; what doesn't work with one gauge of wire may be successful with another.

Direction is important, too. If a stitch looks better worked in one direction than to and fro, work in one direction or in the round. You can cut the piece later and attach the edges to a border wire. Wire doesn't unravel easily.

Enjoy the investigation, and be sure to stretch your hands frequently.

Crochet with wire is a two-handed art; sometimes you push, sometimes you pull. Getting the wire through the loop is easier if you use both hands, since a little pushing distorts the wire less than simply pulling it through with the hook. Try rolling the hook up the wire as it emerges from the chain, to coax it out to the length you want. Let the spaces be spacious, and develop the skill of making stitches that are even. Once you know how wire works, plan ahead to get the shape you want.

STITCHES Which stitches work best? It all depends. Single crochet worked in rows produces a round opening and a more dense, regular fabric. Worked in the round (surprise!) it resembles a Brussels lace ground.

Tall stitches have elongated spaces between them and a lot of twists within. To avoid ruining your wire and your temper, *build the height into your stitch as you go*. With wire, things don't just slide into place—you have to put them in place, and that is where they stay.

For example, if the first yarn over of a double crochet is to swirl in the center of the stitch, use the hook at an angle, which puts the bend where you want it. Don't plan to "tighten up" the stitch as you go along. Poke the wire to make it bend where it should. If you don't want a swirl in the center of the stitch, form the yarn over at the top of the stitch by holding the hook level with the top of the stitch, producing a teardrop shape.

Do you want to work in the spaces or through the stitches? Working in the spaces will compress the horizontal zones and emphasize the posts. Working through the stitches allows the horizontal swirls to be accentuated. What about working around the posts? Train your skill to serve your taste.

Experiment with the wire gauge and hook size to see what you can do. But remember, if you have to tug too much on the wire it will distort the other stitches in the piece. You may find this works to your advantage sometimes, or you may not like it at all.

What if you make a mistake? At first you won't be able to tell because it will look like you are crocheting a pot scrubber. Don't be discouraged. After a couple

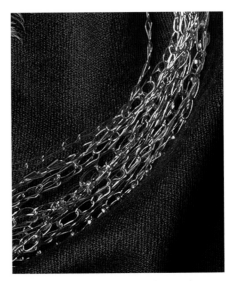

Elegant Wire Jewelry; project instructions on page 116.

of rows you will understand what is going on.

You can pull out a mistake if it is minor. Straighten the wire gently on a flat surface and rework the stitch. But you can't do it more than once or twice in one spot. Wire becomes brittle fast. It may be better to work the piece through, make mistakes, and leave them in. Concentrate on getting the feel of wire and controlling where things happen. When you have worked a swatch, look it over carefully to see if you like the mistakes better than "the other way." Then break off the sample and do things the way you like.

BREAKS AND MENDS are inevitable. Sometimes wires break; sometimes they run out. Either way, you are going to have to add a strand some-time. Practice by cutting the wire in the middle of a stitch and then mending it. That is what your wire sampler is for!

Remove the hook. Use needle-nosed pliers to remove the broken piece and poke around to find the best place to begin a repair. It is easy to start the new wire in a yarn over, the way you would attach any new strand. (Don't worry about working in the end until you have finished the row.) A few pre-made bends will help you position the new wire without tugging. It may not be perfect, but it is pretty close. Insert the hook and carry on.

The origin of the stitch (the horizontal zone) is a good place to anchor the loose ends because there are lots of twists of wire. Make a small hook in the end of the new strand, and crimp or twist it around a wire where it doesn't show.

Make your sampler as long or as short as you like, but don't expect perfection. Samplers are test runs where you learn and experiment. Follow a couple of interesting ideas to see where they lead.

FINISHING A PIECE is simple, and you don't have to worry about starch! Seams can simply be a twist of wire where needed. You don't have to hide ends so much as bend them in. If there is a sharp end you may want to put a drop of solder or epoxy glue on it. Then sit back and admire what your hands have wrought.

Projects for wire crochet: Amulet Necklace and Elegant Wire Jewelry; see pages 114 and 116 for instructions. 🌀

LEFT HANDED

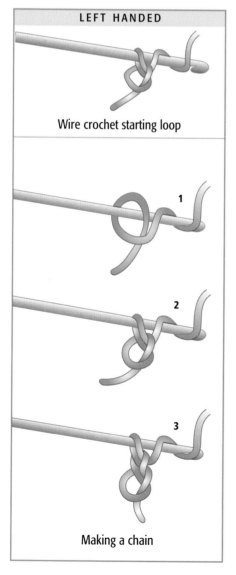

Wire crochet starting loop

1

2

3

Making a chain

WIRE CROCHET STARTING LOOP Use the single-wrap ring to begin.

YARN OVER Crochet with wire is about testing and breaking rules. Yarn over the "wrong" way. Actually, don't yarn over at all; just hook the wire from the front, the way you always wanted when you were first learning crochet. With wire, every bend shows. Your work may not have the uniform stitches of thread crochet, but wire has its own unique beauty.

MAKING A CHAIN As you hook the wire through the starting loop, keep it open and observe the structure. There is a large open loop with a crossing of wire at the side. To make the chain uniform, twist the hook to the right (or the left) each time you pull through a loop of wire. Work at keeping the row of chains even and the twist on the same side in each chain.

RIGHT HANDED

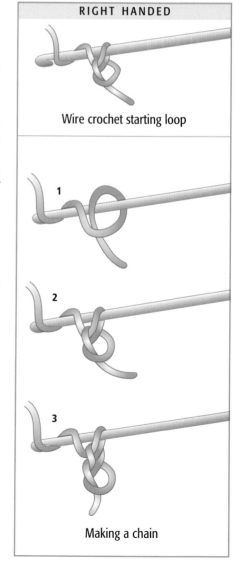

Wire crochet starting loop

1

2

3

Making a chain

tunisian crochet

No one is sure about the origins of Tunisian crochet, but it has been known in the west since 1859, when it was called Princess Frederick William stitch. It has also been called *tricot écossais* (Scottish knitting), railway stitch, idiot stitch, and fool's stitch. The terms *Tunisian crochet* and *afghan stitch* are interchangeable.

Using a special hook, called an afghan hook, cast on stitches in the Forward row and bind off in the Return row. This leaves a layer of warm, insulating loops. The hook length limits width, so large pieces are made in strips. Work is not turned, which makes intarsia color easy, and the square stitch is ideal for cross-stitch decoration.

MATERIALS

THE AFGHAN HOOK is a long crochet hook with a button at the end to keep loops from sliding off. Hold the hook under the palm, rather than like a pencil. Tunisian crochet produces a very dense fabric, so choose a hook a few sizes

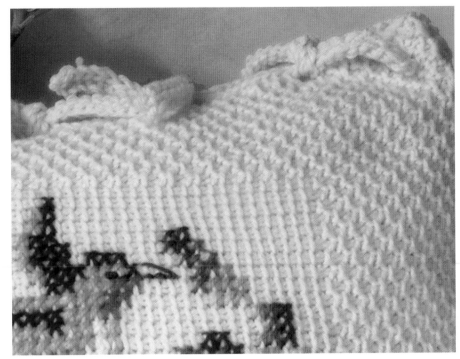

Detail of In a Tunisian Garden pillow; project instructions on page 105.

larger than an ordinary crochet hook for the same yarn.

Afghan hook

TECHNIQUES

TUNISIAN SIMPLE STITCH (TSS)

CHAIN (STARTING) ROW: Make a chain for the number of stitches you need. The first chain from the hook is always skipped and is not charted. Insert the hook into the second chain, yarn over, and draw up a loop. Keep that loop on the hook (two loops on hook). Draw up a new loop in each remaining chain, so that at the end of the row you have a loop drawn up from each chain. At the end of the row do not turn the work.

TUNISIAN RETURN ROW is worked with the front of the work still facing you. Yarn over and draw up one loop. This is the equivalent of the turning chain in regular crochet, but here it is the width that you need. Yarn over again; draw through two loops to bind off the first stitch. Yarn over and draw through two loops at each stitch across the row. At the end of the Return row you will have one complete row and one loop on the hook ready to start the next row.

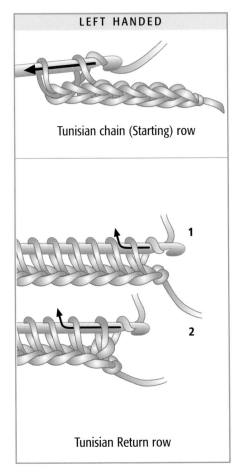

LEFT HANDED

Tunisian chain (Starting) row

Tunisian Return row

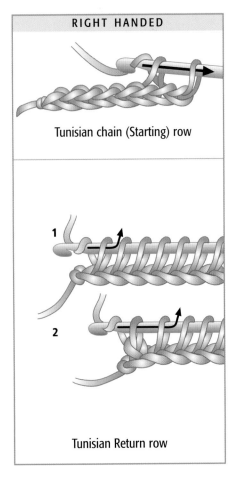

RIGHT HANDED

Tunisian chain (Starting) row

Tunisian Return row

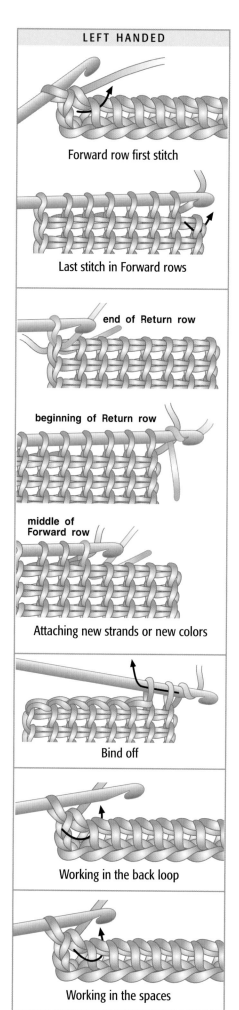

Forward row first stitch

Last stitch in Forward rows

end of Return row

beginning of Return row

middle of
Forward row

Attaching new strands or new colors

Bind off

Working in the back loop

Working in the spaces

FORWARD ROW FIRST STITCH is used to work the "cast-on" rows for the rest of the piece. Insert the hook between the front and back vertical threads of a stitch. Yarn over, draw up a loop, and keep it on the hook. Do this in each stitch.

LAST STITCH IN FORWARD ROW: insert the hook under both vertical end threads, yarn over, and draw up the last loop. This will keep the left and right selvages even.

Alternate the Forward and Return rows for the length of the piece.

ATTACHING NEW STRANDS OR COLORS

Draw up the new color as a yarn over through the last two loops of the Return row. The Forward row will be in the new color.

Within a Forward row, draw up the new color through the vertical loop, as you would any other stitch, and carry the unused color loosely across the back. For the Return row, yarn over with the new color at the first loop of that color.

At the beginning of a Return row draw up the first chain in the new color and work across the row.

BIND OFF at the end of a piece by working a Forward row. Draw up a loop at the second vertical stitch, yarn over and draw through two loops. Continue across the row. After drawing the yarn over through the last two loops, cut the yarn and pull the end through. You can end a row on a Return row, but the Forward row bind-off is preferable because it produces a firmer edge.

OTHER BASIC TECHNIQUES

WORKING IN THE BACK LOOP uses the back part of the vertical stitch.

WORKING IN THE SPACES is working between vertical and horizontal loops.

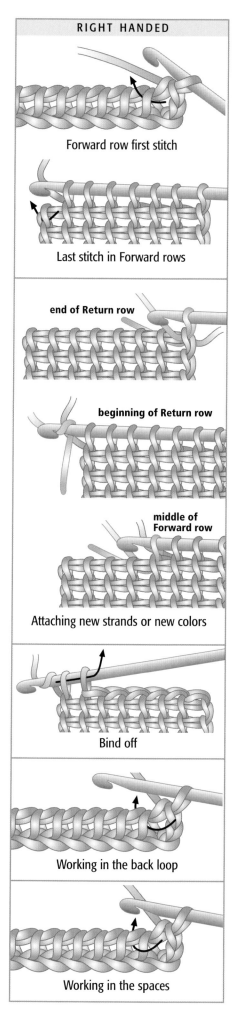

Forward row first stitch

Last stitch in Forward rows

end of Return row

beginning of Return row

middle of
Forward row

Attaching new strands or new colors

Bind off

Working in the back loop

Working in the spaces

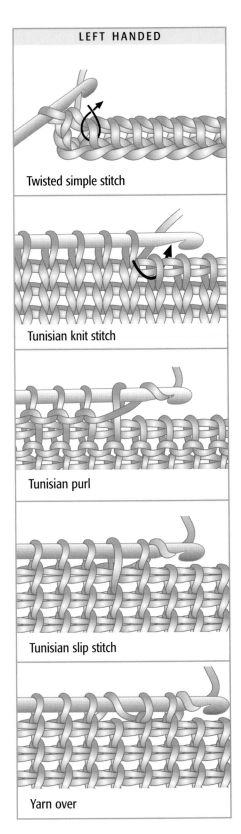

Twisted simple stitch

Tunisian knit stitch

Tunisian purl

Tunisian slip stitch

Yarn over

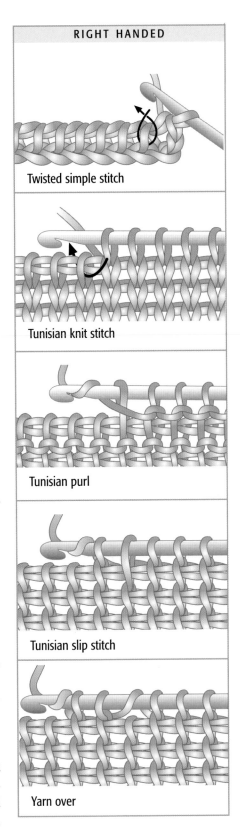

Twisted simple stitch

Tunisian knit stitch

Tunisian purl

Tunisian slip stitch

Yarn over

TUNISIAN STITCHES

TWISTED TUNISIAN SIMPLE STITCH (**TwTss**) uses a twisting technique common in knit stitches. Insert the hook from *left* to *right* (or *right* to *left* for left-handers) in the vertical stitch, yarn over and draw up a loop.

TUNISIAN KNIT STITCH (**Tks**) With yarn in back, insert the hook from front to back between the verticals and under the horizontal strands. Draw up a loop from the back.

TUNISIAN PURL STITCH (**Tps**) With yarn in front, insert the hook as for the Tunisian simple stitch. Yarn over and turn the hook a bit to help draw up a loop.

TUNISIAN SLIP STITCH (**Tsl st**) differs from the slip stitch (see sl st) of ordinary crochet. In Tunisian slip stitch you simply lift the vertical stitch onto the hook and leave it there in the Forward row, working it as usual on the Return row.

YARN OVER is often used for lace stitches. The yarn over makes a hole, which is paired with a decrease to balance the stitch count.

TUNISIAN HALF DOUBLE (**Thdc**), DOUBLE (**Tdc**), AND TREBLE (**Ttr**), etc., are worked in Forward rows. Yarn over and insert the hook, right to left, in the front vertical loop. The rest of the stitch is worked just as it is in regular crochet. Keep the last loop of each stitch on the hook, and work it in the Return row.

BOBBLES, POPCORNS, AND PUFFS are made in the vertical stitch, worked as they are in regular crochet. Keep the last loop on the hook.

LEFT HANDED

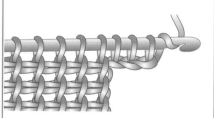

Tunisian internal increase

Tunisian Forward row increase

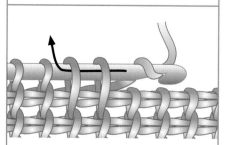

Tunisian Return row

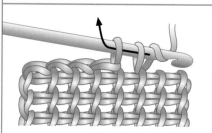

Tunisian Forward row decrease

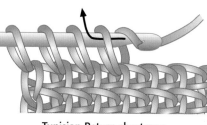

Tunisian Forward short row

Tunisian Return short row

TUNISIAN INCREASES/DECREASES

INCREASES are made by adding stitches between stitches, or by adding extra loops at the ends of rows.

INTERNAL INCREASE (Inc 1 Tss) adds a loop between two other stitches. On the Forward row work twice in one stitch: Insert the hook under the back horizontal strand, then draw up another loop from the vertical part of the stitch. Complete the increase on the Return row by working each loop.

FORWARD ROW INCREASE is made at the end of the Forward row. Chain the required number of loops + 1. Remove the hook from the last loop, pick up the back loop of each chain, then pick up the last loop. Chain 1, yarn over and work the Return row.

TUNISIAN RETURN ROW INCREASE is made at the end of a Return row. Chain the necessary number of stitches. Work the new stitches as you do Chain row stitches, then continue working a Forward row.

DECREASES are made by working 2 or more stitches together, or by skipping stitches in the Forward row and making a short row.

TUNISIAN FORWARD ROW DECREASE (Tss2tog) in a Forward row by inserting the hook between the vertical strands of two stitches. Yarn over and draw through both stitches, leaving one loop to be worked off in the Return row. Three stitches also can be worked together in the same manner, making a decrease of 2 (Tss3tog).

TUNISIAN FORWARD SHORT ROW binds off stitches at the beginning of the row. The last loop of the bound off stitches begins the Forward row.

TUNISIAN RETURN SHORT ROW is made by leaving the desired number of stitches unworked at the end of the Forward row. Work the short Return row as usual.

Projects for Tunisian crochet: In a Tunisian Garden and Child's Tunisian Vest; see pages 118 and 120 for instructions. *pages 118 and 120 for instructions.*

RIGHT HANDED

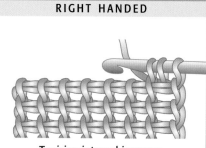

Tunisian internal increase

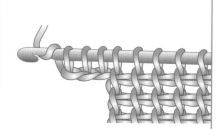

Tunisian Forward row increase

Tunisian Return row

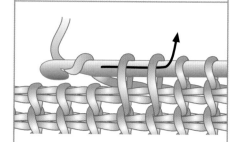

Tunisian Forward row decrease

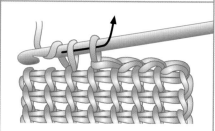

Tunisian Forward short row

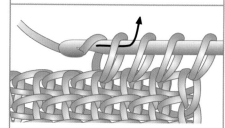

Tunisian Return short row

expert details

As your crochet skill level grows, you may want to challenge yourself by making large garments such as vests, sweaters, cardigans, and coats. You may decide you want fine dressmaking details such as pockets, buttonholes, and decorative edging, yet think they may be daunting. Not so! Pockets, either in-seam or not, are surprisingly easy. The same holds true for buttonholes; we offer them in three styles, as well as two options for attaching buttons to garments so they look as attractive as they are functional. Finally, we show several ways to finish garment edges with decorative stitches for an added *couture* touch.

POCKETS

Pockets can be located in the body of a garment or in the seam. There is very little difference in the construction of each kind. Because crocheted fabric is thick, it is best to use a color-matched woven fabric to make the pocket bag, and to use crochet only on the external pocket details such as the flap, facing, or welt. Welts and facings are often worked in rows of single crochet for sturdiness, but a flap may be worked in a decorative stitch.

IF MAKING A SEAM POCKET, mark an opening in the seamlines the same size as the hemmed opening of the finished fabric pocket. Work the rows of crochet across the seam allowance of the front of the pocket opening, allowing it to extend beyond the seamline if needed. You can tack this extension down with thread on the finished garment. You may do the same for the inside or back edge of the pocket, but it will increase the thickness of the opening, and may look bulky in the finished seam.

Pin the pocket into place. Stitch the inner opening edge to the seamline with thread. (When in doubt choose thread a shade darker than the yarn; it will disappear in the shadows.) Stitch the front of the pocket opening along the edge of the first row of the crocheted facing or welt. You may wish to make a few stitches to hold the pocket in place along the seam allowance of the pocket, to keep it from shifting in the garment.

IF MAKING A HORIZONTAL POCKET in the body of a garment, skip the stitches of the preceding row to make the pocket opening, chaining across the unworked stitches (as shown in the bottom diagram), then continue in pattern to complete the piece.

When you are ready to finish the garment, work a row or two of single crochet on the bottom edge of the pocket opening for a facing or welt. You may crochet the ends of the facing or welt to the garment, or tack them with thread for a less bulky corner. Then sew the fabric pocket to the upper and lower edges of the pocket opening.

Vertical pocket openings may be made by using separate balls of yarn to crochet on either side of the pocket opening. When the opening is the right length, join the two sides again by working across the row with one strand and cutting the other. When possible, work from the exposed edge toward the seam, so that you will be able to hide the yarn ends in a seamline. Work the facing or welt as you would on a seamline pocket, and sew in the pocket using thread.

93

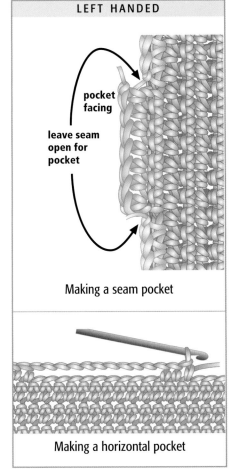

LEFT HANDED

pocket facing

leave seam open for pocket

Making a seam pocket

Making a horizontal pocket

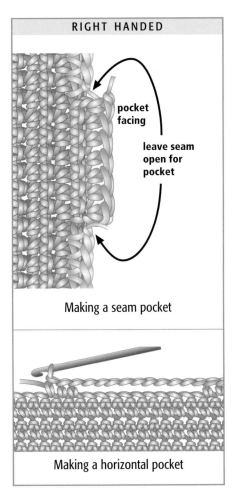

RIGHT HANDED

pocket facing

leave seam open for pocket

Making a seam pocket

Making a horizontal pocket

BUTTONHOLES

Work buttonholes horizontally or vertically by making an opening as you work the fabric, bands, or placket of a garment. In pattern stitches you can use the pattern to provide convenient openings or to disguise them.

When gauging how large to make a buttonhole, remember that crocheted fabric will stretch more than woven fabric. The stitch you are using determines how accurately you can measure your buttonhole. Generally speaking, buttonhole length is about ¾ of the diameter of a button, but if you are working treble crochet, you may not have a lot of control over the basic opening. If a buttonhole ends up a bit too large you can sew it shut a little (using sewing thread) when you finish the edges, or you can indulge in large buttons.

Buttonholes need to be easy to find by touch, especially in lacy fabrics, and need to be sturdy, too. You can reinforce any buttonhole with a finished edge of slip stitch or single crochet. Do this before you continue with the rest of the piece or cut the yarn.

You can also reinforce with a sewn buttonhole stitch after you have completed the garment. If you are using a delicate yarn, you may wish to work with a companion strand of thread or buttonhole twist. Hold the two strands together as you work each stitch.

HORIZONTAL BUTTONHOLES must be made as you crochet the body of the garment or edging. If you are working a crocheted edging around the neck and front of a garment, buttonholes worked horizontally will be vertical. Front and back post ribbing can neatly hide a buttonhole in the transitions.

Skip the stitches you wish to have as the opening. Work one chain for each skipped stitch across the opening. On the return row, work in pattern across the chain. A variation of this is to use the end-of-row increase to work across the space, forming the opening, and finishing it as you work.

VERTICAL BUTTONHOLES in a horizontally-worked garment are worked in two sections. Crochet horizontally up to the opening, then turn and crochet back and forth to that point until the opening is the right height. Remember that both sides of the buttonhole opening must be started on the same side, and worked in the same row-by-row direction, or the patterns will differ.

LOOP BUTTONHOLES are thread-loop semicircles covered with tightly-packed single crochet. Work them either in the last row or the last two rows of edging stitches. Mark the places you want the loops to begin and end.

For two-row loops, on the next-to-last row make a chain just large enough to slip over the button. Continue working the edging, and single crochet over the chain loops in the last row.

To work loops in the last row (shown below), mark the spots along the edge where you want the loops to begin and end. When you come to the place for a loop, crochet past the beginning of the loop, up to the spot you want it to end. Turn and chain back to the spot where you want the loop to begin, making the loop just big enough to slip over the button. Slip stitch the chain to the edge, turn again and work single crochet over the chain loop.

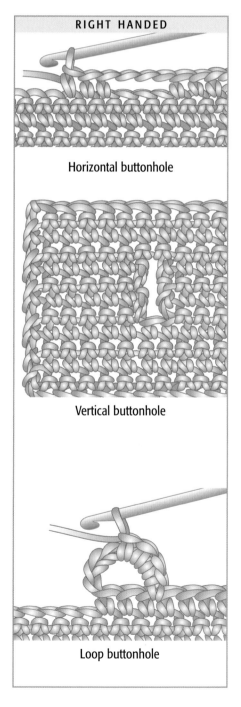

LEFT HANDED

Horizontal buttonhole

Vertical buttonhole

Loop buttonhole

RIGHT HANDED

Horizontal buttonhole

Vertical buttonhole

Loop buttonhole

BUTTONS

BUTTON SHANKS: Crochet is thick, and buttons will need thread shanks to fit comfortably in the buttonholes. To make a shank, leave the threads about $\frac{1}{16}$" to $\frac{1}{8}$" long between the button and the fabric. When you have made all your thread loops through the button, bring the needle down the last time through the top of the button, and wrap the thread tightly around the rest of the threads several times. To finish, push the needle through to the back of the piece, and fasten off.

Buttons needn't be sewn on. To avoid it, make buttonholes on both sides of a garment and use buttons like studs in a dress shirt. Sew two different buttons back to back, one pair for each buttonhole. Use a loop of thread or elastic to make a shank between the two buttons. If you want two different looks for a garment, use two different types of buttons, though they should both have the same diameter. Flip them over to change the button that shows. Use plain buttons behind special buttons that you can remove easily to launder the garment.

WORKING WITH EDGINGS

Trim is useful for surface decoration or finishing touches.

CORDED REVERSE EDGING

Corded reverse edging (also called the crab or shrimp stitch) is a pretty way to cover exposed edges. It is worked backwards, and is fun to do.

Chain one for height. With the yarn in back of the work, insert the hook from front to back at the end of the row. Yarn over and draw up a loop, then yarn over and draw through as usual for a single crochet. Move one stitch to the right. (Move to the left, if you are left-handed.) Continue across the row, and if you decide to go around the corner, work two stitches into the corner stitch; three looks too bunched up.

WORKING ON THE EDGE

Working on the edge, across the ends of the rows, finishes the edges which will be seen. It also stabilizes the fabric in lacy patterns, making seams easier to work and more uniform.

Work stitches at regular intervals across the row ends, using more than one stitch in a space if necessary to keep the stitch size regular. If you are doing this as preparation for a seam, work equal numbers of edge stitches in both pieces. If necessary, use a larger hook size to keep from drawing edge stitches too tightly. ❀

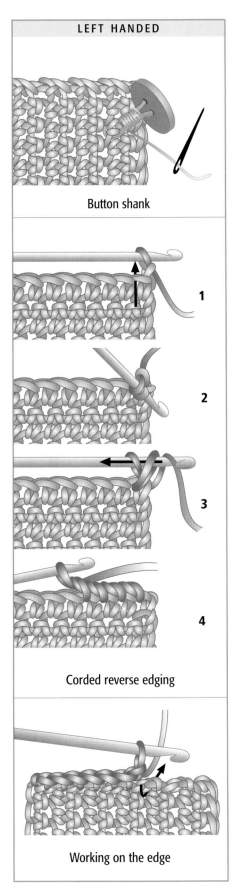

LEFT HANDED

Button shank

1

2

3

4

Corded reverse edging

Working on the edge

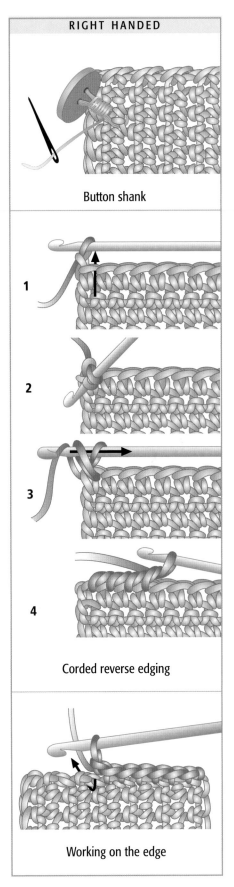

RIGHT HANDED

Button shank

1

2

3

4

Corded reverse edging

Working on the edge

95

lap of luxury

A rich tapestry of navy, wine and teal adds drama to a thick and cuddly afghan. Easy enough for a beginner, it offers a lesson on how to crochet using multiple colors.

DESIGN BY MARSHA HINKSON
Skill level: Beginner
Finished project size: 40" x 58" excluding fringe

MATERIALS
Lion Brand Wool-Ease Thick & Quick, Article #640, 80% acrylic/20% wool yarn (6 ounces/108 yards per ball): 7 balls of Navy (110) for MC; 5 balls each of Claret (143) for color A and Pine (182) for color B

Size N/15 (9.00mm) aluminum crochet hook or size needed to obtain gauge

GAUGE
In Tapestry Crochet, 9 sts and 8 rows = 4" (10.2cm).
Take time to check your gauge.

NOTES
Work the afghan with each row as a right side row. Do not turn at the end of rows.

When working over the unused strand, carry it loosely along top of previous row.

The afghan will stretch along the bias when worked in all RS rows; follow instructions for blocking (see Finishing, below).

STITCH PATTERN
This afghan hides the unused strand of color inside the other single crochet stitches in the row, making color changes quick and neat. The only yarn ends are at the ends of each row, and become fringe. To review the hidden color and tapestry crochet techniques, turn to pages 72 and 73.

INSTRUCTIONS
Foundation: Leaving a 10" tail at beginning, with MC, ch 91. Sc in 2nd ch from hook and in each ch across — 90 sts. Leaving a 10" tail, fasten off. **Do not turn.**

Row 1 (RS): Leaving a 10" tail of MC and A, with the RS facing, join MC with sl st in first sc at right edge, ch 1. Working over color A strand, with MC, sc in same sc as joining and in each of next 9 sc, changing to color A. * With A, sc in next 10 sc and work over the MC strand; with MC, sc in next 10 sc and work over the color A strand. Rep from * across; at end, leaving a 10" strand of each color, fasten off.

Rows 2–10: Rep Row 1.

Row 11 (RS): Leaving a 10" tail of B and MC, with RS facing, join B with sl st in first sc at right edge, ch 1. Working over color MC strand, with B, sc in same sc as joining and in each of next 9 sc, changing to MC. * With MC, sc in next 10 sc and work over the color B strand; with color B, sc in next 10 sc and work over the MC strand. Rep from * across; at end, leaving a 10" strand of each color, fasten off.

Rows 12–20: Rep Row 11.

Row 21: Leaving a 10" tail of A and MC, with the RS facing, join A with sl st in first sc at right edge, ch 1. Working over MC strand, with A, sc in same sc as joining and in each of next 9 sc, changing to MC. * With MC, sc in next 10 sc and work over the color A strand; with A, sc in next 10 sc and work over the MC strand. Rep from * across; at end, leaving a 10" strand of each color, fasten off.

Rows 22–30: Rep Row 21.
Rows 31–40: Rep Rows 1–10.
Rows 41–50: Rep Rows 11–20.
Rows 51–60: Rep Rows 1–10.
Rows 61–70: Rep Rows 11–20.
Rows 71–80: Rep Rows 1–10.
Rows 81–90: Rep Rows 21–30.
Rows 91–100: Rep Rows 11–20.
Rows 101–110: Rep Rows 1–10.

FINISHING
JOINING: With the RS facing, join MC with sl st in first sc at right edge of Row 110. Ch 1, sc in same sc as joining and in each sc across. Fasten off.

BLOCKING: Place afghan onto a flat, padded surface, pinning to measurements. Cover with damp towels and leave until dry.

FRINGE: Beginning at corner, take 2 tails through st, leaving a small lp; take tails through the lp and pull up to form a knot. Rep for each set of 2 tails across each end. 🪻

Marsha Hinkson has been a member of the Kooler Design Studio for the past eleven years as an expert on counted-thread work and embroidery. Her needlework interests and talents include designing easy-to-crochet afghans.

baby bobbles

Decorative bobble patterns lend a chenille-like effect to this blanket made of kitten-soft baby yarn. This beginner's multiple-color project is not difficult, and a true pleasure to crochet.

DESIGN BY MELISSA LEAPMAN
Skill level: Beginner
Finished project size: 36" x 43" excluding fringe

MATERIALS

Coats & Clark RED HEART Baby Fingering, ART. E. 255, 84% acrylic/16% olefin yarn (50 gram/270 yards per skein): 3 skeins each of White (1) for A, Baby Yellow (224) for B, Peach (247) for C, and Pastel Green (680) for D
Size D/3 (3.25mm) aluminum crochet hook or size needed to obtain gauge

GAUGE

In Body Pattern, 17 sts and 12 rows = 3" (7.6cm).
Take time to check your gauge.

STITCH PATTERN

This blanket is worked from side to side, alternating each row of white double crochet with a row of colored bobbles. White (A), yellow (B), peach (C), and

○ chain (ch)

◯ slip stitch (sl st)

+ single crochet (sc)

╪ double crochet (dc)

⬦ bobble: four double crochet cluster

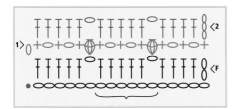

green (D), used in the sequence: A, B, A, B, A, B, A, C, A, C, A, C, A, D, A, D, A, D, A. Each pair is repeated 3 times to create broad stripes of color, with one last row of white for balance. Counting rows is easy, since each color stripe is three bobbles tall.

NOTES

1 BOBBLE: = 4 DC CLUSTER: (yo, insert hook, draw up loop, yo, draw through 2 loops) 4 times; yo, draw through 5 loops on hook.

For ease in finishing, begin and end each row with a 6" tail of yarn; work these tails into the fringe later.

This design is worked sideways.

INSTRUCTIONS

Beginning at the side with A, ch 247.
Foundation Row (RS): Dc in 4th ch from hook, dc in each of next 3 ch. * Ch 1, sk 1 ch, dc in each of next 5 ch. Rep from * across – 245 sts; turn. Fasten off.
Row 1: With the WS facing, join B with sl st in first dc, ch 1, sc in same dc. (Ch 1, sk next dc, sc in next dc) twice. * Bobble in next ch-1 sp, sc in next dc, (ch 1, sk 1 dc, sc in next dc) twice. Rep from * across, ending row with bobble into next ch-1 sp, (sc in next dc, ch 1, sk next dc) twice, sc in 3rd ch of turning ch; turn. Fasten off.

Row 2: With the RS facing, join A with sl st in first sc, ch 3 (counts as dc); (dc in next ch-1 sp, dc in next sc) twice. * Ch 1, sk next bobble, (dc in next sc, dc in next ch-1 sp) twice, dc in next sc. Rep from * across; turn. Fasten off.

Following Color Sequence, rep Rows 1–2 until afghan measures approx 36" from beg, ending after Row 2 has been worked with color B for three consecutive times.

Last row: Rep Row 1 with color A and fasten off.

FINISHING

FRINGE: For each fringe combine color A with the cl color for the row. Cut 7 strands measuring approx. 9" and fold in half to form a lp. With the WS facing, take lp through side edge of one dc; take ends (include rem tails) through lp and pull up to form a knot. * Place next fringe on the side of the cl row, matching colors; rep from * across, ending with one fringe on side edge of the dc row. Trim fringe if desired. Rep for opposite side. 🌀

Melissa Leapman is the author of *Crochet with Style*, *A Close-Knit Family*, and *Seasons of Love: Crocheted Sweaters for the Family* . See her other designs on pages 51, 58, and 61.

delicate filet edging

*You can find exquisite vintage lace like this at estate sales, bed and break-
fast inns, or your grandmother's linen closet—or you can crochet it
yourself! Used here on pillowcases, this traditional leaf-and-acorn
pattern provides a worthy introduction to thread crochet.*

DESIGN BY NANCY NEHRING
Skill level: Intermediate
Finished project size: 40" x 5" to fit a standard, queen, or king pillowcase,
all measuring 20" wide

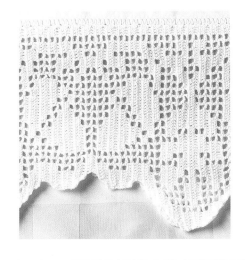

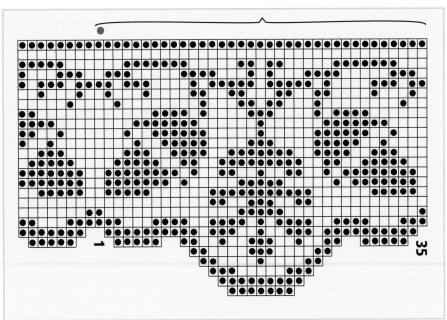

MATERIALS

DMC Cebelia, size 30 (567 yards per ball):
  2 balls, White, for 2 pillowcases
Size 11 (1.10mm) steel crochet hook or
  size needed to obtain gauge

GAUGE

Each 35 mesh repeat measures 5"
  (12.7cm); measuring across the widest
  portion of edging, 26 meshes = 5"
  (12.7cm).
Take time to check your gauge.

STITCH PATTERN

Filet crochet designs are formed by
blocks of solid mesh (filled-in squares,
referred to here as blocks) or open mesh
spaces. This allows two-color designs to
be shown as simple charts. We calculat-
ed the number of chains needed to
begin, and we tell you how we did it—
after that, just follow the chart, using
written instructions to help you become
comfortable with filet crochet techniques. Read from right to left for RS
rows, and from left to right for WS rows.

NOTES

Begin the edging following the written
text, then complete it by following the
chart.

INSTRUCTIONS

Ch 61. (3 chains for each of 19 meshes
plus 1 chain for first double crochet plus
3 chains to turn).

Row 1 (RS): Dc in 4th, 5th, and 6th
chains from hook for initial block. Ch 2,
sk 2 ch, dc in next ch for first sp. (Ch 2,
sk 2 ch, dc in next ch) twice — 2 sp
made. Dc in next 3 ch for block. (Ch 2,
sk 2 ch, dc in next ch) 12 times — 12 sp
made. Dc in each of next 3 ch for block.
Dc in last 4 ch for Ending block; turn.

Row 2: Ch 5, dc in 4th and 5th ch
from hook, dc in next dc — Block
Increase made (block Inc). Dc in each of
next 4 dc — Block over Block made. Ch
2, sk 2 dc, dc in next dc — Sp over
Block made. Ch 2, sk ch-2 sp, dc in next
dc — Sp over Sp made. Dc in next 2 ch
and next dc — Block over Sp made.
Block over Sp twice. (Sp over Sp) 7
times, Block over Sp, Block over Block,
Block over Sp, (Sp over Sp) twice, Block
over Block; turn.

Row 3: Ch 3 (counts as dc), dc in
each of next 3 dc — Beginning Block
made (Beg Block). (Sp over Sp) twice,
Block over Block, (Sp over Block) twice,
Block over Sp. (Sp over Sp) 5 times,
Block over Sp, (Block over Block) 3
times, (Sp over Sp) twice, (Block over
Block) twice. Working into base of last

dc, make 3 dc — Block Inc at End of
Row made; turn.

Rows 4–7: Follow the chart, turning
at the end of each row.

Row 8: Sl st in each of first 3 dc, in
next dc [sl st, ch 3 (counts as dc)] — Beg
Block Dec made. Continue across by
following chart; turn.

Rows 9–22: Follow the chart.

Row 23: Work chart, ending sk last
3 dc — Ending Block Dec made; turn.

Rows 24–36: Work pattern by following the chart, turning at the end of
each row.

Rep Rows 2–36 for 7 total times;
then rep Rows 2–35 once again. Fasten
off. 🌀

Nancy Nehring lectures and teaches needle
arts locally, regionally, and nationally, including the *Crochet Guild of America Chain Link,
Crochet Renaissance, Stitches,* and the
Embroiderers' Guild of America Seminar. See
her other designs on pages 53 and 105.

virginia roses

As if from a Victorian reverie, this remarkable lace motif shows how lovely thread crochet can be. The hexagonal motif stands by itself on a vintage-inspired pincushion or forms a graceful grouping on a dainty dresser mat or doily.

DESIGN BY SHELLEY CARDA
Skill level: Intermediate
Finished project size for dresser mat: 9½" diameter at widest part

DRESSER MAT MATERIALS
J. & P. Coats Opera, size 10 crochet thread (50 grams/230 meters per ball): one ball Color 500 (white)
Size 3 (2.10mm) steel crochet hook
Tapestry needle

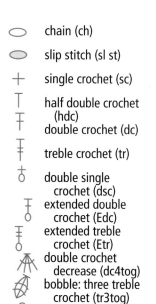

chain (ch)

slip stitch (sl st)

single crochet (sc)

half double crochet (hdc)

double crochet (dc)

treble crochet (tr)

double single crochet (dsc)

extended double crochet (Edc)

extended treble crochet (Etr)

double crochet decrease (dc4tog)

bobble: three treble crochet (tr3tog)

picot

GAUGE
Motif rnds 1 & 2 = 1¾" diameter
Take time to check your gauge.

STITCH PATTERNS
This medallion uses varied techniques to copy the soft shapes of nature. Cluster

stitches (multiple decreases) form the first round of petals, while traditional and extended stitches (see page 45) fan out the petals of the second round. In the airy outer rounds, bobbles flatten out into leaves, and the last stitch of Round 3 is a join which ends in the middle.

DRESSER MAT INSTRUCTIONS
CLUSTER: (Yo, insert hook and draw up loop, yo and draw through 2 loops) 4 times; yo and draw through 4 loops.
PETAL: Over chain-4 (sc, dsc, hdc, dc, Edc, tr, Edc, dc, dsc, hdc, sc).
LEAF CLUSTER: In 1ch * tr3tog; yo, draw through all 4 loops; ch 4; tr3tog; yo, draw through all 4 loops.*

VIRGINIA ROSE MOTIF
Ch 8; join with a sl st to form a ring.

Rnd 1: Ch 2 (counts as first dc), (Cluster, ch 4) 6 times, join with sl st in tip of first cluster.

Rnd 2: Over each ch-4 work Petal. To join, sl st in rnd 1 tch.

Rnd 3: Sl st in (sc, dsc, hdc, dc, Edc, and tr) of first Petal*. *Ch 9, sl st in tr of next Petal*. Repeat from * to * around, ending with ch 4, Etr in last sl st on first Petal (above the tr).

Rnd 4: Ch 3 (count as first tr). In top of Etr work Leaf Cluster. *Ch 6, sl st over tr, ch 6, (Leaf Cluster in 5th ch of ch-9)*. Repeat from * to * 5 times. End with ch 6, sl st over tr, ch 6; sl st in tip of first Leaf.

Rnd 5: Ch 1. *Over ch-4 (3 sc, ch 3, sl st in sc, 3 sc), sl st in tip of leaf; ch 8, sl st in tip of next Leaf.* Repeat 6 times. Fasten off.

MOTIFS 2–7
Repeat Virginia Rose Motif.

FINISHING
With the RSs facing up, place 6 motifs onto a flat surface to form a ring, then add last motif to center. With 2 picots of each motif on the outside of the ring free, join next touching picots together by sewing. Continue in this manner until you have joined all 6 motifs in one location each. Sew center-touching motifs of ring together. Match the remaining motif so that the picots touch the inside connections and sew in place. Dip in tea to dye if desired.

PINCUSHION MATERIALS
Materials listed for Dresser Mat, plus:
⅛ yard solid cotton fabric, coral
⅛ yard print cotton fabric, coral and green
3"-diameter circle of medium-weight card-
    board
⅝ yard of 7 mm-wide silk ribbon, green
Sewing thread, coral
Wool or cotton batting
6 premade ribbon roses, coral

PINCUSHION INSTRUCTIONS
Make a Virginia Rose Motif as instructed for the Dresser Mat. Dip in tea to dye if desired.

FINISHING
Cut two 3½"-diameter circles (top and bottom) from the coral fabric. Cut one 3½" x 33" piece of print fabric (side).

Sew gathering stitches around each fabric circle, ¼" from edges. For the top, center the cardboard circle over the wrong side of one fabric circle, draw up gathering thread snugly, and tie off. Press flat; remove cardboard for top. For the bottom, repeat with the remaining fabric circle but do not remove the cardboard.

Using a ¼" seam allowance and with right sides of fabric facing, sew short edges of side piece together; press seam open. Sew gathering stitches along both long edges of side piece, and along the center (exactly between previous stitching). Measure the circumference of the cardboard unit and pull up all three gathering lines on side piece to the same measurement. Tie off the center gathering stitches on the wrong side of fabric.

With right sides facing, sew one gathered edge of side piece to the top piece along pressed edge. Sewing by hand, repeat with bottom piece, leaving a 2" opening. Fill pincushion firmly with batting, and sew opening shut.

Find center of ribbon and tack to pincushion along center gathering line. Tie ribbon around center of pincushion and tie into a bow (see photo); trim ends.

Tack the six corners of the crochet motif over the pincushion top along seamline. Tack ribbon roses over each lace corner. ❀

Shelley Carda's interest in textiles extends to the care and raising of sheep, whose wool she spins. See her other design on page 57.

irish roses

For over 150 years, the motif known as the Irish Rose has remained one of the most popular crochet patterns, and works beautifully in any size thread or yarn. The buttons pictured here are mounted on half-round button molds to highlight the three-dimensional effect of this classic design.

DESIGN BY NANCY NEHRING
Skill level: Intermediate
Finished project size: see Materials (page 106)

MATERIALS

For small rose: (1³⁄₈" diameter)
Anchor pearl cotton* #12, colors 47 & 923
Size 11 crochet hook
Size #36 (⁷⁄₈") half-round metal button
    mold
1½"-square yellow medium-weight fabric
small pin back (optional)

For medium rose: (1½" diameter)
DMC pearl cotton* #8, colors 51 & 702
Size 9 crochet hook
Size #45 (1¹⁄₈") half-round metal button
    mold
2"-square yellow medium-weight fabric
small pin back (optional)

For large rose: (2½" diameter)
DMC pearl cotton* #5, colors 349 & 3346
Size 7 crochet hook
Size #60 1½" half-round metal button
    mold
3"-square yellow medium-weight fabric
small pin back (optional)
*One skein or ball of pearl cotton will
    make multiple roses.

GAUGE

Traditionally, Irish Crochet does not require attention to gauge, and each person's motifs will differ in size. The mesh background hooks into the motifs as necessary and joins all the motifs together. If your rose is too large or too small, change your hook size.

STITCH PATTERN

The base of this classic motif starts as a wheel, with "spokes" of double crochet separating chain stitches. In the next round, fans of petal stitches are worked over the chains. Chain and petal rounds alternate, getting larger. In each chain round, chain segments increase by one chain. In petal rounds, each petal increases by two stitches in each segment. The final rounds are green leaf rounds, and secure the rose around the button.

NOTES

Work over chain loops, not into chain stitches of loops.

Refer to written instructions for placement of slip stitches.

Charted pattern shows only Rows 1–10. Refer to written instructions for Rnds 12–14.

⬯	chain (ch)
⬬	slip stitch (sl st)
+	single crochet (sc)
T	half double crochet (hdc)
⊤	double crochet (dc)
⊤	treble crochet (tr)
⊤	double treble crochet (dtr)

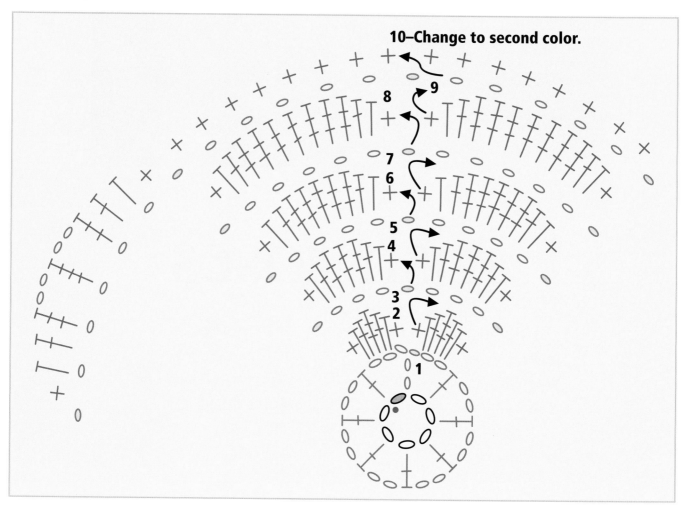

10–Change to second color.

INSTRUCTIONS

Rnd 1: With flower color, ch 6; join with sl st to form ring.

Rnd 2: Ch 5 (counts as dc + ch-2), in ring (dc, ch 2) 7 times; join with sl st in 3rd ch of beg ch-5 – 8 ch-2 sps.

Rnd 3: In each ch-2 sp (sc, hdc, dc, tr, dc, hdc, sc); turn.

Locate the two strands of thread that form an inverted V where two petals join. One is on each side of and directly above the dc from Rnd 2. The V located where the loop on your hook is will not be fully formed yet, so use the first and last threads on the respective sides of the dc.

Rnd 4: Sl st under first and last threads (incomplete V) just below last st from Rnd 3. (Ch 3, sl under next V) 7 times, ch 3, sl under first incomplete V a second time; turn.

Rnd 5: In each ch-3 lp (sc, hdc, dc, 3 tr, dc, hdc, sc) around; turn.

Rnd 6: Same as Rnd 4 except use ch 4.

Rnd 7: In each ch-4 lp (sc, hdc, dc, 5 tr, dc, hdc, sc) around; turn.

Rnd 8: Same as Rnd 4 except use ch 5.

Rnd 9: In each ch-5 lp (sc, hdc, dc, 7 tr, dc, hdc, sc) around. Join with sl st in first sc and fasten off.

Rnd 10: Change to second color. With the WS facing and leaf color, rep Rnd 4 except use ch-5.

Rnd 11: With leaf color, 8 sc in first ch-5 lp; * in next lp (sc, hdc, dc, tr, ch 2, dtr, ch 2, tr, dc, hdc, sc) **, 8 sc in each of next 2 lps, rep from * to ** in each of next 2 lps, 8 sc in last 2 lps. Do not turn or join.

Rnd 12: (Sc in sc, sk 1 sc) 4 times; * ch 5, sk (4 sts, ch-2 sp, dtr, ch-2 sp, and next 4 sts), (sc in next sc, sk 1 sc) 8 times **, ch 5, sc between leaves, rep from * to **.

Add button: Cover button mold with fabric according to instructions on package. Hold covered button in place at back of flower while working remaining rnds. Crochet will collapse around button, capturing it and holding it in place.

Rnd 13: Sc in every other sc and ch around.

Rnd 14: Sc in every other sc around. At end, join with sl st in first sc and fasten off.

If desired, attach a pin back to the leaf crochet to make a brooch.❀

Nancy Nehring designs for DMC, Donna Karan, and *Better Homes and Gardens* magazine. She is the author of three books: *50 Heirloom Buttons to Make, The Lacy Knitting of Mary Schiffmann*, and *Ribbon Trims*. See her other designs on pages 53 and 100.

Button covers, front

Button cover, back

wedding keepsake

This elegant purse accompanies a bride on her wedding day. It's just big enough to hold the essentials for that special occasion, including, of course, a hanky! Crystal beads along the edges and on the drawstring add a touch of glamour.

DESIGN BY JACQUELINE YOUNG
Skill level: Advanced
Finished project size: 7" x 6"

MATERIALS
DMC Cebelia, size 10 crochet thread, (50 grams per ball): 1 ball of White
Size 7 (1.65mm) steel crochet hook or size needed to obtain gauge
Size 11 seed beads, clear with silver lining: 1 hank
Large-eyed beading needle
Sewing needle
Nymo beading thread
Satin cord, white: 1 yard

GAUGE
Rows 1–3 = 1" x 3"
Take time to check your gauge.

STITCH PATTERN
The novel features of this purse start with the gauge swatch: the base chain is in the center. Work rows of chains and shells along the length of base chain, around its end, and up the other long side. The first 3 rows of the purse pattern serve as a gauge swatch, and once the gauge is correct you can continue working the swatch into the finished purse.

NOTES
Before beginning each side of purse, string 250 beads onto crochet thread using the large-eyed beading needle. (If you cannot find this type of needle at your local bead store, stiffen the end of the crochet cotton with clear nail polish and let dry to use as a self-needle.) As you crochet, push the beads down the crochet thread until needed.

INSTRUCTIONS
PURSE FRONT/BACK (MAKE 2)
Row 1: Ch 28. Sc in 2nd ch from hook, (ch 5, sk 3 chs, sc in next ch) 6 times, ch 5, sk 1 ch, in last ch (sc, ch 5, sc). Working along opposite side of chain, ch 5, sk 1 ch, sc in next ch, (ch 5, sk 3 chs, sc in next ch) 6 times, ch 5, sc in ch at base of first sc; turn.

Row 2: * Ch 5, sc in next ch-5 sp, 8 dc in next ch-5 sp, 1 sc in next ch-5 sp **; rep from * to ** again, ch 5, sc in next ch-5 sp, 9 dc in next ch-5 sp, sc in next ch-5 sp. Rep from * to ** twice, ch 2, dc in last sc of row below; turn.

Row 3: Ch 1, sc in first dc, sk ch-2 sp and 1 sc; * [(b-ch, dc) in each of next 8 dc, sc in next ch- 5 sp] twice **, (b-ch, dc, b-ch, dc) in each of next 9 dc, sc in next ch-5 sp. Rep from * to ** along 2nd side; turn.

Row 4: Ch 8; * (sk 3 b-ch, sc in next dc, ch 5, sk 2 b-ch, sc in next dc, ch 5, sk 3 b-ch, hdc in next sc **, ch 5) twice ***. (Sk 2 b-ch, sc in next dc, ch 5) 8 times, sk next 2 b-ch, hdc in next sc, ch 5; rep from * to ***, ending last rep at **; turn.

Row 5: Ch 5; * (sc in next ch-5 sp, 8 dc in next ch-5 sp, sc in next ch-5 sp **, ch 5) 3 times ***, sc in next ch-5 sp, 9 dc in next ch-5 sp, sc in next ch-5 sp, ch 5. Rep from * to ***, ending last rep at **, ch 2, dc in 3rd ch of previous ch-8; turn.

Row 6: Ch 1, sc in first dc, sk ch-2 sp and 1 sc; (dc-picot in each of next 8 dc, sc in next ch-5 sp) 3 times, 2 dc-picots in each of next 9 dc, sc in next ch-5 sp; rep from (to) 3 times; turn.

Row 7: Ch 8; * (sk 3 dc-picot, sc in next dc, ch 5, sk 2 dc-picot, sc in next dc, ch 5, sk next 3 dc-picot, hdc in next sc **, ch 5) 3 times ***. (Sk 2 dc-picot, sc in next ch-5 sp, ch 5) 8 times, hdc in next sc, ch 5, rep from * to ***, ending last rep at **; turn.

Row 8: * (Ch 5, sc in next ch-5 sp, 8 dc in next ch-5 sp, sc in next ch-5 sp) 4 times **. Ch 5, sc in next ch-5 sp, 9 dc in next ch-5 sp, sc in next ch-5 sp, rep from * ending at **, ch 2, dc in 3rd ch of ch-8; turn.

Row 9: Ch 1, sc in first dc, sk ch-2 sp and 1 sc; * (b-ch, dc) in each of next 8 dc, sc in next ch-5 sp; rep from * 3 times more. (B-ch, dc) twice in each of next 9 dc, sc in next ch-5 sp; rep from * 4 times; turn.

Row 10: Ch 8; * (sk 3 b-ch, sc in next dc, ch 5, sk 2 b-ch, sc in next dc, ch 5, sk next 3 b-ch, hdc in next sc **, ch 5) 4 times ***. (Sk next 2 b-ch, sc in next dc, ch 5) 8 times, hdc in next sc, ch 5; rep from * to ***, ending last rep at **; turn.

Row 11: Ch 5; * (sc in next ch-5 sp, 8 dc in next ch-5 sp, sc in next ch-5 sp **, ch 5) 5 times ***. Sc in next ch-5 sp, 9 dc in ch-5 sp, sc in next ch-5 sp, ch 5; rep from * to *** across, ending last rep at **, ch 2, dc in 3rd ch of ch-8, turn.

Row 12: Ch 1, sc in first dc, sk ch-2 sp and 1 sc; (dc-picot in each of next 8 dc, sc in next ch- 5 sp) 5 times, dc-picot in each of next 9 dc, sc in next ch-5 sp; rep from (to) 5 times; turn.

Row 13: Ch 8; * (sk 3 dc-picot, sc in next dc, ch 5, sk 2 dc-picot, sc in next dc, ch 5, sk next 3 dc-picot, hdc in next sc **, ch 5) 5 times ***. (Sk 3 dc-picot, sc in next ch-5 sp, ch 5) twice, hdc in next sc, ch 5; rep from * to *** across, ending last rep at **; turn.

Row 14: * (Ch 5, sc in next ch-5 sp, 8 dc in next ch-5 sp, sc in next ch-5 sp) 5 times **, ch 5, sc in next ch-5 sp, 9 dc in next ch-5 sp, sc in next ch-5 sp. Rep from * across, ending last rep at **, ch 2, dc in 3rd ch of ch-8; turn.

Row 15: Ch 1, sc in first dc, sk ch-2 sp and 1 sc; * (b-ch, dc) in each of next 8 dc, sc in next ch-5 sp **; rep from * 4 times more. (B-ch, dc) twice in each of next 9 dc, sc in next ch-5 sp; rep from * to ** 5 times; turn.

Row 16: Ch 8; * (sk 3 b-ch, sc in next dc, ch 5, sk 2 b-ch, sc in next dc, ch 5, sk next 3 b-ch, hdc in next sc **, ch 5) 5 times ***. (Sk next 2 b-ch, sc in next dc, ch 5) 8 times, hdc in next sc, ch 5; rep from * to *** across, ending last rep at **; turn.

Row 17: Ch 5; * (sc in next ch-5 sp, 8 dc in next ch-5 sp, sc in next ch-5 sp **, ch 5) 13 times, ending last rep at **, ch 2, dc in 3rd ch of ch-8, turn.

Row 18: Ch 1, sc in first dc, sk ch-2 sp and 1 sc; * (ch 1, dc in next dc) in each of next 8 dc, ch 1, sc in next ch-5 sp; rep from * 12 times more. Fasten off.

FINISHING

Block each piece face down on clean cloth with steam iron, stretching gently into shape.

TO JOIN SIDES OF PURSE: string approximately 360 beads onto thread. Pin front and back together with wrong sides facing, sl st through both pieces into first edge stitch on curved side at top edge of purse. * 3 b-ch, sl st into next ch-1 space; rep from * along curved edge of purse. Do not fasten off.

Rnd 1: Continuing along top edge of purse, work 132 sc evenly along top edge of purse.

Rnd 2 (Eyelet Round): Ch 5, sk next 2 sc, dc in next st; * ch 2, sk next 2 sts, dc in next st; rep from * ending ch 2, sl st into 3rd ch of beg ch-5.

Rnd 3: Ch 1, sc in first st; * 2 sc in next ch-2 sp, sc in next dc; rep from * ending 2 sc in next ch-2 sp, sl st into beg sc.

Rnd 4: Ch 1, sc in first st; * ch 5, sk next 3 sts, sc in next st, rep from * ending ch 5, sl st into beg sc.

Rnd 5: Sl st into beg ch-5 sp, ch 3, 7 dc in same ch-5 sp; * sc in next ch-5 sp, ch 5, sc in next ch-5 sp, 8 dc in next ch-5 sp; rep from * ending, ch 5, sc in next ch-5 sp, sl st into 3rd ch of beg ch-3, fasten off.

TASSEL TOPS (MAKE 2)

Rnd 1: Make a loose slip knot, ch 2; 6 sc in 2nd ch from hook.

Rnd 2: 2 sc in each sc around — 12 sc.

Rnds 3–5: Sc in each sc around. At the end of Rnd 5, fasten off.

TO ASSEMBLE DRAWSTRING AND BEADED TASSELS: cut 2 lengths of satin cord 18" long. Wrap both ends of cord with tape to aid in pulling through eyelet round. Beginning at opposite sides, thread each cord through eyelet round. Thread each end of same cord through the loose slip knot on tassel top. With nymo thread and small beading needle, secure both ends of cord; string 50 beads onto thread and secure again to satin cording. Make 3 additional bead loops in same manner. Pull crocheted tassel top over ends of satin cording and secure tassel top in place. ✺

⌒	chain (ch)
+	single crochet (sc)
T	double crochet (dc)
⊽	double crochet increase (dc2tog)
⊙	bead
✤	picot

Jacqueline Young adds teaching to her design credentials, and shares her knowledge of crochet and knitting at national conferences, regional seminars, and yarn shops. She designed this bride's purse for her new daughter-in-law. See her other designs on pages 54 and 114.

III

beaded heart pins

Sweet tokens of love, these two decorative pins provide a feast of lush colors and lavish details. Treat yourself to the tactile pleasure of silk threads, and have fun adding beads, popcorns and dangles for a dazzling effect.

DESIGN BY GWEN BLAKLEY KINSLER
Skill level: Intermediate
Finished project size for larger pin: 1½" x 2"

MATERIALS
FOR LARGER HEART:
Kreinik Silk Serica: one spool each of Dark
    Red (1116) and Lilac (6108)
Size 11 seed beads, dark red and lilac

FOR SMALLER HEART:
DMC Pearl Cotton size 8: one skein each of
    Dark Red (814) and Hot Pink (3805)
Size 11 seed beads, dark red and pink

FOR BOTH:
Size 9 steel crochet hook
Size 11 delica seed beads, red
Beading needle
Small piece synthetic suede, red or black
Small piece quilt batting
Sewing needle and thread
Pin back

GAUGE
8 sc = 1"

STITCH PATTERN
These hearts are crochet "for the fun of it." There is no real stitch gauge, and each pin will be highly individual, even if you follow the directions exactly, because no two hearts "bead" as one.

NOTES
Instructions are for the larger heart. Instructions for the smaller heart are the same except the petal and bobbles are reversed. Also, the smaller heart has 4 bobbles, with one worked in hot pink.

Work this project in rounds.

The beaded side of the stitch is considered the front of the work, even though the beads fall to the back while working the stitches. When working in the round, the front of the work faces away from the crocheter.

INSTRUCTIONS
BEFORE BEGINNING: Wrap three threads with strung beads around a piece of cardboard as follows:

No.1: String 12" of dark red seed beads on red thread (approx. 200)

No. 2: String 12" of lilac (pink) seed beads onto lilac (pink) thread

No. 3: String 5" of red delica seed beads onto red thread

HEART:

Note: Work the stitches that form the point of the heart (sc, hdc, sc) in the center hdc of the previous row. Adjust number of stitches, if necessary, before and after this center point to ensure symmetry.

With No. 1, ch 2 loosely.

Rnd 1: Work 7 bb-sc in 2nd ch from hook; join with sl st in first sc. **Do not turn** — (7 bb-sc).

Rnd 2: (Ch 1, 2 b-ch, 3 bb-dc) in first st, bb-dc in next st, 2 bb-dc in next st, (bb-dc, bb-tr, bb-dc) in next st (tip of heart), 2 bb-dc in next st, bb-dc in next st, (3 bb-dc, bb-hdc) in next st; sl st below next stitch into Rnd 1. Do not turn.

Rnd 3: Make 3 bb-sc in space created between beg ch-3 and next st of Rnd 2, bb-sc in next 7 sts, (bb-sc, bb-hdc, bb-sc) in next st (tip of heart), bb-sc in next

7 sts, 3 bb-sc in next st; sl st below next st into Rnd 2, joining No. 2 at same time. Do not turn.

Rnd 4: Working in FLO with No. 2, sl st in sl st and next sc, (bb-sc, bb-hdc) in next st, (bb-hdc, 2 bb-dc) in next st, 3 bb-dc in next st, (bb-dc, bb-hdc) in next st, bb-sc in next 5 sts. (Bb-sc, bb-hdc, bb-sc) in next st (tip of heart), bb-sc in next 5 sts, (bb-hdc, bb-dc) in next st, 3 bb-dc in next st, (2 bb-dc, bb-hdc) in next st, (bb-hdc, bb-sc) in next st, sl st in next 2 sts; sl st below next 2 stitches and into Rnd 3. Fasten off.

PETAL: With front of heart facing and working in free loops of Rnd 4, attach No. 2 in first free loop at top of heart with sl st. Ch 1, sc in same lp as joining, (sc, hdc) in next st, hdc in next 2 sts, 2 dc in next st, (dc, trc) in next st, tr in next st, dc in next st, hdc in next st, sc in next st, sl st in next stitch and fasten off. Leave remaining free loops unworked.

Rnd 5: Join No.3 at center top of heart on backside. Working this rnd in FLO, bb-sc in next st; bb-hdc in next st, (bb-hdc, bb-dc) in next st, bb-dc in next st, 3 bb-dc in next st, bb-hdc in next 3 sts, (bb-hdc, bb-sc) in next st, bb-sc in next 8 sts, (bb-sc, bb-hdc, bb-sc) in next st (tip of heart). Bb-sc in next 8 sts, (bb-sc, bb-hdc) in next st, bb-hdc in next 3 sts, 3 bb-dc in next st, bb-dc in next st, (bb-dc, bb-hdc) in next st, bb-hdc in next st, bb-sc in next st; sl st below next st into Rnd 4, attaching No.1 at same time.

Rnd 6: With No. 1 in FLO throughout, bb-sl st in first st, bb-sc in next st, 2 bb-sc in next st, 2 bb-hdc in next st, bb-dc in next 2 sts, 2 bb-dc in next st, bb-hdc in next 2 sts, bb-sc in each st to point, (sc, hdc, sc) in next st (point of heart). Bb-sc in next 14 sts, bb-hdc in next 2 sts, 2 bb-dc in next st, bb-dc in next 2 sts, 2 bb-hdc in next st, 2 bb-sc in next st, bb-sc in next st, bb-sl st in last st; sl st in center st of Rnd 5. Fasten off. Carefully weave in all ends.

POPCORN EMBELLISHMENT: **Note:** Work with the back of heart facing so that the beads will fall on outside of popcorn.

Look at the front of the heart to

determine the 3 o'clock and 1 o'clock positions on Rnd 5 and the 3 o'clock position on Rnd 4. With a separate thread, mark each position. Now, with the back of the heart facing, attach No. 1, hooking into unused loop of Rnd 5. Work one 7-bb-dc popcorn in each marked position. Fasten the popcorns down to the front of the heart so they are flat. Secure ends on WS of fabric. Popcorns can also be placed anywhere that is pleasing to you.

Note: For the smaller heart, work three 7-bb-dc popcorns with No. 1 as follows: On Rnd 5 mark the 3 and 5 o'clock positions; on Rnd 4 mark the 3 o'clock position. With No. 2 make a popcorn on Rnd 5 in the 4 o'clock position.

DANGLES: Join No. 1 at tip of heart with sl st, ch 8; 5 bb-dc popcorn in 3rd ch from hook; sl st in each chain back to joining. Ch 11; 5 bb-dc popcorn in 3rd ch from hook; sl st in chain back to joining. Ch 14; 5 bb-dc popcorn in 3rd ch from hook; sl st in chain back to joining. Fasten off.

For variety, make one dangle with No. 2.

FINISHING
Make a paper pattern by laying the finished heart on tissue paper and tracing it. Using pattern, cut shape from synthetic suede and batting, trimming batting a bit smaller. Layer batting and suede against back of heart, pin in place and stitch fabric using whipstitch. Attach pin back to center back with needle and thread. ❁

Gwen Blakley Kinsler is a crochet and beadwork designer whose work has been featured in *Bead & Button, Arts & Crafts, Piecework, Crochet Fantasy*, and *Workbasket* magazines. Books to her credit include *Magical Misers' Purses: Crochet Patterns with Victorian Inspiration* (on beaded purses) and *Kids Can Do It–Crocheting* (to be released in 2003). Gwen was the founding president of The Crochet Guild of America.

amulet necklace

Curious about wire crochet? This tiny amulet necklace allows even a novice to explore this fascinating specialty. The crochet is elementary, as are the petite flowers, thanks to the magic of a few beads.

DESIGN BY JACQUELINE YOUNG
Skill level: Beginner
Finished project size: 2" x 2¹/₄" necklace

MATERIALS

Jewelry Craft Wire, 28-gauge, (24 yards per spool): 1 spool of green

Anchor Pearl Cotton, size 5: one skein each of Dark Green (218), Pale Yellow (301), Rose Pink (77), and Lilac (96)

Size B/2 (2.25mm) and E/4 (3.5mm) aluminum crochet hooks or size needed to obtain gauge

Size 11 seed beads: 15 cream and 500 green

Leaf-shaped beads (10mm): 3 green

Sewing thread, cream and green

Beading needle

Size 24 tapestry needle

GAUGE

With larger hook and wire, 12 sc and 11 rows = 2" (5cm).

Take time to check your gauge.

STITCH PATTERN

Wire brings an interesting texture to simple rows of single crochet stitches. The little flowers are worked in pearl cotton, but are just as simple, with chains and single crochet forming the petals.

INSTRUCTIONS

AMULET

Beginning at the lower edge with larger hook and wire, ch 13.

Foundation Row (RS): Sc in 2nd ch from hook and in each ch across; turn.

Row 1: Ch 1, sc in each sc across; turn.

Rep Row 1 to approximately 4½" from beg. Fasten off.

LARGER FLOWERS

Make one in yellow, one in pink: With smaller hook and pearl cotton, ch 8. In 2nd ch from hook (sc, ch 5, sc); (sc, ch 5, sc) in each ch across — 7 petals; join with sl st in first sc and fasten off. Weave in loose ends on WS of flower.

SMALLER FLOWER

Make one in lilac: With smaller hook and pearl cotton, ch 6. Work as for Large Flowers — 5 petals.

FINISHING

Fold long edge of amulet in half so that WSs are together. Use sewing thread to baste along the fold as a reference point.

Tack flowers and leaf beads to lower left-hand corner of front. With beading needle and matching sewing thread, sew 5 cream-colored beads to the center of each flower.

With RS of amulet facing and smaller hook, join green pearl cotton in lower right corner with a sl st. To join first side, work 11 sc evenly along edge.

FOR NECKLACE; make a 28" chain. Being careful to keep chain untwisted, join with sl st at opposite side of amulet. Working through each layer, ch 1, work 11 sc evenly to lower edge; fasten off. Remove basting.

TO JOIN BEADS: With the RS facing using beading needle and green sewing thread, begin at lower right corner. Sew through first sc and secure. *Slip 5 green beads onto needle, sk 1 sc, join in next sc; rep from * along side **. (Slip 5 green beads onto needle, sk 3 ch, join in next ch) around necklace. Rep from * to ** to join beads along opposite side edge. ❁

Jacqueline Young is the manager of a yarn shop in Fort Wayne, Indiana, where she designs and teaches both crocheted and knitted garments and other wearables. She currently serves as vice president of the Crochet Guild of America (2000–2003). See her other designs on pages 54 and 108.

elegant wire jewelry

Glimmering specialty wire joins beads to enliven this simple but stunning necklace glowing with rich colors. You can't ask for an easier introduction to wire crochet—or jewelry making, for that matter—than this delightful project.

DESIGN BY ARLINE FISCH
Skill level: Intermediate
Finished project size: 30" circumference

MATERIALS
Artistic Wire Ltd., 28-gauge coated copper wire, (40 yards per spool): one spool each of Rose (28s-02), Plum (28s-08), Tangerine (28s-11), Magenta (28-09), and Red (28-14) (The "s" in the color number signifies silver plating under the color)
Size 1 (2.75mm) and size 00 (3.50mm) steel crochet hooks
Size H/8 (5.00mm) aluminum crochet hook
260–300 small round glass beads

STITCH PATTERN
Fourteen individual wire chains of single crochet are bundled together inside a little beaded wire cylinder.

INSTRUCTIONS
CYLINDER
Using size 00 hook and red wire, ch 16; join with sl st to form ring.

Rnd 1: Sc in each ch around 15 sts.

Rnds 2–12: Sc in each sc around. At end of Rnd 12, join with sl st in first sc and fasten off.

Thread 60 glass beads onto the spool of plum wire. * Using size 1 hook, join this wire with sl st at one end of cylinder. 2 bb-sc in each sc around. At end, join with sl st in first sc and fasten off. Thread wire back through one bead. Rep from * for opposite end.

NECKLACE
MAKE 2 CHAINS: Thread 100 beads onto the spool of Plum wire. With size H hook, b-ch 100. Stretch gently to even out stitches and straighten the chain. Fasten off.

MAKE 12 MORE CHAINS: With size H hook, ch 100. Without beads, complete as for Plum Chains. Make 3 each of rose, tangerine, magenta, and red.

FINISHING
* Thread one chain through the cylinder. Join with a sl st to form a ring. Rep from * for rem 13 chains. With any color, make a 6" chain. Holding all the joinings of the chains tog in a bundle, wrap the 6" chain firmly around and around. Scoot the cylinder over the center of wrapped bundle. ✡

Arline Fisch has an extensive academic background in jewelry and metalsmithing. She lectures and conducts workshops on the use of textile structures in metal, and is the author of *Textile Techniques in Metal.* Her work has been exhibited widely in the United States, Europe, and Australia. She is a founding member and past president of the Society of North American Goldsmiths.

in a tunisian garden

A happy marriage of two favorite crafts—crochet and cross-stitch—thrives in this beginner's project. Tunisian crochet in ivory provides the precise geometric "evenweave" ground for the colorful cross-stitched hummingbird design.

DESIGN BY KATHLEEN POWER JOHNSON
Skill level: Beginner
Finished project size: 16" square

MATERIALS

Lion Brand Wool-Ease, Article #620, 80% acrylic/20% wool yarn (3 ounce/85 gram/197 yards per ball): 3 balls of Fisherman (099)

DMC Laine Colbert Tapestry Wool, Art.486, (9 yards/ 8 meters per skein): 1 skein each of colors 7954, 7596, 7205, 7260, 7020, 7032, 7021, 7726, 7040, 7382, 7384, 7347, 7066, and white

Size J-10 (6.00mm) afghan hook or size needed to obtain gauge

Size 18 tapestry needle

Yarn needle

16"-square pillow form

GAUGE

15 sts and 14 rows = 4" (10 cm) in Honeycomb Stitch

Take time to check your gauge.

STITCH PATTERN

The Honeycomb pattern of alternating Tunisian simple and purl stitches creates a rich and easily-worked frame for the embroidered panel in this pillow. Tunisian simple stitch, worked by itself, creates the even-grid fabric which is required for cross-stitch.

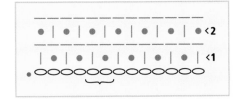

○   chain (ch)

| Tunisian simple stitch (Tss)

●   Tunisian purl stitch (Tps)

—   Tunisian return (R)

INSTRUCTIONS

NOTE: Each "row" refers to both a forward and return Tunisian row.

All return rows are worked as follows: yo, draw up a loop, *yo, draw through 2 loops*; repeat from * to * across row (page 89). Work last Tss under 2 threads in order to produce a chain along the left edge that matches the right edge.

BACK

Ch 62; work forward and return foundation row in Tss. Work 56 rows in honeycomb st as follows:

Symbol	Color
⊞	blue - light
↓	blue - med
■	blue - dark
5	gold
·	white
↑	green - pale
★	green - light
●	green - medium
✖	green - dark
2	teal
I	rose - pale
♥	rose medium
/	brown - dark
/	green - ultra dark
●	brown - dark

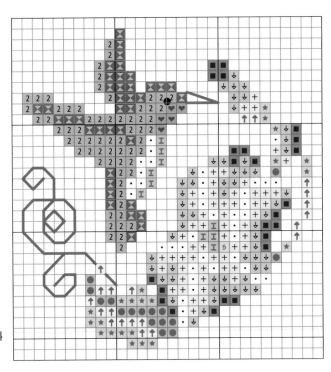

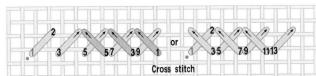

Cross stitch

HONEYCOMB STITCH

Row 1: * Tss, Tps; rep from * across, ending Tss.

Row 2: * Tps, Tss; rep from * across, ending Tss.

Buttonhole row (a forward row): Maintaining pattern st, work 12 sts, (bind off 2 sts, work 10 sts) 4 times, work 2 sts. On following return row, ch 2 over each buttonhole. Bind off all sts, working a slip st into each buttonhole ch.

FRONT

Ch 62; work forward and return foundation row in Tss. Work 12 rows in honeycomb st as follows:

HONEYCOMB STITCH

Row 1: * Tss, Tps; rep from * across, ending Tss.

Row 2: * Tps, Tss; rep from * across, ending Tss.

Next row: Work 15 sts in pattern st (maintaining pattern as established), 32 Tss, 15 sts in pattern st. Cont as established for a total of 34 rows. Work pattern st on 62 sts for 10 more rows. Work buttonhole row and bind off as for back.

EMBROIDERY

Following stitch chart and color key, center design as indicated on chart on 18th st of Tss area, beginning design 2 rows above edge of design area. Use smaller tapestry needle, cross-stitch the bird and flower motifs. Make a small 3-wrap French knot for the eye with brown-dark. With brown-dark, make 3 short straight sts for the underside of the bill and a long straight st for the top side. With green-ultra dark, straight st the green tendril above the lower leaf. When embroidery is complete, hide ends on WS of fabric.

FINISHING

Leaving buttonhole edge open, sew remaining three sides of pillow tops together.

TIES (make 4): With afghan hook, ch 25, work 1 Forward and Reverse Row in Tss then bind off. Thread each tie through opposing front and back buttonholes and tie in loose knot.

Kathleen Power Johnson is a self-taught crochet and knit designer. See her other design on page 120.

child's tunisian vest

Girls just want to have fun with fashion! And they know what colors are cool: it's got to be purple, pink, or blue. Or all of these at once! This easy sweater vest combines color and style with a lesson in Tunisian crochet.

DESIGN BY KATHLEEN POWER JOHNSON
Skill level: Intermediate

Sizes: Children's sizes 1 (2, 4, 6). Model is size 4. Instructions are for smallest size with changes for larger sizes in parentheses. Finished project size:
Chest (buttoned)—20½" (23½", 26", 28"); Back Length—10" (11", 12", 13")

MATERIALS
Paton's Grace, 100% cotton yarn (136 yds/1¾ oz per ball): 2 (2, 2, 3) balls of Viola (60322) for MC; 1 ball each of Sweet Pea (60230) for color A, Ginger (60027) for color B, and Rose (60437) for color C

Size G/6 (4.00mm) afghan hook, or size needed to obtain gauge

Size F/5 (3.75 mm) crochet hook

Tapestry needle

Five ⅝"-diameter buttons

GAUGE
19 sts and 21 rows = 4"/10.2 cm in Tss

22 sts and 24 rows = 4"/10.2 cm in Tattersall Stitch

Take time to check your gauge.

STITCH PATTERN
This vest blends Tunisian crochet tradition with European crochet innovation.

The Tunisian double crochet stitch drops down to form extended (see page 45) front post (see page 41) stitches, creating vertical bars of color which turn stripes into plaid.

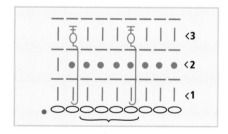

⌒	chain (ch)
|	Tunisian simple stitch (Tss)
●	Tunisian purl stitch (Tps)
—	Tunisian return (R)
	front post extended double crochet (FPE-Tdc)

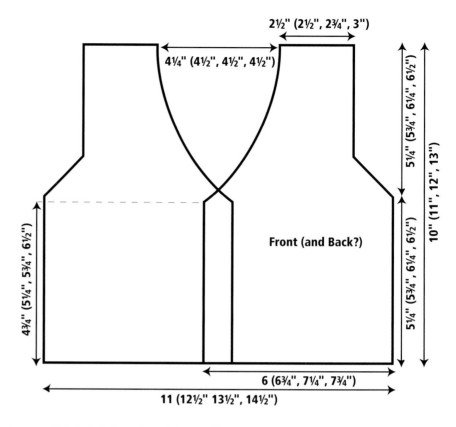

2½" (2½", 2¾", 3")

4¼" (4½", 4½", 4½")

5¼" (5¾", 6¼", 6½")

Front (and Back?)

4¾" (5¼", 5¾", 6½")

5¼" (5¾", 6¼", 6½")

5¼" (5¾", 6¼", 6½")

10" (11", 12", 13")

6 (6¾", 7¼", 7¾")

11 (12½" 13½", 14½")

INSTRUCTIONS

NOTE: Each "row" refers to both a forward and return Tunisian row.

All return rows are worked as follows: yo, draw up a loop, *yo, draw through 2 loops*; repeat from * to * across row (page 89).

Front Post Extended Tunisian double crochet (FPE-Tdc): Working into stitch 3 rows below, yo, insert hook into st, yo, draw loop through, yo, draw loop through first loop on hook, yo, draw loop through 2 loops, leaving remaining loop on hook.

To bind off stitches, work over 2 stitches, pulling loop of 2nd stitch through that of first.

Work last Tss under 2 threads in order to produce a chain along the left edge that matches the right edge.

TATTERSALL STITCH

Multiple of 4 stitches + 1.

ROW 1: (A) Tss across.

ROW 2: (B) Tps across, ending Tss in last st.

ROW 3: (MC) * 3 Tss, FPE-Tdc; rep from * ending Tss.

Repeat rows 1–3 for pattern.

BACK

With MC, ch 54 (62, 66, 71).

Foundation Row: Beginning in 2nd ch from hook, pull up a loop in each ch across — 54 (62, 66, 71) loops. Work return row as usual. Work even in Tss until Back measures approx 4¾ (5¼, 5¾, 6)" from beg. Row 25 (28, 30, 32)

ARMHOLE SHAPING

Tss2tog at the beginning and end of the next 5 (8, 8, 10) rows — 44 (46, 50, 51) sts. Work even until Back measures approx. 9¼" (10¼", 11¼", 12¼") from beg.

BACK NECK SHAPING

Row 1: Work across 13 (14, 15, 16) sts, bind off next 18 (18, 20, 19) sts, work last 13 (14, 15, 16) sts. Working each side separately, work return row.

RIGHT NECK SHAPING

Row 2: Tss across 12 (13, 14, 15) sts.

Row 3: Tss across 11 (12, 13, 14) sts.

Row 4: Bind off 11 (12, 13, 14) sts.

LEFT NECK SHAPING

Row 2: Tss2tog, Tss across.

Row 3: Tss2tog, Tss across.

Row 4: Bind off 11 (12, 13, 14) sts.

RIGHT FRONT

With MC, ch 34 (37, 41, 45) sts and work Row 1 as for Back. In Tattersall Stitch, work buttonhole on 2nd (3rd, 3rd, 3rd) row; then every 6 (6, 7, 7) rows 4 times more. Cont in pattern as established until center edge measures approx. 4½" (5", 5½", 5¾") from beg. Row 27 (30, 33, 34).

BUTTONHOLE

Work 3 sts, bind off 3 sts, cont in pattern as established.

Next return row: Ch 3 over 3 bound off sts.

Next forward row: Pick up loop into each ch. Numbers for armhole shaping and shoulder bind off differ from Back because of the stitch gauge.

NECK SHAPING

Tss2tog at neck edge every row 5 (6, 6, 7) times, then every 2nd row 9 (9, 11, 11) times.

ARMHOLE SHAPING

When side edge measures same as Back, begin shaping.

Tss2tog at end of row 8 (9, 10, 11) times. Work even until Front is same length as Back. Bind off 12 (13, 14, 16) sts.

LEFT FRONT

Work as for Right Front, omitting buttonholes and reversing shaping.

FINISHING

With MC, sew side and shoulder seams. With C and right side facing, attach yarn at side seam with sl st; ch 1, dc in same st. * Skip 1 st, slip st in next st, dc in next st; rep from * around entire vest. At end, join with sl st in first dc and fasten off. Rep around each armhole edge. Sew on buttons opposite buttonholes. ✿

Kathleen Power Johnson is a self-taught crochet and knit designer whose designs and articles have appeared in most of the well-known crochet and knitting magazines. She is a member of The Crochet Guild of America, working in the area of professional development. See her other design on page 118.

MATERIALS

DMC Pearl Cotton size 8: one skein each of Light Rose, #602 (A), Medium Rose, #604 (B), and Dark Rose, #605 (C)
Size 9 (1.40mm) steel crochet hook

STITCH PATTERN

Bobbles, chains, and double crochet fans around a starting ring create this basic medallion. The edge is finished with picots.

INSTRUCTIONS

Ch 4 with color A. Sl st to join.

Rnd 1: Sc 12 in ring. Sl st to join.

Rnd 2: Ch 3 (counts as first dc). *In next sc, dc4tog; ch 4, sk 1 sc*. Repeat around ring 6 times. Sl st in tip of first dc4tog.

Rnd 3: Change to color B. Ch 1. In next ch-4 *sc, 2 dc, ch 3, 2 dc, sc, sk dc4tog;* repeat from * to * around ring. Sl st to join.

Rnd 4: Ch 3. *In next ch-3 [dc, ch 1] 5 times; sk [2 dc, sc], dc between next 2 sc, ch 1, sk [sc, 2 dc]*. Repeat from * to * around. Join with sl st in ch-3.

Rnd 5: Change to color C. Ch 1. Sc in ch-3, *sk dc, 2 dc in ch-1, sk dc, [3 dc in ch-1] twice, sk dc, 2 dc in ch-1, sk dc, sc in ch-1, sk dc, sc in ch-1*. Repeat from * to * around, ending with sc in ch-1, sk dc, sl st in sc to join.

Rnd 6: Ch 1. *BLsc, ch 3, sl st in sc* in each st around. Fasten off. 🪡

⬭	chain (ch)
⬬	slip stitch (sl st)
+	single crochet (sc)
┼	double crochet (dc)
ⵜ	single crochet in back loop (BLsc)
⸛	picot
⬨	double crochet four together (dc4tog)

medallion

Charming little projects like this are fun to make as coasters, ornaments, or clothing embellishments.

DESIGN ADAPTED BY SHELLEY CARDA

Skill level: Intermediate
Finished project size: 3" diameter

123

philosopher's coat

Deep jewel tones join up with multiple intricate patterns for a fabulous tapestry of color and texture. This sweater of distinction—grand enough to be called a coat!—awaits the advanced stitcher for an extraordinary crochet experience.

DESIGN BY RUTH ATKINSON

Skill level: Advanced

Finished project size: 56" bust (buttoned); 33" long.

Instructions are written for size Medium/Large. For a smaller or larger size refer to the charts marked "adjust width" to subtract or add rows. Only one length is given.

MATERIALS

The Philosopher's Wool Co., 2-ply wool, worsted weight yarn (4 oz./122 gm per skein) 16 skeins total. Model uses the following colors:

3 skeins Navy

2 skeins Rust

2 skeins Dark Maroon

2 skeins Wine

1 skein Dark Purple Heather

1 skein Forest Green

1 skein Grape Heather

1 skein Jade Heather

1 skein Black

1 skein Special Red

1 skein Alberta Green

Size G/6 (4.50mm) aluminum crochet hook or size needed to obtain gauge

Size E/4 (3.50mm) aluminum crochet hook

Seven 1"-diameter buttons

Yarn needle

GAUGE

16 sc and 12 rows = 4"/10cm.

Take time to check your gauge.

STITCH PATTERNS

NOTES FROM THE DESIGNER: The philosophy that any color palette (for this model I chose dark jewel tones) is guaranteed to work as long as the crocheter uses all the colors at more or less the same rate. Regardless of palette, the result will be visually similar. The eye digests the colors together rather like a spaghetti sauce... as long as the ingredients are all there, the taste is similar! Close-ups of the coat show how the colors change quite often in fore and background. I try to create very individualistic garments, so I choose not to give exact color changes, but to allow you, the crocheter, to "Color It Your Way."

Begin the sleeve with your darkest, most neutral color for cuff and increase rows. Use a combination of brighter colors for the knurl rows. Repeat the unifying neutral color four or five times throughout the sleeve as knurl rows or overlay colors. Mix all other colors as you wish. Subtle color changes make individual stitch patterns richer. Repeating the neutral color periodically ties everything together and makes it easy to "Color It Your Way."

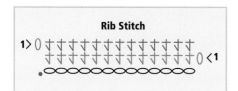

Rib Stitch

RIB STITCH
All rows: Turn. Ch 1. BLsc across.

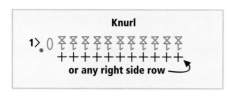

Knurl

or any right side row

KNURL
Work after completing a right side row. For knurl row following another knurl row, work 1 row of BLsc between knurl rows. Any row following a knurl row is worked into the remaining back loops left free behind the knurl row.

Row 1: Do not turn. Ch 1. Working from left to right, corded reverse stitch in front loop only across.

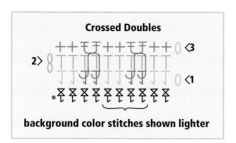

Crossed Doubles

background color stitches shown lighter

CROSSED DOUBLES
Multiple of 2 stitches + 1.
Worked after knurl row.

Row 1: Work into the back loops left free behind the knurl row. Do not turn. Ch 2. * 2 hdc background, 2 hdc overlay*; repeat from * to * across, ending with 1 hdc background.

Row 2: Turn. Ch 2. Hdc background across.

Row 3: With overlay color only. Turn. Ch 1. *2 scs, sk 1 st, FPdc, in skipped st FPdc, skip 2 stitches used by FPdcs*; repeat from * to * across, ending with sc in last st.

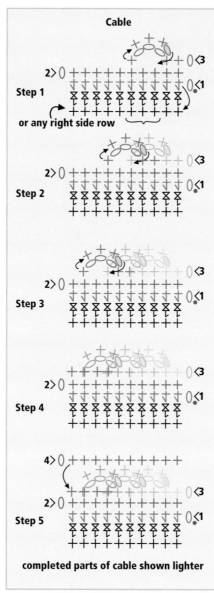

Cable

Step 1
or any right side row

Step 2

Step 3

Step 4

Step 5

completed parts of cable shown lighter

CABLE
Multiple of 3 stitches + 1.
Work after a knurl row. Sc rows are worked in background color. Cable row is worked in overlay color.

Row 1: Work into the back loops left free behind the knurl row. Do not turn. Ch 1. With right side facing, BLsc in remaining loops behind knurl row.

Row 2: Turn. Ch 1. Sc across.

Row 3: Cable row. Turn. Ch 1. 2 scs, *ch 3, sk 2 sts, sc in next, turn, 3 scs over ch-3, sl into sc before ch-3, turn, working behind ch-3 cable just made, sc in each of two skipped sts*; repeat from * to * across until 2 scs remain, 2 scs in next st, sc in last.

Row 4: Turn. Ch 1. Sc across.

Count your stitches. Make another cable row or finish with a row of sc and a row of knurl.

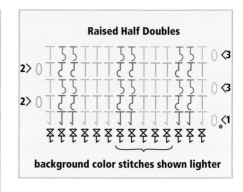

Raised Half Doubles

background color stitches shown lighter

RAISED HALF DOUBLES
Multiple of 5 stitches + 4.
Work after a knurl row. All raised post stitches are raised to the right side. Row 1 sets the color pattern, raised effect starts in Row 2.

Row 1: Work into the back loops left free behind the knurl row. Do not turn. Ch 1. 1 hdc background, 2 hdc overlay, *3 hdc background, 2 hdc overlay*; repeat from * to * across, ending with 1 hdc background.

Row 2: Turn. Ch 2. Hdc background in background and BPhdc around overlay across.

Row 3: Turn. Ch 2. Hdc background in background and FPhdc around overlay across.

Repeat Rows 2 and 3 one more time or to desired size.

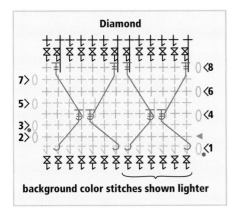

Diamond

background color stitches shown lighter

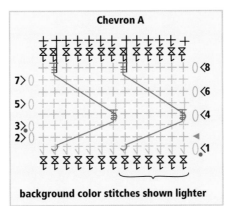

Chevron A

background color stitches shown lighter

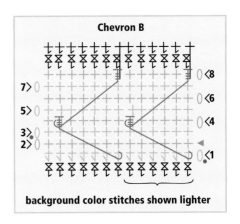

Chevron B

background color stitches shown lighter

DIAMOND

Multiple of 6 stitches + 1.

Work after a knurl row. Rows 1, 2, 3, 5, 6, and 7 are worked in background color. Row 4 uses an overlay color for the treble crochet stitches.

Row 1: Work into the back loops left free behind the knurl row. Do not turn. Ch 1. Sc across.

Row 2: Turn. Ch 1. Sc across. Break yarn.

Row 3: Do not turn. Join yarn where row 2 began (wrong side facing). Ch 1. Sc across.

Row 4: Ch 1. Turn. 2 scs background, FPtr around first st of Row 1, *sk 4 sts of Row 1, FPtr around next st of Row 1, sk 2 sts of Row 3 that are behind FPtrs, 4 sc, FPtr around next st in Row 1*; repeat from * to * until 5 sts remain in Row 3, FPtr around 2nd to last st in Row 1, sk 2 sts of Row 3 that are behind FPtrs, 3 scs.

Row 5: Turn. Ch 1. Sc across except behind trs work scs into scs of Row 3.

Row 6: Turn. Ch 1. Sc across.

Row 7: Turn. Ch 1. Sc across completing last sc in overlay color.

Row 8: Diamond row. Turn. Ch 1. FPtr around first tr in Row 4, sk 1 st of Row 7 that is behind FPtr, 4 sc, FPtr around next tr in Row 4, *FPtr around next tr in Row 4, sk 2 sts of Row 7 that are behind FPtrs, 4 sc, FPtr around next tr in Row 4*; repeat from * to * until 2 background sts in Row 7 remain, sk 1 st of Row 7, sc in last.

For more diamonds, repeat Rows 5–7 and then alternate Rows 4 and 8. Finish with knurl row after Row 8. Sc row between knurl rows secures unused stitches in Row 7.

CHEVRONS A AND B

Multiple of 6 stitches + 1.

Work after knurl row. Background Rows 1, 2, 3, 5, 6, and 7 are the same as in Diamond pattern. Use Chevron A or B as indicated so that all chevrons point toward waist edge.

Chevron A Row 4: Turn. Ch 1. FPdtr around 6th st of Row 1, *sk 1 st of Row 3 that is behind FPdtr, 5 sc, sk 5 sts in Row 1, FPdtr around next st of Row 1*; repeat from * to * until 7 sts remain in Row 3, sk 1 st of Row 3 that is behind FPdtr, 6 sc.

Chevron A Row 8: Turn. Ch 1. 5 sc, FPdtr around first dtr in Row 4, *sk 1 st of Row 7 that is behind FPdtr, 5 sc, FPdtr around next dtr in Row 4*; repeat from * to * until 2 sts remain in Row 7, sk 1 st of Row 7 that is behind FPdtr, sc in last.

Chevron B Row 4: Turn. Ch 1. 5 sc, FPdtr around first st of Row 1, *sk 1 st of Row 3 that is behind FPdtr, 5 sc, sk 5 sts in Row 1, FPdtr around next st of Row 1*; repeat from * to * until 2 sts remain in Row 3, sk 1 st of Row 3 that is behind FPdtr, sc in last

Chevron B Row 8: Turn. Ch 1. FPdtr in first dtr of Row 4, *sk 1 st of Row 7 that is behind FPdtr, 5 sc, FPdtr around next dtr in Row 4*; repeat from * to * until 7 sts remain in Row 7, sk 1 st of Row 7 that is behind FPdtr, 6 sc.

Finish with knurl row after Row 8.

⌒	chain (ch)
⬭	slip stitch (sl st)
+	single crochet (sc)
⊤	back loop single crochet (BLsc)
⊥	front loop single crochet (FLsc)
⊤	half double crochet (hdc)
⌇	front post half double crochet (FPhdc)
⌇	back post half double crochet (BPhdc)
⌇	front post double crochet (FPdc)
⌇	front post treble (FPtr)
⌇	front post double treble (FPdtr)
⊠	corded reverse single crochet
⊠	corded reverse single crochet in front loop

Coat center back

NOTES

Refer to Color Schemes (page 71) to help you choose your own individual color palette.

Work the sleeves first so that you can learn the stitches before going on to the larger pieces.

Work the back from the center panel to each side.

Work the shoulders and sides of the fronts to the side edge, then crochet the neck shaping piece onto the rectangle.

The term overlay (OL) refers here to the raised stitches in a stripe. Work these raised stitches onto or with a background (BG) color or colors.

Count your stitches at the end of each row.

To change color in sc, with present color, draw up a loop in the last stitch before color change, complete the sc with the new color.

When changing color in other stitches, work last stitch before change until 2 loops remain on the hook, then complete the stitch with the new color.

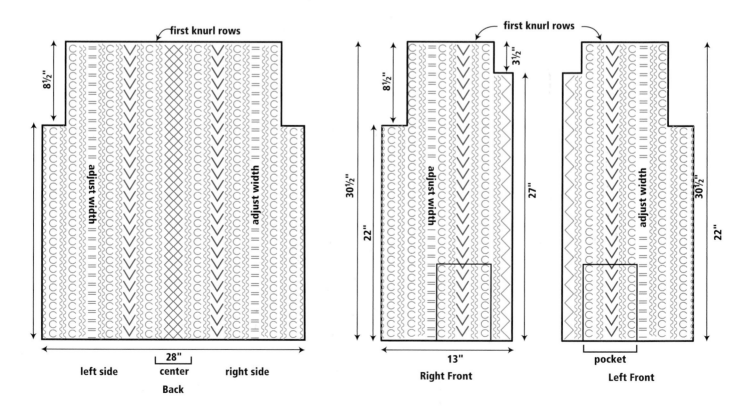

Back

left side   28"   right side
center

Right Front

13"

Left Front

pocket

first knurl rows

8½"   30½"   22"   27"   3½"   adjust width   30½"   22"

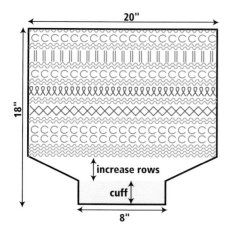

INSTRUCTIONS

SLEEVE

Cuff: Ch 12 sts + 1. Sc across. Work rib stitch until cuff is comfortably snug. Ch 1, turn, start increase rows.

Row 1: Sc 32 sts evenly across top of cuff.

Rows 2, 3, 4, and 5: Increase using hdcs as follows, *1FLhdc, 1BLhdc, 1FLhdc, 2 hdcs in next st*, repeat from * to * across. For firm edge, work first and last sts through both loops. Row 2 — 39 sts, Row 3 — 48 sts, Row 4 — 59 sts, Row 5 — 72 sts, Row 6 — 73 sts.

Refer to sleeve pattern diagram and work pattern stitches as indicated starting with 5 knurl rows at cuff end.

BACK

Start between cable and knurl to left of center back working toward right. Starting chain color and first sc row eventually become part of a cable pattern background.

Ch 109 sts + 1. Turn. 109 sc. Change color.

Make first 2 knurl rows.

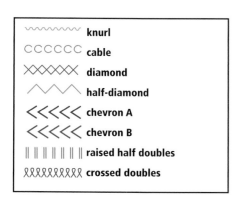

〰〰〰〰	**knurl**
CCCCC	**cable**
✕✕✕✕✕	**diamond**
⌃⌃⌃⌃	**half-diamond**
⟨⟨⟨⟨⟨	**chevron A**
⟨⟨⟨⟨⟨	**chevron B**
‖ ‖ ‖ ‖ ‖ ‖	**raised half doubles**
ꝶꝶꝶꝶꝶꝶ	**crossed doubles**

Coat sleeve

Work diamond pattern. Continue working patterns toward underarm seam as shown in back pattern diagram, adjusting width as follows when you reach the raised half doubles pattern row. Determine final back width from center back to underarm. For small, use 12"; for medium, use 13"; for large, use 14"; or for a custom fit, use bust size divided by 4 plus 4". Work as many rows of raised half doubles so that the width of the piece from center back (center of diamond pattern) to end of raised half doubles is 3.5" less than the desired final back width.

Continue pattern after raised half doubles until 1 cable row and one sc row are completed. Cable pattern should be in same as top cable of sleeve. In next sc row, leave 36 sts unworked for sleeve opening. Continue underarm extension to underarm seam.

To complete left back, turn work wrong side facing. Sc across starting ch to make 2nd background row of cable pattern. Turn to right side for cable row. Continue to underarm seam.

Coat pocket

around bottom. Add 5 knurl rows, decreasing about 5 sts in each sc row that separates the knurl rows. Try on coat after each row, adjusting number of decreases to your liking.

Work 2 knurl rows around entire body of coat, beginning row at a different point on bottom edge each time. At neckline, increase around corners and decrease into curves.

BUTTON BANDS

Row 1: Sc into remaining loops behind knurls.

Row 2: Turn. Ch 2. Hdc across.

Row 3: Turn. Ch 1. Evenly mark placement of 7 buttonholes. Sc across except *ch 2, sk 2 hdc* for buttonholes.

Row 4: Turn. Ch 2. Hdc across. Work 2 hdc over ch-2 buttonholes.

Finish neck edge, including tops of button bands, with 1 row sc and 1 knurl row in same color as button bands.

OPTIONAL RIBBED COLLAR

Join yarn at top of button band. With E (3.5 mm) hook, ch 5 sts + 1. Work rib stitch 5 sts wide joining and turning in remaining loops behind knurl row. Sk 1 or 2 loops at curves.

BLOCK

Set coat in lukewarm water in machine. *Do not agitate.* Use spin cycle to remove excess water. Lay flat and ease into shape. When coat is completely dry, bind edge of each button band with a sl st row.

Use colors as in left back. Starting point is marked on front pattern diagram.

Make pocket front separately on 25 stitches from cable row to cable row including only 1 wrong side background row on each outer edge. If the coat is lengthened, add the same multiple of 6 to the pocket front as to the coat.

Ch 109 sts + 1 to begin front. Work front to wrong side row after cable row. Place pocket on front aligning chevron, cable and bottom edge. Work front and pocket as one on next row. Continue to underarm seam, adjusting size as for back. Turn work and continue to center front. After cable pattern, leave 8 sts unworked at neck edge. Add 1 knurl row and 1 sc row, leaving 2 more sts unworked in each row. Add 1 more knurl row and finish with a diamond pattern up to Row 4.

LEFT FRONT

Work as a mirror image of right front.

FINISHING

Sew shoulder seams.

From right side, work 73 sc evenly across sleeve openings. Follow with a knurl row. With right sides together, join sleeves to openings using a sl st through the remaining back loops behind knurls.

To trim and shape bottom, sc evenly

Ruth Atkinson crochets and produces both one-of-a-kind and kitted designs for Philosopher's Wool of Ontario. Her work has been featured in Threads magazine and has won awards from the Canadian Sewing and Needlework Festival and the Ontario Crafts Council. In addition to teaching workshops, Ruth pursues the arts of spinning and dyeing.

Photographs by Philip Walker.

crochet pattern gallery

A *stitch* is the smallest element in crochet. Each stitch begins and ends with 1 loop on the hook. Crochet is created using a limited number of basic stitches: chain, single crochet, double crochet, treble crochet, slip stitch, etc.

These few basic crochet stitches combine to produce an infinite variety of complex patterns appropriate for textiles, ranging from the finest lace to the thickest carpet. When you repeat a combination of stitches, you develop a *pattern*.

Patterns are named at the whim of the creator, but the name is usually a mental reminder of what the pattern looks like. A name may be descriptive, such as *V Stitch* or *Crossed Stitch*. A name may be chosen because the pattern looks similar to a pattern in another needlework technique, such as *Seed Stitch* in knitting or *Bullion Stitch* in embroidery. The pattern might remind you of another object and so derive its name, such as *Peacock Stitch* or *Catherine's Wheel*.

The name often includes an ending such as *stitch, lace, square, medallion,* or *edging* to indicate the form. The designation *stitch* usually refers to a ground or all-over fabric (not to be confused with the basic stitches like chain and single crochet). *Lace* also refers to an all-over fabric, but one that contains lace holes. *Square* and *medallion* refer to small individual units that are sewn or crocheted together to create a large piece such as a tablecloth, bedspread, or afghan. An *edging* is a narrow band used to decorate the edge of a crocheted or fabric piece.

Many of the simpler crochet patterns have multiple names. For instance, *V Stitch* is also called *Spider Stitch, Begonia Stitch, Cluster Stitch,* and *Rope Stitch*. The simpler patterns have been recreated by different people in different places many times. Each creator gives the stitch a name that is descriptive to her.

The photographs in the gallery show work done by a right-handed person. In some cases, the work will look like a mirror image if done by someone left-handed.

SIMPLE COMBINATIONS

Basic crochet stitches, such as chain, slip, single crochet, half double crochet, double crochet, and treble crochet, work together in simple combinations to produce pattern stitches. You can work a single stitch in groups as in Grit Stitch (page 135) or alternate different stitches as in Seed Stitch (this page).

You can freely substitute single crochet, half double crochet, double crochet or treble crochet stitches for each other in many of these simple combinations. Entire families of stitch patterns are possible with this easy substitution.

These simple patterns are called *grounds*. Use them to create patterned crochet fabric for pillows, blankets, garments, and many other items.

For an explanation of chart symbols, see the inside back cover.

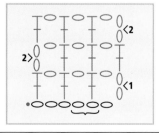

Work edge stitches (turning chains) in one of two ways depending on the application you plan to use. Using the Open Stitch Family as an example (at right), the chart shows the turning chain worked outside of the main body of stitches. For garments, work the turning chains outside the main body of the stitch so that the pattern repeats continuously across seam lines. The chart below shows the turning chain worked within the main body of stitches. When you want even sides on a rectangular piece such as in a blanket, work the turning chain within the main body of stitches. You can convert the patterns in the gallery from one type of turning chain to the other depending on your application.

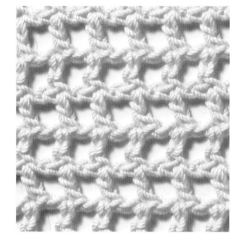

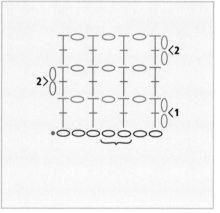

OPEN STITCH FAMILY

INSTRUCTIONS
Chain a multiple of 2 stitches + 1.
Row 1: Turn. Ch 2. Sk tch, *dc in ch, sk 1 ch, ch* across, ending with dc.
Row 2: Turn. Ch 2. *Dc in dc, sk 1 ch, ch* across, ending with dc in dc.
Repeat row 2.

VARIATIONS
Work in tr or taller stitches.

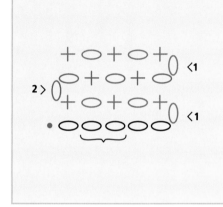

SEED STITCH FAMILY

INSTRUCTIONS
Chain a multiple of 2 stitches + 1.
Row 1: Turn. Ch 1. Sk tch, *sc in st, sk next st, ch 1* across, ending with sc in last st.
Row 2: Turn. Ch 1. *Ch 1, sk sc, sc in ch* across, ending with ch 1.
Repeat rows 1 and 2.

VARIATIONS
Work in hdc, dc, or tr.

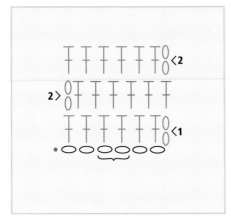

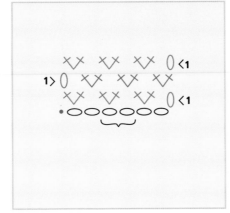

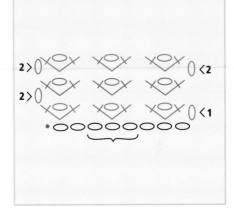

SHALLOW STITCH FAMILY
Other Name: Wide Stitch

NOTES
Work ch loosely to accommodate extra width.

INSTRUCTIONS
Chain a multiple of 1 stitch.

Row 1: Turn. Ch 2. Dc in each ch st across.

Row 2: Turn. Ch 2. Dc below horizontal threads into space between dcs across, ending with dc in tch.

Repeat row 2.

VARIATIONS
Use sc or tr instead of dc.

GRIT STITCH FAMILY
Other Names: Alternate Stitch, V Stitch

INSTRUCTIONS
Chain a multiple of 2 stitches.

Row 1: Turn. Ch 1. Sk tch, *sk 1 st, 2 scs in next* across, ending with 2 scs in last st.

Repeat Row 1.

VARIATIONS
Work in hdc, dc, or tr.

V STITCH FAMILY
Other Names: Spider Stitch, Begonia Stitch, Cluster Stitch, Rope Stitch

INSTRUCTIONS
Chain a multiple of 3 stitches + 2.

Row 1: Turn. Ch 1. Sk tch and 1 ch of base chain, *in next ch (sc, ch, sc), sk 2 chs*; repeat from * to * across, ending with (sc, ch, sc) in last ch.

Row 2: Turn. Ch 1. *Sc, ch, sc* in ch; repeat from * to * across.

Repeat Row 2.

VARIATIONS
Work in hdc, dc, or tr. *Wattle Stitch* is a variation using (sc, ch, dc).

135

crochet pattern gallery

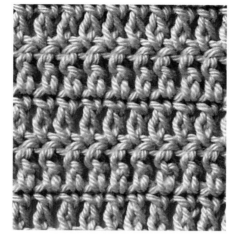

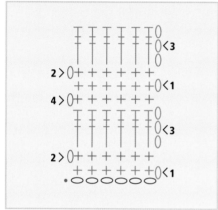

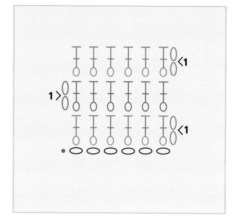

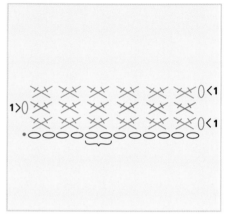

TRACK STITCH FAMILY

NOTES
Use an odd number of rows of a simple stitch like sc between individual rows of a decorative stitch. Then the decorative stitch will always show its right side on the front of the work.

INSTRUCTIONS
Chain a multiple of 1 stitch.
Rows 1 and 2: Turn. Ch 1. Sc across.
Row 3: Turn. Ch 3. Tr across.
Row 4: Turn. Ch 1. Sc across.
Repeat rows 1–4.

VARIATIONS
Use any tall decorative stitch in row 3.

EXTENDED STITCH FAMILY
Other Names: Herringbone Stitch, Elmore Stitch

NOTES
Work the chain used to extend a basic stitch with a single crochet or any taller stitch. Extending a stitch makes a slightly taller stitch and softer fabric than the basic stitch. Extended stitches can also be used in series when increasing height such as sc, hdc, Ehdc, dc, Edc, tr for a smoother increase.

INSTRUCTIONS
Chain a multiple of 1 stitch.
Row 1: Turn. Ch 2. Edc across.
Repeat row 1.

VARIATIONS
Use with single crochet or any taller stitch.

CROSS STITCH

INSTRUCTIONS
Chain a multiple of 2 stitches.
Row 1: Turn. Ch 1. *Sk 1 st, sc in next; working around sc just made, sc in skipped st*; repeat from * to* across.
Repeat row 1.

VARIATION
Work dcs in place of scs.

136

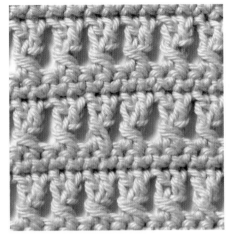

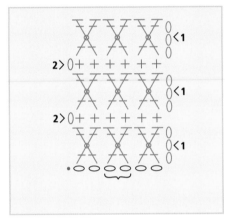
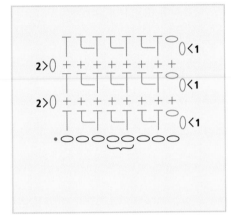
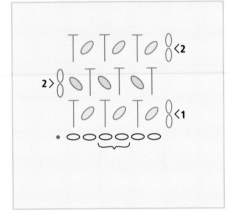

LOCKED CROSS STITCH FAMILY

NOTES

Tall stitches can be crossed and locked together to provide more stability to the stitches. When making the second tr, make the first yo as you normally would. Then pass the hook to the front and the yarn to the back of the first tr. Make the second yo through the hole just above the skipped stitch. Insert hook in the skipped stitch and complete second tr.

INSTRUCTIONS

Chain a multiple of 2 stitches.

Row 1: Turn. Ch 3. *Sk 1 st, tr in next, tr in skipped st working one yo above and one below the first tr* across.

Row 2: Turn. Ch 1. Sc across.

Repeat rows 1 and 2.

VARIATIONS

Use taller stitches, dividing the yarn overs of the second stitch of the crossed pair evenly above and below the cross.

PIGGYBACK STITCH FAMILY

INSTRUCTIONS

Chain a multiple of 2 stitches.

Row 1: Turn. Ch 2. Sk tch, *sk 1 st, hdc, hdc around post of hdc just made*; repeat from * to *across, ending with hdc in last st.

Row 2: Turn. Ch 1. Sc across.

Repeat rows 1 and 2.

VARIATIONS

Work with dc or taller stitches.

CRUNCH STITCH

INSTRUCTIONS

Chain a multiple of 2 stitches.

Row 1: Turn. Ch 2. Sk tch, *sl st, hdc*; repeat from * to * across, ending with hdc in last st.

Row 2: Turn. Ch 2. *Sl st in hdc, hdc in sl st* across.

Repeat row 2.

137

crochet pattern gallery

138

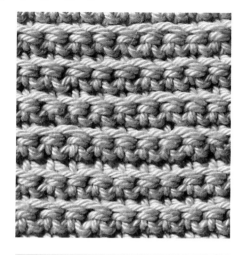

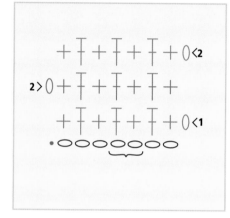

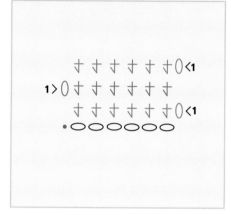

GRIDDLE STITCH
*Other Names: Up and Down Stitch,
Cobble Stitch*

INSTRUCTIONS
Chain a multiple of 2 stitches.
Row 1: Turn. Ch 1. *Sc, dc* across, ending with dc.
Row 2: Turn. Ch 1. *Sc in dc, dc in sc* across.
Repeat row 2.

VARIATION
For more texture, replace dcs with trs.

CRUMPLED GRIDDLE STITCH

INSTRUCTIONS
Chain a multiple of 2 stitches + 1.
Row 1: Turn. Ch 1. *Sc, dc* across, ending with sc.
Row 2: Turn. Ch 1. *Sc in sc, dc in dc* across.
Repeat row 2.

RIB STITCH

INSTRUCTIONS
Chain a multiple of 1 stitch.
Row 1: Turn. Ch 1. Sc in back loop only across.
Repeat row 1.

VARIATION
Work in dc.

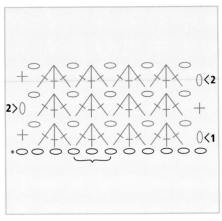

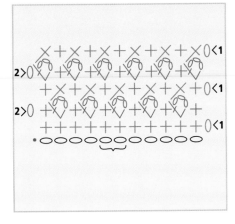

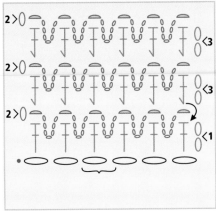

TRINITY STITCH

NOTE
Sc3tog is a cluster stitch composed of three single crochets joined in the last yo.

INSTRUCTIONS
Chain a multiple of 2 stitches + 3.

Row 1: Turn. Ch 2. Sk tch, *over 3 chs sc3tog, ch 1*, insert hook in same ch as previous sc and repeat from * to * across, ending with sc in last stitch.

Row 2: Turn. Ch 2. Beginning in ch, *over (ch, sc3tog, ch) sc3tog, ch 1*, insert hook in same ch as previous sc and repeat from * to * across, ending with sc in tch.

Repeat row 2.

GRANULE STITCH

NOTES
Single-crochet picot — pull up a loop in next st, ch 3 in new loop only, yo, pull through both loops on hook. Push picot to back (right side) of work.

INSTRUCTIONS
Chain a multiple of 2 stitches + 1.

Row 1: Turn. Ch 1. Sc across.

Row 2: Turn. Ch 1. *Sc, single crochet picot*; repeat from * to * across, ending with sc.

Repeat rows 1 and 2.

ASTRAKHAN STITCH
Other Name: Fur Stitch

NOTE
The front loop of the dc in row 2 which is not used becomes the back loop that is used when the fabric is turned in row 3.

INSTRUCTIONS
Chain a multiple of 1 stitch.

Row 1: Turn. Ch 2. Dc across.

Row 2: Turn. Ch 1. *Sl st in back loop of dc, ch 7, push ch loop to back of work (right side)* across, ending with sl st.

Row 3: Turn. Ch 2. Dc in back loop of previous dc across row.

Repeat rows 2 and 3.

VARIATIONS
For thicker fur, substitute a shorter stitch for the dc, such as an hdc. For thinner fur, substitute a taller stitch for the dc, such as a tr.

139

crochet pattern gallery

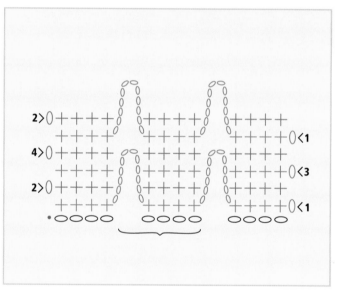

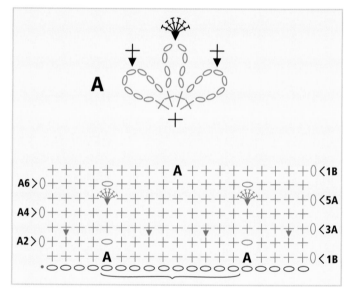

LINKED LOOPS

INSTRUCTIONS

Chain a multiple of 4 stitches.

Row 1: Turn. Ch 1. *Sc 4 times, ch 12* across, rep from * to * ending with 4 scs.

Rows 2, 3, 4: Turn. Ch 1. Sc in each sc across.

Change color after row 4.

Repeat rows 1–4, ending with row 4. Before completing last row, chain loops together by pulling each loop through the one below, beginning at the bottom of row. Crochet through top loop of each row when completing the last row of scs.

THISTLE

INSTRUCTIONS

Chain a multiple of 10 stitches + 9 using color A.

Row 1: Turn. With color B ch 1. Sc 4 times, *[in next stitch (sc, ch 8) 3 times, sc], sc 9 times,* repeat from * to * across, ending with sc 4 times.

Row 2: Turn. With color A ch 1. Sc 4 times, *ch 1, sk ch loops, (sc in sc) 9 times*; repeat from * to * across, ending with sc in last 4 sts.

Row 3: Turn. Ch 1. Sc, *sc through right loop and into next sc, sc 5 times, sc through left loop and into next sc, sc 3 times* repeat from * to * ending with sc in last st.

Row 4: Turn. Ch 1. Sc across.

Row 5: Turn. Ch 1. Sc 4 times,*6 dcs through center loop and into next sc, sc 9 times*; repeat from * to * across, ending with sc 4 times.

Row 6: Turn. Ch 1. Sc 4 times, *ch 1, sk dcs, sc 9 times*; repeat from* to * ending with sc 4 times.

Repeat rows 1–6 offsetting thistle motifs by 5 stitches.

FANS AND SHELLS

Create fans and shells by working multiple stitches in a single stitch of the row below, then skipping several stitches to keep equal numbers of stitches in each row.

Fans and shells can be solid or lacy. Use solid shells as decorative grounds in afghans and garments. Lacy patterns work well for household items like tablecloths and doilies.

For an explanation of chart symbols, see the inside back cover.

Work edge stitches (turning chains) in one of two ways depending on the application you plan to use. Using the Open Stitch Family as an example (Fig. 1), the chart shows the turning chain worked outside of the main body of stitches. For garments, work the turning chains outside the main body of the stitch so that the pattern repeats continuously across seam lines. Fig. 2 shows the turning chain worked within the main body of stitches. When you want even sides on a rectangular piece such as in a blanket, work the turning chain within the main body of stitches. You can convert the patterns in the gallery from one type of turning chain to the other depending on your application.

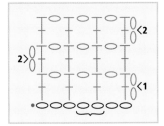

Fig. 1

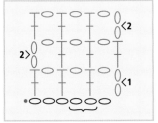

Fig. 2

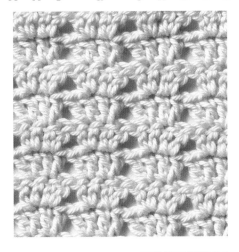

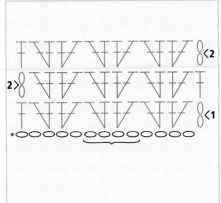

TWIN STITCH

INSTRUCTIONS

Chain a multiple of 4 stitches + 1.

Row 1: Turn. Ch 2. Sk 1 ch of base ch, *(2 dcs in next ch) 2 times, sk 2 chs*; repeat from * to * across, ending with sk 1 ch, dc in last ch.

Row 2: Turn. Ch 2. Sk first 2 dcs, *(2 dcs in next dc) 2 times, sk 2 dcs*; repeat from * to * across, ending with dc in tch.

Repeat row 2.

VARIATIONS

Use hdc or tr.

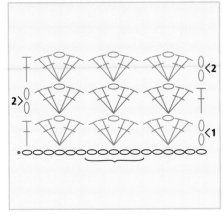

FAN STITCH

INSTRUCTIONS

Chain a multiple of 5 stitches + 2.

Row 1: Turn. Ch 2. Sk 3 chs of base ch, *in next ch (2 dcs, ch 1, 2 dcs), sk 4 chs*; repeat from * to * across, ending with dc in last ch.

Row 2: Turn. Ch 2. Sk 3 dcs, *over ch-1 (2 dcs, ch 1, 2 dcs), sk 4 dcs*; repeat from * to * across, ending with sk 2 dcs, dc in tch.

Repeat row 2.

VARIATIONS

Use hdc or tr.

141

crochet pattern gallery

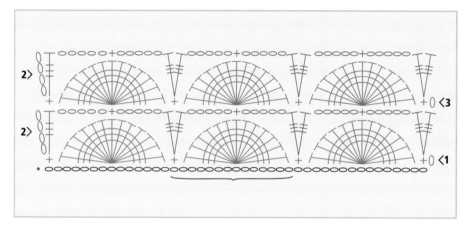

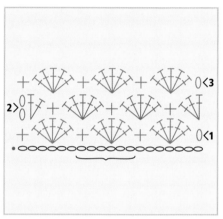

PEACOCK STITCH

INSTRUCTIONS

Chain a multiple of 14 plus + 1.

Row 1: Turn. Ch 1. *Sc, sk 6 chs, 13 dtrs in next ch, sk 6 chs*; repeat from * to * across, ending with sc in last st.

Row 2: Turn. Ch 4 (counts as first dtr). *2 dtrs in sc, ch 5, sc in 7th dtr of fan, ch 5*; repeat from * to * across, ending with 2 dtrs in sc.

Row 3: Turn. Ch 1. *Sc between dtrs, sk 5 chs, 13 dtrs in sc, sk 5 chs*; repeat from * to * across, ending with sc over tch.

Repeat rows 2 and 3, ending with row 2.

SOLID SHELL STITCH

INSTRUCTIONS

Chain a multiple of 6 stitches + 1.

Row 1: Turn. Ch 1. Sk 3 chs of base ch,*5 dcs in next ch, sk 2 chs, sc in next ch, sk 2 chs*; repeat from * to * across, ending with sc.

Row 2: Turn. Ch 2. 2 dcs in sc, *sk 2 dcs, sc in next dc, sk 2 dcs, 5 dcs in sc*; repeat from * to * across, ending with 3 dcs in tch.

Row 3: Turn. Ch 1. Sk 3 dcs, *5 dcs in sc, sk 2 dcs, sc in next dc, sk 2 dcs* repeat from * to * ending with sc in tch.

Repeat rows 2 and 3.

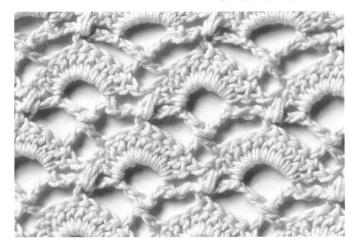

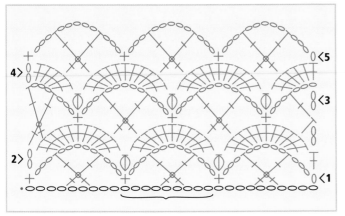
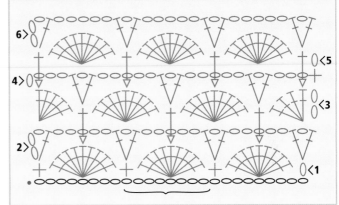

SOFT FAN

NOTE

Locked Cross tr — make first tr as usual. Form 2nd tr with yo, pass hook to front and yarn to back of first tr, yo below first tr, insert hook in st, and complete tr as usual.

INSTRUCTIONS

Chain a multiple of 9 stitches + 1.

Row 1: Turn. Ch 4, tr in 11th ch from hook, ch 5, count back 3 chs on base ch from tr and make 2nd tr of locked cross tr, ch 3, sk 2 chs on base ch from first tr made, sc in next ch, *ch 3, sk 5 chs, tr, ch 5, count back 3 chs on base ch from tr and make 2nd tr of locked cross tr, ch 3, sk 2 chs on base ch from first tr made, sc in next ch*; repeat from * to * across, ending with sc.

Row 2: Turn. Ch 2. *Sk ch-3 and tr, 11 dcs over ch-5, sk tr and ch-3, hdc3tog in sc*; repeat from * to * across, ending with 11 dcs over ch-5, sk tr and ch-3, dc in next ch.

Row 3: Turn. Ch 2. Sk 1 dc, hdc in next, ch 5, dc in hdc just made, ch 3, sk 3 dcs, *sc in next dc, ch 3, tr in 2nd dc of next fan, ch 5, in 10th dc of previous fan make 2nd tr of locked cross tr, ch 3, sk 3 dcs*; repeat from * to * across, ending with tr in tch, ch 3, in 10th dc of previous fan make 2nd tr of locked cross tr.

Row 4: Turn. Ch 2. 5 dcs over ch-3, sk tr and ch-3, hdc3tog in sc, *sk ch-3 and tr, 11 dcs over ch-5, sk tr and ch-3, hdc3tog in sc*; repeat from * to * across, ending with 5 dcs over ch-5.

Row 5: Turn. Ch 4, tr in 2nd dc on next fan, ch 5, in 5th dc

FAN AND V STITCH

INSTRUCTIONS

Chain a multiple of 8 stitches + 1.

Row 1: Turn. Ch 1. Sk 4 chs of base ch, *9 dcs in next ch, sk 3 chs, sc in next ch, sk 3 chs*; repeat from * to * ending with sc.

Row 2: Turn. Ch 3 (counts as first dc and ch). *(Dc, ch, dc) in sc, ch 5, sk fan*; repeat from * to * across, ending with (dc, ch, dc) in tch.

Row 3: Turn. Ch 2. 4 dcs over ch-1, *sk dc, sc over ch-5 and into 5th dc of fan below, sk dc. 9 dcs over ch-1*; repeat from * to * ending with 5 dcs over tch.

Row 4: Turn. Ch 4. *(dc, ch, dc) in sc, ch 5, sk fan*; repeat from * to * across, ending with ch 3, sc in tch.

Row 5: Turn. Ch 1. Sc over ch-3 and into first dc, *sk dc, 9 dcs over ch-1, sk dc, sc over ch-5 and into 5th dc of fan below*; repeat from * to * across, ending with sc over ch-3 and into last dc of half fan below.

Row 6: Turn. Ch 3 (counts as first dc and ch). *(Dc, ch, dc) in sc, ch 5, sk fan* across, ending with (dc, ch, dc) in sc.

Repeat rows 3–6.

---

of previous half fan make 2nd tr of locked cross tr, ch 3, sk 3 dcs, *sc in next dc, ch 3, tr in 2nd dc of next fan, ch 5, in 10th dc of previous fan make 2nd tr of locked cross tr, ch 3, sk 3 dcs*; repeat from * to * across, ending with sc in tch.

Repeat rows 2–5.

143

crochet pattern gallery

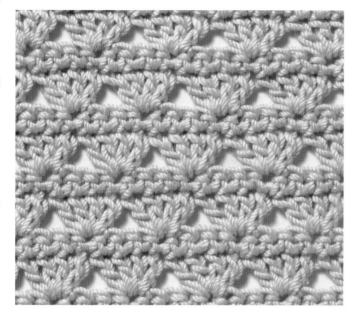

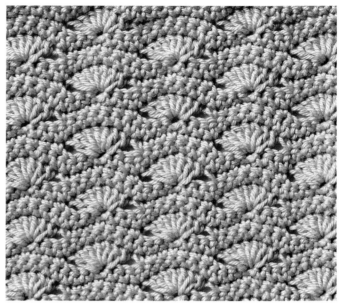

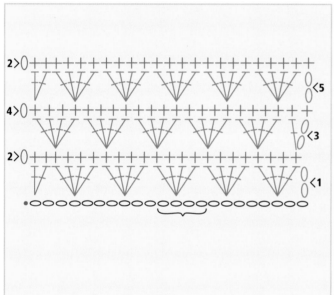

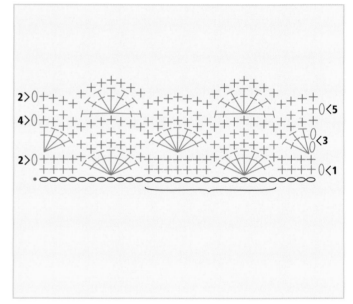

144

SIMPLE SHELL STITCH

INSTRUCTIONS

Chain a multiple of 4 stitches + 2.

Row 1: Turn. Ch 2. Sk 2 chs of base ch, *4 dcs in next ch, sk 3 chs*; repeat from * to * across, ending with 2 dcs in last ch.

Row 2: Turn. Ch 1. Sc across.

Row 3: Turn. Ch 2. Dc in first sc, sk 2 scs, *4 dcs in next sc, sk 3 scs*; repeat from * to * across, ending with 4 dcs in sc, sk 2 scs and tch.

Row 4: Same as row 2.

Row 5: Turn. Ch 2. Sk 2 scs, *4 dcs in next sc, sk 3 scs*; repeat from * to * across, ending with 2 dcs in last sc.

Repeat rows 2–5, ending with row 2 or row 4.

WAVY SHELL STITCH

INSTRUCTIONS

Chain a multiple of 14 stitches + 1.

Row 1: Turn. Ch 1. 4 scs, *sk 3 chs, 7 dcs in next ch, sk 3 chs, 7 scs*; repeat from * to * across, ending with 4 scs.

Row 2: Turn. Ch 1. Sc across, sk tch.

Row 3: Turn. Ch 2. 3 dcs in first sc, *sk 3 scs, 7 scs, sk 3 scs, 7 dcs in next sc*; repeat from * to * across, ending with 4 dcs in last sc.

Row 4: Turn. Ch 1. Sc across, ending with sc in tch.

Row 5: Turn. Ch 1. 4 scs, *sk 3 scs, 7 dcs in next sc, sk 3 scs, 7 scs*; repeat from * to * across, ending with 4 scs.

Repeat rows 2–5, ending with row 2 or row 4.

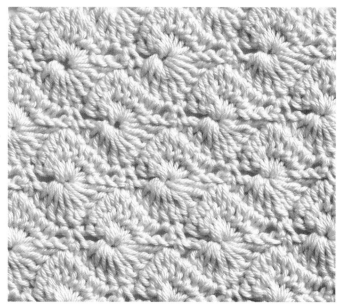

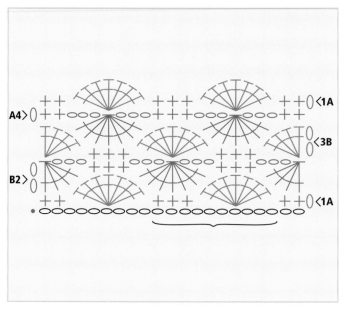

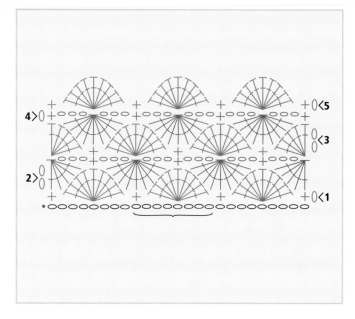

CATHERINE'S WHEEL

INSTRUCTIONS

Chain a multiple of 10 stitches + 1.

Row 1: Turn. With color A ch 1. 2 scs, *sk 3 chs, 7 dcs in next st, sk 3 chs, 3 scs*; repeat from * to * ending with 2 scs.

Row 2: Turn. With color B ch 2. Dc4tog over (sc, sc, dc, dc), *ch 3, 3 scs, ch 3, dc7tog over (dc, dc, sc, sc, sc, dc, dc)*; repeat from * to * across, ending with dc4tog over (dc, dc, sc, sc), sk tch.

Row 3: Turn. Ch 2. 4 dcs in dc4tog, *sk ch 3, 3 scs, sk ch-3, 7 dcs in dc7tog*; repeat from * to * across, ending with 4 dcs in dc4tog, sk tch.

Row 4: Turn. With color A ch 1. 2 scs, *ch 3, dc7tog (over dc, dc, sc, sc, sc, dc, dc), ch 3, 3 scs*; repeat from * to * across, ending with 2 scs, sk tch.

Repeat rows 1–4.

CATHERINE'S DIAMOND

INSTRUCTIONS

Chain a multiple of 8 stitches + 1.

Row 1: Turn. Ch 1. *Sc in ch, sk 3 chs, 9 dcs in next ch, sk 3 chs*; repeat from * to * across, ending with sc in last ch.

Row 2: Turn. Ch 2. Dc5tog over sc and 4 dcs, *ch 3, sc in next dc, ch 3, dc9tog over (4 dcs, sc, 4 dcs)*; repeat from * to * across, ending with dc5tog, sk tch.

Row 3: Turn. Ch 2. 5 dcs in dc5tog, *sk ch-3, sc in sc, sk ch-3, 9 dcs in dc9tog*; repeat from * to * across, ending with 5 dcs in dc5tog, sk tch.

Row 4: Turn. Ch 1. *Sc in dc, ch 3, dc9tog over (4 dcs, sc, 4 dcs), ch 3*; repeat from * to * across, ending with sc in last dc, sk tch.

Row 5: Turn. Ch 1. *Sc in sc, sk ch-3, 9 dcs in dc9tog, sk ch-3*; repeat from * to * across, ending with sc in sc, sk tch.

Repeat rows 2–5, ending with row 2 or row 4.

crochet pattern gallery

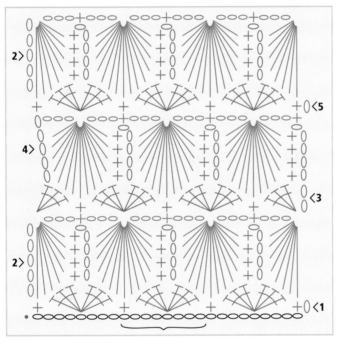

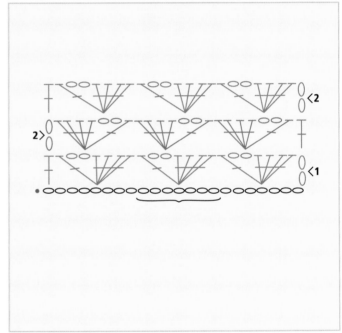

HEXAGON

INSTRUCTIONS

Chain a multiple of 8 stitches + 1.

Row 1: Turn. Ch 1.*Sc in ch, sk 3 chs, in next ch (3 dcs, ch 5, sk 1 of chs just made, sc in next 4 chs, 3 dcs), sk 3 chs*; repeat from * to * across, ending with sc in ch.

Row 2: Turn. Ch 5. Puff stitch over (sc, 3 dcs and 4 scs) pulling loops the height of ch-5, *ch 3, sc in last ch of ch-5, ch 3, puff stitch over (4 chs, 3 dcs, sc, 3 dcs and 4 scs)*; repeat from * to * ending with puff stitch over (4 chs, 3 dcs and sc), sk tch.

Row 3: Turn. Ch 7. Sk 1 of chs just made, sc in next 4 chs, 3 dcs in beginning of half-puff stitch, sk ch-3, *sc in sc, sk ch-3, in puff stitch (3 dcs, ch 5, sk 1 of chs just made, sc in next 4 chs, 3 dcs), sk ch-3*; repeat from * to * ending with 3 dcs in half-puff stitch, ch 5.

Row 4: Turn. Ch 3. *Puff stitch over (5th–8th chs from hook,

ASYMMETRICAL SHELL

INSTRUCTIONS

Chain a multiple of 7 stitches + 1.

Row 1: Turn. Ch 2. Sk 3 chs of base ch, *in next ch (4 dcs, ch 2, dc), sk 6 chs*; repeat from * to * across, ending with sk 3 chs, dc in last ch.

Row 2: Turn. Ch 2. Sk 2 dcs, *over ch-2 (4 dcs, ch 2, dc), sk 5 dcs*; repeat from * to * across, ending with dc in tch.

Repeat row 2.

---

3 dcs, sc, 3dcs, 4 scs), ch 3, sc in last ch of ch-5, ch 3*; repeat from * to * ending with sc in last ch of ch-5.

Row 5: Turn. Ch 1. *Sc in sc, sk ch-3, in puff stitch (3 dcs, ch 5, sk 1 of chs just made, sc in next 4 chs, 3 dcs), sk ch-3*; repeat from * to * across, ending with sc in 5th ch.

Repeat rows 2–5, ending with even row.

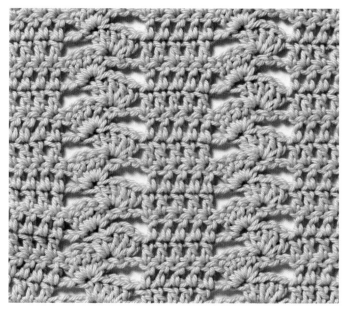

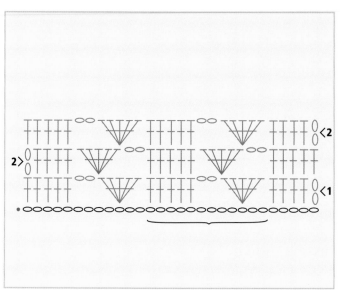

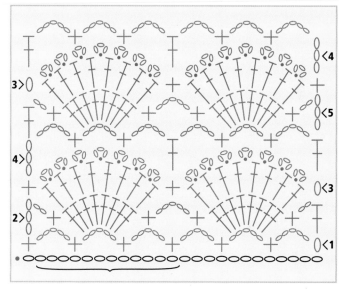

147

BLOCK AND OFFSET SHELL STITCH

INSTRUCTIONS

Chain a multiple of 12 stitches + 5.

Row 1: Turn. Ch 2 (counts as first dc). Sk 1 ch of base ch, *5 dcs, sk 2 chs, 5 dcs in next ch, sk 4 chs, ch 2*; repeat from * to * across, ending with 5 dcs.

Row 2: Turn. Ch 2 (counts as first dc). *5 dcs in dcs, sk ch-2, 5 dcs in first dc of shell, sk 4 dcs of shell, ch 2*; repeat from * to * across, ending with 4 dcs in dcs, dc in tch.

Repeat row 2.

PICOT FAN

NOTE

Picot — ch 3, sl st in first ch of ch-3 just made.

INSTRUCTIONS

Chain a multiple of 12 stitches + 1.

Row 1: Turn. Ch 6. Sk 4 chs of base ch, *sc in next, ch 5, sk 3 chs*; repeat from * to * across, ending with sc.

Row 2: Turn. Ch 5. *Sc over ch-5, 8 dcs over next ch-5, sc over ch-5, ch 5*; repeat from * to * across, ending with ch 2, dc in tch.

Row 3: Turn. Ch 1. *[in dc (dc, picot)] 7 times, dc in dc, sc over ch-5*; repeat from * to * ending with sc in 3rd ch of tch.

Row 4: Turn. Ch 8. *Sk 2 picots, sc in 3rd picot, ch 5, sk 1 picot, sc in next picot, ch 5, sk 2 picots, dc in sc, ch 5*; repeat from * to * across, ending with dc in tch.

Row 5: Turn. Ch 5. *Sc over ch-5, 8 dcs over next ch-5, sc over ch-5, ch 5*; repeat from * to * across, ending with ch 2, dc in 3rd ch of tch.

Repeat rows 3–5, ending with row 4.

crochet pattern gallery

LACE PATTERNS

Crocheted lace usually evokes thoughts of doilies and anti-macassars worked in fine thread, but lace grounds are also possible. Lace grounds worked in yarn are ideal for garments and afghans. Baby layettes often incorporate a single lace pattern in several coordinating pieces. Dressy evening wraps sparkle when you use a metallic yarn. Lace made with thread makes beautiful tablecloths and bedspreads.

For an explanation of chart symbols, see the inside back cover.

For instructions on working edge stitches (turning chains) see sidebar on page 141.

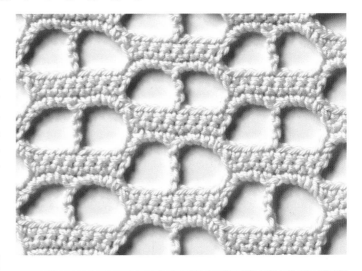

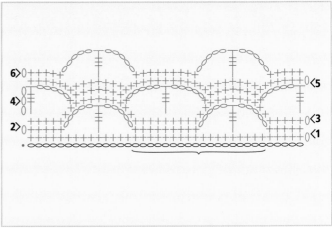

APARTMENT WINDOWS

INSTRUCTIONS

Chain a multiple of 18 stitches + 1.

Row 1: Turn. Ch 1. Sc across.

Row 2: Turn. Ch 1. 5 scs, *ch 5, sk 4 scs, dtr in next sc, ch 5, sk 4 scs, 9 scs*; repeat from * to * across, ending with 5 scs, sk tch.

Row 3: Turn. Ch 1. Sc across working in scs and dtrs and over chs, sk tch at end.

Row 4: Turn. Ch 3. Dtr in first sc, *ch 5, sk 5 scs, 9 scs, ch 5, sk 5 scs, dtr in next sc*; repeat from * to * across, ending with dtr in last sc, sk tch.

Row 5: Turn. Ch 1. Sc across working in scs and dtrs and over chs, sk tch at end.

Row 6: Turn. Ch 1. 5 scs, *ch 5, sk 5 scs, dtr in next sc, ch 5, sk 5 scs, 9 scs*; repeat from * to * across, ending with 5 scs, sk tch.

Repeat rows 3–6, ending with row 3 or row 5.

148

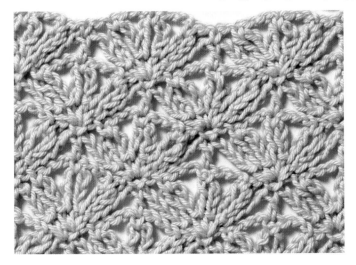

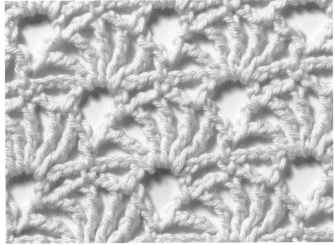

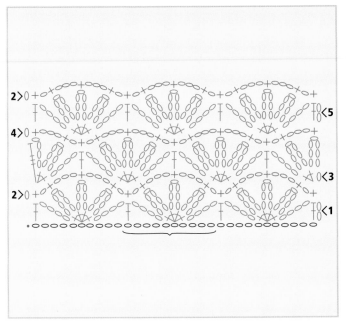

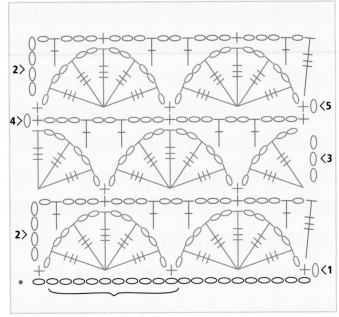

CHAIN LACE

INSTRUCTIONS

Chain a multiple of 10 stitches + 1.

Row 1: Turn. Ch 2. Dc in 3rd ch from hook, *sk 4 chs, ch 4, in next ch (sc, ch 7) 3 times, sc in same ch, sk 4 chs, ch 4, dc in next ch*; repeat from * to * ending with dc.

Row 2: Turn. Ch 1. *Sc in dc, ch 1, (sc in ch-7 loop, ch 3) 2 times, sc in ch-7 loop, ch 1*; repeat from * to * across, ending with sc in dc, sk tch.

Row 3: Turn. Ch 1. In sc (ch 7, sc) 2 times, *sk (ch-1, sc, ch- 3), ch 4, dc in sc, sk (ch-3, sc, ch-1), ch 4, in sc (sc, ch 7) 3 times, sc in same sc*; repeat from * to * ending with (sc, ch 7, sc, ch 4, dtr) in sc, sk tch.

Row 4: Turn. Ch 1. Sc in ch-7 loop, ch 3, sc in ch-7 loop, *ch 1, sc in dc, ch 1, (sc in ch-7 loop, ch 3) 2 times, sc in ch-7 loop*; repeat from * to * across, ending with ch 3, sc in ch-7 loop.

Row 5: Turn. Ch 2. *Dc in sc, sk (ch 3, sc, ch) in sc (sc, ch 7) 3 times, sc in same sc, sk (ch 1, sc, ch 3)*; repeat from * to * ending with dc in sc, sk tch.

Repeat rows 2–5, ending with row 2 or row 4.

OPEN FAN

INSTRUCTIONS

Chain a multiple of 10 stitches + 1.

Row 1: Turn. Ch 1. Sc in 2nd ch from hook, *sk 4 chs, ch 1, in next ch [dtr, (ch 2, dtr) 4 times], ch 1, sc, sk 4 chs*; repeat from * to * across, ending with sc in ch.

Row 2: Turn. Ch 5. Sk (sc, ch, dtr), *dc over ch-2, sk dtr and ch-2, ch 3, sc in dtr, sk ch-2 and dtr, ch 3, dc over ch-2, sk (dtr, ch, sc, ch, dtr), ch 2*; repeat from * to * across, ending with dc over ch-2, ch 1, dtr in sc, sk tch.

Row 3: Turn. Ch 5. In first dtr (dtr, ch 2, dtr) ch 1, sk (ch-1, dc, ch-3), *sc in sc, ch 1, sk (ch-3 and dc), over ch-2 [dtr, (ch 2, dtr) 4 times], ch 1, sk dc and ch-3*; repeat from * to * ending with [(dtr, ch 2) 2 times, dtr] over tch.

Row 4: Turn. Ch 1. *Sc in dtr, sk ch-2 and dtr, ch 3, dc over ch-2, sk (dtr, ch , sc, ch , dtr), ch 2, dc over ch-2, sk dtr and ch-2, ch 3*; repeat from * to * across, ending with sc over tch.

Row 5: Turn. Ch 1. *Sc in sc, ch 1, sk ch-3 and dc, over ch-2 [dtr, (ch 2, dtr) 4 times], ch 1, sk dc and ch-3*; repeat from * to * across, ending with sc in ch.

Repeat rows 2–5, ending with row 2 or row 4.

crochet pattern gallery

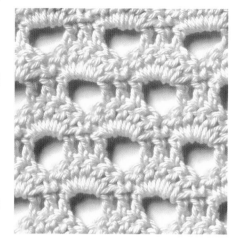

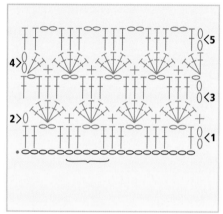

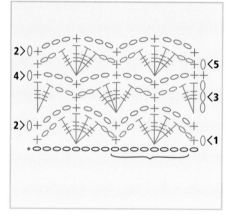

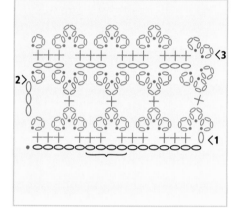

ARCH STITCH

NOTE
Even rows are right side of fabric.

INSTRUCTIONS
Chain a multiple of 5 stitches.

Row 1: Turn. Ch 2. Dc in 3rd ch from hook, *sk 2 chs, ch 2, 3 dcs*; repeat from *to) ending with 2 dcs.

Row 2: Turn. Ch 1. Sk 2 dcs, *5 dcs over ch-2, sk dc, sc in dc, sk dc*; repeat from * to * ending with sc in tch.

Row 3: Turn. Ch 3. Sk dc, *(dc in dc) 3 times, sk (dc, sc, dc), ch 2*; repeat from * to * across, ending with ch 1, dc in tch.

Row 4: Turn. Ch 2. 2 dcs in first dc, sk ch and dc, *sc in dc, sk dc, 5 dcs over ch-2, sk dc*; repeat from * to * across, ending with 3 dcs over tch.

Row 5: Turn. Ch 2. Sk first dc, dc in next, *sk (dc, sc, dc), ch 2, (dc in dc) 3 times*; repeat from * to * across, ending with dc in last dc, dc in tch.

Repeat rows 2–5, ending with row 3 or row 5.

PETAL STITCH

INSTRUCTIONS
Chain a multiple of 8 stitches + 1.

Row 1: Turn. Ch 1. *Sc, sk 3 chs, ch 2, 4 dtrs in next ch, sk 3 chs, ch 2*; repeat from * to * across, ending with sc.

Row 2: Turn. Ch 1. *Sc in sc, sk ch-2 and 1 dtr; ch 3, sc in dtr, sk 2 dtrs and ch-2; ch 3*; repeat from * to * across, ending with sc in sc, sk tch.

Row 3: Turn. Ch 3. 2 dtrs in sc, *sk ch-3, ch 2, sc in sc, sk ch-3, ch 2, 4 dtrs in sc*; repeat from * to * across, ending with 2 dtrs in sc, sk tch.

Row 4: Turn. Ch 1. Sc in first dtr, *sk next dtr and ch-2, ch 3, sc in sc, sk ch-2 and 2 dtrs; ch 3, sc in dtr*; repeat from * to * across, ending with sk ch-2 and dtr, ch 3, sc in dtr, sc in tch.

Row 5: Turn. Ch 1. Sk first sc, *sc in sc, sk ch-3, ch 2, 4 dtrs in sc, sk ch-3, ch 2* repeat from * to * across, ending with sc in last dtr.

Repeat rows 2–5.

DAISY LACE

NOTE
Picot — Ch 4, sl st into first ch.

INSTRUCTIONS
Chain a multiple of 4 stitches.

Row 1: Turn. Ch 1. 3 picots, sk 2 chs, *3 scs, sk 1 ch, 3 picots*; repeat from * to * across, ending with 3 scs, picot.

Row 2: Turn. Ch 3. Picot, *ch 3, picot, make 2 chs of next picot, sc in middle picot of three-picot group in row below, make last 2 chs of picot; rotate last picot down, bring yarn to front of work, sl st in 4th ch from hook to finish picot, picot*; repeat from * to * across, ending with 5 picots attaching 2nd picot to row below.

Row 3: Turn. *Rotate picots at either end of ch-3 down, sc in each of next 3 chs, 3 picots* across, ending with 3 scs, picot.

Repeat rows 2 and 3.

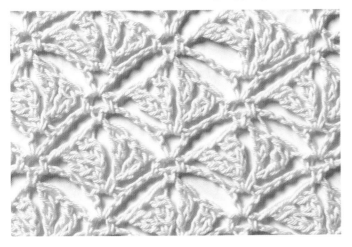

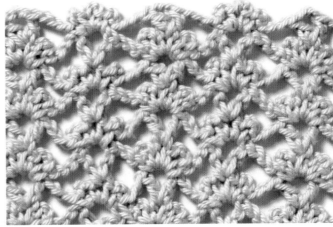

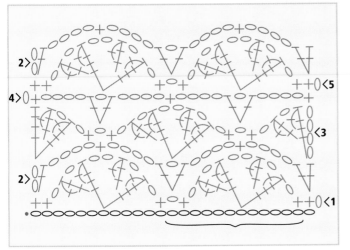

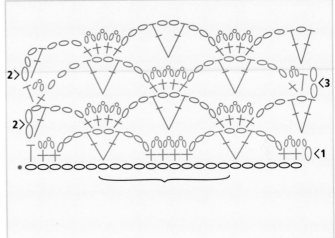

CRAZY DIAMOND

NOTE

Crazy Cluster — dtr in st indicated leaving 2 loops on hook, dc into center wrap of dtr, complete stitch, ch 1, tr into bottom wrap of dtr leaving 2 loops on hook, dc into bottom wrap of tr, complete st.

INSTRUCTIONS

Chain a multiple of 12 stitches + 1.

Row 1: Turn. Ch 1. Sc in 2nd ch from hook, *sc, ch 1, sk 4 chs, in next ch (crazy cluster, ch 2, crazy cluster), ch 1, sk 4 chs, sc in next, sk 1 ch, ch 1*; repeat from * to * across, ending with sc in last st.

Row 2: Turn. Ch 2. Dc in first sc, *sk (sc, ch-1, crazy cluster), ch 4, sc over ch-2, sk (crazy cluster, ch-1, sc); ch 4, over ch-1 (dc, ch 1, dc)*; repeat from * to * across, ending with 2 dc in last sc.

Row 3: Turn. Ch 4. Crazy cluster in first dc, *sk dc; ch 1, sc over ch-4, sk sc, ch 1, sc over ch-4, ch 1, sk dc; over ch-1 (crazy cluster, ch 2, crazy cluster)*; repeat from * to * ending with crazy cluster, dtr in tch.

Row 4: Turn. Ch 1. Sc in dtr, *sk (crazy cluster, ch-1, sc); ch 4; over ch-1 (dc, ch 1, dc), sk (sc, ch-1, crazy cluster), ch 4, sc over ch-2*; repeat from * to * ending with sc in tch.

TRIPLE V PICOT

INSTRUCTIONS

Chain a multiple of 11 stitches + 1.

ROW 1: Turn. Ch 3. Sc in 4th ch from hook, ch 3, *sc, sk 3 chs, ch 3, in next ch (dc, ch 2, dc), sk 3 chs, ch 3, (sc, ch 3) 3 times*; repeat from * to * across, ending with sc, ch 3, sc, ch, hdc.

Row 2: Turn. Ch 3. Dc in hdc, ch 3, *over next ch-2 (sc, ch 3) 4 times, over center ch-3 picot (dc, ch 2, dc), ch 3*; repeat from * to * ending with (dc, ch 1, dc) over tch.

Row 3: Turn. Ch 2. Over ch-1 (hdc, ch 3, sc), ch 3; *over center ch-3 picot (dc, ch 2, dc), ch 3; over next ch-2 (sc, ch 3) 4 times*; repeat from * to * ending with sc, ch 3, hdc over tch.

Repeat rows 2 and 3.

Row 5: Turn. Ch 1. Sc in sc, *sc over ch-4, ch 1, sk dc; in next ch-1 (crazy cluster, ch 2, crazy cluster), ch 1, sk dc, sc over ch-4, sk sc, ch 1*; repeat from * to * across, ending with sc over ch-4, sc in sc.

Repeat rows 2–5, ending with row 4.

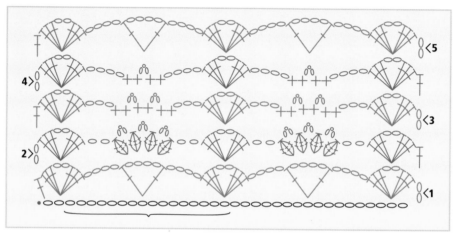

STRAWBERRY

INSTRUCTIONS

Chain a multiple of 16 stitches + 3.

Row 1: Turn. Ch 2. Sk 1 ch of base ch, *in next ch (3 dcs, ch 2, 3 dcs); ch 4, sk 7 chs, in next ch (dc, ch 4, dc); ch 4, sk 7 chs*; repeat from * to * across, ending with (3 dcs, ch 2, 3 dcs) in next ch, dc in last ch.

Row 2: Turn. Ch 2. Sk 4 dcs, over ch-2 (3 dcs, ch 2, 3 dcs), *sk (3 dcs, ch-4 and dc); ch 2, over ch-4 [(tr3tog, ch 3) 3 times, tr3tog]; sk (dc, ch-4 and 3 dcs), ch 2*; repeat from * to * across, ending with (3 dcs, ch 2, 3 dcs) over ch-2, dc in tch.

Row 3: Turn. Ch 2. Sk 4 dcs, *over ch-2 (3 dcs, ch 2, 3 dcs), sk 3 dcs and ch-2, (ch 3, sk tr3tog, 2 scs over ch-3) 3 times; sk (tr3tog, ch-2 and 3 dcs), ch 3*; repeat from * to * across, ending with (3 dcs, ch 2, 3 dcs) over ch-2, dc in tch.

Row 4: Turn. Ch 2. Sk 4 dcs, *over ch-2 (3 dcs, ch 2, 3 dcs), sk (3 dcs, ch 3 and 2 scs); ch 4, 2 scs over ch-3, ch 3, 2 scs over ch-3, ch 4, sk ch-3 and 3 dcs*; repeat from * to * across, ending with (3 dcs, ch 2, 3 dcs) over ch-2, dc in tch.

Row 5: Turn. Ch 2. Sk 4 dcs, *over ch-2 (3 dcs, ch 2, 3 dcs); sk (3 dcs, ch-4, 2 scs); ch 4, over ch-3 (dc, ch 4, dc), sk (2 scs, ch-4, 3 dcs), ch 4*; repeat from * to * across, ending with (3 dcs, ch 2, 3 dcs) over ch-2, dc in tch.

Repeat rows 2–5, ending with row 4.

PINEAPPLE

NOTE

There are 8 dcs in the base of each center pineapple, 6 dcs and a ch 2 or 7 dcs in the base of each pineapple on the left and right.

INSTRUCTIONS

Chain a multiple of 22 stitches + 1.

Row 1: Turn. Ch 2 (counts as first dc). 7 dcs in first ch of base ch, *sk 7 chs, ch 5, sc, (sk 1 ch, ch 3, sc) 3 times, sk 7 chs, ch 5, 8 dcs in next ch*; repeat from * to * across, ending with 7 dcs in last ch.

Row 2: Turn. Ch 4. Sk first dc, sc in dc, (ch 3, sc in dc) 4 times, *sk (dc, ch-5 and sc), ch 5, (sc over ch-3, ch 3) 2 times, sc over ch-3, sk (sc, ch-5 and dc), ch 5, (sc in dc, ch 3) 5 times, sc in dc*; repeat from * to * across, ending with ch 2, dc in tch.

Row 3: Turn. Ch 4. (Sc over ch-3, ch 3) 3 times, sc over ch-3, *sk (sc, ch-5, sc), ch 5, sc over ch-3, ch 3, sc over ch-3, sk (sc, ch-5, and sc), ch 5, (sc over ch-3, ch 3) 4 times, sc over ch-3*; repeat from * to * across, ending with ch 2, dc over tch.

Row 4: Turn. Ch 4. (Sc over ch-3, ch 3) 2 times, sc over ch-3, *sk (sc, ch-5, sc), ch 5, over ch-3 (sc, ch 3, sc); sk (sc, ch-5, sc), ch 5, (sc over ch-3, ch 3) 2 times, sc over ch-3*; repeat from * to * across, ending with ch 2, dc over tch.

Row 5: Turn. Ch 4. Sc over ch-3, ch 3, sc over ch-3, *sk (sc, ch-5, sc), ch 5, 8 dcs over ch-3, sk (sc, ch-5, sc), ch 5, (sc over ch-3, ch 3) 2 times, sc over ch-3*; repeat from * to * across, ending with ch 2, dc over tch.

Row 6: Turn. Ch 4. *Sc over ch-3, sk (sc, ch-5, dc), ch 5, (sc in dc, ch 3) 5 times, sc in dc, sk (dc, ch-5, sc), ch 5, sc over ch-3, ch 3, sc over ch-3, ch 5*; repeat from * to * across, ending with ch 2, dc over tch.

Row 7: Turn. Ch 4. Sc over ch-2, *sk (sc, ch-5, sc), ch 5, (sc over ch-3, ch 3) 4 times, sc over ch-3, sk (sc, ch-5, sc), ch 5, over ch-3 (sc, ch 3, sc)*; repeat from * to * across, ending with (sc, ch 2, dc) over tch.

Row 8: Turn. Ch 2 (counts as first dc). 7 dcs over ch-2, *sk (sc, ch-5, sc), ch 5, (sc, ch 3) 3 times, sc over ch-3; sk (sc, ch-5, sc), ch 5, 8 dcs over ch-3*; repeat from * to * across, ending with 7 dcs over tch.

Repeat rows 2–8, ending with row 4 or row 6.

153

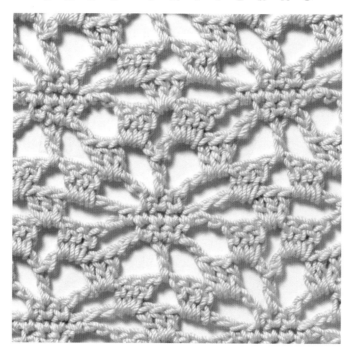

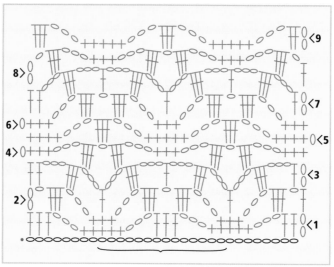

SPIDER WEB LACE

INSTRUCTIONS

Chain a multiple of 14 stitches + 2.

Row 1: Turn. Ch 2. 2 dcs, *sk 3 chs, ch 3, 5 scs, sk 3 chs, ch 3, 3 dcs*; repeat from * to * across, ending with 3 dcs.

Row 2: Turn. Ch 2. *Sk 3 dcs, ch 1, 3 dcs over ch-3, sk sc, ch 3, (sc in sc) 3 times, sk sc, ch 3, 3 dcs over ch-3*; repeat from * to * across, ending with sk 2 dcs, ch 1, dc in tch.

Row 3: Turn. Ch 2. *Dc over ch-1, sk 3 dcs, ch 3, 3 dcs over ch-3, sk sc, ch 3, dc in sc, sk sc, ch 3, 3 dcs over ch-3, sk 3 dcs, ch 3*; repeat from * to * across, ending with dc over ch-1, dc in tch.

Row 4: Turn. Ch 1. (Sc in dc) 2 times, *sc over ch-3, sk 3 dcs, ch 3, 3 dcs over ch-3, sk dc, ch 1, 3 dcs over ch-3, sk 3 dcs, ch 3, sc over ch-3, sc in dc*; repeat from * to * across, ending with sc over ch-3, sc in dc, sc in tch.

Row 5: Turn. Ch 1. *(Sc in sc) 3 times, sc over ch-3, ch 3, sk 3 dcs, 3 dcs over ch-1, ch 3, sk 3 dcs, sc over ch-3*; repeat from * to * across, ending with sc over ch-3, (sc in sc) 3 times, sk tch.

Row 6: Turn. Ch 1. *(Sc in sc) 3 times, sk sc, ch 3, 3 dcs over ch-3, sk 3 dcs, ch 1, 3 dcs over ch-3, sk sc, ch 3*; repeat from * to * across, ending with (sc in sc) 3 times, sk tch.

Row 7: Turn. Ch 2. Dc in 2nd sc, *sk sc, ch 3, 3 dcs over ch-3, sk 3 dcs, ch 3, dc over ch-1, sk 3 dcs, ch 3, 3 dcs over ch-3, sk sc, ch 3, dc in sc*; repeat from * to * across, ending with sk sc, (dc in sc) 2 times, sk tch.

Row 8: Turn. Ch 2. Sk 2 dcs, *ch 1, 3 dcs over ch-3, sk 3 dcs, ch 3, sc over ch-3, sc in dc, sc over ch-3, sk 3 dcs, ch 3, 3 dcs over ch-3, sk dc*; repeat from * to * across, ending with dc in tch.

Row 9: Turn. Ch 2. 2 dcs over ch-1, *sk 3 dcs, ch 3, sc over ch-3, (sc in sc) 3 times, sc over ch-3, sk 3 dcs, ch 3, 3 dcs over ch-1*; repeat from * to * across, ending with 3 dcs over ch-1, sk tch.

Repeat rows 2–9, ending with row 5 or row 9.

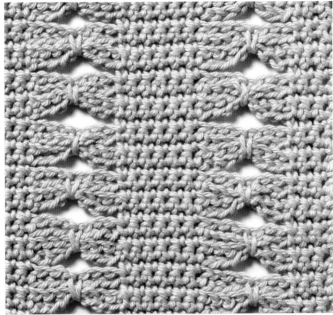

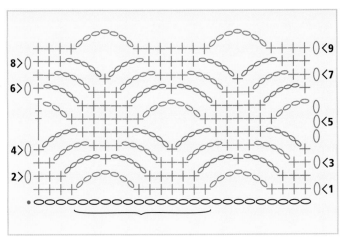

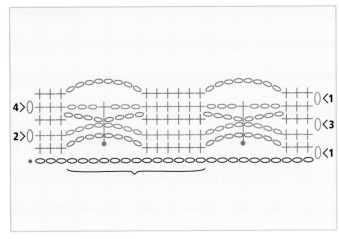

155

STACKED DIAMONDS

INSTRUCTIONS

Chain a multiple of 12 stitches + 1.

Row 1: Turn. Ch 1. 4 scs, *sk 5 chs, ch 7, 7 scs*; repeat from * to * across, ending with 4 scs.

Row 2: Turn. Ch 1. 3 scs, *sk sc, ch 5, sc over ch-7, sk sc, ch 5, 5 scs*; repeat from * to * across, ending with 3 scs, sk tch.

Row 3: Turn. Ch 1. 2 scs, *sk sc, ch 5, sc over ch-5, sc in sc, sc over next ch-5, sk sc, ch 5, 3 scs*; repeat from * to * across, ending with 2 scs, sk tch.

Row 4: Turn. Ch 1. *Sc, sk sc, ch 5, sc over ch-5, 3 scs, sc over ch-5, sk sc, ch 5*; repeat from * to * across, ending with sc, sk tch.

Row 5: Turn. Ch 7. *Sc over ch-5, 5 scs, sc over ch-5, sk sc, ch 7*; repeat from * to * across, ending with sc over ch-5, ch 3, dtr in sc, sk tch.

Row 6: Turn. Ch 1. Sc in dtr, sk ch-3 and sc, *ch 5, 5 scs, sk sc, ch 5, sc over ch-7, sk sc*; repeat from * to * across, ending with sk sc, ch 5, sc over tch.

Row 7: Turn. Ch 1. *Sc in sc, sc over ch-5, sk sc, ch 5, 3 scs, sk sc, ch 5, sc over ch-5*; repeat from * to * across, ending with sk sc, ch 5, sc over ch-5, sc in sc, sk tch.

BOW TIES

NOTE

Even rows are right side of fabric.

INSTRUCTIONS

Chain a multiple of 13 stitches.

Rows 1, 2 and 3: Turn. Ch 1. 3 scs, *ch 8, sk 7 chs, 6 scs*; repeat from * to * across, ending with 3 scs; on all rows except first, sk tch.

Row 4: Turn. Ch 1. 3 scs, *ch 3, sc over ch-8s in three rows below, ch 3, 6 scs*; repeat from * to * across, ending with 3 scs, sk tch.

Repeat rows 1–4.

Row 8: Turn. Ch 1. 2 scs, *(sc over ch-5, sk sc, ch 5, sc in sc, sk sc, ch 5, sc over ch-5, 3 scs*; repeat from * to * across, ending with sc over ch-5, 2 scs, sk tch.

Row 9: Turn. Ch 1. 3 scs, *sc over ch-5, sk sc, ch 7, sc over ch-5, 5 scs*; repeat from * to * across, ending with sc over ch-5, 3 scs, sk tch.

Repeat rows 2–9.

crochet pattern gallery

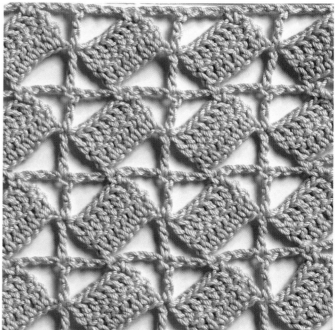

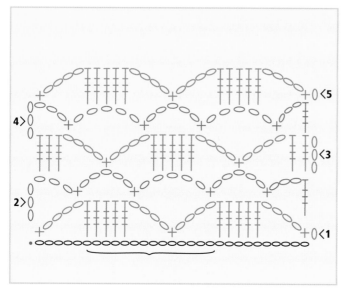

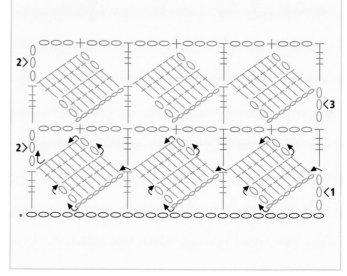

156

SQUARES IN DIAMONDS

INSTRUCTIONS

Chain a multiple of 14 stitches + 1.

Row 1: Turn. Ch 1. Sc, *sk 4 chs, ch 4, (dtr in ch) 5 times, sk 4 chs, ch 4, sc in next ch*; repeat from * to * ending with sc.

Row 2: Turn. Ch 6. *Sc over ch-4, sk 5 dtrs, ch 5, sc over ch-4, sk sc, ch 5*; repeat from * to * across, ending with sc over ch-4, ch 3, dtr in sc, sk tch.

Row 3: Turn. Ch 3. Dtr in dtr, dtr over ch-3, *sk sc, ch 4, sc over ch-5, sk sc, ch 4, 5 dtrs over ch-5*; repeat from * to * across, ending with 3 dtrs over tch.

Row 4: Turn. Ch 6. *Sc over ch-4, sk sc, ch 5, sc over ch-4, sk 5 dtrs, ch 5*; repeat from * to * across, ending with sc over ch-4, ch 3, sk dtr, dtr in dtr, sk tch.

Row 5: Turn. Ch 1. Sc in dtr, sk ch-3 and sc, *ch 4, 5 dtrs over ch-5, sk sc, ch 4, sc over ch-5, sk sc*; repeat from * to * across, ending with sc over tch.

Repeat rows 2–5.

DIAMONDS IN SQUARES

INSTRUCTIONS

Chain a multiple of 8 stitches + 1.

Row 1: Turn. Ch 10 (counts as ch 3 tch and ch 7). Sl st in 15th ch from hook, *turn, ch 2, (dc in next ch of ch-7) 7 times, turn, ch 2, sk first dc, (dc in dc) 6 times, dc in top of ch-2, sk 3 chs of base ch, dtr in next, sk 3 chs of base ch, ch 7, sl st in next ch of base ch*; repeat from * to * across, ending with dtr in last ch.

Row 2: Turn. Ch 6. *Sc between ch-2 and dc at top of diamond made in previous row, ch 3, dtr in dtr, ch 3*; repeat from * to * across, ending with dtr in tch.

Row 3: Turn. Ch 3, [Sk dtr and ch-3, *ch 7, sl st in sc, ch 2, (dc in next ch of ch-7) 7 times; turn, ch 2, sk first dc, (dc in dc) 6 times, dc in top of ch-2, sk 3 chs, dtr in dtr, sk ch-3*; repeat from * to * across, ending with dtr in last ch.

Repeat rows 2–3, ending with row 2.

WAVES, RIPPLES, AND CHEVRONS

Waves, ripples and chevrons produce undulating grounds. Wave patterns are composed of a series of stepped stitches, for instance sc, hdc, dc, tr, dc, hdc, sc. Ripples and chevrons use matched increases and decreases separated by plain stitches.

These simple stitch patterns are ideal for take-along projects. You can easily memorize the pattern so you don't have to carry a pattern booklet. Color changes every few rows are traditional, lending interest to the patterns. Another method of adding interest is to alternate rows of solid and lace stitches as in Textured Wave and Lattice Chevron.

The classic ripple pattern is one of the most beloved afghan patterns, used for baby blankets, throws, and bedspreads. Garments, especially capes, vests, and shawls, also use this variation. Work patterns vertically to add height to the body.

For an explanation of the chart symbols, see the inside back cover.

For instructions on working edge stitches (turning chains) see sidebar on page 141.

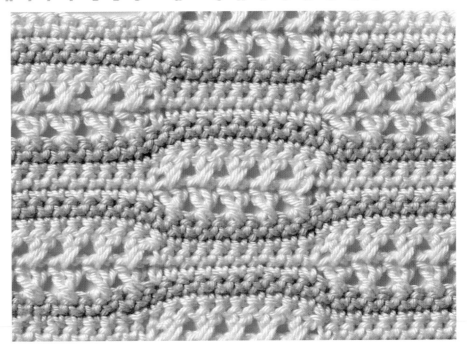

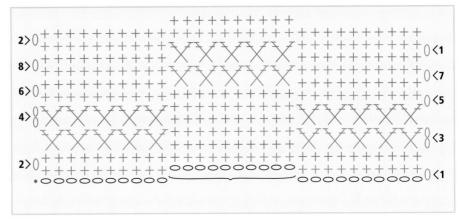

157

TEXTURED WAVE

INSTRUCTIONS

Chain a minimum of 20 stitches with additional stitches in multiples of 10.

Rows 1 and 2: Turn. With color A ch 1. Sc across, sk tch (no tch on first row).

Row 3: Turn. With color B ch 2. *(Sk st, dc in next, dc in skipped st) 5 times, 10 scs*; repeat from * to * across, sk tch.

Row 4: Repeat row 3 working crossed dcs in dcs and scs in scs.

Rows 5 and 6: Turn. With color A ch 1. Sc across, sk tch.

Row 7: Turn. With color B ch 1. *10 scs, (sk st, dc in next, dc in skipped st) 5 times*; repeat from * to * across, sk tch.

Row 8: Repeat row 7 working scs in scs and crossed dcs in dcs.

Repeat rows 1–8.

crochet pattern gallery

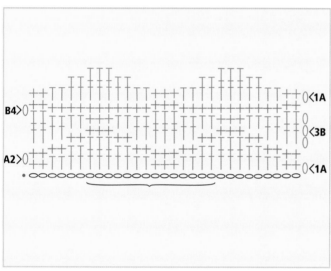

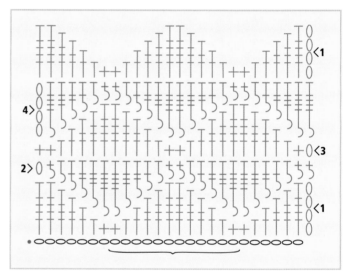

158

LONG WAVE

INSTRUCTIONS

Chain a multiple of 14 stitches + 1.

Row 1: Turn. With color A ch 1. 2 scs, *2 hdcs, 2 dcs, 3 trs, 2 dcs, 2 hdcs, 3 scs*; repeat from * to * across, ending with 2 scs.

Row 2: Turn. Ch 1. Sc across, sk tch.

Row 3: Turn. With color B ch 3. 2 trs, *2 dcs, 2 hdcs, 3 scs, 2 hdcs, 2 dcs, 3 trs*; repeat from * to * across, ending with 2 trs, sk tch.

Row 4: Turn. Ch 1. Sc across, sk tch.

Repeat rows 1–4.

DOUBLE WAVE

INSTRUCTIONS

Chain a multiple of 12 stitches + 1.

Row 1: Turn. Ch 4. Beginning in 5th ch from hook *trtr, dtr, tr, dc, hdc, 2 scs, hdc, dc, tr, dtr, trtr*; repeat from * to * ending with 2 trtrs.

Row 2: Turn. Ch 1. Sk first trtr, *FPsc, FPhdc, FPdc, FPtr, FPdtr, 2 FPtrtrs, FPdtr, FPtr, FPdc, FPhdc, FPsc*; repeat from * to * ending with FPsc, FPsc in tch.

Row 3: Turn. Ch 1. Sk first sc, *sc, hdc, dc, tr, dtr, 2 trtrs, dtr, tr, dc, hdc, sc*; repeat from * to * across, ending with sc, sc in tch.

Row 4: Turn. Ch 4. Sk first sc, *FPtrtr, FPdtr, FPtr, FPdc, FPhdc, 2 FPscs, FPhdc, FPdc, FPtr, FPdtr, FPtrtr*; repeat from * to * ending with FPtrtr in sc, FPtrtr in tch.

Repeat rows 1–4, ending with row 2 or row 4.

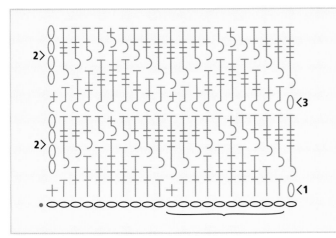

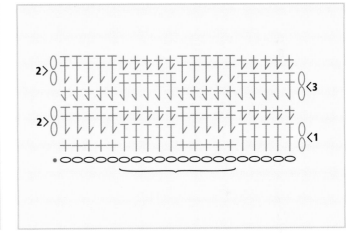

RAISED WAVE

INSTRUCTIONS

Chain a multiple of 10 stitches + 1.

Row 1: Turn. Ch 1. Beginning in 3rd ch from hook *hdc, dc, tr, dtr, trtr, dtr, tr, dc, hdc, sc*; repeat from * to * ending with sc.

Row 2: Turn. Ch 4. Sk sc, *FPdtr, FPtr, FPdc, FPhdc, FPsc, FPhdc, FPdc, FPtr, FPdtr, FPtrtr*; repeat from * to * ending with FPtrtr in tch.

Row 3: Turn. Ch 1. Sk FPtrtr, *BPhdc, BPdc, BPtr, BPdtr, BPtrtr, BPdtr, BPtr, BPdc, BPhdc, BPsc*; repeat from * to * ending with BPsc in tch.

Repeat rows 2 and 3.

UNDULATING WAVES

INSTRUCTIONS

Chain a multiple of 10 stitches.

Row 1: Turn. Ch 2. Beginning in 3rd ch from hook *5 dcs, 5 scs*; repeat from * to * across.

Row 2: Turn. Ch 2. *(FLdc in sc) 5 times, (FLsc in dc) 5 times*; repeat from * to * across, sk tch.

Row 3: Turn. Ch 2. *(BLdc in sc) 5 times, (BLsc in dc) 5 times*; repeat from * to * across, sk tch.

Repeat rows 2 and 3.

crochet pattern gallery

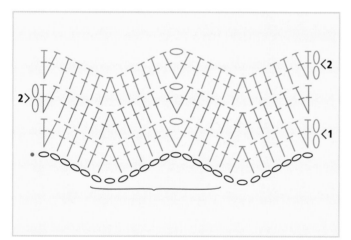

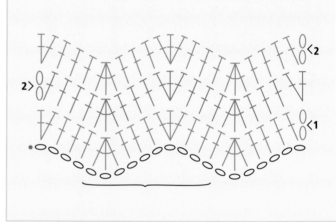

160

CLASSIC RIPPLE

INSTRUCTIONS

Chain a multiple of 12 stitches + 1.

Row 1: Turn. Ch 2. 2 dcs in 3rd ch from hook, *4 dcs, (dc2tog skipping 1 ch between dcs), 4 dcs; in next ch (dc, ch 1, dc)*; repeat from * to * across, ending with 2 dcs in last ch.

Row 2: Turn. Ch 2. 2 dcs in first dc, *4 dcs, (dc2tog skipping dc2tog between dcs), 4 dcs; over ch-1 (dc, ch 1, dc)*; repeat from * to * across, ending with 2 dcs in last dc, sk tch.

Repeat row 2.

VARIATIONS

Alternate 2 or 3 colors.

CLOSED RIPPLE

INSTRUCTIONS

Chain a multiple of 10 stitches + 1.

Row 1: Turn. Ch 2. Dc in 3rd ch from hook, *3 dcs, over 3 chs dc3tog, 3 dcs, 3 dcs in next ch*; repeat from * to * across, ending with 2 dcs in last ch.

Row 2: Turn. Ch 2. Dc in first dc, *3 dcs, over (dc, dc3tog, dc) dc3tog, 3 dcs, 3 dcs in next dc*; repeat from * to * across, ending with 2 dcs in tch.

Repeat row 2.

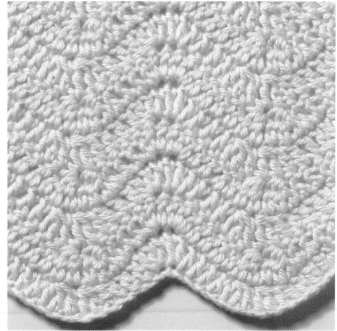

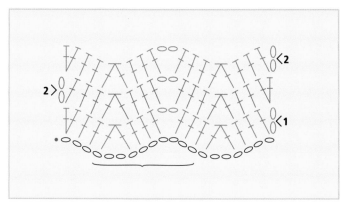

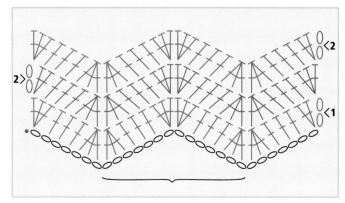

PEEPHOLE CHEVRON

INSTRUCTIONS

Chain a multiple of 10 stitches.

Row 1: Turn. Ch 2. Beginning in 3rd ch from hook *3 dcs, dc2tog skipping 2 chs between dcs, 3 dcs, ch 2*; repeat from * to * ending with 2 dcs in last ch.

Row 2: Turn. Ch 2. Dc in first dc, *2 dcs, dc2tog skipping dc2tog between dcs, 2 dcs, dc over ch-2, ch 2, dc over ch-2*; repeat from * to * ending with 2 dcs in tch.

Repeat row 2.

SHARP CHEVRON

INSTRUCTIONS

Chain a multiple of 14 stitches.

Row 1: Turn. Ch 2. 2 dcs in 3rd ch from hook, *3 dcs, dc3tog 2 times, 3 dcs, (3 dcs in next st) 2 times*; repeat from * to * across, ending with 3 dcs in last ch.

Row 2: Turn. Ch 2. 2 dcs in first dc, *3 dcs, dc3tog 2 times, 3 dcs, (3 dcs in next st) 2 times*; repeat from * to * across, ending with 3 dcs in tch.

Repeat row 2.

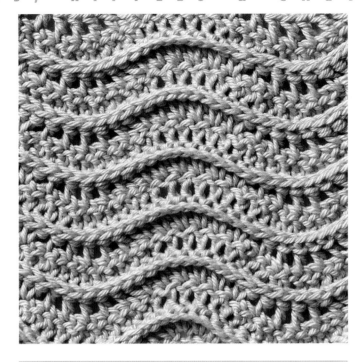

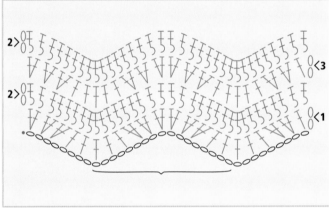

WAVY CHEVRON

INSTRUCTIONS

Chain a multiple of 17 stitches.

Row 1: Turn. Ch 2. Dc in 3rd ch from hook, (2 dcs in next ch) 2 times, *(sk ch, dc) 5 times, sk ch, (2 dcs in next ch) 6 times*; repeat from * to * across, ending with (2 dcs in next ch) 3 times.

Row 2: Turn. Ch 2. FPdc across, ending with FPdc in tch.

Row 3: Turn. Ch 2. Dc in first dc, (2 dcs in next dc) 2 times, *(sk st, dc) 5 times; sk st, (2 dcs in next st) 6 times*; repeat from * to * across, ending with (2 dcs in next st) 3times, sk tch.

Repeat rows 2 and 3.

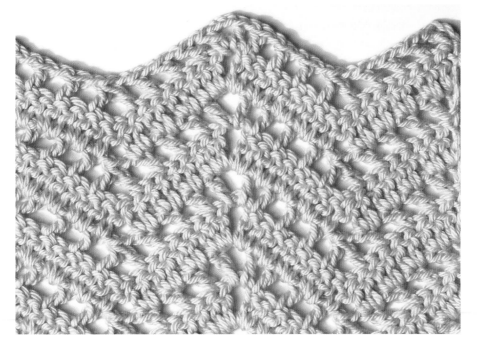

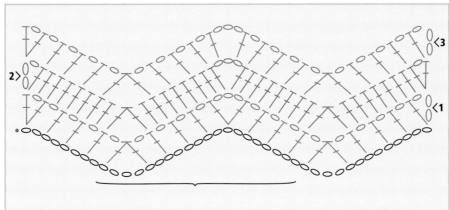

163

LATTICE CHEVRON

INSTRUCTIONS

Chain a multiple of 20 stitches + 1.

Row 1: Turn. Ch 3. Dc in 4th ch from hook, *(sk 1 ch, ch 1, dc) 3 times; sk 1 ch, ch 1, dc2tog skipping 3 chs between dcs; (sk 1 ch, ch 1, dc) 3 times; sk 1 ch, ch 1, in next st (dc, ch 3, dc)*; repeat from * to * ending with (dc, ch, dc) in last ch.

Row 2: Turn. Ch 3. (Dc in dc, dc over ch) 4 times; *dc2tog skipping (ch, dc2tog, ch) between dcs; (dc over ch, dc in dc) 3 times; 2 dcs over ch-3, ch 3, 2 dcs over ch-3, (dc in dc, dc over ch) 3 times*repeat from * to * across, ending with (dc over ch, dc in dc) 3 times, dc over ch; (dc, ch, dc) in tch.

Row 3: Turn. Ch 3. Dc in first dc, sk ch, ch 1, *(dc, sk 1 dc, ch 1) 3 times; dc2tog skipping (dc, dc2tog, dc) between dcs; (sk dc, ch 1, dc) 3 times, ch 1; over ch-3 (dc, ch 3, dc), ch 1*, repeat from * to * across, ending with (dc, ch 1, dc) in tch.

Repeat rows 2 and 3.

ANGLED PATTERNS

Working crochet stitches into previous stitches of the row currently being made forms angled patterns. Angled patterns draw the eye along the diagonal instead of horizontally along the rows as in most crochet.

Fabrics created from angled patterns are more flexible than other crocheted fabrics with the same density of yarn. Because of this, angled patterns are ideal for close-fitting garments. Diagonal lines also add interest to flat items such as scarves, shawls, envelope bags, and afghans.

For an explanation of chart symbols, see the inside back cover.

For instructions on working edge stitches (turning chains) see sidebar on page 141.

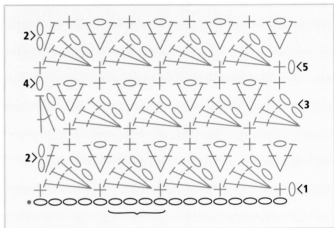

FLYING SHELL

INSTRUCTIONS

Chain a multiple of 4 stitches + 1.

Row 1: Turn. Ch 1. *Sc, ch 2, 3 dcs in sc just made, sk 3 chs*; repeat from * to * across, ending with sc.

Row 2: Turn. Ch 2. Dc in first sc, *sk 3 dcs, sc in top of ch-2, in sc (dc, ch 1, dc)*; repeat from * to * across, ending with (dc, ch 1, dc) in sc, sk tch.

Row 3: Turn. Ch 2. 3 dcs in first dc, *sk ch-1 and dc, sc in sc, ch 2, 3 dcs in sc just made*; repeat from * to * across, ending with sc in sc, ch 2, dc2tog over dc and tch.

Row 4: Turn. Ch 1. Sk dc2tog and ch-2, *in sc (dc, ch 1, dc), sk 3 dcs, sc in top of ch-2*; repeat from * to * across, ending with sc in top of ch-2.

Row 5: Turn. Ch 1. *Sc in sc, ch 2, 3 dcs in sc just made, sk (dc, ch-1, dc)*; repeat from * to * across, ending with sc.

Repeat rows 2–5, ending with row 2 or row 4.

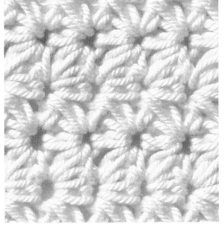

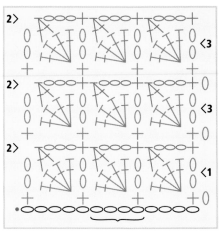

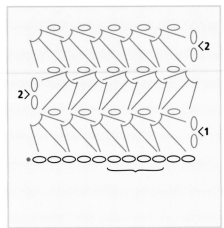

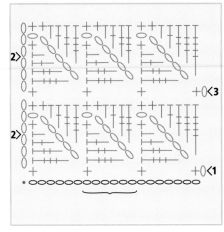

DIAGONAL SHELL

INSTRUCTIONS

Chain a multiple of 4 stitches + 1.

Row 1: Turn. Ch 1. *Sc, ch 2, 4 dcs in sc just made, sk 3 chs*; repeat from * to * across, ending with sc, ch 2.

Row 2: Turn. *Sk dc, dc2tog over next 2 dcs, sk dc, ch 3, sc in top of ch-2*; repeat from * to * across, ending with sc in top of ch-2.

Row 3: Turn. Ch 1. *Sc in sc, ch 2, 4 dcs in sc just made, sk ch-3*; repeat from * to * across, ending with sc, ch 2.

Repeat rows 2 and 3, ending with row 2.

STAR STITCH
Other Name: Marguerite

INSTRUCTIONS

Chain a multiple of 2 stitches + 1.

Row 1: Turn. Ch 3. Puff stitch over (2nd ch from hook, sk 3rd ch, 4th ch from hook, sk next ch, 6th ch from hook), ch 1, *puff stitch over top of puff stitch just made, same ch as last strand of previous puff stitch, sk 1 ch, next ch*; repeat from * to * ending with puff stitch.

Row 2: Turn. Ch 3. Puff stitch over (2nd ch from hook, sk 3rd ch, top of puff stitch, sk ch, top of next puff stitch), *ch 1, puff stitch over (top of puff stitch just made, top of same puff stitch in row below used by last strand of previous puff stitch, sk ch-1, top of next puff stitch in row below)*; repeat from * to * ending with puff stitch over (top of puff stitch just made, top of same puff stitch in row below used by last strand of previous puff stitch, sk ch-1, top of tch).

Repeat row 2.

WEDGES

INSTRUCTIONS

Chain a multiple of 6 stitches + 1.

Row 1: Turn. Ch 1. *Sc, ch 6, working back along ch-6 just made, (sk first ch, sc, hdc, dc, tr, dtr), sk 5 chs of base ch*; repeat from * to * across, ending with sc.

Row 2: Turn. Ch 6. *Working back along same ch-6 used in last row (sc, sc, hdc, dc, tr, dtr)*; repeat from * to * across, ending with trtr in tch.

Row 3: Turn. Ch 1. *Sc in trtr, ch 6, working back along ch-6 just made, (sk first ch, sc, hdc, dc, tr, dtr), sc in sc*; repeat from * to * across, ending with sc in sc, sk tch.

Repeat rows 2 and 3, ending with row 2.

165

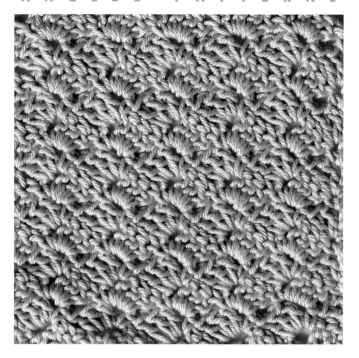

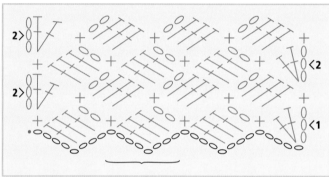

CROSSHATCH

INSTRUCTIONS

Chain a multiple of 8 stitches + 5.

Row 1: Turn. Ch 3. 2 dcs in first ch of base ch, sk 3 chs, *sc in next, ch 2, dc in next 3 chs, sk 4 chs*; repeat from * to * across, ending with sc.

Row 2: Turn. Ch 3. 2 dcs in sc, sk 3 dcs, *sc in top of ch-2, ch 2, 3 dcs over ch-2, sk sc and 3 dcs*; repeat from * to * across, ending with sk sc and 2 dcs, sc in tch.

Repeat row 2.

VARIATION

Change color every row.

SPIKED AND CROSSED STITCH PATTERNS

Spiked and crossed stitches are worked over other stitches to distribute color and/or texture within a piece. Work spiked stitches (also called dropped stitches) over multiple rows. Work crossed stitches over stitches in the same row.

These bold and colorful stitches are ideal for adult garments and accessories such as hats, bags, and purses.

For an explanation of chart symbols, see the inside back cover.

For instructions on working edge stitches (turning chains) see sidebar on page 141.

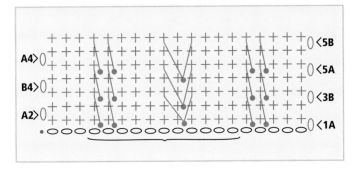

BLOCKS AND VS

NOTES

Work the spike stitch by making a regular sc *except* insert the hook into the space between stitches 2 or 3 rows below. Change yarn color every two rows, after 1 forward and 1 return row. Work the spike stitches on the forward row. The return row is just sc.

INSTRUCTIONS

Chain a multiple of 11 stitches + 8.

Row 1: Turn. With color A ch 1. Sc across.

Row 2: Turn. Ch 1. Sc across.

Row 3: Turn. With color B ch 1. *3 scs, (sc inserting hook into space 2 rows below) 2 times, 3 scs; sc inserting hook 2 rows below and one st ahead, sc; sc inserting hook in same space as previous spike stitch*; repeat from * to * across, ending with 3 scs, sk tch.

Row 4: Same as row 2.

Row 5: Turn. With color A ch 1. *3 scs, (sc inserting hook into space 2 rows below) 2 times; 3 scs, sc inserting hook 3 rows below and one st ahead, sc; sc inserting hook in same space as previous spike stitch*; repeat from * to * across, ending with (sc inserting hook into space 2 rows below) 2 times, 3 scs, sk tch.

Repeat rows 4–5 changing color every 2 rows.

VARIATIONS

Work the pattern with just blocks or just Vs. Vary the spacing between the blocks and/or Vs. For bolder spike stitch, use a dc spike stitch.

167

crochet pattern gallery

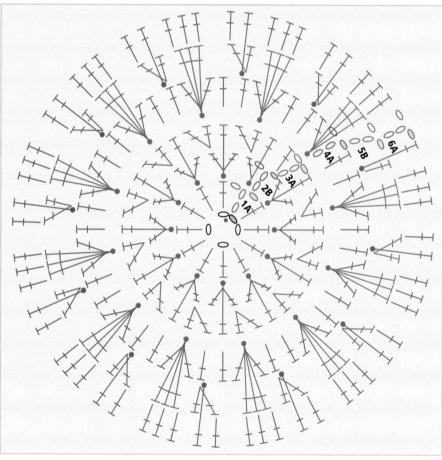

SUNBURST

NOTE
Work the spike stitch by making a regular dc except insert the hook into the top of the dc 2 rows below.

INSTRUCTIONS
With color A ch 4, sl st to join.

Rnd 1: Ch 3. 11 dcs in ring, sl st in 2nd ch of rnd.

Rnd 2: With color B ch 3. Dc in 2nd ch of rnd 1, *2 dcs in dc*; repeat from * to * around ending with sl st in 2nd ch of rnd.

Rnd 3: With color A ch 3. Dc in 2nd ch of previous rnd, dc in 2nd ch of rnd 1, *2 dcs in dc, sk dc, dc in top of dc of rnd 1*; repeat from * to * around ending with dc in top of dc of rnd 1, sk dc, sl st in 2nd ch of rnd.

Rnd 4: Ch 3. Dc in 2nd ch of previous rnd, *2 dcs, 2 dcs in next dc*; repeat from * to * around ending with 2 dcs, sl st in 2nd ch of rnd.

Rnd 5: With color B ch 3. 3 dcs into 3rd ch 2 rows below, *sk dc, 2 dcs in next dc, sk 2 dcs, 3 dcs in dc 2 rows below (same dc as one containing 2 dcs in dc of rnd 4), sk 2 dcs*; repeat from * to * around ending with 3 dcs in 2 rows below, sk dc, dc, sl st in 2nd ch of rnd.

Rnd 6: With color A ch 3. *(dc in dc of spike stitch) 3 times, sk dc, dc in dc 2 rows below (same dc as one containing 2 dcs in dc of rnd 5), dc in dc*; repeat from * to * around ending with (dc in dc of spike stitch) 3 times, sk dc, dc in dc 2 rows below, sl st in 2nd ch of rnd.

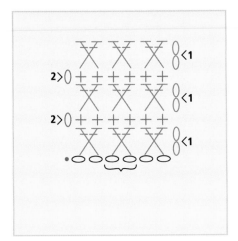

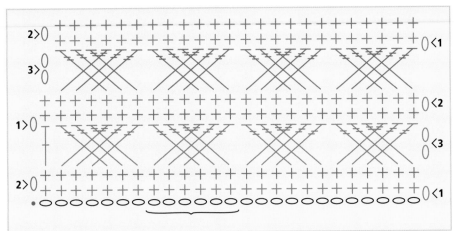

EXCHANGE STITCH

NOTE

Work the second dc behind first dc in each crossed pair.

INSTRUCTIONS

Chain a multiple of 2 stitches.

Row 1: Turn. Ch 2. (Sk 1 st, dc in next, dc in skipped st) across.

Row 2: Turn. Ch 1. Sc across, sk tch.

Repeat rows 1 and 2.

VARIATIONS

Substitute tcs or taller stitches for the dcs in row 1.

CROSSED TREBLES

NOTE

To work tr across trs, yo twice on hook, insert hook from front to back over 3 trs already completed; holding ball yarn behind stitch being worked, yo and pull loop through to front; yo and work off loops 2 at a time.

INSTRUCTIONS

Chain a multiple of 6 stitches + 1.

Rows 1 and 2: Turn. Ch 1. Sc across, on all rows after first row sk tch.

Row 3: Turn. Ch 2. *Sk 3 scs, 3 trs, working around three trs just made tr in each of 3 skipped scs*; repeat from * to * across, ending with dc in last sc, sk tch.

Repeat rows 1–3.

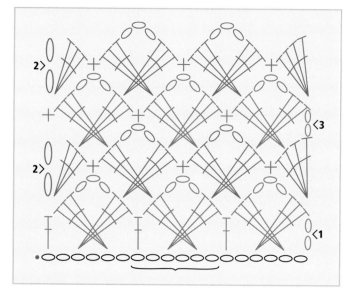

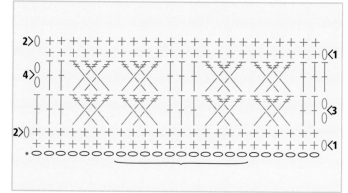

crochet pattern gallery

WOVEN SHELL STITCH

NOTE

Work around dcs by inserting hook from front to back over 3 dcs already completed; with ball yarn in back yo, pull loop through to front and high enough to clear stems of 3 dcs already completed; work off loops 2 at a time.

INSTRUCTIONS

Chain a multiple of 6 stitches.

Row 1: Turn. Ch 2. *Sk 3 chs of base ch, 3 dcs in 4th ch, ch 3, count back 2 chs of base ch; in 2nd of chs skipped work 3 dcs; sk 1 ch from first of ch 3 groups worked, dc in next*; repeat from * to * across, ending with dc in last ch.

Row 2: Turn. Ch 2. 3 dcs in dc, sk 3 dcs, *sc over ch-3, sk 5 dcs, 3 dcs in next; ch 3, in 2nd dc skipped work 3 dcs*; repeat from * to * across, ending with sc over ch-3, 4 dcs in tch.

Row 3: Turn. Ch 2. Sk (4 dcs, sc, dc), 3 dcs in next dc, ch 3, in 3rd dc skipped work 3 dcs, *sc over ch-3, sk (3 dcs, sc, dc), 3 dcs in next dc, ch 3, in 2nd dc skipped work 3 dcs*; repeat from * to * ending with sc in tch.

Repeat rows 2 and 3.

PAIRED CROSSES

NOTES

Make a tr in front of 2 trs already in place — yo 2 times, bring hook and ball yarn to front of work, insert hook in stitch from front to back, fold 2 trs already in place to back and bring hook through gap to front of work, yo, pull yarn through stitch, work off loops 2 at a time.

Make a tr in behind 2 trs already in place — yo 2 times, insert hook in stitch from front to back behind 2 trs already in place, fold 2 trs forward, yo, pull yarn through stitch, work off loops 2 at a time.

INSTRUCTIONS

Chain a multiple of 11 stitches + 2.

Rows 1 and 2: Turn. Ch 1. Sc across, on all rows after first row sk tch.

Row 3: Turn. Ch 2. 2 dcs, *sk 2 scs; work 2 trs; in front of 2 trs just made, work 2 trs in skipped scs; sk 2 scs; work 2 trs; behind 2 trs just made work 2 trs in skipped scs; 3 dcs*; repeat from * to *, ending with 3 dcs.

Row 4: Turn. Ch 2. Sk 1st dc; work 2 dcs, *sk 2 trs, make 2 trs; in front of 2 trs just made work 2 trs in skipped trs; sk 2 trs, work 2 trs in skipped trs; behind 2 trs just made, work 2 trs in skipped trs; 3 dcs in 3 dcs*; repeat from * to *, ending with 2 dcs in last 2 dcs; dc in tch.

Repeat rows 1–4.

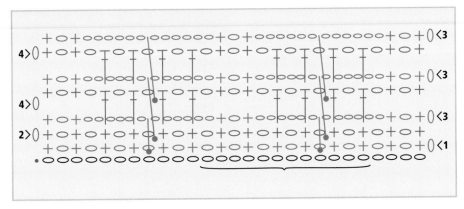

HERRINGBONE

INSTRUCTIONS
Chain a multiple of 12 stitches + 3.

Row 1: Turn. Ch 1. Sc, *sk 1 ch, ch 1, sc in next ch*; repeat from * to * across, ending with sc.

Row 2: Turn. Ch 1. *Sc in sc, sk 1 ch, ch 1*; repeat from * to * ending with sc in sc, sk tch.

Row 3: Turn. Ch 1. *Sc in sc, sk 1 ch, ch 1, sc in sc, ch 6, sk (ch, sc, ch, sc) sl st under next ch 2 rows below, ch 6, sk (sc, ch, sc, ch)*; repeat from * to * ending with sc in sc, sk 1 ch, ch 1, sc in sc, sk tch.

Row 4: Turn. Ch 1. *Sc in sc, sk 1 ch, ch 1, sc in sc, push ch-6s back out of way; working in row 2 (sk 1 ch, ch 1, dc in sc) 4 times, ch 1*; repeat from * to * across, ending with sc in sc, sk 1 ch, ch 1, sc in sc, sk tch.

Repeat rows 3–4.

171

POST STITCHES

Post stitches are worked around the vertical column of a stitch one or more rows below. Post stitches create textures with vertical or diagonal lines, and are often used to mimic textured knitting stitches such as those in Aran sweaters.

Very long post stitches are used to span multiple rows. Work the stitches by making several yarn overs when forming the stitches and then working the yarn overs off 2 loops at a time, just as you would for a treble crochet which has 2 yarn overs. A double treble (dtr) has 3 yarn overs, a triple treble (trtr) has 4 yarn overs, a quadruple treble has 5 yarn overs, and a quintuple treble has 6 yarn overs.

Textured crochet created with post stitches is popular in sweaters, vests and jackets. Home furnishing items such as pillows and afghans often incorporate post stitches. Use post stitches with Tunisian crochet to join sections in strip afghans.

For an explanation of chart symbols, see the inside back cover.

MOCK KNITTING

INSTRUCTIONS

Chain a multiple of 18 stitches + 1.

Row 1: Turn. Ch 2. Dc across.

Row 2: Turn. Ch 2. Sk first dc, *FPdc, sk dc, ch 2, BPdc2tog around next 2 stitches, 10 BPdcs, BPdc2tog around next 2 sts, sk dc, ch 2, FPdc*; repeat from * to * across, ending with hdc in tch.

Row 3: Turn. Ch 2. Sk hdc, *2 BPdcs around next st, sk ch-2, ch 2, FPdc2tog around next 2 sts, 8 FPdcs, FPdc2tog around next 2 sts, sk ch-2, ch 2, 2 BPdcs around FPdc*; repeat from * to * across, ending with hdc in tch.

Row 4: Turn. Ch 2. Sk hdc, *FPdc, 2 FPdcs around next st, sk ch-2, ch 2, BPdc2tog around next 2 sts, 6 BPdcs, BPdc2tog around next 2 sts, sk ch-2, ch 2, 2 FPdcs around next st, FPdc*; repeat from * to * across, ending with hdc in tch.

Row 5: Turn. Ch 2. Sk hdc, *2 BPdcs, 2 BPdcs around next st, sk ch-2, ch 2, FPdc2tog around next 2 sts, 4 FPdcs, FPdc2tog around next 2 sts, sk ch-2, ch 2, 2 BPdcs around next st, 2 BPdcs*; repeat from * to * across, ending with hdc in tch.

Row 6: Turn. Ch 2. Sk hdc, *3 FPdcs, 2 FPdcs around next st, sk ch-2, ch 2, BPdc2tog around next 2 sts, 2 BPdcs, BPdc2tog around next 2 sts, sk ch-2, ch 2, 2 FPdcs around next st, 3 FPdcs*; repeat from * to * across, ending with hdc in tch.

Row 7: Turn. Ch 2. Sk hdc, *4 BPdcs, 2 BPdcs around next st, sk ch-2, ch 2, (FPdc2tog around next 2 sts) 2 times, sk ch-2, ch 2, 2 BPdcs around next st, 4 BPdcs*; repeat from * to * across, ending with hdc in tch.

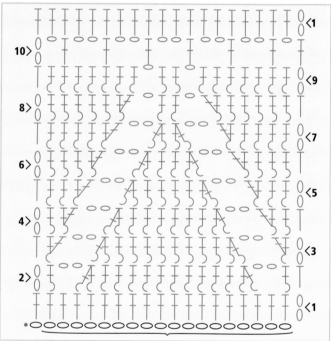

Row 8: Turn. Ch 2. Sk hdc, *5 FPdcs, 2 FPdcs around next st, sk ch-2, ch 1, 2 BPdcs, sk ch-2, ch 1, 2 FPdcs around next st, 5 FPdcs*; repeat from * to * across, ending with hdc in tch.

Row 9: Turn. Ch 2. Sk hdc, *7 BPdcs, sk ch, ch 1, 2 FPdcs, sk ch, ch 1, 7 BPdcs*; repeat from * to * across, ending with hdc in tch.

Row 10: Turn. Ch 3. Sk hdc and BPdc, *dc, sk 2 sts, ch 2*; repeat from * to * ending with dc, sk 1 st, ch 1, dc in tch.

Repeat rows 1–10.

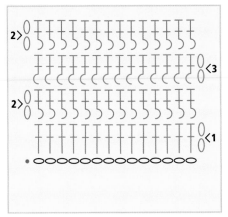

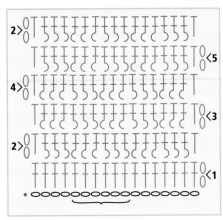

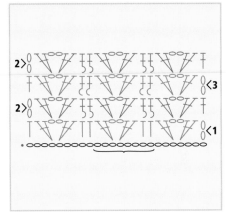

POST RIB

Other Name: Horizontal Relief Rib

INSTRUCTIONS

Chain a multiple of 1 stitch.
Row 1: Turn. Ch 2. Dc across.
Row 2: Turn. Ch 2. FPdc across, sk tch.
Row 3: Turn. Ch 2. BPdc across, sk tch.
Repeat rows 2 and 3.

VARIATIONS

Work with hdc or tr.

BASKETWEAVE

INSTRUCTIONS

Chain a minimum of 6 stitches then a
multiple of 3 stitches + 2.
Row 1: Turn. Ch 2. Dc across.
Row 2: Turn. Ch 2. Hdc, *3 FPdcs, 3
BPdcs*; repeat from * to * across,
ending with hdc, sk tch.
Row 3: Turn. Ch 2. Hdc, *3 BPdcs, 3
FPdcs*; repeat from * to * across,
ending with hdc, sk tch.
Row 4: same as row 3.
Row 5: same as row 2.
Repeat rows 2–5.

SHELLS AND CORDS

INSTRUCTIONS

Chain a multiple of 8 stitches.
Row 1: Turn. Ch 2. Sk 5 chs from hook,
*2 dcs in next, ch 2, 2 hdcs in next
ch, sk 2 chs, 2 dcs, sk 2 chs*; repeat
from * to * across, ending with dc in
last ch.
Row 2: Turn. Ch 2. Sk hdc and 2 dcs,
*over ch-2 work (2 dcs, ch 2, 2 dcs),
(FPdc in hdc) 2 times, sk 2 hdcs*;
repeat from * to * ending with dc in
tch.
Row 3: Turn. Ch 2. Sk 3 dcs, *over ch-
2 work (2 dcs, ch 2, 2 dcs), (BPdc in
dc) 2 times, sk 2 dcs*; repeat from *
to * ending with dc in tch.
Repeat rows 2 and 3.

173

For instructions on working edge
stitches (turning chains) see sidebar
on page 141.

crochet pattern gallery

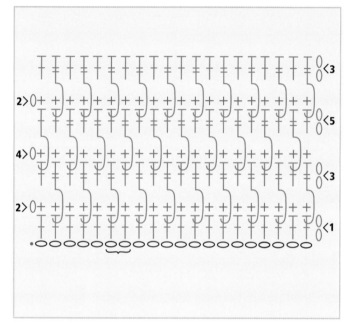

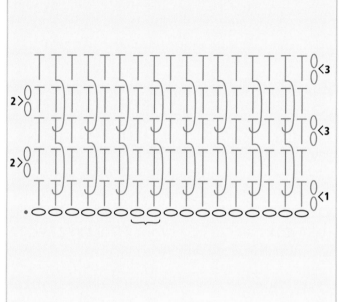

174

ALTERNATING POST
Other Name: Ripple Stitch

INSTRUCTIONS
Chain a multiple of 2 stitches.
Row 1: Turn. Ch 2. Dc across.
Row 2: Turn. Ch 1. Sc across, sk tch.
Row 3: Turn. Ch 2. *FPtr around dc 2 rows below, dc*; repeat from * to * across, ending with dc, sk tch.
Row 4: Turn. Ch 1. Sc across, sk tch.
Row 5: Turn. Ch 2. *Dc, FPtr around dc 2 rows below*; repeat from * to * across, ending with FPtr, sk tch.
Repeat rows 2–5.

PARALLEL POST

INSTRUCTIONS
Chain a multiple of 2 stitches + 1.
Row 1: Turn. Ch 2. Hdc across.
Row 2: Turn. Ch 2. Hdc across, sk tch.
Row 3: Turn. Ch 2. *Hdc, FPhdc around stitch 2 rows below*; repeat from * to * across, ending with hdc, sk tch.
Repeat rows 2 and 3.

VARIATIONS
Work with dc or tr.

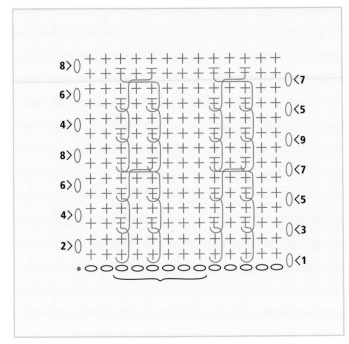

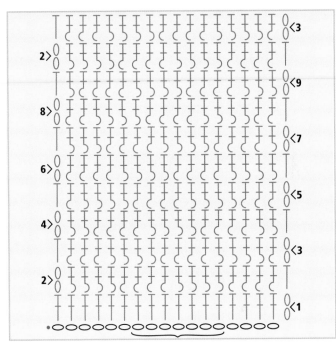

175

TALL CABLES

INSTRUCTIONS

Chain a multiple of 6 stitches + 1.

All even rows: Turn. Ch 1. Sc across, sk tch.

Row 1: Turn. Ch 1. Sc across.

Row 3: Turn. Ch 1. 2 scs, *(FPdc around sc 2 rows below), sk sc behind FPdc, sc, (FPdc around sc 2 rows below), sk sc behind FPdc, 3 scs*; repeat from * to * ending with 2 scs, sk tch.

Row 5: Turn. Ch 1. 2 scs, *(FPdc around FPdc and 2 rows below), sk sc behind FPdc, sc, (FPdc around FPdc 2 rows below), sk sc behind FPdc, 3 scs*; repeat from * to * ending with 2 scs, sk tch.

Row 7: Turn. Ch 1. 2 scs, *(FPdc around sc 2 stitches forward and 2 rows below), sk sc behind FPdc, sc, (FPdc around sc 2 stitches back and 2 rows below), sk sc behind FPdc, 3 scs*; repeat from * to * ending with 2 scs, sk tch.

Row 9: Turn. Ch 1. 2 scs, *(FPdc around FPdc 2 rows below), sk sc behind FPdc, sc, (FPdc around FPdc 2 rows below), sk sc behind FPdc, 3 scs*; repeat from * to * ending with 2 scs, sk tch.

Repeat rows 4–9.

STAIRS

INSTRUCTIONS

Chain a multiple of 8 stitches + 1.

Row 1: Turn. Ch 2. Dc across.

Row 2: Turn. Ch 2. Sk first dc, *4 FPdcs, 4 BPdcs*; repeat from *to * across, ending with hdc in tch.

Row 3: Turn. Ch 2. Sk hdc, BPdc, *4 FPdcs, 4 BPdcs*; repeat from * to * across, ending with hdc in tch.

Row 4: Turn. Ch 2. Sk hdc, 2 FPdcs, *4 BPdcs, 4 FPdcs*; repeat from * to * across, ending with hdc in tch.

Row 5: Turn. Ch 2. Sk hdc, 3 BPdcs, *4 FPdcs, 4 BPdcs*; repeat from * to * across, ending with hdc in tch.

Row 6: Turn. Ch 2. Sk hdc, *4 BPdcs, 4 FPdcs*; repeat from * to * across, ending with hdc in tch.

Row 7: Turn. Ch 2. Sk hdc, FPdc, *4 BPdcs, 4 FPdcs*; repeat from * to * across, ending with hdc in tch.

Row 8: Turn. Ch 2. Sk hdc, 2 BPdcs, *4 FPdcs, 4 FPdcs*; repeat from * to * across, ending with hdc in tch.

Row 9: Turn. Ch 2. Sk hdc, 3 FPdcs, *4 BPdcs, 4 FPdcs*; repeat from * to * across, ending with hdc in tch.

Repeat rows 2–9.

crochet pattern gallery

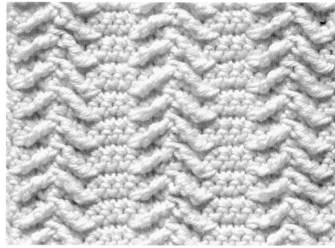

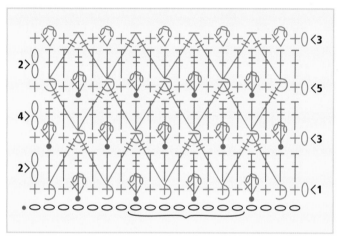

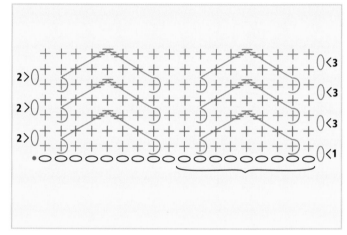

DIAMONDS AND DOTS

NOTES
Single crochet picot — pull up a loop in next st, ch 3 in new loop only, yo, pull through both loops on hook. Pull picot to front of work.

INSTRUCTIONS
Chain a multiple of 8 stitches + 3.

Row 1: Turn. Ch 1. *3 scs, single crochet picot*; repeat from * to * across, ending with 3 scs.

Row 2: Turn. Ch 2. Sk first sc, 2 dcs, *tr in ch behind and below single crochet picot, 3 dcs*; repeat from * to * across, ending with 3 dcs, sk tch.

Row 3: Turn. Ch 1. *Sc, single crochet picot, sc, FPtr2tog around scs 2 rows below — 2 stitches back and 2 stitches forward, sk tr behind FPtr2tog*; repeat from * to * across, ending with sc in tch.

Row 4: Turn. Ch 2. *Tr in dc behind and below single crochet picot, 3 dcs*; repeat from * to * ending with dc in sc, sk tch.

Row 5: Turn. Ch 1. Sc, FPtr in FPtr2tog 2 rows below and 2 stitches forward, sk tr behind FPtr, *sc, single crochet picot, sc, FPtr2tog around FPtr2tog 2 rows below — 2 stitches back and 2 stitches forward, sk tr behind FPtr2tog*; repeat from * to * across, ending with FPtr around FPtr2tog 2 rows below and 2 stitches back, sc in tch.

POST CHEVRONS

INSTRUCTIONS
Chain a multiple of 9 stitches.

All even rows: Turn. Ch 1. Sc across, sk tch.

Row 1: Turn. Ch 1. Sc across.

Row 3: Turn. Ch 1. 4 scs, *FPdtr2tog around stitches 2 rows below — 3 stitches back and 3 stitches forward, 8 scs*; repeat from * to * across, ending with 4 scs, sk tch.

Repeat rows 2 and 3.

Repeat rows 2–5.

VARIATION
For a diamond pattern, replace single crochet picot with sc.

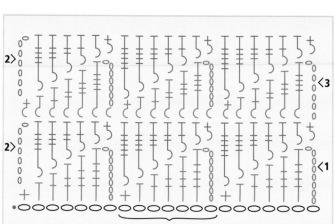

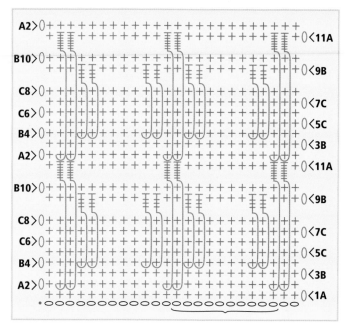

BARN DOORS

NOTE

FPtrtr — yo 4 times, work loops off 2 at a time.

FP quadruple tr — yo 5 times. Insert hook around stitch as indicated. Yo, pull through. Work loops off 2 at a time.

INSTRUCTIONS

Chain a multiple of 7 stitches.

Row 1: Turn. Ch 8. Sk sc, *trtr, dtr, tr, dc, hdc, sc, sl st, ch 7*; repeat from * to * across, ending with sc.

Row 2: Turn. Ch 7. FPtrtr around hdc, FPdtr around dc, FPtr around tr, FPdc around dtr, FPhdc around trtr, FPsc around ch 7, *FP quadruple tr around sc, FPtrtr around hdc, FPdtr around dc, FPtr around tr, FPdc around dtr, FPhdc around trtr, FPsc around ch 7*; repeat from * to * across, ending with FPsc around tch.

Row 3: Turn. Ch 7. *BPtrtr around FPhdc, BPdtr around FPdc, BPtr around FPtr, BPdc around FPdtr, BPhdc around FPtrtr, BPsc around FPquadruple tr, BPsl st around FPsc, ch 7*; repeat from * to * ending with BPsc around tch.

Repeat rows 2 and 3.

FRAMED SQUARES

Other Name: Relief Squares

NOTES

For a FPdtr (front post double treble), wrap the yarn around the hook 3 times. For a FP quintuple treble, wrap the yarn around the hook 6 times.

INSTRUCTIONS

Chain a multiple of 10 stitches + 2.

Row 1: Turn. With color A ch 1. Sc across.

Row 2: Turn. Ch 1. Sc across, sk tch.

Rows 3 and 4: Turn. With color B ch 1. Sc across, sk tch.

Row 5–8: Turn. With color C ch 1. Sc across, sk tch.

Row 9: Turn. With color B ch 1. 3 scs, *(FPdtr around sc 5 rows below) 2 times, 4 scs, (FPdtr around sc 5 rows below) 2 times, 2 scs*; repeat from * to * across, ending with 3 scs, sk tch.

Row 10: Turn. Ch 1. Sc across, sk tch.

Row 11: Turn. With color A ch 1. Sc, *(FP quintuple treble around sc 9 rows below) 2 times, 8 scs*; repeat from * to * across, ending with sc, sk tch.

Repeat rows 2–11.

177

crochet pattern gallery

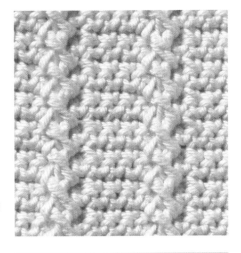

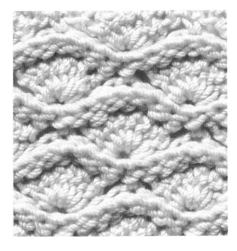

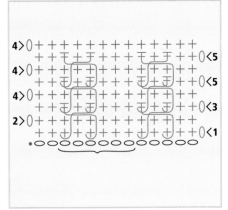

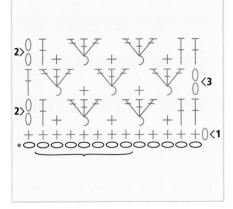

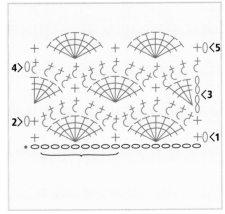

DOUBLE CROCHET CABLES

INSTRUCTIONS

Chain a multiple of 6 stitches + 1.

All even rows: Turn. Ch 1. Sc across, sk tch.

Row 1: Turn. Ch 1. Sc across.

Row 3: Turn. Ch 1. 2 scs, *FPdc around sc 2 stitches forward and 2 below, sk sc behind FPdc, sc, FPdc around sc 2 stitches back and 2 below, sk sc behind FPdc, 3 scs*; repeat from * to * ending with 2 scs, sk tch.

Row 5: Turn. Ch 1. 2 scs, *FPdc around FPdc 2 stitches forward and 2 below, sk sc behind FPdc, sc, FPdc around FPdc 2 stitches back and 2 below, sk sc behind FPdc, 3 scs*; repeat from * to * ending with 2 scs, sk tch.

Repeat rows 4 and 5.

DIVOTS

INSTRUCTIONS

Chain a multiple of 4 + 1.

Row 1: Turn. Ch 1. Beginning in 2nd ch from hook, sc across.

Row 2: Turn. Ch 2. Sk first sc, dc, *sc, sk 1 sc, 3 FPdcs around next sc, sk 1 sc*; repeat from * to * across, ending with sc, 2 dcs.

Row 3: Turn. Ch 2. Sk first 2 dcs, *3 FPdcs around next sc, sc in center dc of 3 FPdcs*; repeat from * to * across, ending with 3 FPdcs around next sc, sk dc, dc in tch.

Repeat rows 2 and 3.

TRIANGLES AND SHELLS

INSTRUCTIONS

Chain a multiple of 8 stitches + 1.

Row 1: Turn. Ch 1. Sc, *sk 3 chs, 7 trs in next ch, sk 3 chs, sc in next ch*; repeat from * to * across, ending with sc.

Row 2: Turn. Ch 1. Sc in sc, BPsc across, ending with sc in sc, sk tch.

Row 3: Turn. Ch 4. 3 dcs in sc, *sk 3 BPscs, sc in next, sk 3 BPscs, 7 trs in next*; repeat from * to * across, ending with 4 dcs in sc, sk tch.

Row 4: Turn. Ch 1. BPsc across, ending with BPsc around tch.

Row 5: Turn. Ch 1. Sc, *sk 3 BPscs, 7 trs in next, sk 3 BPscs, sc in next*; repeat from * to * across, ending with sc in BPsc, sk tch.

Repeat rows 2–5.

178

BOBBLES, POPCORNS, AND PUFFS

Bobbles, popcorns, and puffs — like post stitches — add texture to crochet. But with these stitches, the texture is added in "dots." Work the bobbles, popcorns, or puffs in rows, either vertically or horizontally, or space them in patterns throughout your work.

To create bobbles, popcorns, and puffs, group multiple stitches into the space of a single stitch below and a single stitch above. The excess yarn usually bulges out of the fabric, although sometimes it spreads to fill open space in a lace pattern, as in Little Flowers. You can interchange the three stitches at will in many patterns.

Bobbles, popcorns, and puffs often combine with post stitches. These stitches are popular in hat, scarf, and mitten sets, while lacy patterns are suitable for sweaters, tops, and afghans.

For an explanation of chart symbols, see the inside back cover.

For instructions on working edge stitches (turning chains) see sidebar on page 141.

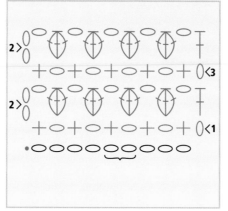

SOFT BOBBLES
Other name: Soft Clusters

INSTRUCTIONS
Chain a multiple of 2 stitches + 1.
Row 1: Turn. Ch 1. *Sc, sk 1 ch, ch 1*; repeat from * to * ending with sc.
Row 2: Turn. Ch 3. Sk sc, *dc3tog over ch, sk sc, ch 1*; repeat from * to * across, ending with sk sc, ch 1, dc in tch.
Row 3: Turn. Ch 1. Sk dc, *sc over ch, sk dc3tog, ch 1*; repeat from * to * across, ending with sc in tch.
Repeat rows 2 and 3.

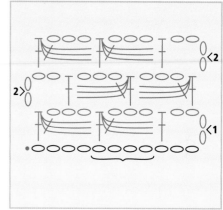

SIDE SADDLE STITCH

INSTRUCTIONS
Chain a multiple of 4 stitches + 3.
Row 1: Turn. Ch 4. Dc in 7th ch from hook, *sk 3 chs, ch 3, dc4tog working the first 3 dcs over the post of dc just made and 4th dc in next ch*; repeat from * to * across, ending with 4th dc in last ch.
Row 2: Turn. Ch 4. Sk dc4tog, dc over ch-3, *sk dc4tog, ch 3, dc4tog working the first 3 dcs over the stem of dc just made and 4th dc over ch-3*; repeat from * to * across, ending with last dc of dc4tog over tch.
Repeat row 2.

179

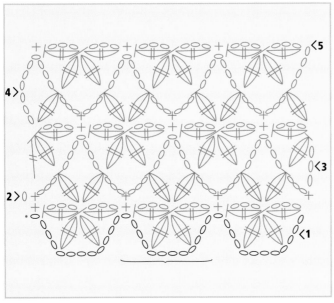

LITTLE FLOWERS

NOTES

Triple bobble in first row — Ch 3, in first of 3 chs just made tr2tog keeping last loop of each tr on hook, sk 3 chs, in next ch tr3tog keeping last loop of each tr on hook, sk 3 chs, in next ch tr3tog keeping last loop of each tr on hook, yo, pull through all 9 loops on hook.

Triple bobble in all other rows — Ch 3, in first of 3 chs just made tr2tog keeping last loop of each tr on hook, sk 3 chs, in next bobble tr3tog keeping last loop of each tr on hook, sk (3 chs, sc, 3 chs), in next bobble tr3tog keeping last loop of each tr on hook, yo, pull through all 9 loops on hook.

INSTRUCTIONS

Chain a multiple of 12 stitches.

Row 1: Turn. *Triple bobble, ch 3, counting ch 3 as a tr tr3tog in top of triple bobble just made, sk 3 chs, sc in next st*; repeat from * to * across, ending with sc.

Row 2: Turn. Ch 1. *Sc in sc, ch 3, tr3tog in top of triple bobble, ch 7, tr3tog in top of same triple bobble just used, ch 3*; repeat from * to * across, ending with sc in last ch of base row.

Row 3: Turn. Ch 3. Sk 3 chs, tr3tog in tr3tog, ch 3, (counting ch 3 just made as a tr) tr3tog in top of tr3tog just made, sk 3 chs, *sc in next, triple bobble, ch 3, counting ch 3 as a tr tr3tog in top of triple bobble just made, sk 3 chs*; repeat from * to * across, ending with sc, ch 3, (counting ch 3 just made as a tr) tr3tog in top 3rd ch from hook keeping last loop of each tr on hook), sk 3 chs, in next bobble (tr3tog keeping last loop of each tr on hook), sk 3 chs, tr in sc pulling last yo through all loops on hook, sk tch.

Row 4: Turn. Ch 10. Tr3tog in top of partial triple bobble, ch 3, *sc in sc, ch 3, tr3tog in top of triple bobble, ch 7, tr3tog in top of same triple bobble just used, ch 3*; repeat from * to * across, ending with sc in sc, ch 3, tr3tog in partial triple bobble, ch 4.

Row 5: Turn. *Triple bobble, ch 3, (counting ch 3 just made as a tr) tr3tog in top of triple bobble just made, sk 3 chs, sc in sc*; repeat from * to * across, ending with sc over tch.

Repeat rows 2–5.

VARIATIONS

Use scalloped beginning and two or three rows of flowers for an edging.

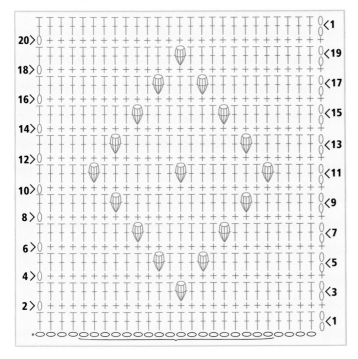

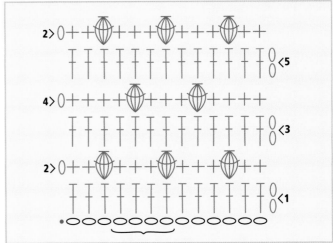

POPCORN DIAMOND

INSTRUCTIONS

Chain a multiple of 18 stitches + 8.

All even rows: Turn. Ch 1. Sk first dc, sc across, ending with sc in tch.

Row 1: Turn. Ch 2. Dc across.

Row 3: Turn. Ch 2. Sk first sc, 12 dcs, 5-dc popcorn, 13 dcs.

Row 5: Turn. Ch 2. Sk first sc, 10 dcs, 5-dc popcorn, 3 dcs, 5-dc popcorn, 11 dcs.

Row 7: Turn. Ch 2. Sk first sc, 8 dcs, 5-dc popcorn, 7 dcs, 5-dc popcorn, 9 dcs.

Row 9: Turn. Ch 2. Sk first sc, 6 dcs, 5-dc popcorn, 11 dcs, 5-dc popcorn, 7 dcs.

Row 11: Turn. Ch 2. Sk first sc, 4 dcs, 5-dc popcorn, 7 dcs, 5-dc popcorn, 7 dcs, 5-dc popcorn, 5 dcs.

Row 13: same as row 9.

Row 15: same as row 7.

BLACKBERRY SALAD STITCH

NOTES

The plain dc rows are the right side of this piece. Push the dc5tog bobbles to the back as they form.

INSTRUCTIONS

Chain a multiple of 4 stitches + 1.

Row 1: Turn. Ch 2. Dc across.

Row 2: Turn. Ch 1. 2 scs, *dc5tog in next dc, 3 scs*; repeat from * to * across, ending with 2 scs, sk tch.

Row 3: Turn. Ch 2. Dc across, sk tch.

Row 4: Turn. Ch 1. 4 scs, *dc5tog in next dc, 3 scs*; repeat from * to * across, ending with 4 scs, sk tch.

Row 5: Turn. Ch 2. Dc across, sk tch.

Repeat rows 2–5.

Row 17: same as row 5.

Row 19: same as row 3.

Repeat rows 1–20.

VARIATIONS

Popcorns can be arranged in a variety of geometric patterns.

crochet pattern gallery

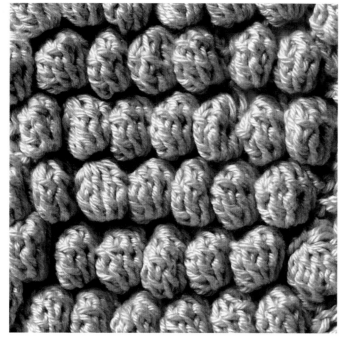

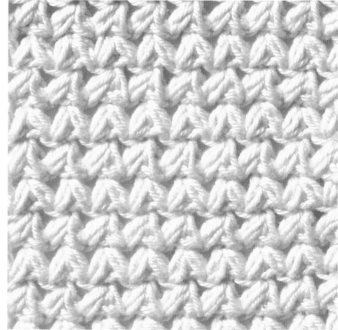

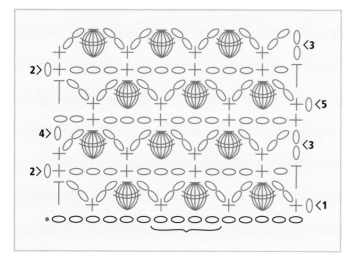

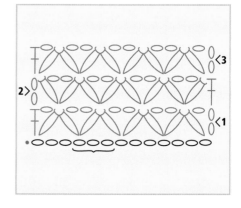

ROCKY ROAD BOBBLES

INSTRUCTIONS

Chain a multiple of 4 stitches + 3.

Row 1: Turn. Ch 1. Sc in 2nd ch from hook, *sk 1 ch, ch 2, tr7tog in next ch, sk 1 ch, ch 2, sc in next ch*; repeat from * to * across, ending with hdc in last ch.

Row 2: Turn. Ch 1. Sc in hdc, *sk (ch-2, sc, ch-2), ch 3, sc in tr7tog*; repeat from * to * across, ending with sc in tr7tog, ch 1, hdc in sc, sk tch.

Row 3: Turn. Ch 4. *Sc in sc, ch 2, tr7tog over ch-3, ch 2*; repeat from * to * across, ending with sc in sc, sk tch.

Row 4: Turn. Ch 3. *Sc in tr7tog, sk (ch-2, sc, ch-2), ch 3*; repeat from * to * across, ending with sc over tch.

Row 5: Turn. Ch 1. Sc in sc, *ch 2, tr7tog over ch-3, ch 2, sc in sc*; repeat from * to * across, ending with hdc over tch.

Repeat rows 2–5, ending with even row.

STARRY EYES

NOTES

Puff Stitch in first row — in ch (yo, pull up loop) 2 times, sk 2 chs, in next ch (yo, pull up loop) 2 times, yo, pull loop through all 9 sts on hook.

Puff stitch in all other rows — in puff st of previous row (yo, pull up loop) 2 times, sk 2 chs, in next puff stitch (yo, pull up loop) 2 times, yo, pull loop through all 9 sts on hook.

INSTRUCTIONS

Chain a multiple of 3 stitches + 1.

Row 1: Turn. Ch 3. In 4th ch from hook, *puff stitch, ch 2; starting in same ch as last st ended*; repeat from * to * across, ending with ch 1, dc in same ch as last st ended.

Row 2: Turn. Ch 2. In first puff st (yo, pull up loop) 2 times, yo, pull through all 5 loops on hook, *ch 2, puff stitch starting in same puff st as last st ended*; repeat from * to * across, ending with ch 2, starting in same st as last puff stitch ended (yo, pull up loop) 2 times, yo, pull through all 5 loops on hook, dc over tch.

Row 3: Turn. Ch 3. Beginning in partial puff st, puff stitch, *ch 2, starting is same puff st as last st ended, puff stitch*; repeat from * to * ending with ch 1, dc in tch.

Repeat rows 2 and 3.

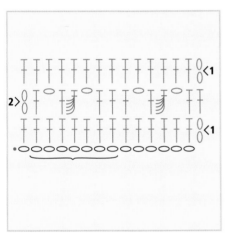

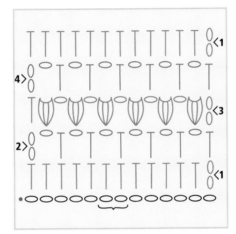

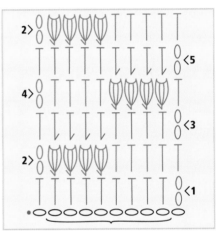

183

OFFSET BOBBLES
Other name: Offset Clusters

INSTRUCTIONS
Chain a multiple of 7 stitches.

Row 1: Turn. Ch 2. Dc across.

Row 2: Ch 2, Sk first dc, dc, *sk dc, ch 1, dc, dc5tog working over post of dc just made, sk dc, ch 1, 3 dcs*; repeat from * to * across, ending with sk dc, ch 1, dc, dc in tch.

Row 3: Turn. Ch 2. Sk first dc, dc across, ending with dc in tch.

Repeat rows 2 and 3.

PUFF STITCH LACE

INSTRUCTIONS
Chain a multiple of 2 stitches + 1.

Row 1: Turn. Ch 2. Hdc across.

Row 2: Turn. Ch 3. Sk 2 hdcs, *hdc, sk hdc, ch 1*; repeat from * to * across, ending with hdc in tch.

Row 3: Turn. Ch 2. *4 strand puff over ch-1, sk hdc, ch 1*; repeat from * to * across, ending with 4 strand puff over ch-1, hdc in tch.

Row 4: Same as row 2.

Repeat rows 1–4.

VARIATIONS
Puff Stitch Lace is a decorative variation of Track Stitch. You can substitute other stitches such as dc or tr for the rows of hdc.

BAGUETTES

NOTE
Even rows are right side of fabric.

INSTRUCTIONS
Chain a multiple of 8 stitches + 2.

Row 1: Turn. Ch 2. Hdc across.

Row 2: Turn. Ch 2. Sk first hdc, *(4 strand puff in back loop) 4 times, 4 hdcs*; repeat from * to * across, ending with hdc in tch.

Row 3: Turn. Ch 2. Sk first hdc, *4 hdcs, 4 hdcs in front loop*; repeat from * to * across, ending with hdc in tch.

Row 4: Turn. Ch 2. Sk first hdc, *4 hdcs, (4 strand puff in back loop) 4 times*; repeat from * to * across, ending with hdc in tch.

Row 5: Turn. Ch 2. Sk first hdc, *4 hdcs in front loop, 4 hdcs*; repeat from * to * across, ending with hdc in tch.

Repeat rows 2—5, ending with odd row.

TAPESTRY, JACQUARD, AND MOSAIC PATTERNS

Tapestry, jacquard, and mosaic are interchangeable crochet terms for designs that feature two or more colors of yarn in each row. Usually one stitch such as single crochet is used throughout the piece. Control of yarns not in use is maintained by working over them, which stiffens the fabric and prevents loose floats on the reverse side.

Tapestry crochet has a definite right side and wrong side. Experts learn to crochet both left- and right-handed so the front of the work always faces them. If you can't crochet with your "off" hand, you can work every other row in reverse single crochet.

This technique can employ simple two-color charted designs for filet crochet (block is one color, open mesh the second color) or for other types of needlework such as cross-stitch. Filet and cross-stitch patterns work for back-and-forth rows, as in Scrolls. Brick patterns, commonly featured in peyote-stitch bead weaving, are ideal for attaching and ending the yarn for each row, as in Triangles.

Tapestry patterns work beautifully for beaded crochet. Instead of alternating two colors of yarn in the pattern, work with just one color of yarn and alternate plain stitch and beaded stitch for the colors in the pattern.

Tapestry crochet is ideal wherever you want a project with a stiff hand. Try it for wall hangings, bags, hats, belts, and rugs. Use lightweight yarns to create pictorial designs in vest backs and afghans.

For an explanation of chart symbols, see the inside back cover.

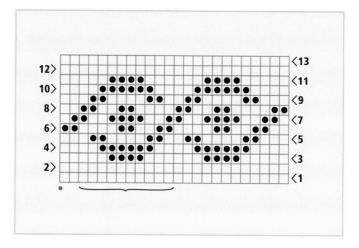

SCROLLS

INSTRUCTIONS

Chain a multiple of 10 stitches + 4.

Work rows back and forth using single crochet on the right side rows and reverse single crochet (or crochet with the opposite hand) on the wrong side rows. Change colors as described in Tapestry Crochet (pages 73–74).

VARIATIONS

Try simple 2-color charted designs for filet crochet (block is one color, open mesh the second color), cross-stitch, or other types of needlework.

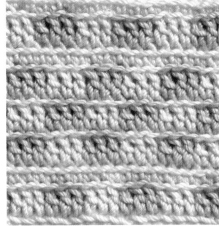

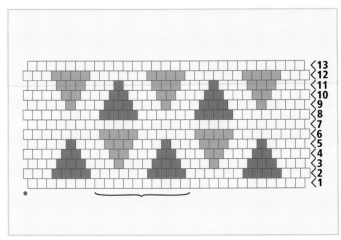

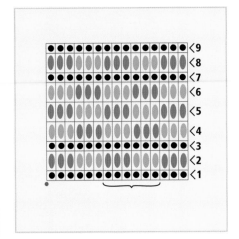

TRIANGLES

INSTRUCTIONS

Chain a multiple of 10 stitches + 9.

Work all rows from right to left (left to right for left-handed people), breaking thread at the end of each row. Change colors as described in Tapestry Crochet (pages 73–74), working each sc over 2 strands.

VARIATIONS

Try simple brick patterns such as peyote-stitch bead weaving patterns.

DOUBLE CROCHET TAPESTRY BLOCKS

INSTRUCTIONS

Chain a multiple of 6 stitches + 3.

Work all rows from right to left (left to right for left-handed people) breaking thread at the end of each row. Work short rows (rows 1, 3, 7, and 9) in single crochet; work tall rows (rows 2, 4, 5, 6, and 8) in double crochet. Change colors as described in Tapestry Crochet (pages 73–74). Work all rows in back loop only. Working in back loop only creates a "line" in the crochet that separates and defines the color changes.

crochet pattern gallery

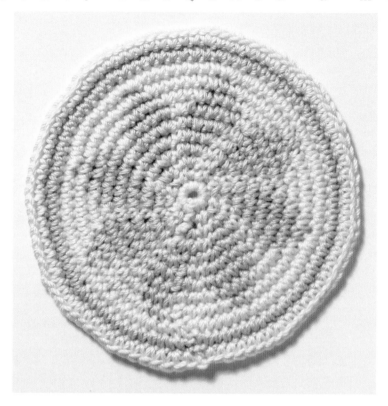

186

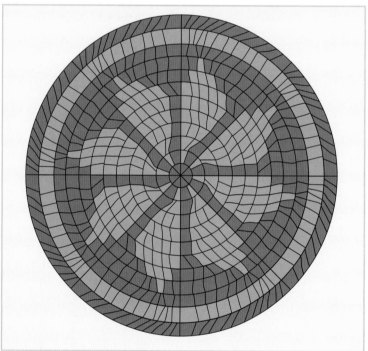

STAR

INSTRUCTIONS

Chain 4 stitches. Sl st to join.

All rnds: Ch 2 (counts as first sc). Sc around according to chart, above, changing colors as described in Tapestry Crochet (page 73–74) and working over second strand of yarn. End round with sl st in 2nd ch of round.

VARIATIONS

For a domed bag bottom, work only six or seven of the repeats instead of all eight. This is an excellent pattern for beads.

NET, MESH, AND TRELLIS PATTERNS

Net, mesh, and trellis patterns are light, airy, open ground patterns. Use either yarn or thread, although fine thread may need starch to give it body.

When working with lacy patterns and long chains, mark the last stitch of the base chain so that you can find it easily when you turn to work the first row.

Net patterns are traditionally worked in fine threads for backgrounds in Irish crochet. When worked in yarn, these grounds create lovely summer wraps for cool evenings. The grounds can be used alone or embellished with crocheted motifs.

For an explanation of chart symbols, see the inside back cover.

For instructions on working edge stitches (turning chains) see sidebar on page 141.

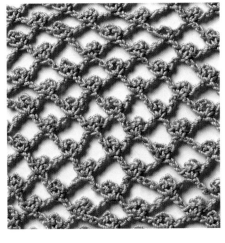

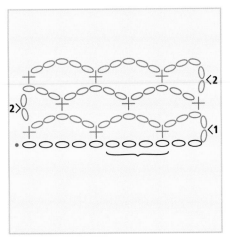

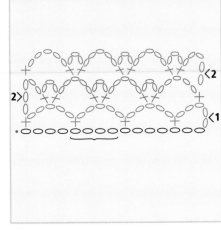

NET STITCH

INSTRUCTIONS
Chain a multiple of 4 stitches + 3.
Row 1: Turn. Ch 5. Sk 2 chs of base ch, *sc in next, sk 3 chs, ch 5*; repeat from * to * across, ending with sc.
Row 2: Turn. Ch 5. *Sc over ch-5, sk sc, ch 5*; repeat from * to * across, ending with sc over tch.
Repeat row 2.

VARIATIONS
Vary the number of chains between single crochets.

PICOT NET STITCH

INSTRUCTIONS
Chain a multiple of 4 stitches + 3.
Row 1: Turn. Ch 5. Sk 2 chs of base ch, *sc in next, sk 3 chs, ch 5*; repeat from * to * ending with sc.
Row 2: Turn. Ch 5. *Into 3rd ch of ch-5 (sc, ch 3, sc)*; repeat from * to * ending with sc in 3rd ch of tch.
Repeat row 2.

VARIATIONS
Vary number of chains between picots.

187

crochet pattern gallery

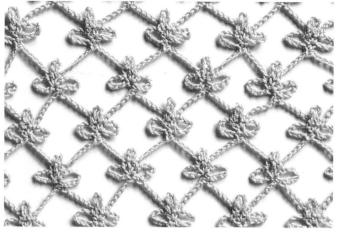

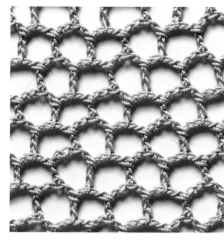

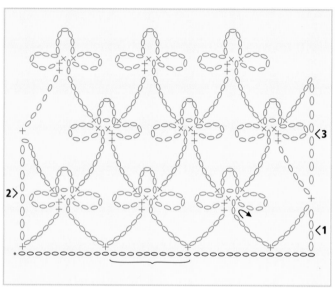

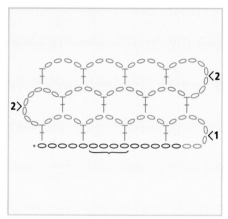

TREFOIL DIAMOND NET

INSTRUCTIONS

Chain a multiple of 10 stitches + 6.

Row 1: Turn. Ch 11. Sk 5 chs of base ch, *sc in next ch, ch 15, in 8th ch from hook sc, (ch 7, sc in same stitch as last sc) 2 times, sc in next ch of ch 15, ch 6, sk 9 scs of base ch*; repeat from * to * ending with sc in base ch.

Row 2: Turn. Ch 15. Sc in sc between first and 2nd ch-7 loop of first trefoil, *ch 1, sc in sc between 2nd and 3rd ch-7 loop of same trefoil, ch 15, in 8th ch from hook sc, (ch 7, sc in same stitch as last sc) 2 times, sc in next ch of ch 15, ch 6, sc in sc between first and 2nd ch-7 loop of next trefoil*; repeat from * to * across, ending with ch 6, sc over tch.

Row 3: Turn. Ch 15. Sc in sc between first and 2nd ch-7 loop of first trefoil, *ch 1 behind trefoil, sc in sc between 2nd and 3rd ch-7 loop of same trefoil, ch 15, in 8th ch from hook sc, (ch 7, sc in same stitch as last sc) 2 times, sc in next ch of ch 15, ch 6, sc in sc between first and 2nd ch-7 loop of next trefoil*; repeat from * to * across, ending with ch 6, sc over tch.

Repeat rows 2 and 3.

HEXAGONAL NET

INSTRUCTIONS

Chain a multiple of 4 stitches + 2.

Row 1: Turn. Ch 8. Sk 1 ch of base ch, *dc, sk 3 chs, ch 4*; repeat from * to * across, ending with dc.

Row 2: Turn. Ch 8. *Dc over ch-4, ch 4*; repeat from * to * across, ending with dc over tch.

Repeat row 2.

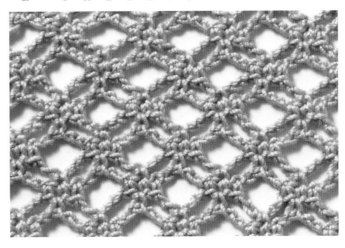

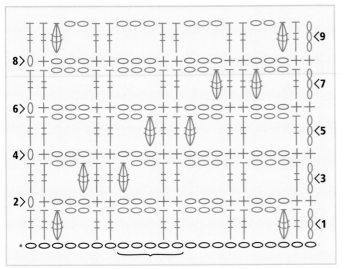

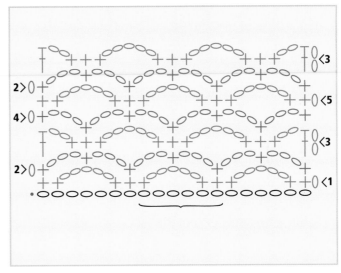

DOUBLE SQUARE NET

INSTRUCTIONS

Chain a multiple of 5 stitches + 2.

All even rows: Turn. Ch 1. Sk first tr, sc in tr, *ch 3, (sc in tr) 2 times*; repeat from * to * across, ending with sc in tr, sc in tch.

Row 1: Turn. Ch 3. Sk first base ch, tr, *tr3tog, sk 2 chs, ch 2, (2 trs, sk 3 chs, ch 3) 2 times, 2 trs, sk 2 chs, ch 2, tr3tog, 2 trs*; repeat from * to * across, ending with 2 trs.

Row 3: Turn. Ch 3. Sk first sc, *tr in sc, [sk ch-3, ch 3, (tr in sc) 2 times] 2 times, sk 2 chs, ch 2, tr3tog in ch, (tr in sc) 2 times, tr3tog in ch, sk 2 chs, ch 2, tr in sc*; repeat from * to *across, ending with tr in sc, tr in tch.

Row 5: Turn. Ch 3. Sk first sc, *tr in sc, sk ch-3, ch 3, (tr in sc) 2 times, sk 2 chs, ch 2, tr3tog in ch, (tr in sc) 2 times, tr3tog in ch, sk 2 chs, ch 2, (tr in sc) 2 times, sk ch-3, ch 3, tr in sc*; repeat from * to * ending with tr in sc, tr in tch.

Row 7: Turn. Ch 3. Sk first sc, *tr in sc, sk 2chs, ch 2, tr3tog in ch, (tr in sc) 2 times, tr3tog in ch, sk 2 chs, ch 2, [(tr in sc) 2 times, ch 3] 2 times, tr in sc*; repeat from * to * ending with tr in sc, tr in tch.

Row 9: Turn. Ch 3. Sk first sc, *tr in sc, tr3tog in ch, sk 2chs, ch 2, [(tr in sc) 2 times, sk ch-3, ch 3] 2 times, (tr in sc) 2 times, sk 2 chs, ch 2, tr3tog in ch, tr in sc*; repeat from * to * ending with tr in sc, tr in tch.

DOUBLE DIAMOND NET

INSTRUCTIONS

Chain a multiple of 6 stitches + 1.

Row 1: Turn. Ch 1. 2 scs, *sk 3 chs, ch 5, 3 scs*; repeat from * to * across, ending with 2 scs.

Row 2: Turn. Ch 1. Sc in first sc, *sk sc, ch 3, sc in 3rd ch of ch-5, sk sc, ch 3, sc in sc*; repeat from * to * across, ending with sk sc, sc in sc, sk tch.

Row 3: Turn. Ch 2. Dc in sc, ch 2, *sc in 3rd ch of ch-3, sc in sc, sc in first ch of ch 3, ch 5, sk sc*; repeat from * to * ending with ch 2, dc in sc, sk tch.

Row 4: Turn. Ch 1. Sc in dc, *ch 3, sk sc, sc in sc, sk sc, ch 3, sc in 3rd ch of ch-5*; repeat from * to * ending with sc in dc, sk tch.

Row 5: Turn. Ch 1. *Sc in sc, sc in first ch of ch-3, sk sc, ch 5, sc in 3rd ch of ch-3*; repeat from * to * ending with sc in 2nd ch of ch-3, sc in sc, sk tch.

Repeat rows 2–5.

Repeat rows 2–9.

VARIATIONS

Omit tr3tog for plain mesh. Position tr3tog in other geometric patterns.

189

crochet pattern gallery

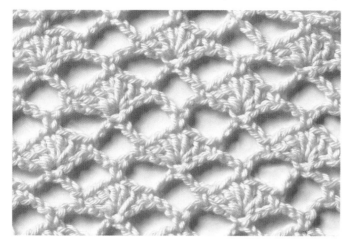

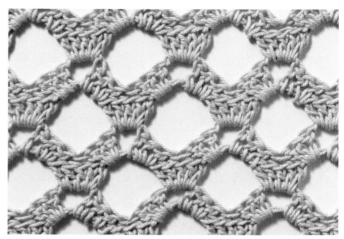

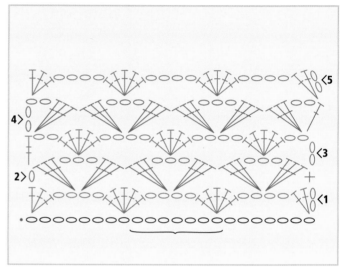

SHELL TRELLIS

INSTRUCTIONS

Chain a multiple of 12 stitches + 1.

Row 1: Turn. Ch 2. 2 dcs in first ch of base ch, *sk 2 chs, sc in next, sk 5 chs, ch 5, sc in next ch, sk 2 chs, 5 dcs in next ch*; repeat from * to * ending with sk 2 chs, 3 dcs in last ch.

Row 2: Turn. Ch 1. Sc in first dc, *sk 2 dcs and sc, ch 5, sc over ch-5, sk sc and 2 dcs, ch 5, sc in 3rd dc of shell*; repeat from * to * ending with sc in tch.

Row 3: Turn. Ch 5. *Sc over ch-5, 5 dcs in sc, sc over ch-5, sk sc, ch 5*; repeat from * to * ending with sc over ch-5, ch 2, dc in sc, sk tch.

Row 4: Turn. Ch 1. Sc in dc, *sk sc and 2 dcs, ch 5, sc in 3rd dc of shell, sk 2 dcs and sc, ch 5, sc over ch-5*; repeat from * to * across, ending with sc over tch.

Row 5: Turn. Ch 2. 2 dcs in sc, *sc over ch-5, sk sc, ch 5, sc over ch-5, 5 dcs in sc*; repeat from * to * ending with 3 dcs in sc, sk tch.

Repeat rows 2–5.

DIAMOND MESH

INSTRUCTIONS

Chain a multiple of 7 stitches + 1.

Row 1: Turn. Ch 2. 2 dcs in first ch of base ch, *sk 6 chs, ch 4, 5 dcs in next ch*; repeat from * to * across ending with 3 dcs in last ch.

Row 2: Turn. Ch 1. *Over ch-4 (3 dcs, ch 3, 3 dcs)*; repeat from * to * across ending with sc in tch.

Row 3: Turn. Ch 4. *5 dcs over ch-3, ch 4*; repeat from * to * across ending with ch 2, tr in tch.

Row 4: Turn. Ch 4. 3 dcs in tr, *over ch-4 (3 dcs, ch 3, 3 dcs)*; repeat from * to * across ending with (3 dcs, ch 2, dc) over tch.

Row 5: Turn. Ch 2. 2 dcs in first dc, *ch 4, 5 dcs over ch-3*; repeat from * to * across ending with 3 dcs over tch.

Repeat rows 2–5.

MOTIFS

Motifs are small individual pieces of crochet that may be combined to form a larger piece. Motifs can incorporate any crochet stitches or patterns and can be any shape: round, square, hexagon, or pentagon. The small pieces are ideal to take as you travel or run errands because a bit of yarn for a motif or two and a hook are easy to carry.

For an explanation of chart symbols, see the inside back cover.

DAFFODIL

NOTES

The center forms a cup that you work from the outside. Attach each petal separately to the center.

INSTRUCTIONS

CENTER

With yellow ch 4, sl st to join.

Row 1: Ch 2, 7 scs in ring, sl st in 2nd ch of rnd.

Rnd 2: Ch 2, sc in 2nd ch of rnd 1, *2 scs in sc*; repeat from * to * around ending with sl st in 2nd ch of rnd.

Rnd 3: Ch 2 (counts as first BLsc), BLsc in each sc around, sl st in 2nd ch of rnd.

Rnds 4–6: Ch 2, sc in each sc around, sl st in 2nd ch of rnd.

Rnd 7: Ch 4, dtr in first ch of previous rnd, 2 dtrs in each sc around, sl st in 3rd ch of rnd. End.

PETALS

With white ch 12, sl st into front loop of a st in rnd 4, working back along ch just made in top loop only [sk 2 chs, hdc, 2 dcs, 4 trs, (2 dtrs in next ch) 2 times, 3 dtrs in end ch], ch 3, sl st in first ch just made, working back along other side of ch (turn work 180 degrees and bottom loop of ch becomes top loop which you work into) [3 dtrs in same ch as dtrs just made, (2 dtrs in next ch) 2 times, 4 trs, 2 dcs, hdc], sk 3 scs of rnd 3, sl st into front loop of next sc, ch 2, sl st in same ch as last hdc. End.

Repeat petals spacing as follows: 2 more petals with 6 unused stitches of rnd 3 between them. Then position last 3 petals evenly between and behind first 3.

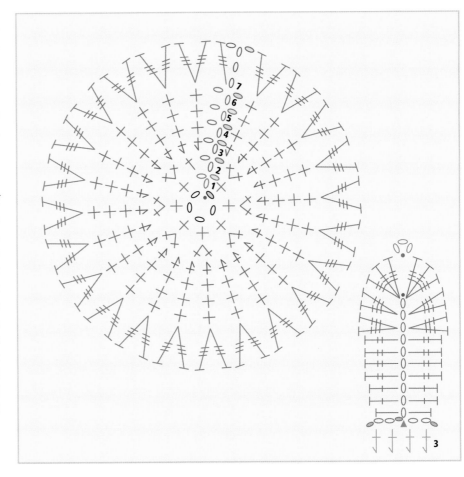

crochet pattern gallery

SUNFLOWER

INSTRUCTIONS

With green ch 6, sl st to join.

Rnd 1: Ch 2, 15 dcs in ring, sl st in 2nd ch.

Rnd 2: Ch 4, *in dc (BLsc, ch 3, BLsc); ch 3, BLsc in next dc, ch 3*; repeat from * to * around ending with ch 3, sl st in first ch of rnd.

Rnd 3: Ch 4, (BLsc in sc, ch 3) 2 times; *in next sc (BLsc, ch 3, BLsc); ch 3; (BLsc in sc, ch 3) 5 times*; repeat from * to * around ending with (BLsc in sc, ch 3) 2 times, sl st in first ch of rnd.

Rnd 4: Ch 4, *in sc (BLsc, ch 3, BLsc), (ch 3, BLsc in next sc) 5 times, ch 3*; repeat from * to * around ending with ch 3, sl st in first ch.

Rnd 5: Ch 4, *BLsc in next sc, ch 3*; repeat from * to * around ending with ch 3, sl st in first ch of rnd. End.

Rnd 6: Attach yellow to last sl st made. Ch 12; working back along ch (sk 3 chs, sc, hdc, dc, 6 trs), *sk 1 sc of center, BPsc around next sc, ch 11, working back along ch (sk 3 chs, sc, hdc, dc, 5 trs), tr in BPsc*; repeat from * to * making 16 leaves and ending with sl st in first ch of rnd.

Rnd 7: Behind rnd 6, ch 2, BPsc around last sc of rnd 5, *ch 11; working back along ch (sk 3 chs, sc, hdc, dc, 5 trs), tr in BPsc, sk 1 sc of center, BPsc around next sc*; repeat from * to * making 16 leaves and ending with sl st in first BPsc of rnd.

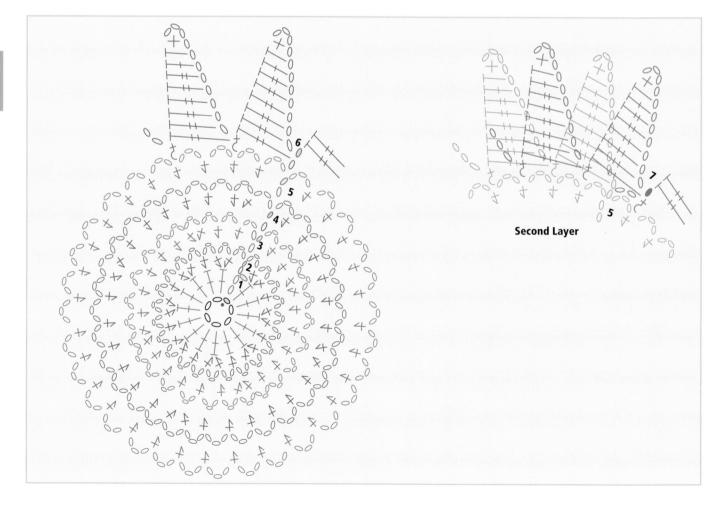

Second Layer

MARGUERITE

NOTE

Make center separately from base and petals and then sew it into place.

INSTRUCTIONS

CENTER

With yellow Ch 4, sl st to join.

Rnd 1: Ch 2, 7 scs in ring, sl st in first ch of rnd.

Rnd 2: Ch 2, BLsc in 2nd ch of rnd 1, *2 BLsc in sc*; repeat from * to * around ending with sl st in first ch of rnd.

Rnd 3: Ch 2, BLsc in 2nd ch of rnd 1, *BLsc in sc, 2 BLsc in next sc*; repeat from * to * around ending with sl st in first ch of rnd.

Rnd 4: Ch 2, *BLsc2tog over 2 scs, BLsc in next sc*; repeat from * to * around ending with sl st in first ch of rnd. End, leaving 12" tail.

BASE AND PETALS

With white ch 4, sl st to join.

Rnd 1: Ch 2, 7 scs in ring, sl st in first ch of rnd.

Rnd 2: Ch 2, *2 scs in sc, sc in sc*; repeat from * to * around ending with sl st in first ch of rnd.

Rnd 3: Ch 2, sc in 2nd ch of rnd 2, *2 scs in sc*; repeat from * to * around ending with sl st in first ch of rnd.

Rnd 4: *Ch 15, working back along ch (sk 1 ch, sc, hdc, 12 dcs), sk ch and sc (sk 2 scs after first leaf), sl st between scs*; repeat from * to * around ending with sl st between scs.

Rnd 5: Sl st over 2nd ch of rnd 4; working behind rnd 4 *ch 15, working back along ch (sk 1 ch, sc, hdc, 12 dcs), sk 2 scs, sl st between scs* repeat from * to * around ending with sl st in first ch of rnd.

ASSEMBLY

Using a #18 tapestry needle, thread the long tail on center, and sew it into place.

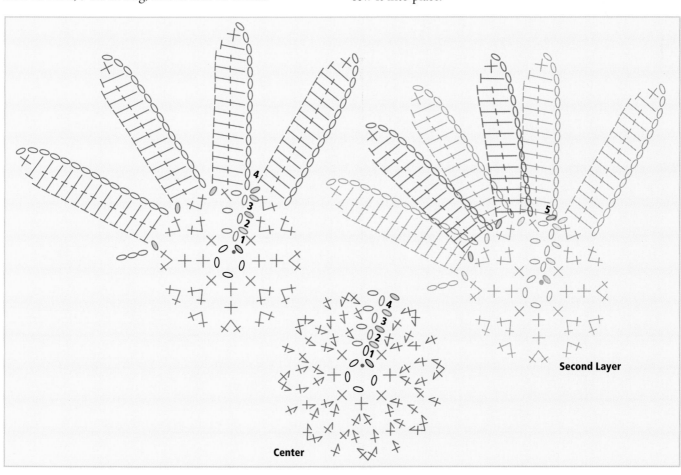

Center

Second Layer

crochet pattern gallery

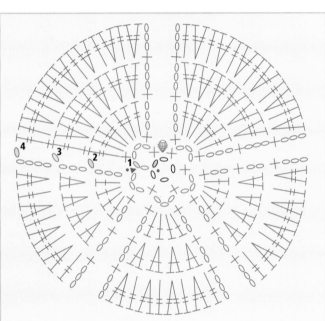

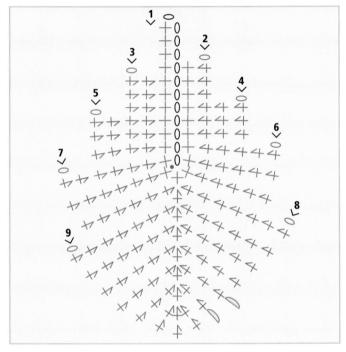

PANSY

INSTRUCTIONS

With green ch 4, sl st to join.

Rnd 1: Ch 4, (sc in ring, ch 3) 3 times, sc in ring, 7-st tr popcorn in ring, sc in ring, ch 3, sl st in first ch of rnd. End.

Rnd 2: With yellow attach yarn in first ch-3, ch 3, over ch-3 (4 dcs, ch 2, sc), [over next ch-3 (sc, ch 2, 4 dcs, ch 2, sc)] 2 times, over next ch-3 (sc, ch 3, 6 trs, ch 3, sc), pass behind popcorn, over next ch-3 (sc, ch 3, 7 trs), sl st to 3rd ch of rnd.

Rnd 3: Ch 3, (2 dcs in dc) 4 times, ch 2, sc in 2nd ch, [sc in 2nd ch, ch 2, (2 dcs in dc) 4 times, ch 2, sc in 2nd ch] 2 times, sc in 3rd ch, ch 3, (2 trs in tr) 6 times, ch 3, sc in 3rd ch, sc in 3rd ch, ch 3, (2 trs in tr) 6 times, tr in tr, sl st in 3rd ch of rnd.

Rnd 4: Ch 4, (2 trs in first dc, 1 tr in next dc) 4 times, ch 3, sc in 2nd ch, [sc in 2nd ch, ch 3, (2 trs in first dc, 1 tr in next dc) 4 times, ch 3, sc in 2nd ch] 2 times, sc in 3rd ch, ch 3, (2 trs in first tr, 1 tr in next tr) 6 times, ch 3, sc in 3rd ch, sc in 3rd ch, ch 3, (2 trs in first tr, 1 tr in next tr) 6 times, tr in tr, sl st in 3rd ch of rnd.

ROSE LEAF

INSTRUCTIONS

Ch 12.

Row 1: Turn. Working in top loop only back along ch just made, sk 1 ch, 10 scs, 5 scs in last ch, rotate work 180 degrees; working in former bottom loop which is now top loop after rotating, work 7 scs.

Row 2: Turn. Ch 1. 9 BLscs, 3 BLscs in next sc, 8 BLscs.

Row 3: Turn. Ch 1. 9 BLscs, 3 BLscs in next sc, 7 BLscs.

Row 4: Turn. Ch 1. 8 BLscs, 3 BLscs in next sc, 7 BLscs.

Row 5: Turn. Ch 1. 8 BLscs, 3 BLscs in next sc, 6 BLscs.

Row 6: Turn. Ch 1. 7 BLscs, 3 BLscs in next sc, 6 BLscs.

Row 7: Turn. Ch 1. 7 BLscs, 3 BLscs in next sc, 5 BLscs.

Row 8: Turn. Ch 1. 6 BLscs, 3 BLscs in next sc, 5 BLscs.

Row 9: Turn. Ch 1. 8 BLscs, 2 BLsl sts.

VARIATIONS

Pad for more texture by working scs over 2 or more strands of the same yarn.

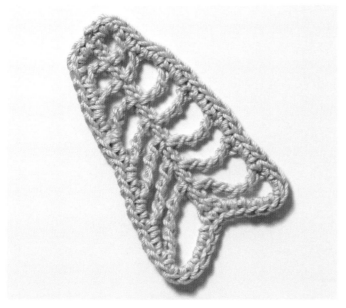

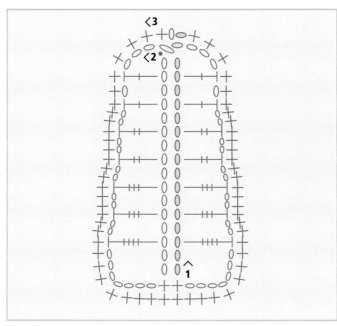

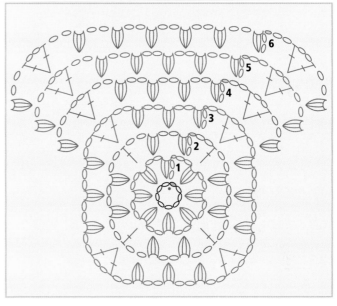

OPEN LEAF

INSTRUCTIONS

Ch 16.

Rnd 1: Turn. Working back along ch just made, 16 sl sts in bottom loop.

Rnd 2: Ch 4, dc in 2nd ch of base ch, ch 1, sk 1 ch, dc in next, (ch 2, sk 1 ch, tr in next) 2 times, (ch 2, sk 1 ch, dtr in next) 2 times, ch 2, sk 1 ch, trtr in next, ch 7, sk 1 ch, sc in next, rotate work 180 degrees and work back along sl sts, sc in first sl st, ch 7, sk 1 sl st, trtr in next, (ch 2, sk 1 sl st, dtr in next) 2 times, (ch 2, sk 1 sl st, tr in next) 2 times, ch 2, sk 1 sl st, dc in next, ch 1, sk 1 sl st, dc in next, ch 3, sl st in first ch of rnd.

Rnd 3: Ch 1, sc over each ch and sc in each sc, dc, tr, dtr or trtr, sl st in first ch of rnd.

VARIATIONS

Pad for more texture by working rnd 3 over 2 or more strands of the same yarn.

HAWAIIAN SQUARE

INSTRUCTIONS

Ch 8, sl st to join.

Rnd 1: Ch 2 (counts as first strand of puff stitch). In ring (4 strand puff stitch, ch 2) 8 times, sl st in top of puff stitch.

Rnd 2: Ch 2 (counts as first strand of puff stitch). Beginning over last ch 2 of rnd 1 and over first ch of ch 2 just made *(puff stitch over ch-2, ch 2) 2 times, dc in next puff stitch, ch 2*; repeat from * to * around ending with sl st into top of puff stitch.

Rnd 3: Ch 2 (counts as first strand of puff stitch). Beginning over last ch 2 of rnd 2 *(puff stitch over ch-2, ch 2) 3 times, in dc (dc, ch 2, dc), ch 2*; repeat from * to * around ending with sl st into top of puff stitch.

Rnd 4: Ch 2 (counts as first strand of puff stitch). Beginning over last ch 2 of rnd 3 *(puff stitch over ch-2, ch 2) 4 times, over ch-2 (dc, ch 2, dc), ch 2*; repeat from * to * around ending with sl st into top of puff stitch.

Rnds 5 and 6: repeat rnd 4 adding one more (puff stitch over ch-2, ch 2) to each side of motif in each round.

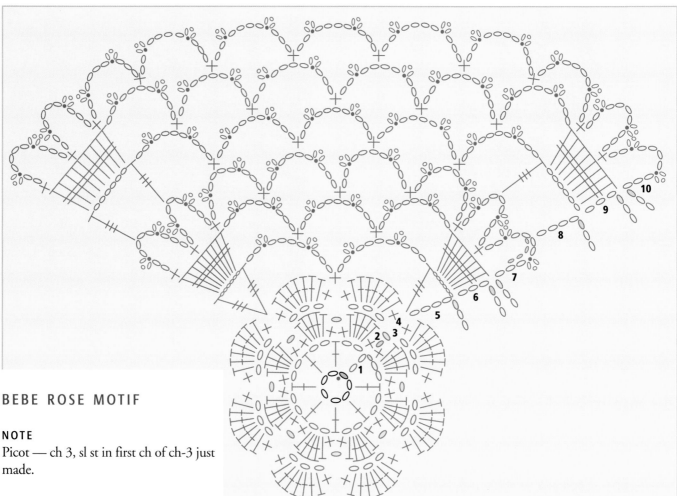

BEBE ROSE MOTIF

NOTE

Picot — ch 3, sl st in first ch of ch-3 just made.

INSTRUCTIONS

Ch 6, sl st to join.

Rnd 1: Ch 4, (dc in ring, ch 2) 7 times, sl st in 2nd ch of rnd.

Rnd 2: *Over ch-2 (sc, hdc, 3 dcs, hdc, sc)*; repeat from * to * around ending with sl st in first sc of rnd.

Rnd 3: *Ch 3, sk (hdc, 3dcs, hdc), sl st between 2 scs*; repeat from * to * around ending with sl st over sl st of rnd 2.

Rnd 4: *Over ch-3 (sc, hdc, 5 dcs, hdc, sc)*; repeat from * to * around ending with sl st in first sc.

Rnd 5: Ch 4 (counts as first dtr). *Dtr between scs, ch 6, dtr between same 2 scs, ch 3, picot, ch 4, picot, ch 2, sc between 2 scs, ch 3, picot, ch 4, picot, ch 2*; repeat from * to * around ending with sl st in 4th ch of rnd.

Rnd 6: Ch 3 (counts as first tr). *9 trs over ch-6, (ch 3, picot, ch 4, picot, ch 2, sc over ch-4) 2 times, ch 3, picot, ch 4, picot, ch 2*; repeat from * to * around ending with sl st in 3rd ch of rnd.

Rnd 7: Ch 3 (counts as first sc and ch 3). *Sc in first tr, ch 3, picot, ch 4, picot, ch 2, sc in 5th tr, ch 3, picot, ch 4, picot, ch 2, sc in 9th tr, (ch 3, picot, ch 4, picot, ch 2, sc over ch-4) 3 times, ch 3, picot, ch 4, picot, ch 2*; repeat from * to * around ending with sl st in first ch of rnd.

Rnd 8: Sl st in first four chs of rnd 7 skipping picot, ch 4 (counts as first dtr). *Dtr over ch-4, ch 6, dtr over next ch-4, (ch 3, picot, ch 4, picot, ch 2, sc over ch-4) 4 times, ch 3, picot, ch 4, picot, ch 2*; repeat from * to * around ending with sl st in 4th ch of rnd.

Rnd 9: Ch 3 (counts as first tr). *9 trs over ch-6, (ch 3, picot, ch 4, picot, ch 2, sc over ch-4) 5 times, ch 3, picot, ch 4, picot, ch 2*; repeat from * to * around ending with sl st in 3rd ch of rnd.

Rnd 10: Ch 3 (counts as first sc and ch 3). *Sc in first tr, ch 3, picot, ch 4,

picot, ch 2, sc in 5th tr, ch 3, picot, ch 4, picot, ch 2, sc in 9th tr, (ch 3, picot, ch 4, picot, ch 2, sc over ch-4) 6 times, ch 3, picot, ch 4, picot, ch 2*; repeat from * to * around ending with sl st in first ch of rnd.

VARIATIONS

Enlarge motif by continuing pattern.

WHEAT EARS

INSTRUCTIONS

Ch 8, sl st to join.

Rnd 1: Ch 3, 23 tr in ring, sl st in 3rd ch of rnd.

Rnd 2: Ch 3 (counts as first tr). *Tr, ch 5, tr in same st as last tr, ch 3, sk 2 trs, dc in next, ch 3, sk 2 trs*; repeat from * to * around ending with sl st in 3rd ch of rnd.

Rnd 3: Ch 3 (counts as first tr). *Over ch-5 (5 trs, ch 5, 5 trs), ch 2, sk ch-3, in dc (tr, ch 3, tr), ch 2*; repeat from * to * around ending with sl st in 3rd ch of rnd.

Rnd 4: Ch 3 (counts as first tr). *Over 5 trs tr5tog, ch 2, over ch-5 (5 trs, ch 5, 5trs), ch 2, over 5 trs tr5tog, ch 2, over ch-3 (tr, ch 3, tr), ch 2*; repeat from * to * around ending with sl st in tr5tog.

Rnd 5: Ch 3 (counts as first tr). *In tr5tog (tr, ch 3, tr), ch 2, over 5 trs tr5tog, ch 2, over ch-5 (5 trs, ch 5, 5 trs), ch 2, over 5 trs tr5tog, ch 2, over tr5tog (tr, ch 3, tr), ch 2, over ch-3 (tr, ch 3, tr), ch 2*; repeat from * to * around ending with sl st in 3rd ch of rnd.

Rnd 6: Sl st into ch 3, ch 3 (counts as first tr). *Over ch-3 (tr, ch 3, tr), ch 2, over tr5tog (tr, ch 3, tr), ch 2, over 5 trs tr5tog, ch 2, over ch-5 (5 trs, ch 3, 5 trs), ch 2, over 5 trs tr5tog, ch 2, over tr5tog (tr, ch 3, tr), ch 2, [over ch-3 (tr, ch 3, tr), ch 2] 2 times*; repeat from * to * around ending with sl st in 3rd ch of rnd.

Rnd 7: Sl st into ch-3, ch 3 (counts as first tr). *[Over ch-3 (tr, ch 3, tr), ch 2] 2 times, over tr5tog (tr, ch 3, tr), ch 2, over 5 trs tr5tog, ch 5, over ch-3 5 trs, ch 5, over 5 trs tr5tog, ch 2, over tr5tog (tr, ch 3, tr), ch 2, [over ch-3 (tr, ch 3, tr), ch 2] 3 times*; repeat from * to * around ending with sl st in 3rd ch of rnd.

Rnd 8: Sl st into ch-3, ch 3 (counts as first tr). *[Over ch-3 (tr, ch 3, tr), ch 2] 3 times, over tr5tog (tr, ch 3, tr), ch 5, over 5 trs tr5tog, ch 5, over tr5tog (tr, ch 3, tr), ch 2, [over ch-3 (tr, ch 3, tr), ch 2] 4 times*; repeat from * to * around ending with sl st in 3rd ch of rnd.

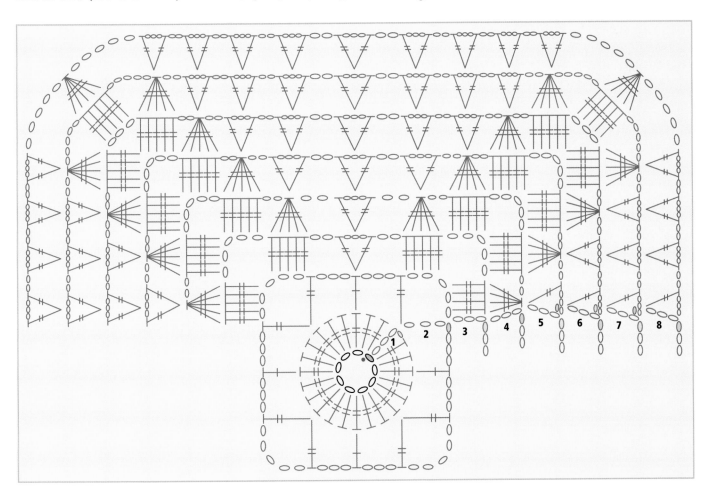

ARROW SQUARE

INSTRUCTIONS

Ch 7, sl st to join.

Rnd 1: Ch 2, 19 dcs in ring, sl st in 2nd ch of rnd.

Rnd 2: Ch 4. *Dc in dc, ch 2*; repeat from * to * around ending with sl st in 2nd ch of rnd.

Rnd 3: Ch 2 (counts as first dc). *Over ch-2 dc5tog, ch 3*; repeat from * to * around ending with sl st in top of dc5tog.

Rnd 4: Ch 2 (counts as first sc). *Over ch-3 3 scs, over next ch 3 3 dcs, over next ch-3 (3 trs, ch 3, 3 trs), over next ch-3 3dcs, over next ch-3 3 scs*; repeat from * to * around ending with sl st in first ch of rnd.

Rnd 5: *Ch 3, (hdc in dc) 3 times, (dc in tr) 3 times, over ch-3 (3 dcs, ch 3, 3 dcs), (dc in tr) 3 times, (hdc in dc) 3 times, ch 3, sc between 3rd and 4th scs*; repeat from * to * around ending by substituting a dc between 3rd and 4th scs for ch 3.

Rnd 6: Sc over stem of dc just made (counts as first sc over ch-3). *Sc over ch-3, ch 5, sc over next ch-3, ch 5, sk 3 hdcs, (dc in dc) 6 times, over ch-3 (3 dcs, ch 3, 3 dcs), (dc in dc) 6 times, sk 3 hdcs, ch 5*; repeat from * to * around ending by substituting (ch 2, dc in sc) for ch 5.

Rnd 7: Sc over ch-2 just made (counts as first sc over ch-5). *(Sc over ch-5, ch 5) 3 times, sk 3 dcs, (dc in dc) 6 times, over ch-3 (3 dcs, ch 3, 3 dcs), (dc in dc) 6 times, sk 3 dcs, ch 5*; repeat from * to * around ending by substituting (ch 2, dc in sc) for ch 5.

Rnds 8–10: Same as rnd 7 except increase (sc over ch-5, ch 5) by one each rnd.

VARIATIONS

Add or subtract outer rounds for desired size.

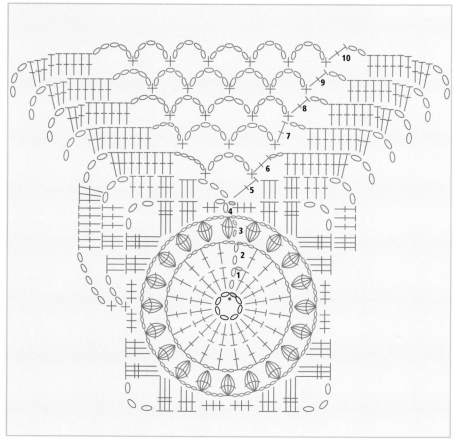

FROZEN STAR

INSTRUCTIONS

Ch 12, sl st to join.

Rnd 1: Ch 2 (counts as first sc). 24 scs in ring, sl st in first ch of rnd.

Rnd 2: Ch 4 (counts as first dtr). Dtr4tog over 4 scs, *ch 7, dtr4tog over 4 scs putting the first dtr in the same sc as the last dtr of previous dtr4tog*; repeat from * to * ending with last dtr in same st as ch-4, ch 7, sl st in top of dtr4tog.

Rnd 3: Ch 5 (counts as sc in dtr4tog and ch 3). *Sc in dtr4tog, (ch 3, sc over ch-7) 3 times, ch 3*; repeat from * to * around ending with ch 3, sl st in 2nd ch of rnd.

Rnd 4: 2 sl sts over ch-3. *Sc over ch-3, ch 3*; repeat from * to * around ending with sl st in first sc of rnd.

Rnd 5: same as rnd 4.

Rnd 6: 2 sl sts over ch-3. *Sc over ch-3, ch 3, sk (sc, ch 3, sc), over next ch-3 (tr4tog, ch 5, dtr4tog, ch 3, sl st in 3rd ch from hook, ch 5, tr4tog), sk (sc, ch-3, sc), (ch 3, sc over next ch-3) 4 times, ch 3*; repeat from * to * around ending with sl st in first sc.

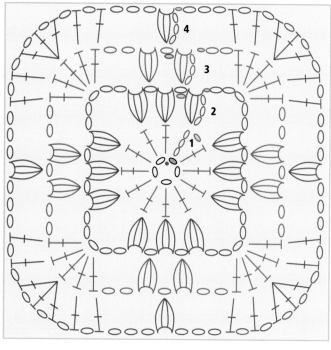

ITALIAN SQUARE

INSTRUCTIONS

Ch 4, sl st to join.

Rnd 1: Ch 3 (counts as first dc). 12 dcs in ring, sl st in 3rd ch of rnd.

Rnd 2: Ch 3 (counts as first strand of puff stitch, ch 3 of rnd 1 counts as first dc). *(4 strand puff stitch in dc, ch 1) 3 times, ch 4 more*; repeat from * to * around ending with ch 4 more, sl st in top of puff stitch.

Rnd 3: Sl st behind first puff stitch and over ch-1, ch 3 (counts as first strand of puff stitch). *4 strand puff stitch over ch, ch 1, 4 strand puff stitch over ch-1, ch 2, 5 dcs over ch-5, ch 2*; repeat from * to * around ending with ch 2, sl st in top of puff stitch.

Rnd 4: Sl st behind first puff stitch and over ch-1, ch 3 (counts as first strand of puff stitch). *4 strand puff stitch over ch, ch 3, sk puff stitch and ch-2, (dc in dc, ch 1) 2 times, in next dc (dc, ch 1, dc, ch 1, dc), (ch 1, dc in dc) 2 times, ch 3, sk ch-2 and puff stitch*; repeat from * to * around ending with ch 3, sl st into top of puff.

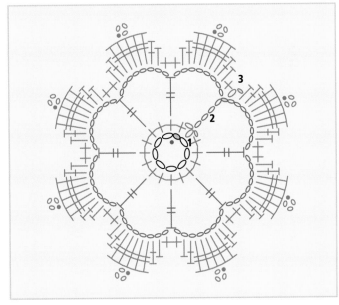

MICA MOTIF

INSTRUCTIONS

Ch 7, sl st to join.

Rnd 1: Ch 5 (counts as first dc and ch 2). In ring (dc, ch 2) 8 times, sl st into 3rd ch of rnd.

Rnd 2: Ch 3 (counts as first dc). *Dc in dc, 4 dcs over ch-2*; repeat from * to * around ending with sl st in 3rd ch of rnd.

Rnd 3: Ch 2 (counts as first dc). *In 4 dcs over ch-2 (dc, sc, sc, dc), sk dc in dc, ch 5*; repeat from * to * around ending with ch 5, sl st in 2nd ch of rnd.

Rnd 4: Ch 2 (counts as first dc). *Over (dc, sc, sc, dc) dc4tog, ch 5, sc over ch-5, ch 5*; repeat from * to * around ending with sl st in top of dc4tog.

Rnd 5: Ch 8 (counts as first dc and ch 5). *Dc in dc4tog, ch 5, sc over ch-5, sc in sc, sc over ch-5, ch 5*; repeat from *

FLEMISH MOTIF

INSTRUCTIONS

Ch 8, sl st to join.

Rnd 1: Ch 2, 15 scs in ring, sl st into first ch of rnd.

Rnd 2: Ch 4 (counts as first tr). *Tr, sk sc, ch 8*; repeat from * to * around ending with sl st in 4th ch of rnd.

Rnd 3: Ch 1, over ch-8 *sc, hdc, dc, 3 trs, ch 3, sl st in 3rd ch from hook, 2 trs, dc, hdc, sc*; repeat from * to * around ending with dc, hdc, sl st in first ch of rnd.

—

to * around ending with sl st in 3rd ch of rnd.

Rnd 6: Ch 10 (counts as first dc and ch 7). *Dc in dc, ch 7, sk ch-5 and sc, sc in next sc, sk sc and ch-5*; repeat from * to * around ending with sl st in 3rd ch of rnd.

Rnd 7: Ch 6 (counts as first dc and ch 3). *In dc (dc, ch 3, dc), (ch 2, dc over ch-7) 2 times, ch 2, dc3tog over (ch-7, sc, ch-7), (ch 2, dc over ch-7) 2 times, ch 2*; repeat from * to * around ending with sl st in 3rd ch of rnd.

crochet pattern gallery

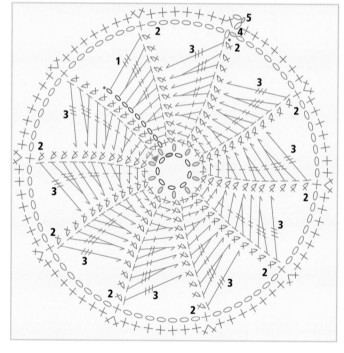

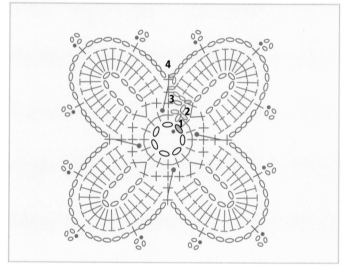

LAZY WHEEL

INSTRUCTIONS
CENTER

Ch 17, sl st in 8th ch from hook to join.

Row 1: Working in ch 9 tail sc, hdc, dc, 2 dcs in next ch, dc, 2 trs in next ch, tr, 2 dtrs in next ch, dtr.

Row 2: Do not turn. Working back along stitches made in row 1, reverse sc in front loop only in each stitch (12 stitches), sl st in center ring.

Row 3: Do not turn. In back loop only sc, hdc, dc, 2 dcs in next st, dc, 2 trs in next st, tr, 2 dtrs in next st, dtr.

Repeat rows 2 and 3 until 10 wedges are completed. End, leaving a 12" tail. Sew first and 10th wedges together.

EDGING

Rnd 4: Attach thread to dtr at point of wedge, ch 1 (counts as

MOORISH MEDALLION

INSTRUCTIONS
Ch 6, sl st to join.

Rnd 1: Ch 2, 15 scs in ring, sl st into first ch of rnd.

Rnd 2: Ch 2, (sc in sc) 2 times, *in next sc (sc, ch 9, sc), (sc in sc) 3 times*; repeat from * to * around ending with sl st in first ch of rnd.

Rnd 3: Ch 2, *sc in sc, sk 1 sc, 21 dcs over ch-9, sk 1 sc*; repeat from * to * around ending with sl st in first sc of rnd.

Rnd 4: Ch 1, *sc in sc of rnd 1 directly below next sc, ch 5, sc into 6th dc, ch 3, sl st in 3rd ch from hook, ch 5, sc into 11th dc, ch 3, sl st in 3rd ch from hook, ch 5, sc into 16th dc, ch 3, sl st in 3rd ch from hook, ch 5*; repeat from * to * around ending with sl st in first sc.

---

first sc). *Sc in dtr at point of wedge, ch 7*; repeat from * to * around ending with sl st in first ch of rnd.

Rnd 5: Ch 2 (counts as first sc). 2 scs in sc, 7 scs over ch-7, repeat around ending with sl st in first ch of rnd.

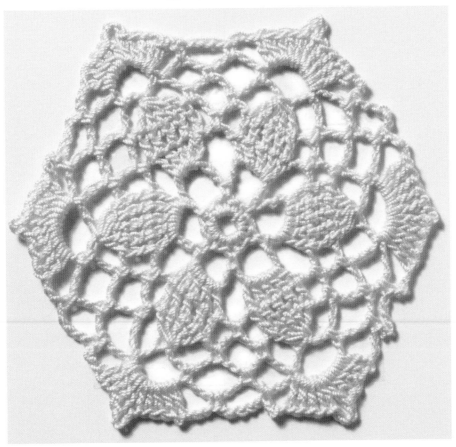

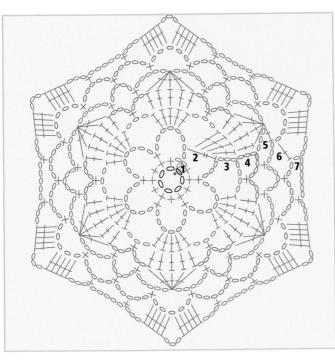

ICE CRYSTAL

INSTRUCTIONS

Ch 6, sl st to join.

Rnd 1: Ch 2, 11 scs in ring, sl st in first ch of rnd.

Rnd 2: Ch 8, *sk 1 sc, sc in next, ch 7*; repeat from * to * around ending with sc in next sc, ch 3, tr in 2nd ch of rnd.

Rnd 3: Ch 3 (counts as first dc). 5 dcs over post of tr, *ch 3, 5 dcs over ch-7*; repeat from * to * around ending with ch 3, sl st in 3rd ch of rnd.

Rnd 4: Ch 3 (counts as first dc). *(Dc in dc) 5 times, ch 3, sc over ch-3, ch 3*; repeat from * to * around ending with ch 3, sc, ch 3, sl st in 3rd ch of rnd.

Rnd 5: Ch 3 (counts as first dc). *Over 5 dcs dc5tog, (ch 5, sc over ch-3) 2 times, ch 5*; repeat from * to * around ending with ch 5, dc in top of dc5tog.

Rnd 6: Ch 6 (counts as sc, ch 5). *Sc over ch-5, ch 5*; repeat from * to * around ending with sc over ch-5, ch 2, dc in first ch of rnd.

Rnd 7: Ch 4. *Over ch-5 (5 dcs, ch 3, 5 dcs), ch 3, sc over ch-5, ch 5, sc over ch-5, ch 3*; repeat from * to * around ending with sc, ch 5, sl st in first ch of rnd.

crochet pattern gallery

BOBBLE HEXAGON
Other name: Cluster Hexagon

INSTRUCTIONS

Ch 6, sl st to join.

Rnd 1: Ch 3, 17 dcs in ring, sl st in 2nd ch of rnd.

Rnd 2: Ch 5 (counts as last dc of this rnd and first ch 3). *Ch 3, (dc in dc) 3 times*; repeat from * to * around ending with ch 3, (dc in dc) 2 times, sl st in 2nd ch of rnd.

Rnd 3: Ch 5 (counts as last dc and first ch 3). *Ch 3, dc over ch-3, dc in dc, dc5tog, dc in dc, dc over ch-3*; repeat from * to * around ending with dc over sl st, sl st in 2nd ch of rnd.

Rnd 4: Ch 5 (counts as last dc and first ch 3). *Ch 3, dc over ch-3, (dc in dc, dc5tog) 2 times, dc in dc, dc over ch-3*; repeat from * to * around ending with dc over sl st, sl st in 2nd ch of rnd.

Rnd 5: Ch 5 (counts as last dc and first ch 3). *Ch 3, dc over ch-3, 3 dcs, dc5tog, 3 dcs, dc over ch-3*; repeat from (to * around ending with dc in dc, dc over sl st, sl st in 2nd ch of rnd.

Rnd 6: Ch 5 (counts as last dc and first ch 3). *Ch 3, dc over ch-3, 9 dcs, dc over ch-3*; repeat from * to * around ending with dc in dc, dc over sl st, sl st in 2nd ch of rnd.

Rnd 7: Ch 5 (counts as last dc and first ch 3). *Ch 3, dc over ch-3, 11 dcs, dc over ch-3*; repeat from * to * around ending with dc in dc, dc over sl st, sl st in 2nd ch of rnd.

Rnd 8: Ch 5 (counts as last dc and first ch 3). *Ch 3, dc over ch-3, (dc, dc5tog) 6 times, dc, dc over ch-3*; repeat from * to * around ending with dc, dc over sl st, sl st in 2nd ch of rnd.

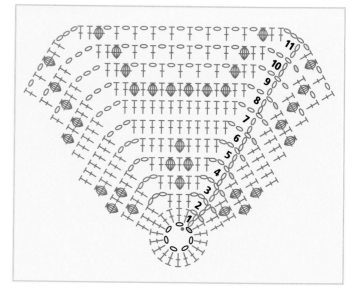

Rnd 9: Ch 5 (counts as last dc and first ch 3). *Ch 3, dc over ch-3, dc, dc5tog, (ch 1, sk dc5tog, dc) 5 times, ch 1, sk dc5tog, dc5tog, dc, dc over ch-3*; repeat from * to * around ending with dc5tog, dc over sl st, sl st in 2nd ch of rnd.

Rnd 10: Ch 5 (counts as last dc and first ch 3). *Ch 3, dc over ch-3, dc, dc5tog, ch 1, sk dc5tog, (dc over ch, ch 1, sk dc) 5 times, dc over ch, ch 1, sk dc5tog, dc5tog, dc, dc over ch-3*; repeat from * to * around ending with dc5tog, dc over sl st, sl st in 2nd ch of rnd.

Rnd 11: Ch 5 (counts as last dc and first ch 3). *Ch 3, (dc over ch-3) 2 times, dc5tog, ch 1, dc in dc5tog, (ch 1, sk ch-1, dc in dc) 6 times, ch 1, dc in dc5tog, ch 1, sk dc, dc5tog, (dc over ch-3) 2 times*; repeat from * to * around ending with (dc5tog, dc) over sl st, sl st in 2nd ch of rnd.

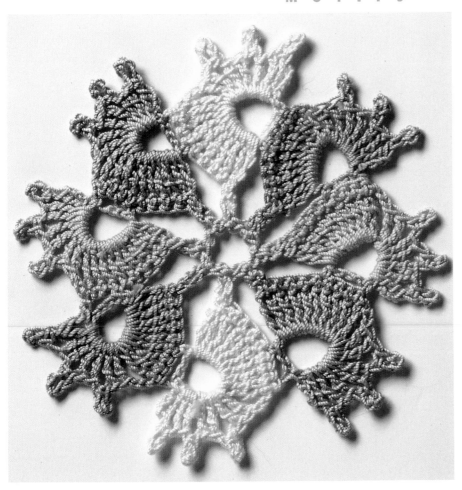

AMANDA WHORL

NOTES

Begin working the segments one at a time, attaching each to the previous as you progress. Alternate four colors for segments (two in each color). Work the center ring last.

INSTRUCTIONS

SEGMENT 1

With color A ch 12, sl st to join.

Row 1: Ch 4, tr in ring, (ch 6, sc in 5th ch from hook, 2 trs in ring), 3 times, ch 2, 10 trs in ring, ch 5, sl st in 4th ch from hook (picot made).

Row 2: Turn. Sk first tr, (sc in tr) 9 times. End.

SEGMENTS 2–7

With next color, attach yarn to last sc of previous segment. Ch 4, sk 3 scs of row 2 of previous segment, sc in next sc, ch 9, sl st in 2nd ch of rnd. Repeat rows 1 and 2 of segment 1.

SEGMENT 8

Work as segment 7 except on row 2 (sc in tr) 5 times, sc in ring of first segment, (sc in tr) 4 times, ch 1, sl st in ring of first segment. End.

CENTER RING

Attach yarn to any picot at center of motif, ch 2. *Sc in picot, sc in side of sc*; repeat from * to * around ending with sl st in first ch of rnd.

205

crochet pattern gallery

SYLVAN CIRCLES

INSTRUCTIONS

Ch 8, sl st to join.

Rnd 1: Ch 3 (counts as first dc). 32 dcs in ring, sl st in 3rd ch of rnd.

Rnd 2: Ch 3 (counts as first dc). In 3rd ch of rnd 1 (dc2tog, ch 3, dc2tog), *ch 7, sk 3 dcs, in next dc (dc2tog, ch 3, dc2tog)*; repeat from * to * around ending with ch 7, sl st in top of first dc2tog.

Rnd 3: Sl st over ch-3, ch 3 (counts as first dc). *Over ch-3 (dc2tog, ch 3, dc2tog), ch 7, sk (dc2tog, ch-7, dc2tog)*; repeat from * to * around ending with sl st in top of first dc2tog.

Rnd 4: Sl st over ch-3, ch 3 (counts as first dc). *Over ch-3 (dc2tog, ch 3, dc2tog), ch 4, sc over ch-7s in rows 2 and 3, ch 4*; repeat from * to * around ending with sl st in top of dc2tog.

Rnd 5: Sl st over ch-3, ch 3 (counts as first dc). *Over ch-3 (dc2tog, ch 3, dc2tog), ch 16, sl st in 12th ch from hook (ring made), ch 3, turn, sl st in last dc2tog, turn, 6 dcs in ring just made, sk ch-4, sl st in sc, 8 dcs in ring, sk ch-4 and dc2tog*; repeat from * to * around ending with sl st in top of first dc2tog.

Rnd 6: Ch 1, over ch-3 (dc2tog, ch 6, sl st in 4th ch from hook, ch 1, dc2tog), ch 1, sl st in top of dc2tog, 16 dcs around outer edge of ring, sl st in dc2tog, repeat around ending with sl st in dc2tog.

SPIRAL PENTAGON

INSTRUCTIONS

Ch 5, sl st to join.

Rnd 1: (Ch 6, sc in ring) 4 times, ch 6, sl st in first ch of rnd.

Rnd 2: Ch 6, 3 scs over ch-6, repeat around ending with 3 scs over ch-6.

Rnd 3: Ch 6, 3 scs over ch-6, (sc in sc) 2 times; repeat around ending with (sc in sc) 2 times.

Rnd 4: Ch 6, 3 scs over ch-6, (sc in sc) 4 times; repeat around ending with (sc in sc) 4 times.

Rnd 5: Ch 6, 3 scs over ch-6, (sc in sc) 6 times; repeat around ending with (sc in sc) 6 times.

Rnd 6: Ch 6, 3 scs over ch-6, (sc in sc) 8 times; repeat around ending with (sc in sc) 8 times.

Rnd 7: Ch 6, 3 scs over ch-6, (sc in sc) 10 times; repeat around ending with (sc in sc) 10 times.

Rnd 8: Ch 5, sc over ch-6, ch 5, sk 1 sc, (sc in sc) 11 times; repeat around ending with (sc in sc) 11 times.

Rnd 9: (Ch 5, sc over ch-5) 2 times, ch 5, sk 1 sc, (sc in sc) 9 times; repeat around ending with (sc in sc) 9 times.

Rnd 10: (Ch 5, sc over ch-5) 3 times, ch 5, sk 1 sc, (sc in sc) 7 times; repeat around ending with (sc in sc) 7 times.

Rnd 11: (Ch 5, sc over ch-5) 4 times, ch 5, sk 1 sc, (sc in sc) 5 times; repeat around ending with (sc in sc) 5 times.

Rnd 12: (Ch 5, sc over ch-5) 5 times, ch 5, sk 1 sc, (sc in sc) 3 times; repeat around ending with (sc in sc) 3 times.

Rnd 13: Ch 5, sc over ch-5, (ch 3, sc over ch-5) 5 times, [ch 3, dc in sc, (ch 3, sc over ch-5) 6 times]; repeat from [to] around ending with ch 3, sl st in 3rd ch of first ch-5.

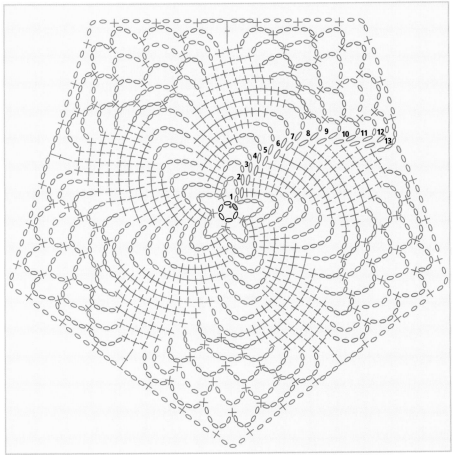

crochet pattern gallery

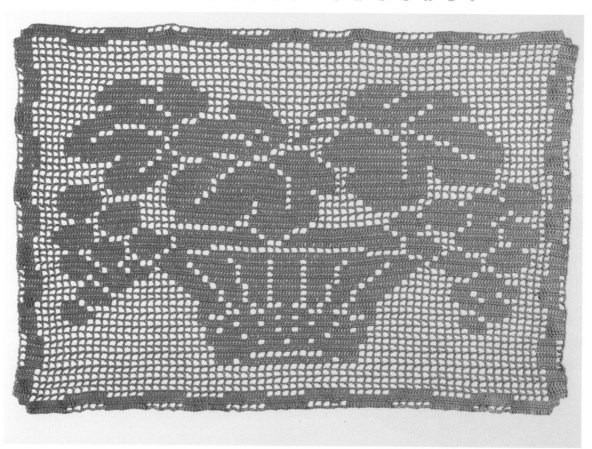

FILET CROCHET

Filet crochet was originally called square crochet because it is composed of open and filled squares (for most crocheters, the squares actually are rectangles as the width and height are not quite identical). It works best in thread because fuzzy yarns obscure the patterns. Filet crochet is popular because the pattern can depict pictures and text. Pictorial filet is best viewed from a distance so the jagged edges of the individual squares blend into the picture.

Traditionally, filet crochet has been used for home furnishing items: wall hangings, curtains, tablecloths, chair back and arm covers, pillows, pillowcase edgings, and doilies. Recently, doily patterns have been worked in smooth sport-weight yarn to create beautiful shawls and afghans.

For stitching instructions refer to Filet Crochet on pages 78–80.

For an explanation of chart symbols, see the inside back cover.

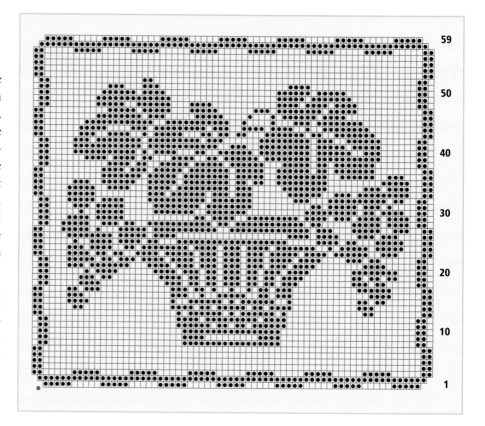

GRAPES IN BASKET

INSTRUCTIONS

69 meshes (or squares) wide x 59 high.

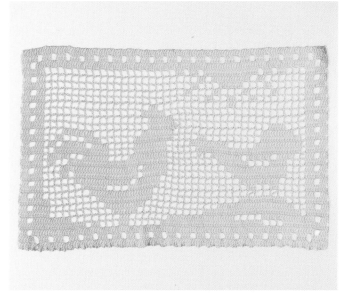

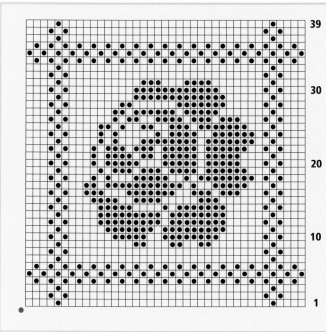

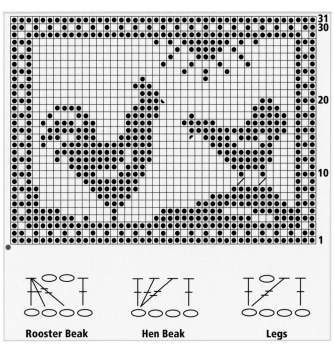

Rooster Beak   Hen Beak   Legs

ROSE

INSTRUCTIONS
39 meshes (or squares) wide x 39 high.

VARIATIONS
This pattern can be worked as a single motif, or the floral motif can be repeated for a larger piece.

CHICKENS

INSTRUCTIONS
43 meshes (or squares) wide x 31 high.

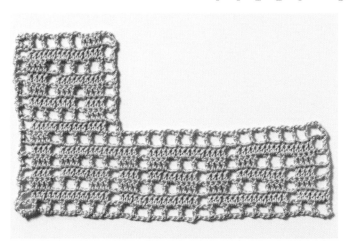

crochet pattern gallery

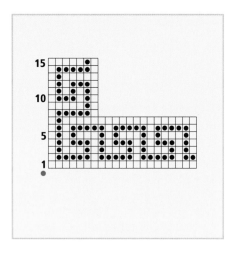

GREEK KEY INSERTION
Other Name: Meander Insertion

INSTRUCTIONS
7 meshes (or squares) wide x a multiple of 7 meshes long.

VARIATIONS
Work edging in a straight piece or create corners.

FILET AND BOBBLE EDGING

NOTES
This pattern is a combination of a filet mesh base with regular crochet stitches. Work regular stitches into mesh as indicated. Single-crochet edging provides a firm edge that helps keep piece flat.

INSTRUCTIONS
8 meshes (or squares) wide x a multiple of 8 meshes long.

Bobble tr5tog into opposite corner of mesh so stitches are diagonal, as shown on chart.

SINGLE CROCHET EDGING
Along both edges work 1 sc into each mesh corner, 1 sc over each chain, and 3 scs over stem of tr.

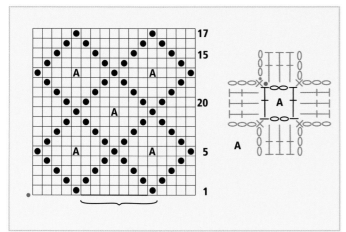

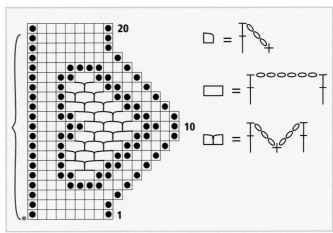

EMBOSSED FLOWER

INSTRUCTIONS

Multiple of 8 meshes + 1.

Work as filet pattern. When you complete mesh around letter A, work counterclockwise around mesh: sc in top of dc just completed, (ch 3, 3 dcs over bar of mesh, ch 3, sc in top of dc); repeat around mesh, ending with sl st in first sc; ch 2 to continue with filet mesh.

FILET AND LACET HEART EDGING

INSTRUCTIONS

16 meshes wide x a multiple of 19 meshes long.

crochet pattern gallery

EDGES, EDGINGS, AND INSERTIONS

Edges, edgings, and insertions are long, narrow pieces of crochet. *Edges* are worked directly onto a piece of crochet to provide strength, stability, and decoration to the edge. *Edgings* are worked separately from a larger piece and have one straight edge for sewing into place. *Insertions* have two straight edges and are inserted into fabric along both edges.

Many ground patterns — fans or lace for example — can be converted into an edge, edging, or insertion by working just two or three rows and finishing one or both edges.

Edges, edgings, and insertions appear extensively on household items: sheets and pillowcases, cupboard edgings, towels, and curtains. Lace patterns are popular on garments as petticoat edgings, collars, cuffs, and decorative insertions. And every afghan is finished with an edge.

You can work edgings separately from or directly onto fabric. The edgings shown here are worked separately on a row of chain stitches. Edgings can be blind-stitched to fabric. You may also eliminate the row of chain stitches and work row 1 directly onto hemstitched fabric.

For an explanation of chart symbols, see the inside back cover.

212

DOUBLE CHAIN EDGE
Other Name: Bicolor Cable Edging

INSTRUCTIONS
Work on base of 3 stitches + 2 or required distance so edge lies flat.

Row 1: With color A (sc, ch 5, sk 2 sts or required distance), repeat.

Row 2: With color B (sc in st to left of sc in row 1, ch 5, drop st from hook, pass hook through loop of color A, pick up loop of color B, sk 2 sts), repeat.

VARIATIONS
Work with 3 colors; vary number of chs for larger or smaller loops as desired.

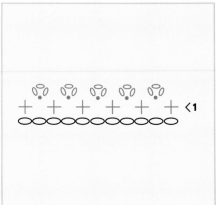
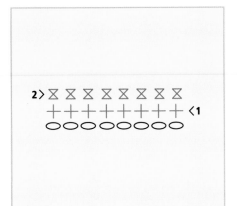
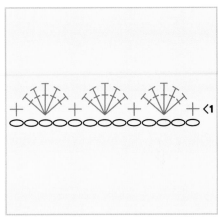

PICOT EDGE

INSTRUCTIONS

Work on base of 2 stitches + 1 or required distance so edge lies flat.

Row 1: (Sc, ch 3, sl st in 3rd ch from hook, sk 1 st or required distance), repeat.

CRAB STITCH EDGE

Other Names: Corded Reverse Stitch, Corded Edging, Lobster Stitch, Shrimp Stitch

INSTRUCTIONS

Work on base with any number of stitches.

Row 1: Sc in each stitch or at required distance so edge lies flat.

Row 2: Do not turn. Sc in last stitch of row 1, sc in 2nd to last st of row 1 (a twist forms in the yarn creating a decorative bump), continue working back along row 1.

SHELL EDGE

Other Name: Scallop Edging

INSTRUCTIONS

Work on base of 4 stitches + 1 or required distance so edge lies flat.

Row 1: Sc, sk 1 st or required distance so edge lies flat, 5 dcs in next st, sk 1 st or required distance so edge lies flat), repeat.

213

crochet pattern gallery

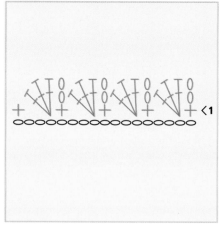

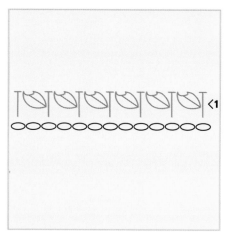

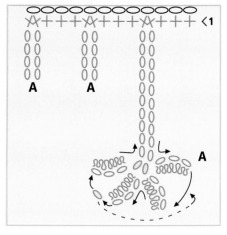

214

TRIANGLE EDGE

INSTRUCTIONS

Work on base of 4 stitches + 1 or required distance so edge lies flat.

Row 1: (Sc, ch 2, 3 dcs in next st, sk 2 sts or required distance so edge lies flat), repeat.

PUFF EDGE

Other Name: Pineapple Edge

INSTRUCTIONS

Work on base of 2 stitches + 1 or required distance so edge lies flat.

Row 1: [Hdc, 3 strand puff stitch over post of hdc just made (7 loops on hook before completing stitch), sk 1 st or required distance so edge lies flat], repeat.

WINDING STITCH FRINGE

NOTES

Work the winding stitch over a short chain: ch 3 in this pattern. Yo, (draw up a loop underneath ch 3, yo on top of ch 3) 9 times, yo, draw loop through all loops on hook. Do not work this stitch too tightly. To get hook through loops, hold the ch 3 and loops between left index finger and thumb, push hook toward chain while drawing hook and last loop through.

INSTRUCTIONS

Work on base of 4 stitches or required distance so tassels don't overlap.

Row 1: (4 scs or required distance so tassels don't overlap, ch 13, winding stitch over last 3 chs made, ch 3, winding stitch over last 3 chs made, sl st in 10th ch of ch-13, ch 3, winding stitch over last 3 chs made, sl st between first two winding stitches, ch 3, winding stitch over last 3 chs made, sl st in 10th ch of ch-13, ch 10, sc in same st as last sc), repeat.

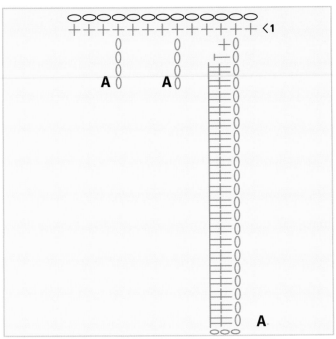

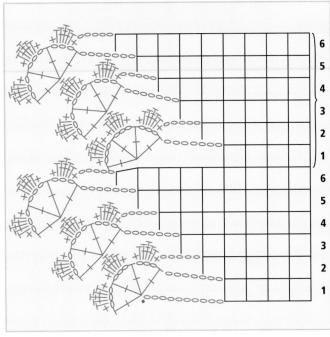

CORKSCREW FRINGE

INSTRUCTIONS

Work on base of 4 stitches or required distance so tassels
  don't overlap.

Row 1: [2 scs or required distance so tassels don't overlap, ch
  25, turn, sk 3 chs, (2 dcs in next ch) 20 times, hdc, (sc in
  ch) 2 times], repeat.

VARIATIONS

Use sc, dc or tr depending on the width of corkscrew you want.
Work 1, 2, or 3 stitches into each chain—the more stitches in
each chain, the more twist.

SHAMROCK EDGING

NOTES

Shamrock Edging is a combination of filet and regular crochet.
Work squares on chart above as filet meshes.

INSTRUCTIONS

Ch 23.

Row 1: 4 meshes, ch 7, in first ch made in base row [(dc, ch 3)
  3 times, dc].

Row 2: Turn. (Over ch-3, sc, hdc, dc, tr, dc, hdc, sc) 3 times,
  ch 5, sk 4 chs of ch-7, dc in next, 5 meshes.

Row 3: Turn. 6 meshes, ch 7, in tr of center group [(dc, ch 3)
  3 times, dc].

Row 4: Turn. (Over ch-3, sc, hdc, dc, tr, dc, hdc, sc) 3 times,
  ch 5, sk 4 chs of ch-7, dc in next, 7 meshes.

Row 5: Turn. 8 meshes, ch 7, in tr of center group [(dc, ch 3)
  3 times, dc].

Row 6: Turn. (Over ch-3, sc, hdc, dc, tr, dc, hdc, sc) 3 times,
  ch 5, sk 4 chs of ch-7, dc in next, 9 meshes.

Repeat rows 1–6.

crochet pattern gallery

SCALLOPED EDGING

INSTRUCTIONS

Chain a multiple of 16 stitches + 9 or, if working directly onto a piece, work over sufficient stitches so edge lies flat and rnd 1 comes out with correct number of repeats.

Rnd 1: Ch 1, (counts as first sc). *Sc, sk 3 chs, 11 trs in next, sk 3 chs, (sc in next, ch 9, sk 7 chs, sc in next)*; repeat from * to * around, ending with sl st in first ch. At corner, replace (to) with sc in corner ch, ch 11, sc in corner ch again.

Rnd 2: Sl st to 6th dc, ch 1 (counts as first sc). {Sc in 6th dc of fan, ch 2, *over ch-7 [(tr3tog, ch 2) 4 times, tr3tog]*, ch 2}; repeat from { to } around ending with ch 2, sl st in first ch of rnd. At corner, replace * to * with over ch-9 [(tr3tog, ch 2) 6 times, tr3tog].

Rnd 3: Sl st into top of tr3tog, ch 2 (counts as first dc). [*(Dc3tog in tr3tog, sk ch-2, ch 4) 4 times, dc3tog in tr3tog*, sk ch-2, ch 2, sc in sc, sk ch-2, ch 2)]; repeat from [to] around, ending with sl st in top of first dc3tog. At corner, replace * to * with (dc3tog in tr3tog, sk ch-2, ch 4) 6 times, dc3tog in tr3tog.

Rnd 4: Ch 1. [Over ch-4 (sc, hdc, 3 dcs, hdc, sc)]; repeat from [to] around, ending with sl st in first ch. At corner, work same pattern as along side.

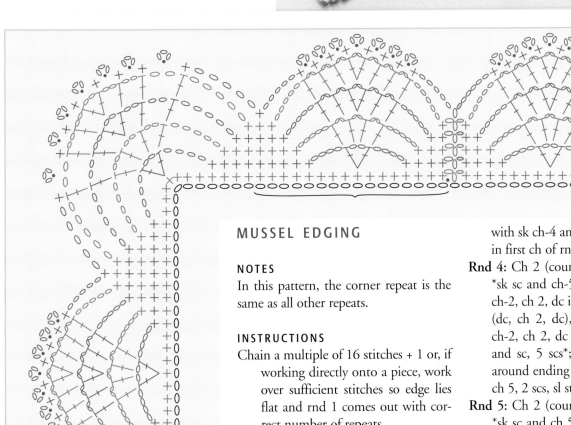

MUSSEL EDGING

NOTES

In this pattern, the corner repeat is the same as all other repeats.

INSTRUCTIONS

Chain a multiple of 16 stitches + 1 or, if working directly onto a piece, work over sufficient stitches so edge lies flat and rnd 1 comes out with correct number of repeats.

Rnd 1: Ch 2 (counts as first sc). Sc in each stitch around, sl st in first ch of rnd.

Rnd 2: Ch 2 (counts as first sc). 5 scs, *sk 3 scs, ch 4, in next sc (dc, ch 2, dc), sk 3 scs, ch 4, 9 scs*; repeat from * to * around ending with sk 3 scs, ch 4, 4 scs, sl st in first ch of rnd.

Rnd 3: Ch 2 (counts as first sc). 4 scs, *sk sc and ch 4, ch 5, dc in dc, ch 2, (dc over ch-2, ch 2) 2 times, dc in dc, sk ch-4 and sc, ch 5, 7 scs*; repeat from * to * around ending with sk ch-4 and sc, ch 5, 3 scs, sl st in first ch of rnd.

Rnd 4: Ch 2 (counts as first sc). 3 scs, *sk sc and ch-5, ch 5, dc in dc, sk ch-2, ch 2, dc in dc, ch 2, over ch-2 (dc, ch 2, dc), ch 2, dc in dc, sk ch-2, ch 2, dc in dc, ch 5, sk ch-5 and sc, 5 scs*; repeat from * to * around ending with sk ch-5 and sc, ch 5, 2 scs, sl st in first ch of rnd.

Rnd 5: Ch 2 (counts as first sc). 2 scs, *sk sc and ch 5, ch 5, (dc in dc, sk ch-2, ch 2) 2 times, dc in dc, ch 2, over ch-2 (dc, ch 2, dc), ch 2, (dc, sk ch-2, ch 2) 2 times, dc in dc, sk ch-5 and sc, ch 5, 3 scs*; repeat from * to * ending with sk sc and ch-5, ch 5, sc, sl st in first ch of rnd.

Rnd 6: Ch 1 (counts as first sc). *Ch 5, (sc in dc, ch 3, sl st in 3rd ch from hook, sk ch-2) 7 times, sc in dc, sk ch-5 and sc, ch 5, sc, sk sc and ch 5*; repeat from * to * ending with sk ch-5 and sc, ch 5, sl st in first ch of rnd.

217

crochet pattern gallery

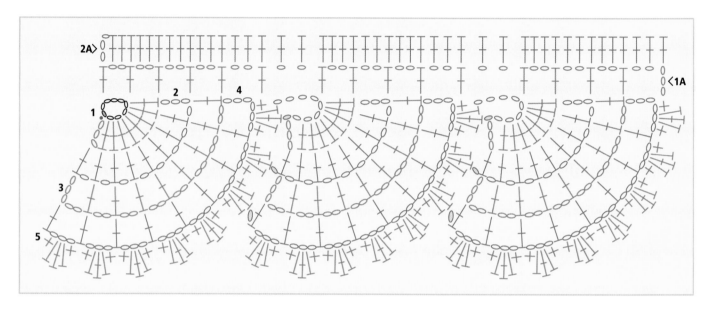

PIRANESI EDGING

NOTE
Work repeats consecutively to desired length.

INSTRUCTIONS
FIRST REPEAT
Ch 8, sl st to join.
Row 1: Ch 3 (counts as first dc). 9 dcs in ring.
Row 2: Turn. Ch 4. Sk first dc, *dc in dc, ch 1*; repeat from * to * across, ending with dc in 3rd ch of tch.
Row 3: Turn. Ch 5. Sk first dc and ch-1, *dc in dc, sk ch, ch 2*; repeat from * to * across, ending with dc in 3rd ch of tch.
Row 4: Turn. Ch 6. Sk first dc and ch-2, *dc in dc, sk ch-2, ch 3*; repeat from * to * across, ending with dc in 3rd ch of tch.

Row 5: Turn. *Over ch-3 (sc, hdc, dc, hdc, sc)*; repeat from * to * across, ending with sc.

ADDITIONAL REPEATS
Turn, ch 8, sk hdc, sl st in dc of previous repeat.
Repeat rows 1–5. Do not end, continue with heading.

HEADING
Row 1A: Ch 5, *dc in top of last dc of row 3, ch 2, dc in 3rd ch of row 2, ch 2, dc in top of last dc of row 1, ch 2, dc in ring, ch 2, dc in last sc of row 4 of previous repeat*; repeat from * to * along edging ending with dc in ring, ch 2, dc in ring again.
Row 2A: Turn. Ch 3. Dc in each st.

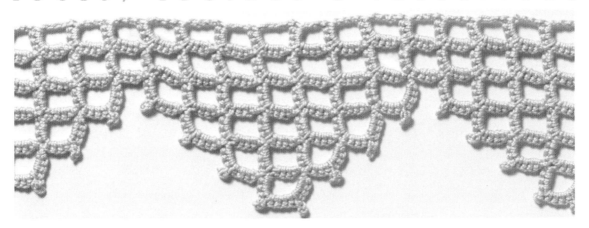

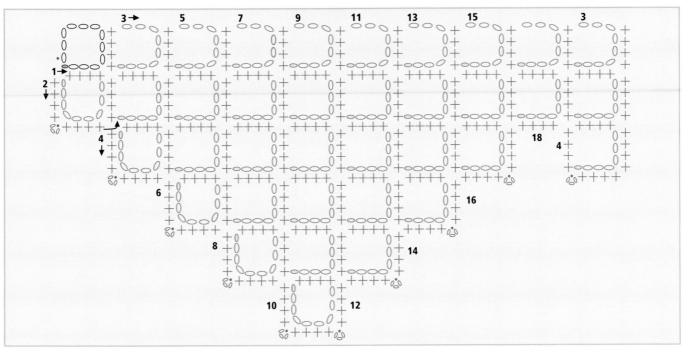

HARDANGER EDGING

INSTRUCTIONS

Ch 12, sl st to join.

Row 1: 4 scs in ring, ch 8, turn, sl st in first sc of row.

Row 2: Turn. 4 scs in ring, (ch 3, sl st in 3rd ch from hook — picot), 8 scs in ring, 4 scs in previous ring.

Row 3: Turn. Ch 8. Working back along row of scs made in previous row, sl st in 4th sc, turn, 4 scs in ring just made, ch 6, turn, sk 3 scs in previous row, sl st in 4th sc, turn, 4 scs in ring just made, ch 8, turn, sl st in 4th sc from hook.

Row 4: Turn. 4 scs in ring just made, picot, 8 scs in ring, 4 scs over chs in each remaining ring made in previous row.

Row 5: Turn. Ch 8. Working back along scs made in previous row, (sk 3 scs,

sl st in 4th sc, turn, 4 scs in ring just made, ch 6, turn) 2 times, sk 3 scs, sl st in 4th sc, turn, 4 scs in ring just made, ch 8, turn, sc in 4th sc from hook.

Repeat rows 4–5, increasing one ring in each odd row until there are 6 rings, then decrease 1 ring each row until there are only 2 rings. Except:

Row 10: Turn. (4 scs in ring just made, picot) 2 times, 4 scs in ring, 4 scs over chs in each remaining ring made in previous row.

All even-numbered decrease rows: Turn. 4 scs in ring just made, picot, 4 scs in ring, 4 scs over chs in each remaining ring made in previous row.

Repeat rows 3–18 to desired length.

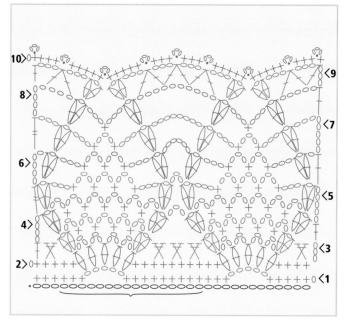

crochet pattern gallery

220

PINEAPPLE EDGING

NOTES
V-chain — (dc2tog, ch 1, dc2tog)

INSTRUCTIONS
Chain a multiple of 16 + 15.

Row 1: Turn. Ch 1. 5 scs, *sk 4 chs, ch 5, 12 scs*; repeat from * to * ending with 6 scs.

Row 2: Turn. Ch 1. 5 scs, *sk 1 sc, over ch-5 [(dc2tog, ch 3) 4 times, dc2tog], sk 1 sc, 10 scs,* repeat from * to * across, ending with sk 1 sc, 4 scs, sk tch.

Row 3: Turn. Ch 3. Sk first sc, dc in next, dc in skipped sc, *sk 2 scs, in dc2tog V-chain, (ch 3, sc over ch-3) 4 times, ch 3, in dc2tog V-chain, sk 3 scs, dc in next, dc in last skipped sc, (sk 1 unused sc, dc in next, dc in skipped sc) 2 times*; repeat from * to * across, ending with sk 3 scs, dc in next, dc in last skipped sc, dc, sk tch.

Row 4: Turn. Ch 4. Sk 3 dcs and dc2tog, *over ch-1 V-chain, (ch 3, sc over ch-3) 5 times, ch 3, sk dc2tog, over ch-1 V-chain, ch 3, sk (dc2tog, 6 dcs and dc2tog)*; repeat from * to * across, ending with over ch-1 V-chain, dc in tch.

Row 5: Turn. Ch 5. Sk dc2tog, *over ch-1 V-chain, sk (dc2tog, ch 3 and sc), (ch 3, sc over next ch-3) 4 times, sk (sc, ch-3 and dc2tog), ch 3, over ch-1 V-chain, (sk dc2tog, ch-3 and dc2tog), ch 3*; repeat from * to * across, ending with over ch-1 V-chain, tr in tch.

Row 6: Turn. Ch 5. Sk dc2tog, *over ch-1 V-chain, sk (dc2tog, ch-3 and sc), (ch 3, sc over next ch-3) 3 times, ch 3, sk (sc, ch-3, and dc2tog), over ch-1 V-chain, sk (dc2tog, ch-3 and dc2tog), ch 6*; repeat from * to * ending with over ch-1 V-chain, ch 1, dc in tch.

Row 7: Turn. Ch 8. Sk (dc, ch, and dc2tog), *over ch-1 V-chain, sk (dc2tog, ch-3 and sc), (ch 3, sc over next ch-3) 2 times, sk (sc, ch-3 and dc2tog), ch 3, over ch-1 V-chain, sk (dc2tog, ch-6 and dc2tog), ch 8*; repeat from * to * across, ending with over ch-1 V-chain, ch 3, tr in 4th ch of tch.

Row 8: Turn. Ch 8. Sk (tr, ch-3, and dc2tog), *over ch-1 V-chain, ch 3, sk (dc2tog, ch-3 and sc), sc over ch-3, sk (sc, ch-3 and dc2tog), ch 3, over ch-1 V-chain, sk (dc2tog, ch-8 and dc2tog), ch 10*; repeat from * to * across, ending with over ch-1 V-chain, ch 5, dc in 5th ch of tch.

Row 9: Turn. Ch 3. Sk 1 ch, dc in next, ch 3; dc2tog (in same ch as last dc, sk 2 chs, in next ch), *ch 3, sk dc2tog, in ch-1 V-chain, sk (dc2tog, ch-3, sc, ch-3, dc2tog), in ch-1 V-chain, sk dc2tog, ch 3; dc2tog (in next ch, sk 2 chs, in next ch), [ch 3, dc2tog (in same ch as last dc, sk 2 chs, in next ch)] 2 times*; repeat from * to * across, ending with in ch-1 V-chain, sk dc2tog, ch3; dc2tog (in next ch, sk 2 chs, in next ch); ch 3, dc in 4th ch of tch.

Row 10: Turn. Ch 1. Sc in dc, (ch 3, sl st in 3rd ch from hook - picot), 3 scs over ch-3, picot, sk dc2tog, *3 scs over ch-3, sc in dc2tog, sc over ch, picot, sk 2 dc2togs, sc over ch, sc in dc2tog, (3 scs over ch-3, picot, sk dc2tog) 3 times*; repeat from * to * across, ending with 3 scs over ch-3, picot, sc in dc.

VARIATION
Work it in the round.

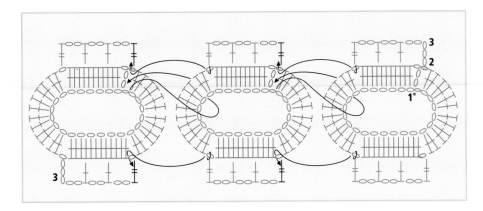

WEDDING RING INSERTION

NOTE
Work circles consecutively to desired length.

INSTRUCTIONS
FIRST CIRCLE
Rnd 1: Ch 24, sl st to join.

Rnd 2: Ch 3, 11 dcs in ring, ch 1, (12 dcs in ring, ch 1) 3 times, sl st in 3rd ch of rnd. End.

ADDITIONAL CIRCLES
Rnd 1: Ch 24, slip tail of ch through previous completed circle from front to back, sl st to join.

Rnd 2: Ch 3, 11 dcs in ring, ch 1, (12 dcs in ring, ch 1) 3 times, sl st in 3rd ch of rnd. End.

HEADING
Row 3: Attach yarn to ch-1 of circle, ch 6, *(sk 3 dcs, dc in next, ch 2) 2 times, overlap 2 circles so the ch-1 spaces line up, tr over ch-1 through both circles, ch 2, working in next circle*; repeat from * to * across, ending with tr over last ch 1.

Repeat heading for other side of insertion.

VARIATIONS
Work it in the round.

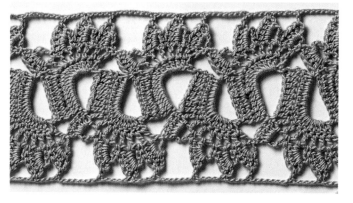

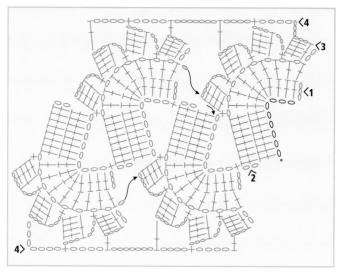

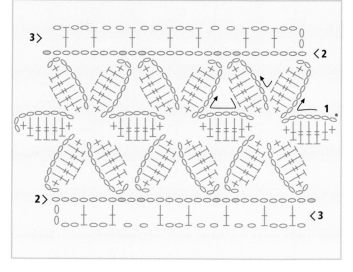

ARCHES INSERTION

NOTE
Work repeats consecutively to desired length.

INSTRUCTIONS
FIRST REPEAT
Ch 9.

Row 1: Turn. Ch 3. Dc in first ch of base ch, 14 dcs over ch, dc in last ch.

Row 2: Turn. Ch 2. (Dc in dc) 8 times, (ch 1, dc in dc) 8 times, sk tch.

Row 3: Turn. Ch 2. (Dc in ch, ch 3, 4 dcs over stem of dc just made, sc in next ch, ch 3) 3 times, dc in ch, ch 3, 4 dcs over stem of dc just made, sc in next ch, ch 9, sk 7 dcs, sc in last dc, sk tch.

SECOND REPEAT
Same as rows 1–3 of first repeat.

ADDITIONAL REPEATS
Row 1: Turn. Ch 3. Dc in first ch of base ch, 14 dcs over ch, dc in last ch.

Row 2: Turn. Ch 2. (Dc in dc) 8 times, (ch 1, dc in dc) 8 times, sk tch, sl st into 3rd ch of last ch-3 in row 3.

Row 3: Turn. Ch 2. (Dc in ch, ch 3, 4 dcs over stem of dc just made, sc in next ch, ch 3) 3 times, dc in ch, ch 3, 4 dcs over stem of dc just made, sc in next ch, ch 9, sk 7 dcs, sc in last dc, sk tch.

CLEMATIS INSERTION

INSTRUCTIONS
FLOWERS
Row 1: *Ch 16, sk 2 chs, sc, dc, 3 trs, dc, sc, ch 9, sk 2 chs, sc, dc, 3 trs, dc, sc*; repeat from * to * for desired length of insertion, ch 9, sc, dc, 3 trs, dc, sc, working back along other side of chains, *(ch 9, sk 2 chs, sc, dc, 3 trs, dc, sc) 2 times, in 7 unused chs made in first half of row (sc, dc, 3 trs, dc ,sc)*; repeat from * to * across. End.

HEADING
Row 2: On wrong side attach yarn to tip of petal, *ch 7, sl st in tip of next petal, ch 1, sl st in tip of next petal*; repeat from * to * across.

Row 3: Turn with front side up. Ch 4. (Sk 2 chs, dc in next, ch 2); repeat across.

Repeat heading on other side of insertion.

VARIATIONS
To use as an edging, omit one heading.

HEADING
Row 4: Attach yarn to 3rd ch of first ch-3 (point) in row 3, ch 7, *sc in next point in row 3, ch 4, dc in next point row 3, ch 7, dc in first point of row 3 in next repeat, ch 4*; repeat from * to * across.

Repeat on other side of insertion.

SPIDER INSERTION

INSTRUCTIONS

Ch 39.

Row 1: Turn. Ch 2. Dc across.

Row 2: Turn. Ch 2. Sk first dc, 3 dcs, sk 1 dc, ch 1, dc, (sk 3 dcs, ch 3, dc) 2 times, sk 3 dcs, ch 2, 3 dcs in next dc, sk 3 dcs, ch 11, 3 dcs in next dc, sk 3 dcs, ch 2, dc, (sk 3 dcs, ch 3, dc) 2 times, sk 1 dc, ch 1, 3 dcs, dc in tch.

Row 3: Turn. Ch 2. Sk first dc, 3 dcs, (ch 3, dc over ch-3) 2 times, ch 2, 3 dcs in 2nd ch of ch-2, ch 6, sc over ch-11, ch 6, 3 dcs in first ch of ch-2, ch 2, dc over ch-3, ch 3, dc over ch-3, sk dc and ch-1, ch 3, (dc in dc) 3 times, dc in tch.

Row 4: Turn. Ch 2. Sk first dc, 3 dcs, ch 1, dc over ch-3, ch 3, dc over next ch-3, ch 2, 3 dcs in 2nd ch of ch-2, ch 6, sc over ch-6, sc in sc, sc over ch-6, ch 6, 3 dcs in first ch of ch-2, ch 2, dc over ch-3, ch 3, dc over ch-3, ch 1, (dc in dc) 3 times, dc in tch.

Row 5: Turn. Ch 2. Sk first dc, 3 dcs, ch 3, dc over ch-3, ch 2, 3 dcs in 2nd ch of ch-2, ch 6, sc over ch-6, (sc in sc) 3 times, sc over ch-6, ch 6, 3 dcs in first ch of ch-2, ch 2, dc over ch-3, ch 3, (dc in dc) 3 times, dc in tch.

Row 6: Turn. Ch 2. Sk first dc, 3 dcs, ch 1, dc over ch-3, ch 2, 3 dcs in 2nd ch of ch-2, ch 6, sc over ch-6, (sc in sc) 5 times, sc over ch 6, ch 6, 3 dcs in first ch of ch-2, ch 2, dc over ch-3, ch 1, (dc in dc) 3 times, dc in tch.

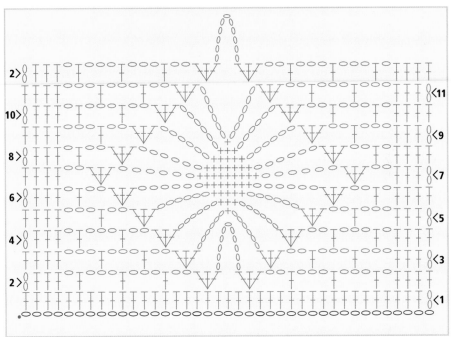

Row 7: Turn. Ch 2. Sk first dc, 3 dcs, ch 2, 3 dcs in 2nd ch of ch-2, ch 6, sc over ch-6, (sc in sc) 7 times, sc over ch-6, ch 6, 3 dcs in first ch of ch-2, ch 2, sk dc, (dc in dc) 3 times, dc in tch.

Row 8: Turn. Ch 2. Sk first dc, 3 dcs, ch 1, dc over ch-2, ch 2, 3 dcs in first ch of ch-6, ch 6, sk sc, 7 scs, sk sc, ch 6, 3 dcs in last ch of ch-6, ch 2, dc over ch-2, ch 1, (dc in dc) 3 times, dc in tch.

Row 9: Turn. Ch 2. Sk first dc, 3 dcs, ch 3, dc over ch-2, ch 2, 3 dcs in first ch of ch-6, ch 6, sk sc, (sc in sc) 5 times, sk sc, ch 6, 3 dcs in lst ch of ch-6, ch 2, dc over ch-2, ch 3, (dc in dc) 3 times, dc in tch.

Row 10: Turn. Ch 2. Sk first dc, 3 dcs, ch 1, dc over ch-3, ch 3, dc over ch-2, ch 2, 3 dcs in first ch of ch-6, ch 6, sk sc, (sc in sc) 3 times, sk sc, ch 6, 3 dcs in last ch of ch-6, ch 2, dc over ch-2, ch 3, dc over ch-3, ch 1, (dc in dc) 3 times, dc in tch.

Row 11: Turn. Ch 2. Sk first dc, 3 dcs, (ch 3, dc over ch-3, ch-3, dc over ch-2, ch 2, 3 dcs in first ch of ch-6, ch 6, sk sc, sc in sc, sk sc, ch 6, 3 dcs in last ch of ch-6, ch 2, dc over ch-2, ch 3, dc over ch-3, ch 3, (dc in dc) 3 times, dc in tch.

Repeat rows 2–11.

Last row: Turn. Ch 2. Dc across.

TUNISIAN CROCHET

Tunisian crochet is a cross between crochet and knitting, and requires a special hook to form the stitches. It's longer than a standard crochet hook, so you can hold the last loop of each stitch on the hook as you work on the row. It's often called an *afghan* hook. The Forward row of stitches is picked up like knitting and the Return row is worked off with a crocheted slip stitch.

Tunisian crochet is usually worked with the front of the work facing you, and is not turned at the end of the row. Tunisian crochet is slightly different than regular crochet. The last chain of the base chain becomes the first stitch of row 1 (page 108). It is charted as the first stitch of row 1 so the base chain appears to have one less stitch on the chart than is indicated in the written instructions. Likewise, the first stitch in each later row is the loop that remains on the hook at the end of the previous row. It is charted as the first stitch of the next row.

Tunisian crochet is also called *afghan* stitch and, from its name, you can guess one of its main uses is for afghans. It can also be used for garments like vests and coats, durable pillows, and, if worked tightly, thick hotpads.

224

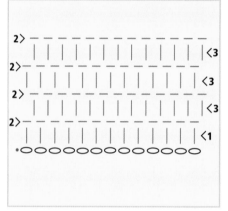

TUNISIAN SLANT STITCH

INSTRUCTIONS

Chain a multiple of 1 stitch + 1.

Row 1: Sk first ch, pick up a loop in each ch.

Row 2: Ch 1, *yo, draw through 2 loops*; repeat from * to * across.

Row 3: Pick up loop between vertical bars in previous forward row, repeat across.

Repeat rows 2 and 3, ending with row 2.

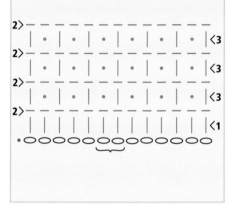

TUNISIAN MOSS STITCH

INSTRUCTIONS

Chain a multiple of 2 stitches + 1.

Row 1: Sk first ch, pick up a loop in each ch.

Row 2: Ch 1, *yo, draw through 2 loops*; repeat from * to * across.

Row 3: *Tss, Tps*; repeat from * to * across, ending with Tss.

Repeat rows 2 and 3, ending with row 2.

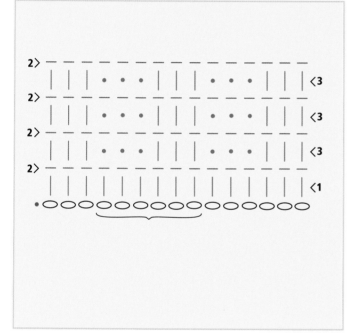

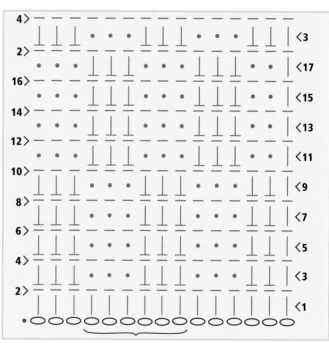

225

TUNISIAN RIB STITCH

INSTRUCTIONS

Chain a multiple of 6 stitches + 4.

Row 1: Sk first ch, pick up a loop in each ch.

Row 2: Ch 1, *yo, draw through 2 loops*; repeat from * to * across.

Row 3: *3 Tss, 3 Tps*; repeat from * to * across, ending with 3 Tss.

Repeat rows 2 and 3, ending with row 2.

TUNISIAN BASKETWEAVE STITCH

INSTRUCTIONS

Chain a multiple of 6 stitches + 4.

All even rows: Ch 1, *yo, draw through 2 loops*; repeat from * to * across.

Row 1: Sk first ch, pick up a loop in each ch.

Rows 3, 5, 7 & 9: Tss, 2 Tks, 3 Tps, *3 Tks, 3 Tps*; repeat from * to * across, ending with 3 Tks.

Rows 11, 13, 15 & 17: Tss, 2 Tps, *3 Tks, 3 Tps*; repeat from * to * across, ending with 3 Tps.

Repeat rows 2–17, ending with even row.

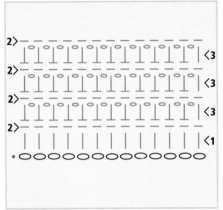
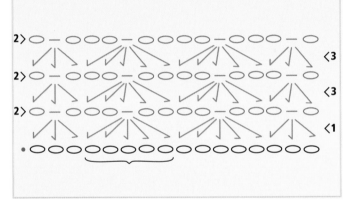

TUNISIAN SHAKER STITCH

INSTRUCTIONS

Chain a multiple of 1 stitch.

Row 1: Sk first ch, pick up a loop in each ch.

Row 2: Ch 1, *yo, draw through 2 loops*; repeat from * to * across.

Row 3: Tss, *ch 1, Tks in next st*; repeat from * to * across, ending with Tks.

Repeat rows 2 and 3, ending with row 2.

TUNISIAN CLUSTER STITCH
Other Name: Tunisian Lace Stitch

INSTRUCTIONS

Chain a multiple of 5 sts + 2.

Row 1: Sk first ch, pick up a loop through top back loop only in each ch across.

Row 2: Ch 2, (yo, draw through 4 loops), (ch 3, yo, draw through 6 loops), *ch 4, yo, draw through 6 loops*; repeat from * to * across, ending with ch 3, yo, draw through 4 loops, ch 1.

Row 3: Pick up a loop through top back loop only in each st across.

Repeat rows 2 and 3, ending with row 2.

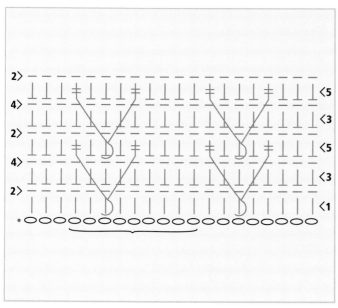

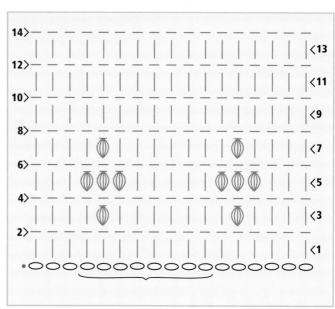

227

TUNISIAN POST CHEVRON

INSTRUCTIONS

Chain a multiple of 9 stitches + 3.

All even rows: Ch 1, *yo, draw through 2 loops*; repeat from * to * across.

Row 1: Sk first ch, pick up a loop in each ch.

Row 3: Tks across.

Row 5: 3 Tks, *tr around vertical bar of st 2 odd rows below and 2 sts forward, 3 Tks, tr around same vertical bar just used, 4 Tks*; repeat from * to * across, ending with 3 Tks.

Repeat rows 2–5, ending with row 2.

TUNISIAN PUFFS

INSTRUCTIONS

Chain a multiple of 8 stiches + 2.

All even rows: Ch 1, *yo, draw through 2 loops*; repeat from * to * across.

Row 1: Sk first ch, pick up a loop in each ch.

Row 3: 4 Tss, *5-strand puff st, 7 Tss*; repeat from * to * across, ending with 4 Tss.

Row 5: 3 Tss, *3 5-strand puff sts, 5 Tss*; repeat from * to * across, ending with 3 Tss.

Row 7: same as row 3.

Rows 9, 11 & 13: Tss across.

Repeat rows 2–13, ending with row 2.

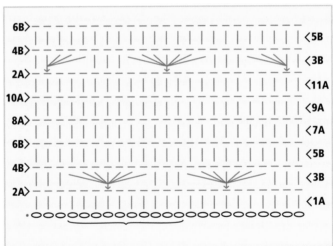

TUNISIAN FANS

INSTRUCTIONS

Chain a multiple of 10 stitches + 4.

All even rows: Ch 1, *yo, draw through 2 loops*; repeat from
* to * across.

Row 1: With color A sk first ch, pick up a loop in each ch.

Row 3: With color B *3 Tss, sk 3 sts, 7 Tss in top loops of next
st, sk 3 sts*; repeat from * to * ending with 3 Tss.

Row 5: With color B simple st across.

Rows 7, 9 & 11: With color A Tss across.

Repeat rows 2–11, offsetting fans by 5 stitches.

resources & suppliers

Artistic Wire (wire)
1210 Harrison Avenue
La Grange Park, IL 60526
Phone: 630-530-7567
Fax: 630-530-7536
Email: artwire97@aol.com

Big Sky Studio and Gallery (yarns and materials)
961 'C' Moraga Road
Lafayette, CA 94549
Phone: 925-284-1020
Fax: 925-284-2624
E-mail: BigSkys@PacBell.Net
Website: www.bigskystudio.com

Coats & Clark (Anchor, Susan Bates, Red Heart, Coats)
Consumer Services
P.O. Box 12229
Greenville, SC 29612-0229
Phone: 800-648-1479
Website: www.coatsandclark.com

Crochet Guild of America (CGOA) (national organization)
2502 Lowell Road
Gastonia, NC 28054
Phone: 877-852-9190
Fax: 704-852-9776
Website: www.crochet.org

Kreinik Mfg. Co., Inc. (threads)
3106 Lord Baltimore Drive, Suite 101
Baltimore, MD 21244
Phone: 800-537-2166
Fax: 410-281-2519
Email: kreinik@kreinik.com
Website: www.kreinik.com

Lacis (threads and materials)
3163 Adeline St.
Berkeley, CA 94703
Phone: 510-843-7178
Fax 510-843-5018
E-mail: staff@lacis.com
Website: www.lacis.com

Lion Brand Yarn (yarns)
34 15th Street
New York, NY 10011
Phone: 800-258-9276
Website: www.lionbrand.com

Mill Hill Beads (beads)
P.O. Box 1060
Janesville, WI 53547
Fax: 608-754-0665
Email: millhill@millhill.com
Website: www.millhillbeads.com

Nordic Needle, Inc. (threads and materials)
1314 Gateway Dr. SW
Fargo, ND 58103
Phone: 800-433-4321
Fax: 701-235-0952
E-mail: info@nordicneedle.com
Website: www.nordicneedle.com

Patternworks (yarns, threads, materials)
P.O. Box 1618
Center Harbor, NH 03226-1618
Phone: 800-438-5464
Email: knit@patternworks.com
Website: www.patternworks.com

Philosopher's Wool Co. (wool and kits)
Inverhuron, Ontario
NOG 2T0 Canada
Phone: 519-368-5354
Website: www.philosopherswool.com

NOTES FOR THE HISTORY OF CROCHET
(PAGES 10–21)

1. Lis Paludan, *Crochet: History and Technique* (Interweave Press, Loveland, CO, 1988), pp. 20–21.

2. Elizabeth Wayland Barber, *Women's Work: the First 20,000 Years* (Norton, New York, 1994), pp. 43-45. The string skirt that the figure wears is clearly shown frayed at the bottom edge, and each thread has carefully carved twist marks, indicating twisted fiber rather than hide or sinew strips.

3. Elizabeth Wayland Barber, *Prehistoric Textiles* (Princeton University Press, Princeton, NJ) pp. 53, 58–59, 69, 121.

4. Lynn S. Teague, Curator, Arizona State Museum, University of Arizona, Tucson, AZ, private correspondence, 2001. "Reports of a crocheted foundation for Pima pottery are unfounded. Both the Pima, or Akimel O'odham (river people), and their relatives the Tohono O'odham (desert people) make pottery using the paddle and anvil method, a method also used for many centuries by their prehistoric Hohokam ancestors. The origin of the misconception that a crocheted base was used may be found in a relatively minor practice by some potters. In Pima pottery making, the base of a new pot is shaped by molding wet clay against the base of an existing pot. Some potters place a piece of cloth over the base of the older pot, so that the clay of the new vessel won't stick to the old. The new pot base is then removed from the existing base. After drying to a leather-like consistency, the base is shaped by using a wooden paddle to mold the clay against a stone anvil, and the vessel is completed using coils of added clay and temper. The cloth impression left in the interior bottom of vessels when potters use fabric between the new pot base and the old may be the origin for the erroneous reports of a crocheted base for Pima pottery."

5. Paludan, op. cit., p. 15.

6. The word "crotchet" is used consistently throughout the book, indicating that the pronunciation at that time was like the well-attested English word used in architecture and music, among other disciplines. It referred to a small hook, such as seen on an eighth note in music, or as an ornamental device. But within a year of the publication of A Winter Gift, the word had been standardized to "crochet," indicating that the French pronunciation was preferred. If crochet had been a long-familiar pastime, especially one already known as "shepherd's knitting," there would have been no need to come up with new words to describe it, and certainly no indecision between English and French versions of the word.

7. Paludan, op. cit., p. 59. Paludan cites some patterns which require the yarn to be broken at the end of each row and reattached, so that the work is always done right to left. This technique appears alongside turned work patterns, so was seemingly done for aesthetic reasons. The uni-directional approach virtually died out at the end of the 19th century in favor of the more efficient turning approach, though there are still uni-directional pattern stitches and techniques.

8. Pat Earnshaw, *A Dictionary of Lace* (Shire Publications, (Shire Publications, Buckinghamshire, UK, 1982), p. 30; and Judith Gwynne, Illustrated Dictionary of Lace (Lacis, Berkeley, CA, 1997), p. 62.

9. Paludan, op. cit., p. 10.

10. Richard Rutt, Bishop of Leicester, *A History of Hand-knitting*, (Interweave Press, Loveland, CO, 1987), pp. 23–24.

11. Elizabeth Wayland Barber, op. cit., p. 5.

12. Ibid. pp. 292–293.

13. Elaine Merritt, "Precious Lace," (*Piecework*, Interweave Press, Loveland, CO, January/February 2001), pp. 29–32.

14. Michael and Ariane Batterberry, *Fashion: the Mirror of History*, (Greenwich House, NY, 1977), pp. 87–88.

15. Annette Feldman, *Handmade Lace & Patterns*, (Harper & Row, NY, 1975), p. xiii; Susan Temme Grob, "Bobbin Lace: Intrigue and Hard Work," *Piecework, Interweave Press*, Loveland, CO, January/February 2001), p. 27.

16. Patricia Wardle, *Victorian Lace*, (Praeger Publications, NY, 1968), p. 186.

17. Paludan, op. cit., p. 20.

18. Ibid.

19. Susan Burrows Swan, *Plain and Fancy: American Women and Their Needlework, 1650-1850*, (Holt, Rhinehart, and Winston, Austin, TX, 1975), p. 84, Plate 10.

20. Paludan, op. cit., p. 20

21. Freiherr Alfred von Henneberg, *The Art and Craft of Old Lace*, (E. Weyhe, NY, 1931), p. 42.

22. Paludan, op. cit., p. 24.

23. Nancy Nehring, private correspondence, June 2001.

24. Ibid.

25. Paludan, op. cit., p. 15.

26. Miss Frances Lambert, *My Crochet Sampler* (D.M. Peyser, NY, 1846), Interpreted and worked by Nicole Scalessa, Historic Reflections in Crochet, The Library Company of Philadelphia, 2001, pp. 36-37, Color Plate 8. Exhibition catalog.

27. Scalessa, op. cit., p. 40.

28. Edwin Hubbell Chapin, *Duties of Young Women* (George W. Briggs, Boston, MA, 1848), p. 8.

29. Nicole H. Scalessa, "The Hook and the Book," Exhibition at The Library Company of Philadelphia, June–September, 2001.

30. Ibid.

31. Freiherr Alfred von Henneberg, *The Art and Craft of Old Lace* (E.Weyhe, NY, 1931), pp. 42–43.

32. Wardle, op. cit., p. 52.

33. Charlotte Elizabeth Tonna, *The Wrongs of Woman, Part IV, The Lace Runners*, 1844. Cited in Exhibition, "The Hook and the Book," Library Company of Philadelphia, June–September, 2001. Though Tonna's work dates prior to the blossoming of crocheted lace in Ireland, but the taint of immorality clung to lace-making throughout the Victorian era. It was openly expressed in *The English Illustrated Magazine* of June, 1890. Alan S. Cole, writing on Irish lace-making, says "Crochet was readily bought up, but it as quickly earned a bad name—not merely on account of its artistic deficiencies, but also because of its demoralizing effects. Godly people held the crochet-maker in horror." Wardle, op. cit., p. 197. This may be a possible origin of the word "hooker" as referring to a prostitute.

34. Wardle, op. cit., p. 84.

35. Wardle, op. cit., 187.

36. Ibid.

37. Wardle, op. cit., p. 188.

38. Ibid.

39. Ibid.

40. Ibid.

41. Barnes, Galer, Britton "Irish Crochet of Clones" (*Piecework*, July/August 1997), pp. 44-47.

42. Paludan, op.cit., p.15.

43. Paludan, ibid., p. 72.

44. Wardle, op. cit., p. 197.

45. Ibid.

46. Wardle, op. cit., pp. 198–199.

47. Ibid.

48. Wardle, op. cit., p. 65.

49. Paludan, op. cit., pp. 74–75.

50. Thérèse de Dillmont, *Encyclopedia of Needlework*, (Mullhouse, Alsace, France, n.d.), p. 316.

bibliography

GENERAL

Barber, Elizabeth Wayland. *Women's Work: the First 20,000 Years.* Norton, New York, 1994.

An American Lady (editor). *A Winter Gift for Ladies, Being Instructions in Knitting, Netting, and Crotchet [sic] Work, Containing the Newest and Most Fashionable Patterns from the Latest London Edition.* G. B. Zieber and Company, Philadelphia, 1847.

Barber, Elizabeth Wayland. *Prehistoric Textiles.* Princeton University Press, Princeton, NJ, 1991.

Barnes, Galer Britton. "Irish Crochet of Clones." Piecework, Interweave Press, Loveland, CO, July/August 1997. pp. 44-47.

Batterberry, Michael and Ariane. *Fashion: The Mirror of History.* Greenwich House, NY, 1977.

Blakley-Kinsler, Gwen and B.J. Licko-Keel. *Magical Miser's Purses.* DMC, South Kearny, NJ, 1999.

Brock, Delia and Elaine Bodger. *The Adventurous Crocheter.* Simon & Schuster, NY, 1972.

Carroll, Alice (editor). *The Good Housekeeping Needlework Encyclopedia.* Rhinehart & Company, NY, 1947.

Chapin, Edwin Hubbell. *Duties of Young Women.* George W. Briggs, Boston, 1848.

Cosh, Sylvia and James Walters. *The Crochet Workbook.* St. Martin's, Griffin, NY, 1989.

Decorative Crochet. Number 81, Les Editions de Saxe S.A., Danbury, CT, May 2001.

Decorative Crochet. Les Editions de Saxe S.A., Danbury, CT, Number 82, July 2001.

Decorative Crochet. Les Editions de Saxe S.A., Danbury, CT, Number 84, November 2001.

de Dillmont, Thérèse. *Encyclopedia of Needlework.* DMC, Mulhouse, Alsace, France, n.d.

————. *Masterpieces of Irish Crochet.* Dover Press, NY, 1986.

Dittrick, Mark. *Hard Crochet.* Hawthorn Books, NY, 1978.

Dubin, Lois Sherr. *The History of Seed Beads, from 30,000 B.C. to the Present.* Harry Abrams, NY, 1987.

Earnshaw, Pat. *A Dictionary of Lace.* Shire Publications, England, 1982.

Eaton, Jan. *A Creative Guide to Crochet.* New Holland, London, 1994.

Elwell, Bart. "Ioana Bodrojan's Romanian Point Lace." *Piecework*, Interweave Press, Loveland, CO, January/February 2001. pp. 43–44

————"Ioana Bodrojan and Narcissa Webb, A Romanian Point-lace Butterfly to Make," *Piecework*, Interweave Press, Loveland, CO, January/February 2001. pp. 45–47

Feldman, Annette. *Crochet and Creative Design.* Harper & Row, NY, 1973.

————. *Handmade Lace & Patterns.* Harper & Row, NY, 1975.

Fournier, Jane. "A Beaded Purse to Crochet." *Piecework*, Interweave Press, Loveland, CO, September/October 1996. pp. 56-57

Grob, Susan Temme. "Bobbin Lace: Intrigue and Hard Work." *Piecework*, Interweave Press, Loveland, CO, January/February 2001. p.27.

Gwynne, Judyth L. *Illustrated Dictionary of Lace.* Berkeley, CA, Lacis, 1997.

Harding, Mary, (editor). *Crochet Fashions for the Whole Family.* Phoebus Publishing/BPC Publishing Ltd., 1975–1977.

Harmony Guides. *220 More Crochet Stitches, Vol. 7.* Collins & Brown Ltd., London, 1998.

Harmony Guides. *300 Crochet Stitches, Vol. 6.* Collins & Brown Ltd., London, 1998.

Henneberg, Freiherr Alfred von. *The Art and Craft of Old Lace.* E. Weyhe, NY, 1931.

Kliot, Jules and Kaethe. *Irish Crochet Lace.* Some Place Publications, Berkeley, CA, 1980.

Lacis Publications (compiled). *The Art of Crocheting With Relief Crochet.* Berkeley, CA, Lacis, 2000.

Lambert, Miss Frances. *My Crochet Sampler.* D.M. Peyser, NY, 1846.

Lammer, Jutta. *The Reinhold Book of Needlecraft.* Van Nostrand Reinhold, NY, 1973.

Lane, Rose Wilder. *Woman's Day Book of American Needlework.* Simon and Schuster, NY, 1963.

Leapman, Melissa. *Crochet with Style.* Taunton Press, Newtown, CT, 2000.

Lee, Ramona. *Victorian Purses and Amulet Bags*. HB Publications, Spokane, WA, 1999.

Leisure Arts. *The Complete Guide to Thread Crochet*. Leisure Arts, Little Rock, AR, 2000.

Leisure Arts. *I Can't Believe I'm Crocheting*. Leisure Arts, Little Rock, AR, 2000.

Leisure Arts. *63 "More" Easy-To-Crochet Pattern Stitches Combine To Make An Heirloom Afghan*. Leisure Arts Leaflet #2146. Leisure Arts, Little Rock, AR, 2000.

Lenthe, Sue. "Very Special Editions: Crochet Sample Books." *Piecework*, Interweave Press, Loveland, CO, May/June 1997. pp. 45-48.

MacKenzie, C.D. *New Design in Crochet*. Van Nostrand Reinhold, NY, 1972.

McGoveran, Mary. *Crocheted Buttonholes, Hand-knitting Techniques from Threads Magazine*. Taunton Press, Newtown, CT, 1991.

Magic Crochet. Les Editions de Saxe S.A., Danbury, CT, no. 96, June 1995.

Magic Crochet. Les Editions de Saxe S.A., Danbury, CT, no. 131, April 2001.

Magic Crochet. Les Editions de Saxe S.A., Danbury, CT, no. 133, August 2001.

Marsh, Heidi (compiled by). *Knit, Net Crochet and More of the Era of the Hoop*. Privately printed, Greenville, CA, distributed by Lacis, 1993.

Meadors, Kay. *Booties by the Dozen*. Leisure Arts Leaflet #3243. Leisure Arts, Little Rock, AR, 2000.

Merritt, Elaine, "Precious Lace," *Piecework*, Interweave Press, Loveland CO, January/February 2001. pp.29-32.

Mon Tricot Knitting Dictionary. Crown Publishers, New York, NY. 1972.

Norton, Carol. *Tapestry Crochet*. Dos Tejedoras, St. Paul, MN, 1991.

Paludan, Lis. *Crochet: History and Technique*. Interweave Press, Loveland, CO, 1995.

Perreault, Denise. "The Secrets of Seed Bead Manufacturing." *Beadwork*, Interweave Press, Loveland, CO, October/November 2001. pp. 45–47.

Pfeuffer, Augusta. *Crocheted Art Edgings and Insertions*. Some Place, Berkeley, CA 1975.

Piecework. "Irish Crochet of Cones." Interweave Press, Loveland, CO, July/August 1997. pp. 44–47.

Piecework. "Trimmings: a Sampling of Old Patterns." September/October 1996. pp. 12–16.

Potter, Annie Louise. *A Living Mystery: the International Art and History of Crochet*. A.J. Publications International, 1980.

Probert, Christina. *Lingerie in Vogue Since 1910*. Abbeville Press, NY, 1981.

Righetti, Maggie. *Crocheting in Plain English*. St. Martin's Press, NY, 1988.

Ross, Mabel. *The Encyclopedia of Hand Spinning*. Interweave Press, Loveland, CO, 1988.

Rutt, Richard, Bishop of Leicester. *A History of Hand-knitting*. Interweave Press, Loveland, CO, 1987.

Scalessa, Nicole. *Historic Reflections in Crochet*. The Library Company of Philadelphia, 2001.

Sims, Darla. *63 Easy-To-Crochet Pattern Stitches Combine to Make an Heirloom Afghan*, Leisure Arts Leaflet #555. Leisure Arts, Little Rock, AR, 2000.

Swan, Susan Burrows. *Plain and Fancy: American Women and Their Needlework, 1650–1850*. Holt, Rhinehart, and Winston, Austin, TX, 1975.

Textile Arts Center of McHenry County (IL) College and the Crochet Guild of America, "Chain Reaction:" a juried and invitational traveling exhibition of contemporary crochet that challenges traditional expectation, Chicago, 2000.

Tracy, Gloria and Susan Levin. *Crochet Your Way*. Taunton Press, NY, 2000.

Pauline Turner. *How to Crochet*. Collins & Brown, Ltd., London, 2001 (Distributed by Sterling Publishing).

Waldrep, Mary Carolyn (editor). *Irish Crochet Designs and Projects*. Dover Press, NY, 1988.

Walters, James. *Crochet Workshop*. Sidgwick & Jackson, London, 1979.

Wardle, Patricia. *Victorian Lace*, Praeger Publications, NY, 1968.

Weiss, Rita (editor). *Traditional Edgings to Crochet*. Dover, NY, 1987.

index

For a complete list of crochet patterns see the Pattern Index on pages 238–240.